Politics of the Theological

American University Studies

Series VII
Theology and Religion

Vol. 133

PETER LANG
New York • Washington, D.C./Baltimore • San Francisco
Bern • Frankfurt am Main • Berlin • Vienna • Paris

Barry Harvey

Politics of the Theological

Beyond the Piety
and Power
of a World
Come of Age

PETER LANG
New York • Washington, D.C./Baltimore • San Francisco
Bern • Frankfurt am Main • Berlin • Vienna • Paris

Library of Congress Cataloging-in-Publication Data

Harvey, Barry.
 Politics of the theological: beyond the piety and power of a world come
of age / Barry Harvey.
  p.   cm. — (American university studies. Series VII, Theology and
religion; vol. 133)
 Includes bibliographical references and index.
  1. Theology—Methodology. 2. Consciencei—Religious aspects—
Christianity. 3. Baptists—Doctrines. 4. Theology, Doctrinal—
Introductions. I. Series.
BR118.H38   230'.01—dc20   94-13600
 ISBN 0-8204-1874-9
 ISSN 0740-0446

Die Deutsche Bibliothek-CIP-Einheitsaufnahme

Harvey, Barry:
Politics of the theological: beyond the piety and power of a world come of
age / Barry Harvey. - New York; Washington, D.C./Baltimore; San Francisco;
Bern; Frankfurt am Main; Berlin; Vienna; Paris: Lang.
 (American university studies: Ser. 7, Theology and religion; Vol. 133)
 ISBN 0-8204-1874-9
NE: American university studies / 07

The paper in this book meets the guidelines for permanence and durability of
the Committee on Production Guidelines for Book Longevity of the
Council on Library Resources.

© 1995 Peter Lang Publishing, Inc., New York

Printed in the United States of America.

To My Parents, James H. and Esther B. Harvey

CONTENTS

Preface   ix

Introduction   1

Chapter 1
Science, Conscience, and the Politics of Theology   19
    Theologians of "Science" and the Ethos of Modernity   21
    Science and the Positivism of Modern Western Culture   27
    Theologians of "Conscience" and the Ethos of Pietism   39
    From "Science" to "Conscience"
        The Implications for Theology   45

Chapter 2
The Story of Conscience: I   59
    "For the Sake of Conscience"
        The Apostle Paul on Conscience   60
    "My Conscience is Captive to the Word of God"
        Martin Luther on Conscience   68

Chapter 3
The Story of Conscience: II   85
    "The Aboriginal Vicar of Christ"
        John Henry Newman's Doctrine of Conscience   85
    Conscience in the Pedagogy of the Oppressed
        Paulo Freire's Doctrine of Conscientization   94

The Habits and Relations of Conscience
in the Story of Theology   104

Chapter 4
Laboratory of the Living Word   109
The Dilemma of Conscience in (Post)Modern Culture   109
The Church as the Context for Conscience   111
Conscience, Transfiguration, and the Politics of God 123

Chapter 5
The Hermeneutics of the Politics of God   141
Power and the Age of Anxiety   141
Politics, Confrontation, and Transfiguration   149
Power in the Age of Maturity   160

Chapter 6
Language, Truth, and Power   169
The "The-Anthropological" Focus of Theology   169
A Pragmatic Construal of Theology   181
The Living Word of Truth   188

Chapter 7
Poetics of the Theological   201
The Metaphorical Directives of the Politics of God   202
The Narrative Configuration of the Politics of God   210
The Dogmatic Grammar of the Politics of God   218

Conclusion   239

Bibliography   249

Index   261

PREFACE

The title of the present work is derived from a key phrase in Clodovos Boff's book, *Theology and Praxis*. In it Boff emphasizes that he wishes to craft "a theology of the political," in order to elaborate the methodological contours of liberation theology. While I am largely sympathetic with Boff's motivations, I nonetheless contend that this emphasis is misdirected, for it ultimately perpetuates the modern assumption that religious faith is a private, largely inchoate, and essentially emotive type of consciousness with no intrinsic (i.e., historical, material, or social) relationship to the concerns and celebrations that make up everyday life. Consequently, Boff tacitly relies on the modern conception of politics, and with it the practices, relations and institutions, the images, descriptions and conversations, that comprise what Max Weber calls the "iron cage" of liberal capitalist society. Boff's theology of the political thus fails, ironically, to discern the liberating politics of God narrated in Scripture.

Theological inquiry, I shall argue here, is always vested in some particular political configuration. Christian theology, accordingly, relies principally on that community called the church. Only within this set of practices and relations do theologians have access to the intellectual and moral context that informs the discourses of theology with their interpretive sense and intelligibility. What one acquires within this practical configuration is a way of being and acting in the world, i.e., a performative grasp of a field of possibilities, that embodies a radically different story about creation and the place of human beings within it.

The assertion that only the church provides the proper context for theological reflection produces a hostile reaction in many people. For some, it conjures up dark images of the late medieval church and its corrupt, authoritarian practices. For others, the contingency inextricably involved in such statements undercuts the universal scope of the gospel. Still others, fearful of sectarian intolerance, object to its distinctly "undemocratic" ring, hearing it as a claim that the Christian community "possesses" the truth in a unique way which entitles them to impose their beliefs on everyone else. Some ask, "Which church?", implying that unless and until all the various Christian bodies cross their liturgical "t's" and dot their doctrinal and ethical "i's" in the same way, such claims for the church cannot be consistently upheld (curiously, inquiries into the fundamental tenets of liberal democracy are rarely asked to meet this kind of stringent requirement).

Each of these objections either traffics in misconceptions, is unwilling to seriously entertain questions about its own political assumptions, or both. Having said this, I must nonetheless acknowledge that the problems which accompany my position are many and complex. This book is an attempt to address at least some of them. To the degree that I can persuade my readers to at least attend to these issues and questions, I shall have in like measure achieved an important objective.

No undertaking of this magnitude is ever accomplished without the support and encouragement of innumerable people and institutions. The Graduate School of Duke University and the Andrew Mellon Foundation both provided me with fellowships that allowed me to pursue my graduate education. But it is always the relationships which any institution of higher education fosters that mark graduate studies as a meaningful time. Many different people could be mentioned in this regard, but I shall restrict my comments to Frederick Herzog, my mentor. Not only did his wise counsel and gracious spirit give shape to my intellect, but his unflagging devotion to the church of Christ awakened a similar passion in me.

Several people at Baylor University have contributed in various ways to this project. I cannot imagine a more supportive Dean than William Cooper or department chair than Glenn Hilburn. C. W. Christian, Daniel McGee, Bob Patterson, and John Wood have been invaluable as friends and colleagues in the division of theological studies. Finally, my students consistently provide the enthusiasm, and ultimately the rationale, for this book.

To my wife Sarah I owe an inestimable debt. Her wisdom, devotion, grace, humor, labor, and encouragement underwrite every page of this book. She exemplifies in her work as a teacher and minister the type of conscience that everyone in the church needs to nurture.

Our daughter Rachel and son John are my joy and delight. They constantly remind me of what is truly important in God's creation. In the final analysis, they are our most precious legacy, not the reading and writing of books. Finally, I am thankful for my brothers and their families, who have helped me to be aware of, and to appreciate, the things that finally matter.

This book is dedicated to my parents. The family is, as one theologian has recently noted, the paradigm for all political communities in that they exist to nurture a particular kind of life. I cannot begin to describe the depth of feeling, the care and discipline, that I received from my parents. As Paul Lehmann said of his parents, is from my father and mother that I first learned freedom in believing, and obedience in freedom. I thank God for their love and friendship.

Waco, Texas
January 1994

INTRODUCTION

In the introduction to *Criticism and Social Change*, Frank Lentricchia tells the reader what his book is about, "at its polemical core," by citing a distinction which he attributes to John Dewey by way of Kenneth Burke. The distinction is between "education as a function of society" and "society as a function of education." This is a way of dividing the world between those who have a place of their own in society and those who do not. According to Lentricchia,

> If you are at home in society, you will accept it, and you will want education to perform the function of preparing the minds of the young and the not-so-young to maintain society's principles and directives. Such a relationship between society and its educational institutions Burke calls "normal," and what he intends by this is roughly the irony that Michel Foucault extracts from the term—education will involve itself in a process of "normalization," of making normal, of ensuring that its pedagogical subjects will be trained (taken through the human equivalent of the process of dressage) so that they will be happy, useful, productive, and safe subjects, in the social and political sense of the term: they will be cunningly "subjected."

If you subscribe to this intra-societal role for education, writes Lentricchia, you are a conservative, "but if you think the order should be reversed, you are a radical or that strange, impossible utopian, the radical in reverse gear we call a reactionary." (Liberals are nervous conservatives, "governed by an irresistible impulse to tinker, though when the chips are down, they usually find a way to resist their need to mess with the machine.") The radical, on the other hand, has no ultimate stake in the present social order, and seeks to reverse the roles: "To say that 'society' should be a function of 'education' is to say, in effect, that the principles and directives of the prevailing society are radically askew (that the society has been despoiled of its reasonableness) and that education must serve to remake it accordingly."[1]

The primary concern of my book, with a core that will strike many as polemical but which ultimately seeks to be conciliatory, rests upon a similar distinction. The crucial juxtaposition for the theologian, however, is not the relation between education and society, but between "the church as a function of society" and "society as a function of the church." If you are basically at home in our (post)modern[2] world, you will want the church to serve the practices, institutions, and goals that determine the possibilities for everyday life within our society; in short, you will want the church to be edifying. The church will then, inevitably and inextricably, invest itself in an analogous process of "normalization," i.e., it will be drawn into the process of making "normal citizens" fit for the present order of things. If, however, you agree with John Milbank's assertion that the primary task of the church "is the establishment of a new, universal society, a new *civitas*, in which...intimate relationships are paradigmatic: a community in which we relate primarily to the neighbour, and every neighbour is mother, brother, sister, spouse,"[3] then you will see the goals, institutions, and practices of the church in a very different light.

The church in North America has for the most part been confined by the processes of normalization. The Christian community is generally very much at home in the present social order, and only perceives the need to tinker with its basic social connections. The politics of liberal capitalism has largely gone unchallenged in determining both what is at stake for the church and what possibilities are open to Christians in a (post)modern age. Consequently, the differences between so-called conservatives and liberals within the church—e.g., between Pat Robertson and John Spong, or "pro-life" and "pro-choice" groups—are in the end simply variations between species belonging to the same genus, or as Alasdair MacIntyre puts it, debates between conservative liberals, liberal liberals, and radical liberals.[4]

Stanley Hauerwas, in his inimitable way, pinpoints the predicament facing the normal church:

> The church seems caught in an irresolvable tension today. Insofar as we are able to maintain any presence in modern society we do so by being communities of care...Any attempt in such a context for the church to be a disciplined and disciplining community seems antithetical to being a community of care. As a result the care the church gives, while often quite impressive and compassionate, lacks the rationale to build the church as a community capable of standing against the powers we confront.
>
> That the church has difficulty being a disciplined community or even cannot conceive what it would mean to be a disciplined community, is not

surprising given the church's social position in developed economies. The
church exists in a buyer's or consumer's market, so any suggestion that in
order to be a member of a church you must be transformed by opening your
life to certain kinds of discipline is almost impossible to maintain...The
church is very good at providing the kinds of services necessary to sustain
people through the crises in their personal lives, but this simply reflects the
fact that the church has become the privatized area of our culture...

    [Consequently], the church cannot help become a life-style enclave
and/or an umbrella institution where people are giving us the opportunity to
associate with other people with their similar interests...that are not in any
way shaped by Christian convictions.[5]

In such circumstances, if the church is to recover the kind of critical traction it needs to distinguish itself over against a (post)modern society, some
type of radical shift—what Paul Lehmann refers to as "transfiguration"—is
called for in the piety, politics, and style of reasoning within the Christian
community.

What would it mean for the church to acknowledge and embrace its
"abnormality" in the present ordering of creation? Or to put the matter in
terms of the title of a recent book co-authored by Hauerwas and William
Willimon, how can the body of Christ concretely realize within the (post)-
modern context its status as "resident aliens"?[6] Unfortunately, when we
turn to the present array of options contained within contemporary theology in hopes of addressing this question, what we encounter is a handful of
techniques which continue to "tinker" with the dominant tendencies of
(post)modern thought and practice rather than providing a way of articulating what is involved in the reconfiguration of the church's fundamental
way of being in, and dealing with, the world.

The field of contemporary Christian theology is presently dominated
by four basic methodological strategies. Two of these strategies—revisionist theology and deconstruction—explicitly presuppose the modern doctrine
of the subject as the basis for defining the identity of the self, but then each
develops this doctrine in opposite directions. Revisionist theology, as one
critic has observed, "seeks to carry on the tradition of Schleiermacher and
liberal theology, with its nineteenth century optimism appropriately chas-
tened by the insights of neo-orthodoxy, indeed by the whole grim history
of the twentieth century. Revisionist theologians tend to think that both
theological language and Scripture symbolically convey a religious dimension of experience or a possibility for human existence."[7] In spite of devastating criticisms from anti-foundationalists and social theorists, however,
revisionist theologians have generally been unable or unwilling to offer any

kind of persuasive rejoinder to their critics, nor have they provided any kind of argument for the coherence and intelligibility of their own positions. What we find in place of such arguments are vague, sweeping statements claiming apologetically that revisionist theology "is not only more adequate to our experience but also more genuinely postmodern."[8]

In one respect, I agree completely with this last statement. Revisionist theology, in some significant ways, is more adequate to "our" experience and thus more genuinely postmodern. It would be difficult to overestimate the contribution of liberal and revisionist theology to the construction of our normalized North American culture. However, when one takes into account the political fragmentation and poverty of imagination that characterizes the "postmodern experience," this is a rather dubious accolade. In general, revisionists have lapsed from Immanuel Kant's rhetoric of frankness (*sapere aude!*), and have instead reverted to what Stanley Rosen calls rhetorical esotericism, "the accommodation of truth to political expediency." Seldom do they confront the truth about the contradictions inherent in the modern doctrine of subjectivity, the fact that "*there is no liberal solution to the aporia of the Enlightenment, because liberalism (and a fortiori socialism) is itself the crystallization of that aporia.*"[9] Nicholas Lash puts into capsule form the revisionist dilemma:

> On liberal assumptions, the life of the church (as of the wider society) is thought to resemble an unending academic seminar. But those who take part in the seminar, frequently unmindful of the social and economic privilege which makes their performance possible, tend to overlook the extent to which theoretical disagreement is but the abstract expression, in the order of ideas, of conflicts which, outside the seminar room or the "salon," frequently find harsher and more concrete form. In other words, the weakness of theological, as of political, liberalism lies in its neglect of the calculus of power and in the inadequacy of its analysis of the grounds and sources of conflict and contradiction.[10]

By contrast, deconstruction is well known for its endless demonstrations that the modern doctrine of the subject is incoherent, but beyond this it is apparently incapable of evaluating other possibilities.[11] Cornel West's devastating assessment of deconstructionist strategies is to the point: "This version of relentless skepticism toward logical consistency and theoretical coherence, which refuses to entertain or encourage novel reconstructions, may be symptomatic of the relative political impotence of marginal peoples, their inability to creatively transform and build on the ambiguous legacy of the Age of Europe."[12] Deconstruction, in other words, finds innumerable ways to tell us that all attempts at epistemology, metaphysics, and ethics—disciplines which in the (post)modern era are grounded in the self as subject—will never achieve what they set out to accomplish, but it cannot find one way to say anything else. In the final analysis, says West,

> deconstructions are, like the Left-Hegelian critiques of Marx's own day, interesting yet impotent bourgeois attacks on the forms of thought and categories of a "dead" tradition, a tradition that stipulates the lineage and sustains the very life of these deconstructions…[It] is not simply that these attacks valorize textuality at the expense of power, but more important, that they are symbiotic with their very object of criticism: that is, they remain alive only as long as they give life to their enemy. In short, deconstructionist assaults must breathe life into metaphysical, epistemological, and ethical discourses if their critiques are to render these discourses lifeless.[13]

Because deconstruction inexplicably identifies any reference to the self with the doctrine of modern subjectivity, departing at a most curious and inopportune moment from its otherwise unqualified celebration of *différance*, it invariably (though inadvertently) reconstructs itself in the mutated form of an impotent liberal or revisionist subject. As William Poteat states in reference to the deconstruction of modern axioms,

> This terrible pathos of not being God deeply afflicts us. All because the venue remains unchanged, all because after we have exposed the chimera of an eternal, ahistorical truth, we still perceive and evaluate the realm of the pretensions and retrotensions of time as from the perspective of eternity— static and changeless as the printed word is when compared with the spoken. So we think of ourselves as being left with "only" the realities and Being that are disclosed in time, and left "only" with history.[14]

Rosen thus has good reason to conclude that the cluster of movements commonly grouped under the banner of postmodernity simply perpetuates the basic tendencies of modernity: "Postmodernism has no more rejected Kant than Kant rejected the Enlightenment. We are now living through the rhetorical frenzy of the latest attempt of the self-contradictory nature of the Enlightenment to enforce itself as a solution to its own incoherence."[15]

Jeffrey Stout appropriately describes the third basic approach within contemporary theology—postliberal theology—as "the quest, initiated in recent years by the most interesting American followers of Karl Barth, to get beyond all forms of modernism in theology; either a *cul de sac* or the harbinger of a new theological age (too soon to tell)."[16] According to its most widely-read proponent, Yale University professor George Lindbeck, postliberal theology seeks to provide an alternative account of religion and religious doctrine to those offered by revisionist theologians, an account, moreover, that does not concede to deconstruction the possibility of obtaining some measure of coherence and intelligibility. Labelling his account a cultural-linguistic approach, Lindbeck maintains that "religions resemble languages together with their correlative forms of life and are thus similar to cultures (insofar as these are understood semiotically as reality and value systems---that is, as idioms for the construing of reality and the living of life.)" Speaking primarily to revisionist theologians, Lindbeck argues that religions and religious language cannot be construed as formalizable symbolic systems. Theologians should instead view a religion and its teachings as though it were a distinct culture, seeking to give a "thick description" of that religion, treating it "[as an] interlocked system of construable signs," that is, as a context within which social events, behaviors, institutions, and processes may be intelligibly described. For example, he argues that "The cross is not to be viewed as a figurative representation of suffering nor the messianic kingdom as a symbol of hope in the future; rather, suffering should be cruciform, and hopes for the future messianic."[17]

Many who see themselves in line with the classical tradition of Christianity, and are therefore unwilling to go along with liberal and revisionist efforts to "translate" this tradition into existential or experiential categories which supposedly hold across cultures and traditions, are attracted to postliberal theology. Nevertheless, numerous and substantial problems exist in the way Lindbeck and his associates carry out this project. In particular, their conception of religious doctrine may allow us to acknowledge the *historicity* of a tradition's beliefs and principles, but it does not give us any way of accounting for the *history* of that tradition. A cultural-linguistic schema does not deal with historical contexts or social locations; indeed, it is incapable of accounting for these irreducible radices of our creaturely existence. In short, Lindbeck promises to deliver a thick description of religious discourse, but instead we are handed a thin and formal historicism that masks rather than exhibits the actual production of ourselves as embodied agents within the configurations of social practices constituting historical communities.

Ironically, it is Lindbeck himself who unwittingly tips us off to this philosophical bait-and-switch. He labors diligently to undermine the modern doctrine of epistemological foundations and "the myth of the transcendental ego," but his admission that a cultural-linguistic model may be construed as "a kind of quasi-transcendental (i.e., culturally formed) *a priori* for the possibility of experience" covertly reintroduces these concepts in modified form.[18] In short, Lindbeck does not dispel this myth, but simply transfers the site where this "ego" or "subject" is located from the individual human being to the "culture" or "religion." In ways that are reminiscent of Jürgen Habermas's interminable efforts to locate normative foundations for critical social theory which are partly transcendental and partly empirical, Lindbeck is trapped, as it were, between heaven and earth. He seeks to distance himself from the kinds of rhetorical appeals to "universal criteria," "the transcendental ego," "foundations," and "intuitive religious experience" that permeate liberal and revisionist theology, and yet he fashions an account that simply transfers the function of these artifacts of modernity to "religion" or "culture." There is, in other words, as much "liberal" as "post" to postliberal theology.

And finally there is the so-called conservative or classicist theology in all its variant forms (including Roman Catholic intregalists and Protestant evangelicals and fundamentalists). In some ways this mode of theological reasoning has the potential to foster a counter-societal outlook, as Harvey Cox notes in *Religion in the Secular City*, but it is constantly dissipated by its reactionary impulses. As a result, classicist theology assimilates the very tendencies it opposes, particularly (post)modernity's instrumental conception of rationality. In the final analysis, classicist theology promotes what West terms a neo-hegemonic culture: "it postures as an oppositional force, but, in substance, is a new manifestation of people's allegiance and loyalty to the status quo."[19]

What I hope to do in this book, therefore, is to set forth an account of theology that will contribute to the formation of a community that truthfully narrates a counter-history to the story implicated in the techniques and tendencies of (post)modernity, thus offering to the world an alternative range of possibilities for the practice of everyday life. My supporting cast is relatively small. The first member of this troupe, which performs the role of interlocutor (although often on an implicit level), is my own church tradition, located within the life and thought of those most peculiar people known as Baptists. The purpose of beginning with my own tradition is *not* to formulate a position that is primarily addressed to those of similar conviction and practice. Lash rightly states that such a tightly defined focus "can engender narrowness and parochialism...[that] stands in need of permanent corrective pressure from the 'catholic' impulse."[20] Rather, I want to raise issues and advance claims for all Christians to consider. However, as most involved in ecumenical discussions readily acknowledge, we presently encounter the "catholic" tradition only as it is manifested in particular Christian communities. Insisting at the outset that one particular tradition does fully represent the normative heritage of the church universal—even if, in the providence of God, there is a group that closely embodies in its teachings and practices "the Tradition"—is not only premature but counterproductive as well, given the present status of ecumenical relations.

The first chapter will thus begin with a typology of Baptist theology, in which I shall juxtapose two basic procedures for construing the process and goal of theological inquiry. I shall focus in particular upon the relationship between how theology is conceived as a mode of critical inquiry by these theologians, on the one hand, and the relation of the church's practices, skills, texts, and goals to those of (post)modern society, on the other. As with any typology, this distinction functions heuristically; in this case, it is to help us take note of how particular forms of "scientific" discourse invest twentieth-century Baptist thought as found in some of its preeminent representatives. (It is therefore not intended to serve as a definitive or exhaustive analysis of Baptist theology.)

The first type is the one most often associated with serious theological reflection, and as such it constitutes the dominant form within the academy.[21] This type has embraced, often with only minor reservations, the techniques and tendencies of contemporary Western culture. A second type, though not normally recognized as theological discourse in its own right, reaches back to Baptist origins in the seventeenth century Pietist movement, with its characteristic emphasis upon the *praxis pietatis*,[22] and reconfigures this tradition within the context and challenges of the modern world. The inherent tendencies of the *praxis pietatis* place this second type, in varying degrees,[23] in a critical relationship over against dominant societal tendencies. The strength of the first type lies in its conceptual precision and coherence, but it gains these attributes at the expense of a self-critical examination of the habits, relations, and goals it unwittingly assimilates along with its systematic detail. The second type strives for a conscientious understanding of Christian faith in continuity with its formative roots, and therefore with a measure of suspicion toward the social practices of the modern world, but it lacks (with one notable but problematic exception[24]) any sustained attempt to set forth and explicate the theological terms of the church's engagement with the world. The need for theological critique and self-criticism in Baptist life is thus stymied between the confinement of the first type within questionable modes of inquiry, on the one hand, and the absence of a coherent tradition of theological inquiry to inform the second type, on the other.

Fortunately, the theological legacy of Baptists does not begin and end with the Pietist tradition. Of particular interest to me is the recent work of James McClendon. McClendon locates Baptist life and thought in the first volume of his systematic theology within a broader theological tradition, for which he coins the term *baptist* to distinguish it from its more conventional use. The primary characteristic of "baptists," writes McClendon, consists of the recognition of a vital link that exists between the church of the apostles and our own, which he expresses in a hermeneutical motto, "[the] shared awareness of *the present Christian community as the primitive community and the eschatological community.*"[25] Contrary to what is often said of the baptist position, McClendon does not ignore historical developments that occur after the first century, nor does he propose a simplistic restitution of "primitive" Christianity. It has principally to do, as John Howard Yoder puts it, with the one trait that characterizes all Protestants, "from 'mainstream' to 'radical'," which is the conviction

> that in the earlier history of Christianity something had gone wrong. For some, the corrective change that would be needed should be minimal, limited to those points "necessary for salvation," with no intention to call into question the inherited church order. For others, the change needs to be sweeping. But that there needs to be critical change at all means in any case that our…reasoning cannot proceed unself-critically. We can never simply stand on the shoulders of an unquestioned consensus from the past, claiming it to be "catholic" and assuming its acceptability simply by virtue of the claim that it has been believed always everywhere by everyone.[26]

McClendon's "baptist vision," its seems to me, moves the discussion regarding the role of theological inquiry in the right direction, and so from time to time it will emerge in my deliberations.[27]

There is a second reason for beginning with Baptist life and theology, albeit a negative one. Harold Bloom, in his latest book, *The American Religion*, is uncomfortably close to the target when he argues that "Southern Baptists call themselves Christians, but like most Americans they are closer to ancient Gnostics than to early Christians."[28] Baptists thus afford an ideal setting for examining the techniques of normalization which confront the church in a (post)modern world. Kenneth Cauthen, for example, has identified crucial links between the Pietist emphases embodied in Baptist life, and the prevalence of liberal and revisionist theology in most American churches. In particular, he cites the rejection of creedal conformity and the freedom of the individual to interpret the Scriptures for herself, plus the stress in frontier revivalism on the importance of conversion and the experience of salvation, which shifts attention away from correct dogmatic assent and focuses it on individual experience. Cauthen correctly concludes that "In the light of this background it is not surprising that some of the most influential leaders of liberal thought in America came out of a Baptist, pietistic environment which had already laid the groundwork for some of the most distinctive liberal emphases."[29] Moreover, as McClendon says, it was also this groundwork which "permitted alien thought forms to supplant the baptist vision, which is at the true center of this way of life."[30] Contemporary Baptist life and thought thus provide an ecclesial microcosm —a laboratory microworld for theology, if you will—in which to isolate and identify some of the problematic threads within the social fabric of the (post)modern church.

Yet another reason for examining this microcosm has to do with developments in communions outside of the Baptist tradition. Theologians within the so-called mainline or magisterial churches have recently begun to seriously reexamine various aspects of the free church tradition which were once summarily disparaged as sectarian. Beginning with historical inquiries into the early church's baptismal practices and the concept of a regenerate church membership, and extending to a variety of contemporary issues—the precise nature of the relationship between the church and liberal capitalism, doubts about a just war in a nuclear age, the character of the diaspora existence which Christians now face in an increasingly post-Christian age—practices and relations that once were dismissed out of hand are now being carefully reassessed by these other traditions.[31] With or without their knowledge or consent, the contribution of baptists to the faith and practice of the church catholic is finally being realized.

In the final analysis, though, whatever is signified by the word baptist must be consonant with the "catholic" substance of the church and the Christian faith. Nothing that I shall advocate in this book will be as controversial with my fellow Baptists as this last statement. All manner of accusations will likely be leveled against me, and charges of "creedalism," "clericalism," and "sacerdotalism," coupled with stirring reaffirmations of "soul liberty" and the "autonomy" of the local church, will no doubt reverberate in protest. Yet there is no Christian people more entangled as a group in the habits and relations of (post)modern culture than Baptists are. Anti-creedalism has ironically become the most stringent and impoverished creed that anyone calling themselves Christian has ever devised. If there is any group that is more dogmatic than Baptist fundamentalists, it is the so-called moderates, only their dogma, as Bloom has documented, is more indebted to the Cartesian anthropology of William James and Ralph Waldo Emerson than it is to Scripture, Nicaea, and Chalcedon.[32]

My concern with the catholicity of theological inquiry may help to explain why I, a Baptist (or baptist) theologian, do not deal in depth with the subject of baptism in this book, but discuss time and again the Eucharist (or as my tradition calls it, the Lord's Supper). I have particularly found Nicholas Lash to be a complementary and, on occasion, corrective voice to the others in my research. The writings of David Burrell, Avery Dulles, Gustavo Gutiérrez, Alasdair MacIntyre, Herbert McCabe, John Milbank, and Rowan Williams have also provided me with considerable insight into the fundamental themes of theology's catholic heritage.

The chief protagonist in this work, however, is Paul Lehmann. A sustained and rigorous engagement with Lehmann's theology, located in chapters four to seven, provides both the content and the form for the present study. As I hope to demonstrate, Lehmann's approach to theological inquiry is well suited to the task at hand. First, he embodies many of the concerns of the early Baptist Pietists. He shares their commitment to an intensely personal and holistic relationship to God, but he also extends and deepens the scope of this commitment. More specifically, Lehmann positions the *praxis pietatis* within the *koinonia*, the fellowship or communion of the Christian community, contending that the formative practices of the church shape its piety and distinctive style of life. Above all else, he asserts that the *koinonia* is preeminently a eucharistic achievement.

Lehmann forges a creative link between the practice of piety and the everyday life of the Christian *koinonia* in terms of the political dynamics of God's presence and activity in the world. While the correlation of piety with politics may seem at odds with traditional conceptions of spirituality, Lehmann persuasively argues that an Aristotelian definition of politics—"activity, and reflection upon activity, which aims at and analyzes what it takes to make and keep human life human in the world"—places the sense of the biblical metaphors describing God's creative and redemptive activity within its proper context. Messianic politics, as a result, frames the biblical contours and directions of a mature Christian spirituality. Piety apart from politics, on the other hand, "loses its integrity and converts into apostasy; whereas politics without piety subverts both its divine ordination and its ordering of humanness, perverts justice, and converts into idolatry."[33]

Lehmann also shares with Baptists their commitment to the scriptural basis of Christian piety. He constantly strives to nurture within the church a "biblical imagination [which can] give pointed expression to what God is doing in the world."[34] However, unlike many later-day Pietists, Lehmann does not regard the Bible as a timeless repository of perfect, propositionally formed truths or as the symbolic representation of a people's religious experience. Instead he contends that Scripture, through the imaginative use of metaphor within an overarching narrative, juxtaposes "inconfusedly and inseparably" the ways of God and the activities and achievements of humankind. The penultimate chapter of the biblical narrative is the story of the eucharistic community in the world, through whom, "by the operative (real) presence and power of the Messiah-Redeemer in the midst of his people, and through them of all people," God labors to fashion an alternative history for creation. The church thus exhibits to the present order of things the contours and content of God's providential care for the world: the new humanity and the age to come.[35] Lehmann's approach to Scripture supports a style of theological inquiry which is prepared not only to disclose the idolatry in other perspectives, but also for the collapse of its own idols, while at the same time providing the church with the skills it needs to discern something of God's providential ordering of creation.[36]

Lehmann's theology also shares a great deal with baptist thought. This continuity is often overlooked by many baptist theologians, such as Yoder, Hauerwas, and McClendon, due perhaps to a natural tendency on their part to associate Lehmann's work with that of his American contemporaries, H. Richard and Reinhold Niebuhr, rather than with that of his close friend and Union Seminary classmate, Dietrich Bonhoeffer.[37] Even where baptists do disagree with Lehmann—particularly over such troublesome questions as the nature of the church's involvement in the violence of the present age—the differences are not incommensurable, and thus the engagement of these two perspectives creates opportunities for determining how the church might go on and go further on these important issues. In any event, engaging Lehmann's theology from a baptist perspective has proven to be an interesting and productive endeavor.

The rhetorical *leitmotif* of this study is the notion of conscience, for which Lehmann provides an innovative account in his writings. According to Lehmann, it is only as human motivation and human judgment actually converge within conscience that God and humans "have directly and insistently to do with one another [as] the aims and the direction, the motivations and the decisions, the instruments and the structures of human interrelatedness are forged into a pattern of response—a style of life."[38] As a result, only as the sentience, motility, and intentionality of our bodies are shaped and directed within this distinctive style of life (the effect of a social configuration inaugurated by God's redemptive presence in history), is it possible to attend truthfully to the mystery of our existence. While the idea of conscience does not often provide the basis for ordering in a coherent fashion the many concerns and tasks of theology, there are precedents for it in the history of Christian theology. Chapters two and three, therefore, will examine four noted theologians who, over the centuries, made effective use of the idea of conscience to focus and direct their thought.

In many respects, however, it is chapter five, dealing with the relationship of conscience and power, that forms the core of this book. Most modern inquires into the question of power, whether liberal or Marxist, posit a radical distinction between power and knowledge. I shall argue that this is a misleading dichotomy. Power, as one philosopher of science recently put it, cannot be regarded either as external to knowledge or as its antithesis; rather, power is the mark of knowledge.[39] Thus the question of how to construe the intrinsic relation between conscience and power is both crucial and complex. Lehmann's thoughts on this matter, while in need of elaboration, help to break down this unhealthy dichotomy.

One final comment is in order. This book is not an intellectual history of Lehmann's thought,[40] nor a work on early Pietism or Baptist theology. With respect to Lehmann, I find him at certain key points in need of elaboration or correction. With respect to traditional Baptist positions, as noted above, I shall often side with what I have called the catholic tradition. For example, I agree with Lehmann's assertion that the fundamental relatedness of individuals within the church is a eucharistic achievement. This book *is* about the role of Christian theology, of theologians such as myself, and about the contribution we make—or fail to make—to the ongoing life of the church in a (post)modern world. An underlying premise of this book, therefore, has to do with what I take to be the primary concern of theological inquiry, namely, that it is inextricably interwoven with the church's continuing struggle with both its tradition *and* its own social and historical context for the practice of everyday life.[41] The metaphor of arbitration, rather than the popular images of dialogue and conversation, best express the practical—and thus the political—character of theology's deliberations. The idea of arbitration allows, or rather *compels* us to be mindful of the interrelatedness of power and knowledge intrinsic to human affairs.

I shall close with another citation from Lentricchia, an author of Italian-American ancestry whom a fellow critic once dubbed the "dirty Harry" of literary theory. In an animated discussion with another well-known and controversial literary critic about the social role of "theory," Lentricchia offers a humorous midrash on a notorious fictional character in a popular novel and movie that may help the reader get at what I take to be the role of theology within the life of the church. Perhaps, suggests Lentricchia, theologians could

> learn a lesson from our godfather, Vito Corleone, who believed that one (preferably someone else) had to "answer" for one's actions. Don Corleone was a connoisseur of reason (as in "I will reason with him"; or as in "But no one can reason with him"). But the Don was no Kantian. Unlike [theologians and other scholars] who assign self-consciousness no historical role, he knew that the sort of worry synonymous with self-reflection takes place in a context of other wills, not in some self-contained transcendental inner sphere, but in a context of situations that make vivid, sometimes vividly red, the consequences of taking "unreasonable" positions. Critical self-consciousness, in other words, is not a pointless activity of intellectuals too enamored of philosophical idealism, but a necessity for getting on with others in the world—a necessity even for intellectuals.[42]

We do indeed need to realize that humans must "answer" for their actions, and therefore it is incumbent upon theologians to be connoisseurs of reason. The connoisseurship of reason, however, does not refer to a self-contained, transcendental sphere of religious experience, nor does it reside in pious generalizations about the semiotic conditions of "unconstrained conversation" or in thick descriptions of quasi-transcendental symbol systems. The primary context of theological rationality is not the cordial yet deceptive confines of the seminar room. Like the reasonableness of Don Corleone, self-critical theological reflection functions within what William James once called the "blooming, buzzing confusion" of everyday life. When practiced from the standpoint of the messianic community, the bewilderingly unpredictable, frequently traumatic, and often tragic character of our existence does make vivid, and sometimes vividly red, the consequences of taking unreasonable or abnormal positions. Theology, in other words, is not a pointless activity of intellectuals enchanted by the abstractions of academia, but a necessity for the church which properly regards itself as "the corporate structure of God's activity in the world."[43] Moreover, when Lentricchia refers to "a context of situations that make vivid, sometimes vividly red, the consequences of taking 'unreasonable' positions," he not only illumines Jesus' statement that Christians are to be as "wise as serpents" (Matthew 10[16]), he also sheds unexpected light on what frequently happens when Christians demonstrate unreasonable fidelity to Jesus' insistence that we are also to be as "harmless as doves." Herbert McCabe puts the matter in a concise and straightforward manner:

> The gospels…on many occasions insist upon two antithetical truths which express the tragedy of the human condition: the first is that if you do not love you will not be alive; the second is that if you *do* love you will be killed. If you cannot love you remain self-enclosed and sterile, unable to create a future for yourself or others, unable to live. If, however, you do effectively love you will be a threat to the structures of domination upon which our human society rests and you will be killed.[44]

NOTES

[1]Frank Lentricchia, *Criticism and Social Change* (Chicago: The University of Chicago Press, 1983), 1–2; Kenneth Burke, *Attitudes Toward History*, 3d ed. (Berkeley: University of California Press, 1984), 331–32.

[2]The parenthetical rendering of this term is my way of emphasizing what I take to be the fundamental continuity between so-called postmodern doctrines of the text and the social and intellectual contours of modern Western society.

[3]John Milbank, *Theology and Social Theory: Beyond Secular Reason* (Cambridge, MA: Basil Blackwell Inc., 1990), 228.

[4]Alasdair MacIntyre, *Whose Justice? Which Rationality?* (Notre Dame, IN: University of Notre Dame Press, 1988), 392.

[5]Stanley Hauerwas, *After Christendom?* (Nashville, TN: Abingdon Press, 1991), 93–96.

[6]Stanley Hauerwas and William H. Willimon, *Resident Aliens: Life in the Christian Colony* (Nashville, TN: Abingdon Press, 1989).

[7]William Placher, "Revisionist and Postliberal Theologies and the Public Character of Theology," *The Thomist* 49 (July 1985): 392. I would include under the banner of revisionist theology Gregory Baum, Clodovis Boff, John Cobb, Edward Farley, Langdon Gilkey, David Ray Griffin, Gordon Kaufman, Hans Küng, Sallie McFague, Wolfhart Pannenberg, Schubert Ogden, Rosemary Ruether, Susan Thistlethwaite, and David Tracy. While some may be surprised to see the names of noted liberation and feminist theologians on this list, it is my contention that much of liberation and feminist theology has become entangled in the normalizing tendencies of (post)modern thought, thus emptying it of much

its revolutionary content and unwittingly perpetuating what may be appropriately called neo-patriarchy.

[8]David Ray Griffin, Introduction to SUNY Series in Constructive Postmodern Thought, *Primordial Truth and Postmodern Theology*, by David Ray Griffin and Huston Smith (Albany, NY: State University of New York Press, 1989), xiii; cf. John B. Cobb, "Two Types of Postmodernism: Deconstruction and Process," *Theology Today* 48 (July 1990): 149–58.

[9]Stanley Rosen, *Hermeneutics as Politics* (New York: Oxford University Press, 1987), 15, 28. For more sustained criticisms of liberal-revisionist strategies, see Paul Giurlanda, *Faith and Knowledge* (Lanham, MD: University Press of America, 1987), 256–97; and Frederick Herzog, *Justice Church* (Maryknoll, NY: Orbis Press, 1980), 55–71.

[10]Nicholas Lash, *Theology on the Way to Emmaus* (London: SCM Press Ltd, 1986), 21–22. Michel Foucault levels a similar indictment against revisionist attempts to revive the liberal project, only more directly: "'Dialectic' is a way of evading the always open and hazardous reality of conflict by reducing it to a Hegelian skeleton, and 'semiology' is a way of avoiding its violent, bloody and lethal character by reducing it to the calm Platonic form of language and dialogue." Michel Foucault, *Power/Knowledge*, ed. Colin Gordon (New York: Pantheon Books, 1980), 114–15.

[11]The writings of Jacques Derrida provide the point of departure for deconstructionist theology. Among those who explicitly approach the field of Christian theology from a deconstructionist perspective are Thomas Altizer, Gary Percesepe, Carl Raschke, Robert Scharlemann, Mark C. Taylor, and Charles Winquist.

[12]Cornel West, *The American Evasion of Philosophy* (Madison: The University of Wisconsin Press, 1989), 236.

[13]Cornel West, "Ethics and Action in Fredric Jameson's Marxist Hermeneutics," *Postmodernism and Politics*, ed. Jonathan Arac (Minneapolis: University of Minnesota Press, 1986), 139.

[14]William H. Poteat, *A Philosophical Daybook: Post-Critical Investigations* (Columbia: University of Missouri Press, 1990), 65.

[15]Rosen, *Hermeneutics as Politics*, 49.

[16]Jeffrey Stout, *Ethics After Babel* (Boston: Beacon Press, 1988), 301. I would include within the category of postliberal theologians Brevard Childs, Hans Frei, Garrett Green, Paul Holmer, George Hunsinger, David Kelsey, George Lindbeck, William Placher, Ronald Thiemann, and Charles Wood.

[17]George Lindbeck, *The Nature of Doctrine* (Philadelphia: The Westminster Press, 1984), 18, 115, 118.

[18]Lindbeck, *The Nature of Doctrine*, 33, 36, 126.

[19]Harvey Cox, *Religion in the Secular City: Toward a Postmodern Theology* (New York: Simon and Schuster, 1984), 11–82; Cornel West, *Prophesy Deliverance!* (Philadelphia: The Westminster Press, 1982), 120.

[20]Lash, *Theology on the Way to Emmaus*, 200.

[21]This predominance in the academy is documented among Southern Baptists, for example, by noting the leading theologians listed by Thomas Langford, "Theology (Southern)" in *Encyclopedia of Religion in the South*, ed. Samuel S. Hill (Macon, GA: Mercer University Press, 1984), 775–77.

[22]F. Ernest Stoeffler, *The Rise of Evangelical Pietism* (Leiden: E. J. Brill, 1965), 5, 9.

[23]It is important to recognize that the representatives of the second type were not thoroughly self-critical in their dealings with the normalizing tendencies and techniques of modernity, a propensity which, as has been often noted, creates ambiguities, distortions and problematic assertions in their thought. But as Lehmann has observed, a theology that aims at a creative iconoclasm must be ready for the collapse of the idolatries in its own perspective as well as those of the views it is criticizing. Paul Lehmann, "On Doing Theology: A Contextual Possibility," *Prospect for Theology: Essays in Honor of H. H. Farmer*, ed. F. G. Healy (Digswell Place: James Nisbet and Co., Ltd., 1966), 136.

[24]Walter Rauschenbusch, *A Theology for the Social Gospel* (New York: The Macmillan Co., 1917). However inadequate we judge this work to be for the task it undertakes, it does set an important precedent in the history of Christian thought for the place of a theology of conscience in the dogmatic reflections of the church. As Rauschenbusch's biographer comments: "At least he gave the social gospel a chair in the house of Christian theology." Dores Robinson Sharpe, *Walter Rauschenbusch* (New York: The Macmillan Co., 1942), 354.

[25]James William McClendon, *Ethics: Systematic Theology* (Nashville, TN: Abingdon Press, 1986), 31.

[26]John Howard Yoder, *The Priestly Kingdom* (Notre Dame, IN: University of Notre Dame Press, 1984), 16.

[27]I differ from McClendon's understanding of "baptist" in one significant respect: I argue that the "baptist vision" is finally not a "vision" at all, i.e., it does not primarily subsist as an explicit set of convictions in terms of which we "gaze" at the world, but as a distinctive configuration of social practices and relations that offers an alternative range of possibilities for creation to those provided by the polity and policies of "normal" society and culture. I would prefer, in other words, to speak of "baptist politics."

[28]Harold Bloom, *The American Religion: The Emergence of the Post-Christian Nation* (New York: Simon & Schuster, 1992), 22. The links between the emergence of this new form of gnosticism and Puritan Pietism have recently been explored in a most interesting way by Charles Taylor in his recent book, *Sources of the Self: The Making of the Modern Identity* (Cambridge, MA: Harvard University Press, 1989), 211–47.

[29]Kenneth Cauthen, *The Impact of American Religious Liberalism*, 2d ed. (Washington: University Press of American, 1983), 62. Unlike early Pietism, Cauthen ascribes the main locus of authority to personal experience in later Baptist thought, which represents a departure from original Puritanism and reflects the inroads made into Pietism by the ethos of the Enlightenment. Stoeffler, *The Rise of Evangelical Pietism*, 14–15.

[30]McClendon, *Ethics: Systematic Theology*, 27.

[31]See Yoder, *The Priestly Kingdom*, 5–6, and Terrence Tilley, "Why American Catholic Theologians Should Read 'baptist' Theology," *Horizons* 14 (1987): 129–137.

[32]Bloom, *The American Religion*, 191–217.

[33]Paul L. Lehmann, *Ethics in a Christian Context* (New York: Harper & Row, 1963), 65, 85, 90–95; Paul Lehmann, *The Transfiguration of Politics* (New York: Harper & Row, 1975), 234; see also 32, 233, 258, 269–270.

[34]Lehmann, *Ethics*, 90.

[35]Lehmann, *Ethics*, 86–101; "On Doing Theology," 123, 133–34.

[36]Paul Louis Lehmann, "The Formative Power of Particularity," *Union Seminary Quarterly Review* 18 (March 1963): 318; "On Doing Theology," 136; *Transfiguration*, 282–84.

[37]See Stanley Hauerwas, "The Politics of Charity," *Interpretation* 31 (July 1977): 252; McClendon, *Ethics*, 259–66.

[38]Lehmann, *Ethics*, 288.

[39]Joseph Rouse, *Knowledge and Power: Toward a Political Philosophy of Science* (Ithaca, NY: Cornell University Press, 1987), 19.

[40]Nancy J. Duff's book, *Humanization and the Politics of God: The Koinonia Ethics of Paul Lehmann* (Grand Rapids, MI: Wm. B. Eerdmans Publishing Co., 1992), does a commendable job of summarizing Lehmann's theology.

[41]See Michel de Certeau, *The Practice of Everyday Life*, trans. Steven F. Rendall (Berkeley: The University of California Press, 1984).

[42]Frank Lentricchia, *Ariel and the Police* (Madison: The University of Wisconsin Press, 1988), 133.

[43]Lehmann, *Ethics*, 58; cf. 47, 68.

[44]Herbert McCabe, O.P., *God Matters* (London: Geoffrey Chapman, 1987), 218. The conclusion to this chapter is adapted from my "Insanity, Theocracy, and the Public Realm: Public Theology, the Church, and the Politics of Liberal Democracy," *Modern Theology* 10 (January 1994): 52–53.

Chapter 1

SCIENCE, CONSCIENCE, AND THE POLITICS OF THEOLOGY

"To be or not to be—that is indeed the first and indispensable question for everything and everyone, and for man in particular. But with respect to Being, does God have to behave like Hamlet?" With this allusion to the famous soliloquy of Hamlet, Jean-Luc Marion begins a rigorous mode of inquiry into the "God without Being," that is, the God who is not determined by the relation to Being. Ultimately, argues Marion, the issue at hand for theology is not whether it is possible for God to attain to Being, "but, quite the opposite, the possibility of Being's attaining to God." David Tracy, in the book's foreword, uses Marion's thesis as the basis upon which to distinguish between the "two basic theological strategies on the proper Christian response to modernity." The first and more familiar of these procedures, and the one that Tracy advocates, is a revisionist or correlational strategy, an approach that seeks in manifold ways to correlate the claims of "reason" and the disclosures of "revelation." Tracy associates Marion with a second strategy, which in its various manifestations contends that reason as such is an idol that is incapable of "iconically disclosing God."[1]

In this chapter I shall address a set of issues that runs parallel to Marion's construal of the relationship between the category of Being and the God without Being. My concern, however, is to critique the concept of Knowledge as it functions in modern and (post)modern thought. In particular, I shall argue that our relation to God is not determined by our epistemological or hermeneutical strategies (which I locate under the category of science) but rather that our knowledge is determined by our performative relation to God and our fellow creatures (which I shall deal with under the category of conscience). As Scripture puts it, it is not possible for humans to know the mystery of God, but in Christ we are known by God, and are thereby empowered to share in the knowledge of God. Knowledge of God, in this sense, is not a subject's categorical grasp of an object. McCabe correctly observes that "our faith seems not like an increase of knowledge but, if anything, an increase of ignorance. We become more acutely aware of our inadequacy before the mystery as we are brought closer to it." The knowledge of God, states Rowan Williams, is "sharing what God is—more boldly, you might say, sharing God's 'experience'. God is known in and by the exercise of crucifying compassion; if we are like him in that, we know him. And we know 'as we are known', 'as I have been fully understood' (1 Cor. 13[12]), since God knows the human condition in loving it."[2]

However, rather than speaking of God's "experience" of the world to describe our knowledge of God, I argue that to share what God is requires that we share God's "conscience." Moreover, as Lash says, "If the God who always has to do with us (whether or not we advert to the fact, or have been educated to recognition of the fact) is to be named as 'holy mystery', then it follows that *all* our actions and relationships—domestic and political, cultural and scientific—must be disciplined and qualified by...reticence and reverence."[3] In other words, only to the extent that we come to share in the conscience of God are humans capable of a non-instrumental (and therefore non-idolatrous) form of science as knowledge of the world.

However, if we are to make the transition from science to conscience, theologians must first dispense with the metaphysics of the subject that has virtually dictated every aspect of both (post)modern ontology and epistemology. What will emerge in its place can be specified only in relation to the practical networks that determine for Christians both the range and the character of its responses to the world. In order to make sense of the difference between "science" and "conscience," therefore, I need to elaborate on what is implied by the former concept in the context of modern and (post)modern thought, and especially in relation to the modern dogma of the human subject. To do this I shall address certain developments within Baptist thought connected to the conception of theology as a science, and then compare this emphasis on scientific knowledge with an alternative tradition of inquiry emphasizing the notion of conscience. Ironically, both models are firmly rooted in the movement which gave birth to Baptists— Puritanism and its distinctive conception of the *praxis pietatis*. In spite of their common origins, however, these models focus on and develop radically different aspects of this tradition. In the final section I shall attempt to briefly indicate how a carefully crafted understanding of conscience offers us an alternative basis upon which to develop a coherent account of how humans are truthfully related both to the mystery of God and of every other person and thing with whom we share creation.

Theologians of "Science" and the Ethos of Modernity

We can detect within late nineteenth and twentieth century Baptist thought two contrasting procedures concerning the response of theology to the modern world. One approach typifies the writings of those most commonly accepted as properly doing the work of the theologian. Numbered among this group are many of the theologians who formed the main conduit through which the developments and directions of Protestant liberalism were mediated to North America. William Newton Clarke, Harry Emerson Fosdick, Shailer Mathews, Douglas Clyde Macintosh, Crawford H. Toy, William Rainey Harper, Shirley Jackson Case and George B. Foster make up what may be called the liberal wing of this first type. Also included in this first group of Baptist theologians are those who, while more conservative and therefore cautious in their use of the methods and conclusions of the mentality which found theological expression in Protestant liberalism, nevertheless took advantage in varying degrees of these methods' insights and contributions to theological inquiry. Walter T. Conner, Dale Moody, Edgar Young Mullins and Augustus Hopkins Strong are some of the names to be noted in this context.[4]

A brief look at a few of these scholars will show how thoroughly the practice of theology was thought to fall within the purview of the "scientific method." Indeed, it is of great concern to them to demonstrate the scientific character of theology. The position of Clarke, whose book *An Outline of Christian Theology* was a standard text in systematic theology in many Protestant seminaries at the turn of the century, is typical:

> Theology is the study of religion and nothing else, and thus its field possesses such unity as a science requires. Its work is the investigation and classification of facts; it employs both the inductive and the deductive method, and it seeks to hold whatever is legitimately ascertained and nothing more. Thus as to field and methods it is related to its material, the facts

of religion, much as botany is related to the facts of plant-life, or astronomy to the facts of celestial matter and motion, and ranks with them among sciences…Theology claims that its facts are ascertainable in a reasonable degree, and capable of scientific treatment…As the science of religion, it seeks to discover and make known the true, rational, abiding foundation of real and eternal religious life for man.[5]

Strong concurs with Clarke's estimation of theology as a science, although he prefers to call it "the science of God and of the relations between God and the universe," rather than the science of religion. He says further that "In defining theology as a science, we indicate its aim. Science does not create, it discovers. Theology answers to this description of a science. It discovers facts and relations, but it does not create them." Strong also extends Clarke's understanding of science to include its systematizing character: "Science is not only the observing, recording, verifying and formulating of objective facts; it is also the recognition and explication of the relations between these facts, and the synthesis of both the facts and relational principles which unite them in a comprehensive, rightly proportioned and organic system."[6]

The concern for the scientific character of theological inquiry also prevails among more conservative Southern Baptist theologians. Mullins, arguably the most influential theologian Baptists have ever produced in North America, agrees with Strong that theology is a science that deals with God and God's relation to humanity, although like Clarke this entails a necessary connection to religion as the primary object of investigation.[7] Moody also grounds his understanding of Christian doctrine in a methodology which seeks to harmonize and systematize the historical and natural sciences in a cultural apologetic for the Christian Bible. He thus sets out to "illustrate how the historical-critical study of the Scriptures is the best way to relate the Scriptures to modern science and society."[8]

While some express reservations about how appropriate the notion of science is in relation to the primary aims of theology, for the most part these Baptist theologians, as well as their colleagues in virtually every other tradition in the West, are enchanted by, and therefore warmly embraced, the modern ethos of "science." Few thought it necessary to seriously question the fundamental soundness of this epistemic strategy or the anthropology implicit in its governing assumptions. Most eagerly expected a harvest of knowledge to be gleaned from the commonly accepted definition of science. Lacking any kind of detailed hermeneutics of suspicion,[9] the epistemic model of science and its correlative construal of the human subject came to dominate the theological scene.

In one sense we should not be surprised by their enthusiasm. As scholars located within the highly regarded universities and seminaries of North America and Europe, the dominant intellectual assumptions of these institutions also establish for this first type of theological inquiry the essential structures and directions of the epistemic strategy of science. Richard Rorty accurately describes the conventional wisdom that has characterized the contemporary academic setting since the period of the Enlightenment, especially as it is embodied in the foundational discipline of philosophy:

> In every sufficiently reflective culture, there are those who single out one area, one set of practices, and see it as the paradigm human activity. Then they try to show how the rest of culture can profit from this example. In the mainstream of the Western philosophical tradition, this paradigm has been knowing—possessing justified true beliefs, or, better yet, beliefs so intrinsically persuasive as to make justification unnecessary. Successive philosophical revolutions within this mainstream...are so many attempts to refashion the rest of culture on the model of the latest cognitive achievement.[10]

The paradigm of "knowledge" was thought to be warranted by the spectacular successes of the natural sciences, a set of disciplines that most believed could dictate where and how and under what conditions one could make claims to truth, goodness, beauty, and divinity. Habermas, for example, observes that "Knowledge is implicitly defined by the achievement of the sciences. Hence transcendental inquiry into the conditions of possible knowledge can be meaningfully pursued only in the form of methodological inquiry into the rules for the construction and corroboration of scientific theories."[11] In his book *The Empire of Reason*, historian Henry Steele Commager describes the scientistic ethos in which not only Baptist theology but virtually all of modern Christian thought was cultivated:

> It was the age of science, it was the age of philosophy, it was the age of enlightenment. Everywhere the scientists were philosophers, and most of the philosophers were scientists, while all were enlightened. They had emancipated themselves from all but the classical past (which was not really past at all, but viewed as contemporary)—the past of ignorance, credulity and superstition—and now with tireless curiosity and feverish impatience they hurled themselves upon a new world and a new universe. They were not interested in the next world; they were interested in the world about them, the world of Nature, society, politics, and law; they were interested in Man...

"Order," they knew, "is Nature's first law," and they made it their
own, for they were in harmony with Nature. They organized, they system-
atized, they classified, they codified, and all Nature, the universe itself, fell
into order at their bidding...

There was order even in religion...Indeed, God Himself was admon-
ished to abide by fixed laws, for as Jonathan Mayhew of Boston reminded
Him, "The power of the Almighty is *limited by law*...by the eternal *laws* of
truth, wisdom and equity, and the everlasting *tables* of right reason."[12]

Charles Taylor notes that the scientific revolution found in Puritan
theology, and particularly in their affirmations regarding the sacredness of
work and ordinary life, a hospitable environment. Like most Protestant
groups, Puritans (out of whom the first Baptists emerged) rejected the sacramental view of the late medieval Catholic Church and the corrupt notion
that a monastic vocation was somehow higher or more spiritual than the
concerns of everyday life on the part of the laity. Marriage and secular
vocation were raised to a quasi-sacramental status (a status they possess,
moreover, apart from the life of the church). To be a valid calling, one's
labor had only to be of benefit to humankind, giving rise to the well-known
Puritan stress on personal discipline and diligence (what Max Weber labels
its "innerworldly asceticism"). The things of this world, including a person's relationships with other people, existed not for themselves, and therefore they had no inherent significance and were not to be enjoyed except in
the proper spirit, i.e., as instruments to serve and glorify God. Moreover,
there was

a profound analogy in the way the proponents of both Baconian science and
Puritan theology saw themselves in relation to experience and tradition.
Both saw themselves as rebelling against a traditional authority which was
merely feeding on its own errors and as returning to the neglected sources:
the Scriptures on one hand, experimental reality on the other. Both ap-
pealed to what they saw as living experience against dead received doctrine
—the experience of personal conversion and commitment, or that of direct
observation of nature's workings.[13]

Puritan theology also helped to give birth to modernity's instrumental
view of reason. The traditional view of science, says Taylor, which sought
to contemplate the overall order in creation, "came to be seen as vain and
misguided, as a presumptuous attempt to escape the hard work of detailed
discovery." Bacon's insistence that science must serve humankind, rather
than striving toward speculative ideas which result in unresolvable disputes,
found a receptive ear in Puritanism's emphasis on productive efficacy in

every form of human labor, so that as God's elect stewards of creation they might repair the disorder caused by sin to the world. Taylor suggests that "where Protestant theology had made the circumspect and sober use of the things which surround us to the ends of our preservation and the glory of God, the spiritually correct way to be in the world, Bacon develops a view of the physical universe which makes this essential to the *epistemically* correct way as well...Our aim must be to use things in the way God intended, and this has yet to be (re)discovered in our fallen condition...Baconian science, in other words, gains a pious purpose within the framework of Puritan spirituality..."[14]

Within this enlightened and sanctified framework, most theologians drank deeply from the well of the reason of science. They were for the most part thoroughly enchanted by the cultural demand that theology be rigorously scientific in its reflections and representations. With few exceptions, theologians sought to duplicate with their own object of inquiry the paradigm of *scientia* as it was generally understood by modernity, as can be seen in the ways they identified problems, formulated solutions, and pursued methodological refinements. It was hoped that the systematic order which this approach seemed to offer could yield the kind of manageable control for the theological disciplines that had been demonstrated (most felt conclusively) in the natural sciences.

The emergence of the so-called human sciences, first in certain key social institutions of early modernity, and then later on within the academy, may also be linked to the prevailing scientism of the period. The scientific management of human beings, i.e., of the *faits sociales* and of the human consciousness, did not lag far behind the development of the natural sciences. Milbank notes that "[the] bond between 'natural' and 'social' science is here perfect, and present even as far back as Pierre d'Ailly, for whom an exclusively positive character of legal obligation reflects a natural causality which is the merely accidental regularity of divine, legally imposed connections, between entirely discrete particulars." And in France, writes Commager, "La Mettrie—Voltaire called him the 'King's Atheist in Ordinary'—announced that Man was a Machine, neither more nor less; and indeed if the whole world was a machine, why not man?" It is therefore not surprising to learn that "for Hobbes, Wilkins and Locke, ethical understanding is more susceptible to geometrization or probabilization than physics because here alone technical control can be coextensive with the object of understanding."[15]

To be sure, the supposition that Christian thought should be practiced under the rubric of science is not an innovation of the twentieth century nor strictly an intellectual heirloom of the Enlightenment. On the contrary, the idea of theological science occupies a well-established position in the Christian tradition extending back to at least the thirteenth century. Etienne Gilson, commenting on Thomas Aquinas' declaration at the beginning of the magisterial *Summa Theologica* that "*sacra doctrina est scientia,*" claims that "There is no question of maintaining—no one has ever maintained—that faith is a kind of cognition superior to rational cognition. It is quite clear, on the contrary, that belief is a *succedaneum* of knowledge, and that to substitute science for belief, wherever possible, is always a positive gain for the understanding." Lev Shestov, exploring the relationship between faith, reason, and revelation in the history of Christian thought in its anthropological context, traces the genealogy, if not the terminology, of theological science back to the dawn of the Middle Ages: "Already in St. Augustine, it is clearly established that faith is subject to the control of reason, that it almost seeks this control." It must be conceded, therefore, that the scientific posture of modern theology does appear to have rhetorical warrants in the Christian tradition.[16]

However, in the decades following the Enlightenment the notion of science acquired a sense and significance which differed in important respects from its earlier, pre-Enlightenment connotations. According to both classical and medieval thought, knowledge consists in the relation between the self and that which is known, whereas modern thought assign epistemic and metaphysical priority to the knowing subject, thereby redefining knowledge as that which securely bridges the rift between the subject and all that is "outside" it. In effect, the mind of the isolated "I" became the exclusive site of all knowledge and understanding. This paradigm shift constituted a fundamental restructuring of what it meant to make a legitimate claim that one had scientifically acquired knowledge.[17] When nurtured in the soil of the Puritan theology of work and ordinary life, and formulated by such philosophers as René Descartes, John Locke, David Hume and, most influentially, Immanuel Kant, "science" gradually was shrouded in a mystique of objectivity, so that one who had proceeded scientifically possessed hard, rational knowledge, that is, knowledge which putatively was value-neutral, detached, certain (or at least highly probable), and definitive. The difference between the entities which the sciences sought to comprehend and the theories which were developed to facilitate that comprehension was progressively obscured in both the popular mind and in the philosophical discussions of the day by the conviction that there was a prevailing identity between the two.[18]

It should not surprise anyone, then, if theologians were either so impressed or intimidated by the compelling achievements of the natural and human sciences that their continued existence within the academy was felt to depend on whether they could demonstrate, in ways that were methodologically appropriate for their object of investigation, a similar scientific character that marked Newtonian mechanics, Darwinian biology, or political economy.[19] It was widely thought that the only alternative to this scientistic impulse was to be relegated to the subjective and emotive (that is, the irrational and chaotic) realm of what was considered to be a primitive (that is to say, pre-scientific) form of (not quite) human existence that was best left behind.[20] The possibility that such notions are themselves positivistic, and are thus properly subject to rigorous scrutiny, did not occur to many.

Science and the Positivism of Modern Western Culture

The meaning of the term positivism has shifted markedly since the nineteenth and early twentieth centuries. Whereas the French tradition of sociology, represented by such figures as Emile Durkheim and Auguste Comte, and the philosophical movement known as logical positivism, represented pre-eminently by the so-called Vienna Circle, had enthusiastically embraced the positivist designation, Dietrich Bonhoeffer's contention that Karl Barth's theology had deteriorated from its initial promise into a kind of revelational positivism demonstrates a shift to a more pejorative use of the term.[21] In order to adequately characterize this shift in meaning, we may begin with Wolfhart Pannenberg's definition: "Every form of positivism takes some fact or institution as the ultimate basis of its argument." Furthermore, Pannenberg states, these facts or institutions "are not open to question."[22] In other words, a positivist approach invariably establishes as the *a priori* principle of rational inquiry what ought to be the subject of historical investigation. A positivist mode of inquiry thus begins with an uncritical, fideistic acceptance of some contingent social arrangement of relations and forces, and then insists that this arrangement forms the irreducible norms for determining questions of truth, knowledge and meaning.

In the (post)modern context the concept of science most suitably names the distinctive type of positivism that permeates the practices, techniques, and social roles of modernity. The scope of modernity's positivistic reach is not confined to particular disciplines or institutions, but represents

> a saturation of the whole process of living—not only of political and economic activity, nor only of manifest social activity, but of the whole substance of lived identities and relationships, to such a depth that the pressures and limits of what can ultimately be seen as a specific economic, political, and cultural system seem to most of us the pressures and limits of simple experience and common sense...It is a whole body of practices and expectations, over the whole of living: our sense and assignments of energy, our shaping perceptions of ourselves and our world. It is a lived system of meanings and values—constitutive and constituting—which as they are experienced as practices appear as reciprocally confirming. It thus constitutes a sense of reality for most people in the society, a sense of absolute because experienced reality beyond which it is very difficult for most members of the society to move, in most areas of their lives.[23]

My use of the term science to describe modernity's polity and policies, tendencies and techniques, represents a move away from the popular definition of science as simply a set of "universal laws, valid at all times and places...[which] can be applied to particular situations...by using various bridge principles and by determining the relevant facts about the situation that need to be included in this instantiation of the law."[24] In the final analysis, modernity's positivistic conception of science is rooted in its refusal to self-critically examine its anthropological context, assumptions and consequences. Walker Percy, a novelist and philosopher who deals with the adverse effects of the Enlightenment upon our humanity, contends that the "scientific method" is inherently incapable of adequately coming to terms with the contingency and purposefulness of human existence, a fact that creates an irresolvable methodological antinomy.[25]

As noted above, during the Enlightenment the cultural authority of science and the scientific method extended beyond their original contexts, permeating every aspect of modern society. Matthew Lamb accurately portrays the cultural influence of the scientific ethos:

> The "success" of mathematics and natural sciences meant their methods became the canon of all exact knowledge for the human sciences—what could not be quantified somehow lacked meaning. The "success" of technology meant that the machine became the model of rational order—what

could not be programmed somehow should not exist. Human sciences began to treat humanity as made in the image of its own mechanical products.
Organic and psychic processes were no more than highly complex physical-
mechanical events. Mind and consciousness were dismissed as illusory,
sooner rather than later to be mapped out in cybernetic, bio-computer input-
output schemata. Work was "Taylorized" into mechanistically regulated assembly line productivity. Interpersonal relations became techniques of suc-
cessful role playing. Community values took a back seat to the demands of
mobility with urbanization and industrialization.[26]

The social hegemony of science exerted tremendous positivisitic pressure
not only within the intellectual cloister of the academy but throughout
every dimension of culture, constantly striving to refashion humanity in its
own oppressive image, which Herbert Marcuse has aptly labeled the "one-
dimensional man."[27]

The parturition of modernity's scientism was brought full term with
the entrenchment within Enlightenment thought of the rhetorical picture of
the self as an autonomous, self-possessing subject. This picture, initially
proposed by the French philosopher René Descartes, consolidated and extended the legitimacy that modernity would acquire from the technological
triumphs of the natural sciences to set the parameters of what properly
constitutes knowledge. The primary social effect of the modern doctrine
of subjectivity, writes West, was that philosophy "became the queen of the
emerging scientific disciplines within this new paradigm as a metadiscipline
which provided objective and valid grounds for knowledge claims put for-
ward in the newer disciplines, especially physics. This turn in philosophy
granted science a monopoly on truth in the marketplace of ideas, to the dis-
may of both artists and theologians."[28] The fusion of the Cartesian turn to
the knowing subject with the technical wonders of the so-called "hard" sciences was secured for at least two centuries by its partnership with Isaac
Newton's mechanistic conception of the universe. This alliance seemed to
promise the possibility that all reality would one day be completely mas-
tered. The human self, when depicted as the knowing subject, had become
that through which all reality, including the being of God, was necessarily
mediated.[29]

Descartes's formal philosophical doctrines, such as the mind-body dualism and the quest for absolute certainty, are routinely criticized in philosophy seminar rooms, and just as routinely repudiated. What has not been
repudiated by either modern or (post)modern scholars, however, is the

representation of the self as knowing subject. The Cartesian picture of the
subject, writes William Poteat,

> is comprised of a coherent system of mutually implicative images, meta-
> phors, and analogies, that represent man's relation to nature, to his own
> body, to the world of material objects, to time and history, to his acts of re-
> flection, to his decisions, to his intellect, *even to his own ego*; and these re
> lations are analogous to the relation that God is conceived to have to the
> world that he has made out of nothing. Man is here depicted...as spectators
> of a distanced spectacle, disembrangled from the moil and ruck of the world
> like discarnate gods.[30]

This picture has rooted itself in the imagination of the West, where it
has undergone countless mutations, and in these mutated forms it implicitly
provides the basic presuppositions of modernity's intellectual repertoire.
Thus while Cartesianism as an explicit philosophical system is virtually
without effect in our culture, "it functions however at a tacit level like a
repetition compulsion; it is ubiquitous and pervades the atmosphere of our
life like chronic depression."[31]

In formulating this picture of the knower, Descartes establishes a distinctive, if somewhat peculiar, relationship between the *res cogitans* and the
res extensa. On one hand, the human being as a thinking thing is distinguished by its prior ontological and self-conscious detachment from the remainder of reality. Thus what is variously termed "thinking," "mind,"
"reason," or "self-consciousness" is divorced from and prior to (either log-
ically or ontologically) embodied, social existence in the world. On the
other hand, the primary function of this self-positing subject is to extend itself over the rest of reality through the act of knowing, thus bridging the
chasm separating itself from the world through the generation of precise
representations of objective reality in the mind, consciousness, or (in its
latest philosophical manifestation) in language. From its privileged position of detached priority, the ego or "I think" of isolated human subjectivity seeks to exert itself over the remainder of reality which now stands
over against it as object, that is, as a world which belongs to the subject as a
"stock of resources on hand for the fulfillment of what we value."[32] This
extension of the disembodied, ahistorical subject is accomplished in the activity of knowing, an activity that is formalized and provided with normative criteria in modern culture by science and the scientific method. When
knowing is formed by the scientific method, not only the knowing subject

or self is determined in all its aspects, but also the nature of the known object or world.[33]

The Cartesian dogma of subjectivity, having split the self into two distinctive entities, created an unanticipated abyss between the human being as thinking thing and as extended thing. By making the autonomous subject the starting point for philosophical inquiry into the foundations of knowledge, the intellectual and moral tradition inaugurated by Descartes implicitly assumes that some kind of identity would eventually be secured between an individual's mental or linguistic representations and the alienated objects of the world to which those representations conceptually correspond. Modern thinkers have occupied themselves ever since by trying to build reliable bridges across this abyss, transforming practical problems of knowledge and ethics into "pseudomechanical problems of 'mental engineering'."[34] When the assumption that these "engineering projects" would eventually span the gap is undermined from a variety of viewpoints, thus striping the subject of its intellectual moorings, (post)modern thought is left standing before "the dread chasm that has rent the soul of Western man ever since the famous philosopher Descartes ripped body loose from mind and turned the very soul into a ghost that haunts its own house."[35]

One of the more problematic features of the Cartesian picture is its account of the relationship between knowledge and power, an account shared by liberal, Marxist, and postmodern thinkers alike. According to conventional (i.e., Cartesian) wisdom, power is something that is possessed and used by specific subjects (individuals, institutions, and social classes) who occupy positions of prestige and privilege. Each exercise of power is discrete and relatively self-contained, and is therefore directed against specific individuals, classes and institutions at specific times and places. With respect to epistemic matters, power and knowledge remain distinct in all their interactions. In the best of circumstances, power can assist the quest for knowledge indirectly by securing the social conditions in which open inquiry can proceed unhindered by the repressive use of power. It is usually the case, however, that the use of power constrains or distorts the search for knowledge, forcing those who hold non-traditional beliefs to set them aside in favor of those held by ruling interests. According to this account, however, power never directly contributes to the production of knowledge.

The bifurcation of knowledge and power in conventional accounts of science can also be seen in many of those who have labored to make explicit the historical dimensions of knowledge in the field of hermeneutics, such as Hans-Georg Gadamer and Martin Heidegger. West argues that while these scholars take seriously the *historicity* of thought, that is, the temporally situated nature and bias of texts and interpretations, they fail to take *history* seriously, "to dig into the depths of the cultural contexts of texts and interpreters." In the final analysis, says West, "it is impossible to historicize philosophy without partly politicizing (in contrast to vulgarly ideologizing) it."[36]

Michel Foucault's later work represents a sustained attempt to undermine the conceptual split between power and knowledge by politicizing the modern imagination. In particular, he recommends that we

> abandon a whole tradition that allows us to imagine that knowledge can exist only where the power relations are suspended and that knowledge can develop only outside its injunctions, its demands and its interests...[We] should abandon the belief that power makes mad and that, by the same token, the renunciation of power is one of the conditions of knowledge. We should admit rather that power produces knowledge (and not simply by encouraging it because it serves power or by applying it because it us useful); that power and knowledge directly imply one another; that there is no power relation without the correlative constitution of a field of knowledge, nor any knowledge that does not presuppose and constitute at the same time power relations. These "power-knowledge relations" are to be analysed, therefore, not on the basis of a subject of knowledge who is or is not free in relation to the power system, but...the subject who knows, the objects to be known and the modalities of knowledge must be regarded as so many effects of these fundamental implications of power-knowledge and their historical transformations.[37]

Knowing and doing, from Foucault's standpoint, are not extrinsically related activities, for the exercise of the intellect is always vested in a determinate field of power. As Joseph Rouse says, "power itself becomes the mark of knowledge."[38]

Foucault has charted the reciprocal relationship between knowledge and power most thoroughly in the area of the human sciences. The "sciences of man" were made possible by the development of a series of disciplinary mechanisms within key institutions of modern society (prisons, schools, hospitals, and factories). The initial purpose of these disciplines was to neutralize dangers, control useless or disturbed conduct, or manage large numbers of people. Military discipline, for example, was originally intended solely to prevent looting, desertion and the refusal to carry out orders; quarantines were imposed to prevent the spread of disease; in the workshop discipline was designed to enforce respect for rules and authority figures, and to prevent losses due to theft. It was discovered, however, that these disciplines could play a positive role as well, namely, to increase the possible utility of individuals and to optimize their productive potential through the efficient ordering of their multiplicities. By the end of the eighteenth century, these disciplines crossed a "technological threshold," so that as they were combined and generalized "they attained a level at which the formation of knowledge and the increase of power regularly reinforce one another in a circular process...an epistemological 'thaw' through a refinement of power relations; a multiplication of the effects of power through the formation and accumulation of new forms of knowledge."[39]

These relations of power/knowledge, as Foucault calls them, were not confined to the particular institutions in which they initially developed, but swarmed outward to permeate every aspect of modern society. In particular, they formed the tacit protocols for the human sciences, which were quickly becoming a fixture in the modern academy. He does not wish to say that the human sciences simply

> emerged from the prison. But, if they have been able to be formed and to produce so many profound changes in the episteme, it is because they have been conveyed by a specific and new modality of power: a certain policy of the body, a certain way of rendering the group of men docile and useful. This policy required the involvement of definite relations of knowledge in relations of power; it called for a technique of overlapping subjection and objectification; it brought with it new procedures of individualization. The carceral network constituted one of the armatures of the power-knowledge that has made the human sciences possible. Knowable man (body, individuality, consciousness, conduct, whatever it is called) is the object-effect of this analytical investment, of this domination-observation.[40]

It has long been argued, and is still widely believed today, that the natural sciences are exempt from the basic implications of power/knowledge. Mary Hesse summarizes the prevailing view (a view, by the way, to which she does not subscribe), which maintains that any reference to the effects of power on knowledge in the natural sciences must be "confined to the pathology of belief: to irrationality, or error, or deviance from rational norms...*Correct* use of reason, and true grounded belief, need no causal explanation, whereas error does need it."[41] I contend, however, that the wide-spread refusal to acknowledge the relation of power to knowledge in natural science betrays a growing uneasiness that the cherished neutrality and objectivity of scientific knowledge might no longer be tenable.

The men who began the modern scientific tradition did not think it necessary to exempt the natural sciences from the inherent relationship between the activity of knowing and the exercise of power. West commends Francis Bacon, an early advocate of the scientific revolution, for his meta-philosophical honesty in acknowledging the intrinsic connection between power and scientific knowledge: "For [Bacon] the aim of philosophy was to give humankind mastery over nature by means of scientific discoveries and inventions." And Milbank remarks that as far back as the seventeenth century scholars acknowledged that "the specificity of modern 'scientific' knowledge is to do with an 'artificial' method and an infallible knowledge of artifice...(although there were divergent sceptical, rationalist and 'experimentalist' versions of this specificity)."[42]

In recent years there have been numerous attempts to return the practice of natural science to its original metaphilosophical honesty. Literary theorists, neo-pragmatists, and the new empiricists have collaborated with continental hermeneutics and poststructuralism in an ongoing effort to disclose the types of power relations that inform the natural sciences. Rouse, combining the analytical insights of these traditions of inquiry, persuasively argues that science is principally an interrelated network of activities and achievements that gives us a practical mastery of locally situated phenomena. Power is an essential characteristic of this field rather than a thing or relation within it. The relations of power constituted in the practice of science, Rouse maintains,

> impose constraints upon us and compel actions from us in ways arguably far more extensive and intensive than the more traditionally recognized forms of political domination...They shape the practical configuration within which our actions make sense, both to ourselves and to one another. This shaping occurs most directly through their effects upon the kinds of equipment available to us, the skills and procedures required to use that equipment available to us, the skills and procedures required to use that equipment, the related tasks and equipment that use imposes upon us, and the social roles available to us in performing these tasks. Through this process, they change our understanding of ourselves and our lives...[We] cannot reconfigure the field of our possible actions in these ways without changing our understanding of who we are and what is at stake in our lives. We understand ourselves in terms of the world we encounter around us, which provides the context within which we work out who we are.[43]

Modernity's reluctance to come to terms with the concrete relationship between knowledge and power, in itself a problematic philosophical issue, is compounded by the way that science has contributed to the political formation of modern society. Michael Polanyi summarizes in a concise and accurate manner the primary aim of scientific research in modernity: "The avowed purpose of the exact sciences is to establish complete intellectual control over experience in terms of precise rules which can be formally set out and empirically tested."[44] But as I said earlier, intellectual control cannot be divorced from practical mastery. West is therefore on target when he observes that "the...clamor for scientific standing discloses the will to power which rests at the center of European modernity: the will to cognition and control, manipulation and mastery."[45] The scientific ethos of modernity both presupposes and masks a distinctive type of formal rationality, which Marcuse calls the specific socio-historical project of advanced industrial society. Within this ethos the passionate quest for domination, control, mastery underwrites the entire cognitive enterprise.[46]

In short, the type of knowledge that is produced by science does not primarily consist in the bracketing of intellectual activity from nature and history, but in a distinctively structured intrusion into reality, tacitly governed at all levels by "a continual striving for increased control and more precise determination of ourselves and the world, that is *never* subordinated to any other concern."[47] Scientific reflections have assumed the façade of "reality" itself, so that *epistemic representations* are gradually realized as *political representations* as well. Cultural hegemony is exhibited in the way "science" and "reality" function in both academic and popular discourse as virtually synonymous, interchangeable terms.

Initially modernity only sought to subject nature to human mastery through the knowledge gleaned by science. It was believed, in retrospect quite naively, that this control over nature would provide for the increasing common good of humanity, the "safeguarding of life against 'accidents' and 'blows of fate'...to be independent of nature."[48] Indeed, there is little question that this passion for mastery greatly enhanced the power of the human masters, leading to "advances in science, exploration of distant lands, conquest and enslavement of peoples throughout the globe, and development of techniques for mass production and distribution of goods."[49] This orientation toward the mastery of nature in the ethos of modern culture was a departure from earlier conceptions of the relation of science and nature. According to Fritjof Capra,

> From the time of the ancients the goals of science had been wisdom, understanding the natural order and living in harmony with it. Science was pursued "for the glory of God"...[As a result] the organic world view of the

> Middle Ages had implied a value system conducive to ecological behavior...
> These cultural constraints disappeared as the mechanization of science took
> place. The Cartesian view of the universe as mechanical system provided a
> "scientific" sanction for the manipulation and exploitation of nature that has
> become typical of Western culture. In fact, Descartes...shared Bacon's
> view that the aim of science was the domination and control of nature, af-
> firming that scientific knowledge could be used to "render ourselves the
> masters and possessors of nature."[50]

Lamb vividly describes the effects to nature in a society enchanted by
the will to mastery, as

> the very tools of science and technology which were supposed to save us
> from the terrors of nature are, through industrialization, polluting and de-
> stroying environment after environment. Nature, as Hegel observed, is be-
> ing sucked up into history. But Hegel hardly envisaged the megamachine
> of modern industry which would turn nature into a resource reservoir feed-
> ing the rapacious appetite of the megamachine...a dumping site where the
> machine would spew its toxic wastes.[51]

The drive to control and manage nature not only leads to tragic ecological
consequences, but also involves a corresponding tendency to subject humanity to the interests of modernity's unfettered striving for domination.
Human needs, desires, values, community, freedom, in short, everything
that makes for a truly human way of life, must be made subservient to a
society and culture determined by the will to mastery through a political
"pacification of existence."[52] Socio-economic domination,[53] the management of the productive forces of labor as governed by the technological
concern for mastery over nature, comprises the primary mode of domination and exploitation of humanity in modern culture, particularly over
the vast majority of humans who are politically and economically powerless and thus who exist on the periphery of society. The control of human
life, unfortunately, is not confined to economic means alone, but interacts
on several levels with other forms of social supervision. These other
forms of human management, in their reductionistic treatment of human
beings, are able to absorb traditional, even antagonistic, visions of human
life and reconfigure them into components of modernity's cultural ethos.[54]

According to Rouse, one of the most interesting effects of our culture's addiction to science is "an ambiguous sense of ourselves as knowing
subjects and known objects, as powerful agents and docile targets of power,
as constrained and manipulated but also as the ones for whose sake the manipulation is performed and whose values its supposedly implements." As

a result, we find ourselves in the ironic position of possessing a kind of knowledge through which we have access to a wide variety of manipulative capabilities, supposedly reflecting choices and decisions we have made, but which is embodied in practices, equipment, social roles, and skills "that in a sense come to possess us." Rouse argues that "the effects of these practices upon us and our form of life...need to be understood in terms of power and call for an explicitly political interpretation and criticism. The forms of power/knowledge embodied in the natural sciences help reshape our world as a field of possible action and fundamentally influence what is at stake in our lives."[55]

Marcuse provides a capsule analysis of this shift in the will to mastery from nature to humanity in the scientistic ethos of modernity:

> The principles of modern science were *a priori* structured in such a way that they could serve as conceptual instruments for a universe of self-propelling, productive control: theoretical operationalism came to correspond to practical operationalism. The scientific method which led to the ever-more-effective domination of nature thus came to provide the pure concepts as well as the instrumentalities for the ever-more-effective domination of man by man through the domination of nature. Theoretical reason, remaining pure and neutral, entered into the service of practical reason. The merger proved beneficial to both. Today, domination perpetuates and extends itself not only through technology but as technology, and the latter provides the great limitation of the expanding political power, which absorbs all spheres of culture.[56]

The consequences of modern culture's captivation by the ethos of science, and its distorted determination of who the human person is, are apparent throughout the modern world. Bonhoeffer correctly diagnoses the problem: "Nature was formerly conquered by spiritual means, with us by technical organization of all kinds. Our immediate environment is not nature, as formerly, but organization. But with this protection from nature's menace there arises a new one—through organization itself. But the spiritual force is lacking. The question is: What protects us against the menace of organization?"[57]

"Unless the question of the meaning of the human project is confronted," Gibson Winter rightly observes, "there can be no escape from the domination and injustice that follow upon the drive for mastery." The legacy of the project of modern industrial society, in which reason functions as the scientific instrument of domination, has important implications for the way theologians understand and carry out their responsibilities. Rubem

Alves vividly illustrates the predicament of modernity in its captivity to the positivistic ethos of science in a parable that humorously outlines the dilemma facing contemporary theology:

> Once upon a time a lamb, with a love for objective knowledge, decided to find out the truth about wolves. He had heard so many nasty stories about them. Were they true? He decided to get a first hand report on the matter. So he wrote a letter to a philosopher wolf with a simple and direct question: What are wolves? The philosopher-wolf wrote a letter back explaining what wolves were: shapes, sizes, colours, social habits, thought, etc. He thought, however, that it was irrelevant to speak about the wolves' eating habits since these habits, according to his own philosophy, did not belong to the essence of wolves. Well, the lamb was so delighted with the letter that he decided to pay a visit to his new friend, the wolf. And only then he learned that wolves are very fond of barbecued lamb.[58]

Has theology's rather uncritical acceptance of, and attachment to, the scientistic ethos placed it in the position of the unsuspecting lamb, whose zeal for objective knowledge led to its initial deception and eventual ingestion by modernity's predatory eating habits? Can Christian theologians embrace the paradigm of science without fundamentally affecting its own intrinsic character and loyalties? In view of the problematic nature of science as a form of cultural positivism that is at best deficient in its conception of the relationship between knowledge and power, and which all too often manifests itself as a field of practices that is determined in its his basic orientations by a will to mastery, perhaps Christian thought should refuse to submit uncritically to the positivity of such a cultural ethos, and engage it instead in terms of its own basic accountabilities to God and the church? In short, should not the formation of a community which "represents genuine opposition to the hegemonic culture," a people who seek to foster an alternative set of habits, relations, and sensibilities "that cannot possibly be realized within the perimeters of the established order"[59] in response to God's liberating activity in Jesus Christ, be the primary concern of Christian theology?

Theologians of "Conscience" and the Ethos of Pietism

A different approach to theological inquiry, one that responds in a distinctive manner to the peculiarities of the modern world—what I shall refer to as a theology of conscience—is represented in Baptist circles by the works of Walter Rauschenbusch, Clarence Jordan, and Martin Luther King, Jr. The description of these three as theologians of conscience is not based on a detailed theory of conscience in their writings. To my knowledge no such account exists, although all three frequently employ the term in their sermons, books, and other writings. Nor are they mainly known for their work as academic theologians (although in Rauschenbusch's case this role is an important part of his story). Each of these Baptists, however, exhibits a profound awareness of the ambiguities and mystifications embedded in the practical configurations of modernity. It is the kind of awareness, moreover, that typifies what Antonio Gramsci calls an organic intellectual, and forms the basis for an alternative account of theological reflection.[60]

I would also argue that it is no coincidence that King, Jordan, and Rauschenbusch exemplify the distinctive characteristics of the Evangelical Pietist tradition that has nurtured Baptist life and thought since its inception, and usually in a less diluted fashion, than those theologians enchanted by a scientific conception of knowledge. The identification of Pietism as a key influence in their lives and theology is not intended to deny or slight the other voices that contribute to their development as theologians. It is rather to note how Pietism informs every aspect of their lives, permitting these other voices to enrich their labors in distinctive ways. The impact of Pietism on Rauschenbusch's life and thought has received the greatest attention, but its significance as an essential facet in the lives of King and Jordan can also be discerned.[61] Because of their tacit reliance on this heritage, they perpetuate in their personal lives and in their writings a viable foundation for developing an alternative approach to theological inquiry that is not thoroughly compromised by the ethos of science.

The term that I have used to distinguish a very different side of the Puritan tradition from that dicussed by Taylor is taken from F. Ernest Stoeffler's important study of the Pietist movement in seventeenth century Protestantism, *The Rise of Evangelical Pietism*. Not only did the Pietist strain within Puritanism give birth to Baptists, but it also nourishes the practical and intellectual labors of King, Rauschenbusch, and Jordan. Stoeffler contends that the term Pietism cannot properly be restricted to a movement within Lutheranism and thereby confined to the Continent, but should be used to refer to a widespread phenomenon within both the Reformed and Lutheran traditions. This movement was not characterized by one particular system of doctrine, although they generally adhered to the basic theology of the Reformation. Nor did these groups share a common polity, liturgy or geographical boundaries. According to Stoeffler, seventeenth century Pietists are properly identified by a profoundly experiential spirituality and an intense ethical sensitivity and rigor. Their labors centered around the stimulation and cultivation of the *praxis pietatis*, thus preserving what they believed to be the principal motif of the Reformation. The concern for the *praxis pietatis* stood in contrast to what they considered to be a dead orthodoxy and society's accommodation to prevailing cultural norms of thought and moral conduct: "What [the Pietists] endeavored to do was to correct the then current dry-as-dust orthodoxy in favor of the Christianity of the reformers, which was a living, vital, and hence affectively satisfying faith."[62]

According to Stoeffler, four basic tendencies set Pietism apart as a distinctive tradition within the history of Protestantism. First, for Pietists the essence of Christianity resided in a personally meaningful relationship of the individual to God. This experiential and intensely personal dimension of Pietism was consciously contrasted to the abstract formalism of scholastic disputes over doctrine or the preoccupation with the liturgy. This essential aspect of Christian faith was expressed through some type of inner identification and experiential oneness with God, being filled with the Holy Spirit, the indwelling Christ, or being grafted into Christ.[63] The experiential emphasis in Pietism accounts for its great influence in contemporary styles of Christian worship and the general life of the church, as seen in their contributions in the areas of hymnody, devotional literature and the resurgence of dynamic preaching in Protestant churches. It would be inaccurate, however, to equate the Pietist concern for the experiential dimension of Christian faith with the kind of religious subjectivity inculcated by nineteenth century liberalism and American frontier revivalism. With but a few exceptions early Pietists combined a recognition of the importance of an unassailable source of authority that lies beyond the individual for the life and faith of the church with the recognition that the only authority that makes this faith personally significant is always experiential. As Stoeffler notes, "The majority of [Pietists]...had no time for a religious faith which might tend to aim solely at pleasurable emotions."[64]

A second mark of Pietism was its idealistic or perfectionistic thrust. They were highly critical of the nominal culture Christianity of their time, in which anyone who was baptized and maintained a formal connection to the territorial church through participation in the sacraments, verbal assent to its creeds, and adherence to its liturgical forms was considered a Christian. Pietists considered such an understanding of Christianity shallow and superficial. They were particularly disturbed by its ethical equivocation and accommodation to the status quo. The stress in preaching was thus placed upon conversion and sanctification, apart from which an individual's faith meant little or nothing. Moreover, justification was more than a forensic act on the part of God; it needed to be personally appropriated as a fiducial commitment. Those who made such a commitment were referred to on the continent as "whole," "perfect" or "entire" Christians, while Puritan Pietists typically distinguished between "professors" and "believers." This idealist thrust manifested itself in their deep concern for evangelistic and missionary outreach, and also accounts for the enormous social impact of Pietism in its opposition to slavery, its advocacy of prison reform, the creation of Sunday Schools (which initially provided educational opportunities for impoverished youths, and only later were devoted strictly to religious education), support for Bible societies and the general advancement of education, renewed emphasis on the place of the laity within the life of the church, and advocacy of freedom of conscience and its expressions.[65]

Stoeffler makes two interesting observations concerning Pietism's perfectionist tendencies in relation to the shaping forces of Baptist life and thought. He notes first that Calvinist groups historically possessed a more critical attitude toward the cultural status quo and its religious and ethical complacency than did its Lutheran counterparts. Taylor also draws attention to this aspect of Reformed life, stating that "Calvinism is marked out by a militant activism, a drive to reorganize the church and the world...it aspired to a far-reaching regulation of the conduct of those who lived under church discipline. Calvinist movements aspired to build a new, proper order of things." Baptist Pietists thus inherited a counter-hegemonic or prophetic orientation from the Reformed tradition, and cultivated a radical opposition to any institution or other social condition which impeded an individual's break with the old life and her thorough-going commitment to the new life in Christ. Stoeffler also comments upon the fact that the Pietists made effective use of conventicles, gathering small groups of earnest believers together for the purpose of stimulating true piety, a practice to which the magisterial churches in various degrees objected. Pietists believed that a territorial church, in which all who were baptized due to their birth in that geographical location were counted as Christian, did not meet the requirements of a true and intense spirituality. Within their Sunday afternoon conventicles the discussion was "practical, deeply ethical rather than theological, fervent, urgent, Biblical and sometimes legalistic."[66]

The third characteristic of the Pietist ethos, in contrast to the rationalism and orthodoxy of Protestant scholasticism, was their commitment to a biblically informed manner of thought and life, particularly in relation to the concerns and celebrations of everyday life. Pietists did not trust the unrestrained power of reason, that is, reason that was not subordinate to the authority of Scripture. They were therefore suspicious of theologians and their convoluted scholastic debates. In their adherence to biblical norms for ordinary life, invariably exhibiting a strong ethical orientation, usually austere and occasionally legalistic, Pietists regarded the revealed law of God as "the authoritative disclosure of God's design" for human life, and a filial obedience to this law with the guidance and assistance of the Spirit was considered to be the primary obligation of the believer. Stoeffler also believes that it was Pietism's biblical emphasis which elevated the doctrinal status of the priesthood of the believer from dogmatic obscurity in the magisterial churches: "It was this implicit, somewhat naive, trust in the Word, rather than in man's words about the Word, which is also responsible for the fact that Pietists really trusted the religious opinions of theologically untrained laymen. The theory was, of course, that the Spirit of God is able to commend the truth of the Bible to men's minds and hearts without the tortured interpretations of the professionals."[67]

The final distinguishing mark of Pietism is an intrinsic part of any historical movement which earns the suffix of an "ism," i.e., its oppositional character, a deliberate protest against some dominant pattern. The Pietists nurtured a type of piety which formed a counter-hegemonic witness over against the prevailing norms of faith and practice that dominated seventeenth and eighteenth century European culture. While Pietism was rooted in the Protestant Reformation and adhered to its basic doctrinal positions, it held that there was an inextricable link in the territorial churches between what was considered a dead orthodoxy and the ethical equivocation and accommodation to the cultural standards of the masses. The question of insti-

tutional separation, which later became a reality among Baptist congrega-
tions, was always subordinate to the primary concern of being transformed
by the power of God rather than being conformed to this fallen world.[68]

When one studies the lives and labors of Jordan, Rauschenbusch, and
King, the practical, spiritual, and intellectual legacy of Pietism is readily
apparent. The Pietistic understanding of discipleship—in particular, its
prophetic stream, which sets forth a "profound conception of human nature
and human history, a pervasive picture of what one is as a person, what one
should hope for, and how one ought to act"[69]—informs the basic tendencies
of these theologians of conscience. The Pietist tradition provides them with
their basic moral and theological motifs, infusing their thought with spiritual rigor, personal vitality, and ethical integrity.

Pietism's influence on Rauschenbusch, Jordan, and King is best seen in
the ways that their basic themes are grounded in the biblical images which
depict the ways and will of God. H. Richard Niebuhr, for example, says of
Rauschenbusch that "Though his theory of the relation of God and man often seemed liberal he continued to speak the language of the Prophets and
St. Paul." And as Winthrop Hudson has noted, Shailer Mathews, a noted
Baptist theologian at the University of Chicago, faulted Rauschenbusch for
being too rhetorical (and therefore not sufficiently scientific). But the impact of the biblical metaphors on these theologians of conscience goes beyond the rather superficial judgment that their rhetoric relies heavily upon
the imagery of Scripture. Norman Perrin observes, for example, that
Rauschenbusch regards the "ancient myth" of the Kingdom of God as a living reality powerfully manifesting itself in human life, in marked contrast
to Rudolf Bultmann, who held that the these myths could no longer be read
in such a manner, and thus they had to be demythologized. Rauschenbusch
anticipates in this respect Bonhoeffer's criticism of Bultmann, namely, that
"the full content, including the 'mythological' concepts must be kept—the
New Testament is not a mythological clothing of a universal truth; this my-
thology (resurrection etc.) is the thing itself."[70]

In similar fashion King, who at appropriate times would write and
speak in a manner befitting a Ph.D. in theology from Boston University,
exhibits his Pietist heritage at those moments when the pressures and pas-
sions of the justice struggle moved him to set aside the trappings of learned
discourse for that which his heart constantly affirmed, and especially when
he addressed Black audiences in the churches of the South. At these times
his words display more than a rhetorical style; they reveal the *grammar* of

his conscience. McClendon observes that the "Old Testament and New Testament provided Martin with a rich panoply of images, some expressed, others hovering in the background of his thought, guiding, shaping the faith by which he walked."[71]

Pietism's goal of fostering a biblically-informed way of life is most clearly seen, however, in the writings of Jordan, whose "Cotton Patch" paraphrases of the New Testament are his primary mode of public expression. Jordan elevates the colloquial paraphrase of the Bible to the level of a theological genre, offering in the process an incisive analysis and critique of modernity by restating the biblical story from the vantage point of his own social location in the Jim Crow South. He states that the purpose of the Cotton Patch version is for its readers "to be participants in the faith, not merely spectators,"[72] and in the process summarizes the difference between the basic tendencies of a theology of conscience from a theology built around the reified notion of science. Simply put, Jordan is, in the most basic sense of the term, a grassroots narrative theologian.

Stoeffler acknowledges that the way the early Pietists read Scripture was marked by a certain naiveté. In particular, they placed a great deal of trust in the ability of sincere but untrained lay people to interpret the Bible. This practice led to a conception of the Bible as an ahistorical transcription of the mind of God, divorced from any consideration of the historical and social factors involved in the production of texts, and requiring little or no instruction from ecclesiastical authorities, the church's doctrinal and liturgical traditions, or academic theologians. While such naiveté possesses certain liabilities which cannot be quickly overlooked—privatistic and divisive interpretations, the parochialism of a relatively insulated culture, wooden and legalistic application of culturally conditioned pericopes, and neglect or insufficient treatment of questions, problems, and issues which are not directly addressed by the Bible—it also affords some important strengths. In particular, Pietist naiveté unleashed Scripture's powerful prophetic imagery, forged "within the complex history of conflict and clarification which is the history of the Jewish and Christian people."[73] This imagery enabled them to mount an effective critique of the accepted practices and norms of seventeenth century European society.

A similar naiveté related to the biblical witness informs the thought of King, Rauschenbusch, and Jordan, somewhat along the lines of Ricoeur's discussion of "second naiveté."[74] To be sure, these men no longer read the biblical witness exactly as their Pietist forebears had. They clearly exhibit an awareness of modern scholarship and its impact on biblical interpretation. In addition, they recognize that Scripture by itself would not lead to the formation of a people who would embody a set of habits, relations, and sensibilities distinct from those advocated by the modern world, and thus they engage other traditions of inquiry and conduct. Nevertheless, these other traditions—historical criticism, liberal theology, political economy, philosophical personalism, Gandhian *satyagraha*—do not replace the basic tendencies of their biblical heritage, but constitute hermeneutical paths[75] which take them from the immediacy of Pietism's original naiveté, which had been irretrievably lost through exposure to the contours of modern thought, to the mediations of a second naiveté. As they move along their respective paths Rauschenbusch, Jordan, and King labor to reclaim the metaphorical power of the Bible to shape a prophetic conscience capable of discerning the redemptive activity of God in creation. For these theologians of conscience Scripture embodies a surplus of meaning and power that ultimately relativizes the reductive efforts of modern thought to define the true, the good, the beautiful and, most significantly, the divine.[76] Each of these organic intellectuals returns to the "ancient myths" because the truth they narrate surpasses the feeble offerings of the modern myths.

From "Science" to "Conscience"
The Implications for Theology

"The story of modernity," says Rosen, "is...one of the self-thematising and self-reifying *scientism* of modern subjectivity."[77] The much-acclaimed objectivity and universality of our quest for knowledge within this narrative can be deconstructed as "the contingent emergence of imposed interpretations."[78] Unfortunately, over the last few centuries the church has all too often confused its story with the story of modernity, making it increasingly difficult for Christians to discern the "crucial difference...between telling a story differently and telling a different story."[79] As a willing yet often unwitting participant in a world that in its struggle to "come of age" is passing through a tormented and traumatic period of adolescence, the reifying tendencies and techniques of science have consistently scripted the habits, relations, and sensibilities of modern theology.

The habits, relations, and sensibilities of modernity also play a major role in the evolution of the *praxis pietatis* since its inception. Pietists were highly critical of the scholasticism that dominated the theological landscape of their day, and especially of its obsession with doctrinal minutiae. Such rationalistic concerns, they believed, drew attention away from the essential aspects of their faith, exchanging a dead orthodoxy for the daily cultivation of a vital personal piety. Consequently, while early Pietists generally accepted the liturgical patterns and doctrinal norms of the Reformation, their aversion to theological hairsplitting, combined with a well-intentioned but misguided emphasis upon the attitude and inner commitment of the individual believer (laying the groundwork for the impoverished principle of soul competency in this century), deprived them of an adequate appreciation of the important role that certain institutions and forms of discourse have always and of necessity played in the faithful pursuit of the *praxis pietatis*.[80] Latent tendencies were thereby established within Pietist circles that eventually result in the uncritical assimilation of institutional forms and patterns of thought that run counter to the initial aims of the movement.

Later generations of Pietists proved to be susceptible to the relations and techniques which constituted a world that was rapidly coming of age, as Cartesian subjectivity made significant inroads into their conceptions of spirituality. The *praxis pietatis* was gradually reconfigured as "religious experience," a private but universal substance of the human subject that is essentially unrelated to specific traditions or practices, but the effects of which can be kept under public surveillance, and their basic presence and behavior recorded. As a rule Pietists lacked the institutional forms and intellectual skills that they would need to effectively cope with the fragmentation of modern society into autonomous spheres of private value and public fact, and especially with the largely self-imposed confinement of the *praxis pietatis* (now in its reconfigured mode as religious experience) to the marginal status of the private realm.

The gradual privatization of religion in the modern world, in concert with the peculiar alliance forged between the first Puritans and the pioneers of the scientific revolution, led Baptists in North America to embrace ambiguous positions with respect to its social environment. These positions include a dubious reinterpretation of Baptists' traditional advocacy of the separation of church and state, according to which church and state as *institutions* continue to be formally distinguished, but in such a way as to unwittingly authorize a new and more powerful civil alliance between Christian

identity and nationalist sentiments.[81] But perhaps the most troubling development among late nineteenth and twentieth century Baptists was the metamorphosis of the Reformation doctrine of the priesthood of the believer—
in which the production of the self did not occur apart from corporate
practices, skills, and social roles—into the privatistic notion of soul competency. This unfortunate transmutation of the Reformation's conception of
all believers to function as priests to their neighbors reveals the extent to
which the *praxis pietatis* was assimilated into the habits, relations, and sensibilities of modern and (post)modern society. The chief architect of soul
competency was Mullins, a noted Baptist theologian who sought a scientific
basis for theology. Mullins carefully crafts this doctrinal mutation in *The
Axioms of Religion*, explicitly citing the modern narrative of freedom and
scientific progress for its rational warrants.[82]

The writings of King, Rauschenbusch, and Jordan are also not exempt
from these developments in the *praxis pietatis*, although the ways in which
they reflect these processes varies between them. In particular, their debt
to the liberal theologies of Schleiermacher, Brightman, DeWolf, Mullins,
Ritschl, and Tillich is well-documented. Moreover, Pietism's traditional
suspicion of institutional structures and intellectual traditions largely denies
them access to the critical skills that they afford. With these skills they
might have more readily discerned the full effect of modern polity and policy on the cultivation of personal piety. As a result, the influence of the
various systems of thought and practice which comprise the hermeneutical
paths along which these theologians of conscience move from a primitive to
a second naiveté in their interpretation of Scripture becomes a matter of
concern in our quest for an alternative account of theological reflection, as
their writings retain certain aspects of these systems and practices that mask
and impoverish the integrity of accountable Christian piety. In particular,
at times they cannot distinguish between the style of life made possible by
God's gracious activity in Christ and the form of existence nurtured by liberal capitalism.

In short, the greatest threat to the *praxis pietatis* is no longer posed by
a dead orthodoxy, but by the reifying effects of Cartesian subjectivity and
the instrumental rationality of a (post)modern society. This society pre-
serves and promotes its operative rationale in the artifact of "science," ap-
propriating traditional (pre-Enlightenment) concerns such as the *praxis pietatis*, and subjecting them (in both the epistemological and political senses
of that term) to alien (and alienating) techniques and modes of inquiry.

The promise of the "Age of Enlightenment," unfortunately, is not commensurate with its consequences nor with the human reality its strives to comprehend. As Lamb puts it, "We can no longer live with the illusion of pure reason because of its manifold victims."[83]

The sense and direction of our everyday existence can no longer be said to reside in what Kierkegaard aptly calls the "pathos of subjectivity," that is, in the solitude of the contemplative, introspective ego and the universal dictates of "reason" and "religion," notions which are invariably rooted in one way or another in the Cartesian subject. Pietism's goal of nurturing a personal spirituality vitally engaged with the concerns and celebrations of everyday life, therefore, cannot be divorced from certain corporate habits, relations, and sensibilities. As Lash puts it, "human persons are not what we initially, privately and 'inwardly' are, but what we may (perhaps) together hope and struggle to become." The cultivation of a corporate existence in which a mature and accountable personal spirituality can flourish demands institutional form and sustained intellectual endeavor. Again Lash states the reason for the complications of institutions and critical inquiry:

> [T]he Church *requires* the complications of theology, its endless and often irresolvable disputes, its tentative and fragmentary character, not in order to render our confusion even more obscure, but because only thus, only through engagement in such complexity (whether—as for most people— primarily at the practical level, or also at more reflective levels) can we be brought to that wisdom which enables us patiently to live out our human lives in trustful relationship to the absolute simplicity of the mystery of God.[84]

Paul Lehmann also contends that the conditions under which theologians carry out their responsibilities "are neither discernible nor describable ...in terms of the subject-object or self-world relation. This relation has haunted Cartesian and post-Cartesian habits of mind with the schizoid spectre of an abyss between metaphysics and epistemology, between a theory of reality and a theory of knowledge and its possibilities." While Lehmann is aware of the basic incoherence of Cartesian subjectivity and the edifice of science that is constructed upon it, he is also sensitive to the church's need for an account for the human self in its manifold relations both to God and the world to which it belongs: "What is required is a context...which conjoins the focus of divine activity and the focus of human responsiveness in such a way as to provide behavior with direction and decisiveness."[85]

One of the principal ways that Lehmann strives to fashion this context for theological inquiry is through an innovative understanding of the notion of conscience. He begins with the initial appearance of this idea in the epistles of Paul, where he contends it is drawn into the semantic horizon of the Hebrew term for "heart," *leb*, "the organ of thinking and knowing in the cognitive sense of 'mind' or 'intelligence' and also in the reflexive or intensive sense of the involvement of the self in the act of thinking or knowing. Cognition and the response of the self are thus conjoined in the act of knowing." In this semantic context, Lehmann says, conscience names the fulcrum of human responsiveness, "that delicate conjunction of the inner springs of human motivation and of human judgment," which is ultimately determined by the contours and dynamics of the divine activity. Conscience, when placed within this context, designates "the pivotal personal center of man's total response to the dynamics, direction, and personal thrust of the divine claim upon him."[86]

Lehmann acknowledges that this definition of conscience is closer to French than to standard English usage: "In the French...'conscience' comprehends both consciousness and responsibility for what one is conscious of ...In French, you cannot really know, you cannot be aware, in a neutral way. You cannot have consciousness without taking responsibility for what you are conscious of. There is a moral dimension intrinsic to knowledge." Lehmann seeks with this term to make explicit the inseparability of cognition and personal involvement, describing the *knowing-in-relation* which characterizes the human being as a historical, embodied agent rather than as an ahistorical, disembodied subject, that is, as a self who is concretely involved in history and culture in a response, on the one hand, to the God whose messianic claim upon all creation is ultimately the foundation of our humanity and on the other, to her fellow creatures, who have a claim upon her as a consequence of the divine claim.[87]

When used in this fashion, says Lehmann, conscience names the activity both of knowing and of doing which "expresses and exposes the connection between...the environment of humanization and the obedient response to this environment," i.e., "the living link between the order by which human life is sustained and the personal response of obedience to this order." As the performative intersection of motivation and judgment, the living unity of the affective, volitional, and cognitive dimensions of our day-to-day existence, conscience enables us "to discern in, with, and under the concrete course of human events the presence and power of God at work,

giving shape to human life," providing "specific knowledge of what God
expects of humanity and of what humanity owes to God." And in contrast
to the Cartesian portrait of human subjectivity, piety and reason may be
distinguished within conscience, but they can never finally be separated. In
short, conscience, like the Hebrew notion of the "heart," refers to the performative relation or bond between the mystery of God and the practice of
everyday life within the community of faith.[88]

The shift from science to conscience has profound implications for the
way one approaches theology as disciplined inquiry, i.e., as second-order
discourse. According to Lehmann, Christian thought, rightly conceived, is
not reflexive, (that is, "reason in the act of thinking about itself, about the
structure of the mind, or about the laws of thought"), but instrumental or
performative, i.e., responsive to the presence and power of God in the
world to make and keep human life human.[89] The use of the idea of conscience (*con-scientia*) to refer to the fulcrum of human responsiveness calls
into question the concept of a pure cognition (*scientia*) removed from or
prior to the practice of everyday life, and ultimately exposes it as an uncritical and erroneous presumption founded upon the deceptive picture of
the Cartesian ego.

The turn away from knowing as an activity of discarnate, ahistorical
subjectivity "alters the priorities in the possibility and the order of inquiry.
The science of 'human things' takes precedence over the sciences of knowing and of being; in short, anthropology is the clue to, and the criterion of,
epistemology and ontology (or metaphysics)." The knowledge of human
things for Lehmann is not an autonomous field of thought within the rationalized configurations of modern existence, but subsists as an aspect of
politics, which he defines as "activity, and reflection upon activity, which
aims at and analyzes what it takes to make and to keep human life *human* in
the world." Politics, in other words, should not be confused with the modern discipline of political science, which imagines "the political" as a field
of pure, autonomous power. Politics has principally to do with those relations and habits that govern the practice of everyday life, thereby giving
shape and direction to human existence, and as Lash states, it is "in the adventure of human existence [that] we have to do with the 'absolute mystery'
of God."[90]

However, before we examine how Lehmann develops various facets of
this innovative *leitmotif* for theology, we shall take a short detour through
the history of Christian thought, and identify others in this tradition who

pursue a similar understanding of theological inquiry. By first familiarizing ourselves with the role that the idea of conscience has played at crucial points within the intellectual tradition of the church, thus making explicit themes, emphases, and shortcomings which historically have informed this idea, we shall be in a better position to evaluate its sense and significance for our (post)modern circumstances.

NOTES

[1]Jean-Luc Marion, *God Without Being: Hors-texte*, trans. Thomas A. Carlson (Chicago: The University of Chicago Press, 1991), xix–xx; David Tracy, Foreword to *God Without Being*, by Jean-Luc Marion, ix–xi.

[2]McCabe, *God Matters*, 20; Rowan Williams, *The Wound of Knowledge*, 2d ed. (Boston: Cowley Publications, 1990), 14.

[3]Lash, *Easter in Ordinary*, 240.

[4]The liberal or revisionist tradition of Baptist thought continues in the work of Kenneth Cauthen, Harvey Cox, Langdon Gilkey, Bernard Loomer and Bernard Meland. Carl F. H. Henry, Clark Pinnock and Bertrand Ramm represent the more "conservative" branch of this first type of Baptist thought.

[5]William Newton Clarke, *An Outline of Christian Theology*, 18th ed. (New York: Charles Scribner's Sons, 1909), 4–5.

[6]Augustus Hopkins Strong, *Systematic Theology* (Philadelphia: Judson Press, 1907), 1–2.

[7]Edgar Young Mullins, *The Christian Religion in its Doctrinal Expression* (Philadelphia: The Judson Press, 1917), 1–2. It is interesting to note that Walter Conner, a student of Mullins and Strong who was quite influential among Baptists in the Southwestern portion of the United States, came to reject, at least nominally, the modern preoccupation of theology with science as the all-encompassing discipline in the academy: "There was never a more vain idea than the one that all of reality, so far as man could know it, could be brought under the head of science, in the modern and technical sense of that noble term. It is time that theology declared its independence of science and stood on its own feet." Walter T. Conner, Preface to *The Gospel of Redemption* (Nashville: Broadman Press, 1945). Conner never came to a clear understanding of what this independence might consist and thus, in spite of his resolve, continued to work within the scientific molds cast by his teachers.

[8]Dale Moody, *The Word of Truth: A Summary of Christian Doctrine Based on Biblical Revelation* (Grand Rapids: William B. Eerdmans Publishing Company, 1981), xi, 1–2.

[9]See Paul Ricoeur "The Critique of Religion." *Union Seminary Quarterly Review* 23 (Spring 1973): 205–12. This article may also be found in a collection of Ricoeur's essays, *The Philosophy of Paul Ricoeur: An Anthology of his Work*, eds. Charles E. Reagan and David Stewart (Boston: Beacon Hill Press, 1978), 213–22.

[10]Richard Rorty, *Philosophy and the Mirror of Nature* (Princeton: Princeton University Press, 1979), 366–67.

[11]Jürgen Habermas, *Knowledge and Human Interests*, trans. Jeremy J. Shapiro (Boston: Beacon Press, 1971), 67. Rorty observes that in Western culture "the assumption that scientific discourse was normal discourse and that all other discourse needed to be modeled upon it has been the standard motive for philosophizing." Rorty, *Philosophy and the Mirror of Nature*, 387.

[12]Henry Steele Commager, *The Empire of Reason: How Europe Imagined and America Realized the Enlightenment* (Garden City, NY: Anchor Press/ Doubleday, 1977), 1–3.

[13]Taylor, *Sources of the Self*, 230.

[14]Taylor, *Sources of the Self*, 213, 225–26, 231–32.

[15]Milbank, *Theology and Social Theory*, 10–11; Commager, *The Empire of Reason*, 46.

[16]Thomas Aquinas, *Summa Theologica* 1a.1.2.; Etienne Gilson, *The Spirit of Medieval Philosophy*, trans. by A. H. C. Downes (New York: Charles Scribner's Sons, 1936, 1940), 35; Lev Shestov, *Athens and Jerusalem*, trans. by Bernard Martin (Athens, OH: Ohio University Press, 1966), 297. See Wolfhart Pannenberg's inquiry into the status of theology as a science prior to the modern era in *Theology and the Philosophy of Science*, trans. by Francis McDonagh (Philadelphia: The Westminster Press, 1976), 7–14, 228–50.

[17]Kenneth Surin, *Theology and the Problem of Evil* (New York: Basil Blackwell Inc., 1986), 47, 35 (n. 42). For a cogent treatment of the historical metamorphosis of meaning in the term *scientia*, see Jeffrey Stout, *The Flight from Authority: Religion, Morality, and the Quest for Autonomy* (Notre Dame: University of Notre Dame Press, 1981), 38–50.

[18]For sustained critiques of the identity logic which undergirds modern conceptions of knowledge, see Theodor W. Adorno, *Negative Dialectics*, trans. E. B. Ashton (New York: Continuum Publishing Company, 1973), and Adorno and Max Horkheimer, *Dialectic of Enlightenment*, trans. John Cumming (New York: Continuum Publishing Company, 1972).

[19]While there are innumerable studies that attempt to correlate the methodologies of the natural sciences and theology, some of the more consciously self-critical inquiries are to be found in a collection of essays edited by A. R. Peacocke, entitled *The Sciences and Theology in the Twentieth Century* (Notre Dame: University of Notre Dame Press, 1981).

[20]What has been designated "scientism" here is similar to but not identical to what is often referred to as "positivism," which is most characteristically exemplified by the position of Alfred Jules Ayer in *Language, Truth and Logic*, 2d ed., (New York: Dover Publications, Inc., 1952). The term scientism has been substituted for positivism in the present discussion because I contend that recent efforts by philosophers of religion and theologians to move beyond the logical and/or empirical verificationism of explicit forms of positivism are by and large still ensnared in the more deeply-seated positivism of modern Western culture, for which the notion of "science" functions as rhetorical *leitmotif.*

[21]Auguste Comte, *Cours de philosophie positive* (Paris: Baillière, 1864); Alfred Jules Ayer, ed., *Logical Positivism* (New York: The Free Press, 1959); Dietrich Bonhoeffer, *Letters and Papers from Prison*, ed. Eberhard Bethege, enlarged edition (New York: Macmillan Publishing Company, 1971), 280, 286, 329. It is not necessary here to rehearse the philosophical justifications for, critiques about, or defenses against these assertions. My concern is rather to establish a general sense for the term that will be useful in the examination of intellectual developments that have thoroughly charmed Western culture.

[22]Pannenberg, *Theology and the Philosophy of Science*, 29. Ironically, Pannenberg unwittingly indicts his own approach to theology with this definition, in which he never seriously questions the historical basis of his own conceptions of meaning, truth, or logic.

[23]Raymond Williams, *Marxism and Literature* (New York: Oxford University Press, 1977), 110.

[24]Joseph Rouse, *Knowledge and Power: Toward a Political Philosophy of Science* (Ithaca, NY: Cornell University Press, 1987), 21.

[25]Walker Percy, "Culture: The Antinomy of the Scientific Method," *The Message in the Bottle* (New York: Farrar, Straus and Giroux, 1954), 215–42. Another incisive treatment of the contradictions inherent in modern culture is found in Max Horkheimer and Theodor W. Adorno, *Dialectic of Enlightenment*, trans. John Cumming (New York: Herder and Herder, Inc., 1972).

[26]Matthew Lamb, *Solidarity with Victims* (New York: Crossroads Publishing Company, 1982), 15–16. See also Gibson Winter, *Liberating Creation* (New York: Crossroad Publishing Company, 1981), ix–xiv, 1–6.

[27]Herbert Marcuse, *One-Dimensional Man* (Boston: Beacon Press, 1964).

[28]West, *Prophesy Deliverance!*, 28; cf. 51–52.

[29]Eberhard Jüngel identifies a critical aporia in the theological determination of the essence and existence of God in this mode of thought. This is a result of simultaneously conceiving of the essence of God as that being upon which human existence is posited and yet whose own divine existence is established only through the self-certainty of the thinking human ego. Eberhard Jüngel, *God as the Mystery of the World: On the Foundation of the Theology of the Crucified One in the Dispute between Theism and Atheism*, trans. Darrell L. Guder (Grand Rapids: William B. Eerdmans Publishing Company, 1983), 111–26, 150, 186.

[30]William H. Poteat, *Polanyian Meditations: In Search of a Post-Critical Logic* (Durham, NC: Duke University Press, 1985), 252–53, 267.

[31]William H. Poteat, *A Philosophical Daybook: Post-Critical Investigations* (Columbia: University of Missouri Press, 1990), 5.

[32]Rouse, *Knowledge and Power*, 66.

[33]In this context Marcuse writes: "Modern scientific philosophy may well begin with the notion of the two substances, *res cogitans* and *res extensa*—but as the extended matter becomes comprehensible in mathematical equations which, translated into technology, 'remake' this matter, *res extensa* loses its character as independent substance." Marcuse, *One-Dimensional Man*, 152.

[34]Nicholas Lash, *Easter In Ordinary: Reflections on Human Experience and the Knowledge of God* (Charlottesville: University Press of Virginia, 1988), 94; cf. 69, 96.

[35]Walker Percy, *Love in the Ruins* (New York: Farrar, Straus & Giroux, Inc., 1971; Avon Books, 1978), 181.

[36]Cornel West, review of *In Memory of Her*, by Elisabeth Schüssler Fiorenza, in *Religious Studies Review*, 11 (January 1985): 2; Cornel West, "The Politics of American Neo-Politics," *Post-Analytic Philosophy*, eds. John Rajchman and Cornel West (New York: Columbia University Press, 1985), 269.

[37]Michel Foucault, *Discipline and Punish*, trans. Alan Sheridan (New York: Random House, 1979), 27–28.

[38]Rouse, *Knowledge and Power*, 19. I am deeply indebted to Rouse for this general account of the interaction of power and knowledge.

[39]Foucault, *Discipline and Punish*, 224.

---

[40]Foucault, *Discipline and Punish*, 305.

[41]Mary Hesse, *Revolutions and Reconstructions in the Philosophy of Science* (Bloomington: Indiana University Press, 1980), 32.

[42]West, *Prophesy Deliverance!*, 51; Milbank, *Theology and Social Theory*, 11. Fritjof Capra notes the dubious ethical character which accompanies Bacon's metaphilosophical honesty: "The terms in which Bacon advocated his new empirical method of investigation were not only passionate but often outright vicious. Nature...had to be 'hounded in her wanderings', 'bound into service', and made a 'slave'. She was to be 'put into constraints' and the aim of the scientist was to 'torture nature's secrets from her.'" Fritjof Capra, *The Turning Point* (New York: Simon and Schuster, 1982), 56.

[43]Rouse, *Knowledge and Power*, 246.

[44]Polanyi, *Personal Knowledge*, 18, italics mine.

[45]West, *Prophesy Deliverance!*, 100.

[46]Marcuse, *One-Dimensional Man*, xvi.

[47]Rouse, *Knowledge and Power*, 261.

[48]Bonhoeffer, *Letters and Papers from Prison*, 380.

[49]Winter, *Liberating Creation*, x, 3.

[50]Capra, *The Turning Point*, 55–56, 60–61. The citation is from René Descartes's *Discourse on Method*.

[51]Lamb, *Solidarity with Victims*, 6. In Jüngel's words, "The necessary consequence of the Cartesian understanding of man as the 'thinking thing' who secures the existence of what is through representation is the mastering of the world, guided by man's thinking and planning." Jüngel, *God as the Mystery of the World*, 177–78.

[52]Marcuse, *One-Dimensional Man*, 16.

[53]Lamb insightfully notes that "the apparent contradiction between late capitalism and state socialism tends to mask the underlying commitments of both to identity domination. Today they offer us the cynical choice between monopoly controlled states or state controlled monopolies." Lamb, *Solidarity with Victims*, 36.

[54]See Nicholas Wolterstorff, *Until Justice and Peace Embrace* (Grand Rapids: William B. Eerdmans Publishing Company, 1983), 23–41, and Arthur F. McGovern, *Marxism: An American Christian Perspective* (Maryknoll, NY: Orbis Books, 1980), 135–71.

[55]Rouse, *Knowledge and Power*, 247.

[56]Marcuse, *One-Dimensional Man*, 158.

[57]Bonhoeffer, *Letters and Papers from Prison*, 380.

[58]Winter, *Liberating Creation*, xi; Rubem Alves, "On the Eating Habits of Science," *Faith and Science in an Unjust World*, vol. 1, ed. Roger L. Shinn (Philadelphia: Fortress Press, 1980), 41.

[59]West, *Prophesy Deliverance!*, 120.

[60]According to Cornel West, organic intellectuals "are those who, because they are organically linked to prophetic movements or priestly institutions, take the life of the mind seriously enough to relate ideas to the everyday life of ordinary folk. Traditional intellectuals, in contrast, are those who revel in the world of ideas while nesting in comfortable places

far removed from the realities of the common life." West adds that while this distinction between organic and traditional intellectuals "is too broad and vague to do full justice to the complexity of intellectual activity, it is useful in distinguishing the social location of such activity." Cornel West, "On Christian Intellectuals," *Prophetic Fragments* (Grand Rapids, MI: William B. Eerdmans Publishing Co., 1988), 271–72.

[61]For more information on Rauschenbusch's Pietism, see Winthrop S. Hudson, "Walter Rauschenbusch and the New Evangelism," *Religion in Life* 30 (Summer 1961): 413–14, and Reinhart Müller, *Walter Rauschenbusch: ein Beitrag zur Begegnung des deutschen und des amerikanischen Protestantismus* (Leiden: E. J. Brill, 1957), 9–12, 107–08, 110. Except for Dallas Lee's journalistic biography, *The Cotton Patch Evidence* (New York: Harper & Row, 1971), and a few sketchy articles there are only a few good analyses of Clarence Jordan's work. See Joel Snider, *The "Cotton Patch" Gospel: The Proclamation of Clarence Jordan* (Lanham, MD: University Press of America, 1985), 7–30, and James Wm. McClendon, Jr., *Biography as Theology* (Nashville: Abingdon Press, 1974), 112–39. There is a conspicuous lack in the various intellectual histories about King concerning the influence of Baptist Pietism on his life and thought. Even King's strong empathy for the social theology of Rauschenbusch does not trigger the Pietist connection. Neither John J. Ansbro's intellectual history, *Martin Luther King, Jr.: The Making of a Mind* (Maryknoll, NY: Orbis Books, 1982), nor James H. Cone's recent book, *Martin & Malcolm & America: A Dream or a Nightmare* (Maryknoll, NY: Orbis Books, 1991) deal seriously with King's Pietist roots. Such omissions seem odd, especially in light of Cornel West's strong assertion that "Afro-American thought must take seriously the most influential and enduring intellectual tradition in its experience: evangelical and pietistic Christianity." West, *Prophesy Deliverance!*, 15. Cf. Allan Boesak, *Coming in out of the Wilderness: A Comparative Interpretation of the Ethics of Martin Luther King, Jr. and Malcolm X* (Kampen: J. H. Kok, 1976), Lehmann, *The Transfiguration of Politics*, 179–94, and McClendon, *Biography as Theology*, 65–86.

[62]Stoeffler, *The Rise of Evangelical Pietism*, 6–9, 11. In the final analysis, a complete picture of Puritanism would need to reconcile Stoeffler's insights with those of Taylor in *Sources of the Self*.

[63]"By ingrafting they obviously did not mean any formal connection with the visible Church, but the living, organic relationships of the individual believer with Christ whose mystical body is the Church." Stoeffler, *The Rise of Evangelical Pietism*, 15.

[64]Stoeffler, *The Rise of Evangelical Pietism*, 14.

[65]Stoeffler, *The Rise of Evangelical Pietism*, 3–5, 19. The kind of tolerance championed by the Pietists is spoken of favorably by Herbert Marcuse in his critical essay concerning indiscriminate toleration, "Repressive Tolerance," *A Critique of Pure Tolerance*, with Robert Paul Wolff and Barrington Moore, Jr. (Boston: Beacon Press, 1969), 81–123.

[66]Stoeffler, *The Rise of Evangelical Pietism*, 16–17, 20; Taylor, *Sources of the Self*, 227–28. For more information into historic Calvinism's social activism see Andre Bieler, *The Social Humanism of Calvin*, trans. Paul T. Fuhrmann (Richmond: John Knox Press, 1964), and W. Fred Graham, *The Constructive Revolutionary: John Calvin and his Socio-Economic Impact* (Richmond: John Knox Press, 1971). For an intriguing example of how the Calvinist critique of culture has consciously evolved in the present see Wolterstorff, *Until Peace and Justice Embrace*.

[67]Stoeffler, *The Rise of Evangelical Pietism*, 20–22. Stoeffler's incidental comment that Pietism's trust in the Bible was "somewhat naive" will be shown to disclose a powerful dynamic in a theology of conscience.

[68]Stoeffler, *The Rise of Evangelical Pietism*, 22–23, 29. For a more detailed description of how this oppositional nature developed into separatism in Baptist life see Robert G. Torbet, *A History of the Baptists*, 3d ed. (Valley Forge, PA: Judson Press, 1963), 29–57.

[69]West, *Prophesy Deliverance!*, 16.

[70]H. Richard Niebuhr, *The Kingdom of God in America* (New York: Harper and Brothers, 1935), 194; Winthrop Hudson, "Walter Rauschenbusch and the New Evangelism," 416–20; Norman Perrin, *Jesus and the Language of the Kingdom* (Philadelphia: Fortress Press, 1976), 70–71, 198–99; Bonhoeffer, *Letters and Papers from Prison*, 329. Max L. Stackhouse details the contrast between Rauschenbusch's and Bultmann's use of Scripture for theological reflection in his introduction to *The Righteousness of the Kingdom* by Walter Rauschenbusch, (Nashville: Abingdon Press, 1968), 45–59.

[71]McClendon, *Biography as Theology*, 85. The biblically-formed discourse favored by both Rauschenbusch and King has often been criticized. King's famous "Dream Speech" was ridiculed by one of his biographers for being "rhetoric almost without content." David L. Lewis, *King: A Critical Biography* (Baltimore, Penguin Books, 1970), 228.

[72]Clarence Jordan, *The Cotton Patch Version of Paul's Epistles* (Piscataway, NJ: Association Press, 1968), 7. Besides the Cotton Patch translations of the New Testament there were only a few books, including an exposition on the Sermon on the Mount by the same title, a few articles, sermons and assorted recordings. For a comprehensive bibliography see McClendon, *Biography as Theology*, 113 (n.1).

[73]Lash, *Easter in Ordinary*, 276.

[74]Paul Ricoeur, *The Symbolism of Evil*, trans. by Emerson Buchanan (New York: Harper & Row, 1967), 350–52.

[75]These "hermeneutical paths" are naturally subject to critical scrutiny. To identify King, Jordan, and Rauschenbusch as starting points for modelling a theology of conscience does not imply a blanket acceptance of their respective "paths."

[76]Winthrop Hudson has captured the dynamics of this second naiveté for the theologians of conscience in a comparison of Rauschenbusch's and Shailer Mathews's understanding of God: "Mathews thought of God, in large part at least, as a fact which 'must be treated seriously', a necessary 'corollary', a 'universal will' or a kind of 'Natural Law' to be studied and defined and heeded. For Rauschenbusch, God was always a living presence to be experienced—demanding repentance, promising forgiveness, and through a miracle of grace enabling one to walk in newness of life." Hudson, "Walter Rauschenbusch and the New Evangelism," 418.

[77]Rosen, *Hermeneutics as Politics*, 11, my emphasis.

[78]Hubert L. Dreyfus and Paul Rabinow, *Michel Foucault: Beyond Structuralism and Hermeneutics*, 2d ed. (Chicago: The University of Chicago Press, 1983), 108.

[79]Lash, *Theology on the Way to Emmaus*, 183.

[80]Stoeffler, *The Rise Of Evangelical Pietism*, 23.

[81]See John H. Yoder, *The Original Revolution: Essays on Christian Pacifism* (Scottdale, PA: Herald Press, 1970, 1977), 146–53; Yoder, *The Priestly Kingdom*, 141–44, 174–75.

[82]E. Y. Mullins, *The Axioms of Religion: A New Interpretation of the Baptist Faith* (Philadelphia: American Baptist Publication Society, 1908), 59–69.

[83]Lamb, *Solidarity with Victims*, 15.

[84]Lash, *Easter in Ordinary*, 86, 266.

[85]Lehmann, "On Doing Theology," 123; *Ethics*, 316.

[86]Lehmann, *Ethics*, 316, 353 (n. 2), 354. For a more detailed discussion of Old Testament anthropology, see Hans Walter Wolff, *Anthropology of the Old Testament*, trans. Margaret Kohl (Philadelphia: Fortress Press, 1974), 40–58.

[87]Paul Lehmann, "Messiah and Metaphor," *Religious Studies in Higher Education*, ed. Emerson I. Abendroth (Philadelphia: The Division of Higher Education of the United Presbyterian Church, 1967), 26; *Ethics*, 248, 353.

[88]Lehmann, *Ethics*, 79 (n. 3), 350, 336; *Transfiguration*, 234, 36.

[89]Lehmann, "The Formative Power of Particularity," 309.

[90]Lehmann, *Transfiguration*, 230; *Ethics*, 85; Lash, *Easter in Ordinary*, 239. Regarding the conception of politics as a field of pure, autonomous power, see Milbank, *Theology and Social Theory*, 9–26.

Chapter 2

THE STORY OF CONSCIENCE: I

My use of the idea of conscience to counter the picture that invests scientific rationality, "a picture of ourselves as spectators of a distanced spectacle, disembrangled from the moil and ruck of the world like discarnate gods,"[1] may well be confusing to some. In contemporary usage this idea usually refers to a mental faculty of moral introspection and judgment, "an internal register or principle enjoining good acts and dissuading evil, a universal standard of judgment, an inner voice built into the human psyche."[2] Conscience is commonly thought to be an intellectual faculty, or the peculiar use of the intellect, which supplies an innate apprehension of, or applies from some other source, the natural moral law that informs human conduct; or in a more negative estimation, it is dismissed as the residue of the tension which emerges from the confrontation between egoistic desires and the necessary but enforced socialization of conduct through acculturation. This definition of conscience is reinforced by a rigid division in the faculty of reason in modern thought, restricting its semantic range to the moral or practical, as opposed to the theoretical or cognitive, dimension of thought. This division, in turn, reinforces the abyss between thought and power, knowing and doing, thinking and acting, the life of the mind and the life of the body, which both accompanies and perpetuates the inherent tendencies of modernity.

Using the idea of conscience to provide a framework for addressing the many concerns and tasks of theology, while not standard methodological procedure, has important precedents in the history of Christian thought, as I shall attempt to demonstrate in the ensuing two chapters. According to Lehmann, however, the significance of this idea within the Christian tradi-

tion cannot be understood in abstraction, but only in terms of two dialectically intertwined stories that together have determined the role which conscience plays in the Western world. The first story narrates the semantic
pilgrimage of conscience that began with the Greek tragedians of the fifth
century B.C.E. and concludes with the psychoana-lytic theory of Sigmund
Freud. Lehmann describes this story as a "tortuous record of decline and
fall." The decline of conscience refers to the lost persuasiveness and force
that negates the ability of conscience to shape and direct human life through
the interrelation of judgment and action, while the fall of conscience signals
its ultimate rejection as essential to human life. But Lehmann states that a
second story unfolds within the Christian tradition over that same time-
span, narrating a real possibility for the liberation and empowerment of
conscience. These two stories confront theology with a sharp alternative
with respect to the question of conscience. It must either acquiesce to the
(post)modern rejection of conscience altogether, or if it believes that the
conscience which has declined and fallen is not the one which is intrinsic to
human life and activity, it must provide an account of conscience that radically transforms the understanding of its nature, function and significance.[3]

In the two ensuing chapters I shall relate and expand on Lehmann's
chronicle of the pilgrimage of conscience through the intellectual tradition
of the West. More specifically, I shall survey the writings of four key figures in the history of Christian thought who deal extensively with the idea
of conscience as a primary point of departure for theological reflection: the
apostle Paul, Martin Luther, John Henry Newman, and Paulo Freire. The
recurring themes and emphases that mark these efforts to set forth a "theology of conscience" will be of particular interest. In addition, I shall identify what I consider to be the shortcomings in their accounts of conscience,
in order to address them self-critically in later chapters.

"For the Sake of Conscience"
The Apostle Paul on Conscience

The term conscience makes its first appearance in Christian writings in
the epistles of the apostle Paul.[4] As with virtually every other aspect of his
thought, Paul offers no systematically developed doctrine of conscience,

and it is only one of the many terms which he appropriates from both Hebraic and Hellenistic cultures to speak of the rationality and responsiveness
of the human being within the sphere of God's redemptive activity in Jesus
Christ. Nevertheless, his use of the idea of conscience is one of his more
provocative adaptations, for he frequently appeals to its imperious witness
at crucial junctures in his letters. While Paul's use of conscience is a biblical warrant for the term which is admittedly far more suggestive than it is
systematic, it is "a step of momentous significance" which "raises the whole
problem of act, being and knowledge in anthropology,"[5] and hence points
to a formative paradigm for accountable Christian inquiry.

Before we can delve into Paul's use of the notion of conscience, however, we must note its semantic context in the first century Greco-Roman
world. The term has no direct equivalent in Hebrew, nor is there a consistent pattern when it is used sparingly to render a variety of terms in the
Septuagint. Not surprisingly, it appears more frequently in intertestamen-
tal Jewish literature, most notably in the works of Philo of Alexandria,
with whom it functions as the *elenchos*, an inner forum provided by God
that accuses and instructs the individual in the struggle against sin and for a
virtuous life before God.[6]

What we are to conclude from the lack of conceptual equivalents is a
matter of debate. W. D. Davies, for example, argues that a fundamental
incommensurability in anthropological perspectives between Hebraic and
Hellenistic cultures is uncovered with this absence. The Hellenistic world,
says Davies, focuses upon the introspective, human-centered consciousness
of the human being, while Hebrew thinking is theocentric, emphasizing
God as king and the human as God's obedient servant. "Not the knowledge
of the self (including the conscience)," writes Davies, "but the fear of the
Lord is the beginning of wisdom." Davies's argument on this point echoes
Krister Stendahl's well-known distinction between the "theocentric" perspective of the Hebrew world view and the "introspective" approach of the
Greek-speaking world.[7]

David Daube counters Davies and Stendahl by noting that the absence
of a term in a culture's working vocabulary often implies a "previous self-
understoodness of what it expresses," and offers several examples to show
that new words are coined or adopted to emphasize the striking, the excep-
tional, or the disputed, not the ordinary. Even if one begins with the modern definition of conscience, Daube argues, one can show that writers in
the Old Testament were quite familiar with inner struggle and conflict.

Many biblical authors were well aware of the phenomenon, if not the concept, of conscience, particularly as one was called to accountability before God by the radical demands of the covenant.[8]

The term Paul uses, *syneidesis*, originated in the market discourse of the Greek-speaking world around the fifth century B.C.E., and along with the terms *syneidos* and *synesis* it has its etymological roots in the verb *synoida* (*tini ti*), "to have knowledge (of something) with" [another]. All three substantives are derived from the reflexive form *synoida emauto*, bringing together in the same person the one who knows and the one who shares in this knowledge. While the term *syneidesis* was subject to variety of usages through the first century C.E., Christian Maurer contends that underlying the inevitable fluctuations in meaning there is the common perception of a polarity or tensive awareness within the self. This polarity, however, is not limited to what is commonly regarded in modern thought as a moral conscience. Socrates, for example, uses the reflexive verb form, *synoida emauto*, when he refers to an awareness of his own ignorance as the beginning of all wisdom.[9]

In any case, a relatively stable use of the term had evolved within its native Hellenistic environment by the time the New Testament books were being written. *Syneidesis* in the Greek vernacular was normally associated with the fixed order of reality, designating a link that is often traced to the gods or God as the rulers of the cosmos. Conscience reflects this order within human nature, where it principally functions in two ways. First, conscience always refers to specific acts which are in the past; second, it functions as a painful reminder of those acts which transgressed the fixed moral order. Lehmann forcefully describes this understanding of conscience as "the enemy of humanization," for it signifies

> that human nature is so constituted that if man oversteps the moral limits of his nature he is certain to feel the pain of *tes syneideseos*. Just as the delight of a journey lies in the absence of mishap, so the absence of conscience is a great joy. As a nurse or governess will watchfully guard her charges, so the proper office of conscience is to protect man from physical and moral harm. What is to be noted above all is that according to the original semantic environment of conscience, the ethical significance of conscience is not that it is a teacher of morals. Its ethical significance is that it resides in human nature as the bearer of ethical negation and futility in the relations between man and the order of things in which he lives.[10]

The story of the decline and fall of conscience in Western culture thus begins with the Greek tragedies. In the letters of the apostle Paul, however, one finds an alternative account of conscience and the possibilities at hand for its liberation and empowerment.

The apostle first refers to conscience in the controversy over the eating of meat sacrificed to idols within the Corinthian church (1 Cor. 8^{7-13}, 10^{25-30}). He admonishes those who were flaunting their freedom from dietary restrictions on the basis of their superior "knowledge" to be mindful of those who, having once been accustomed to the worship of idols and therefore new to God's liberating work in Christ, had not yet grasped the full scope of this liberty. Paul exhorts them, "for the sake of conscience," *dia ten syneidesin*, in the weaker brother, to refrain from eating the controversial dishes in situations which could burden or offend one's weaker brother or sister.

Within the body of Christ, then, Paul imposes a restriction with respect to conscience that is, in Maurer's words, "both a liberation and a commitment." On the one hand, Paul deprives conscience of its former office to accuse or excuse (also at 1 Cor. 4^4), regardless of whether it is one's own conscience or that of the neighbor in question, for such judgments belong to the Lord. Yet at the same time the members of Christ's body are inextricably bound to each other through a relation of conscience. The relations which Christians enjoy with their fellow believers cannot be divorced from their own selfhood, an identity secured in and through conscience in keeping with the creation of a new humanity in Christ. Moreover, Paul speaks interchangeably of a person or of a person's conscience. "The attitude to one's *syneidesis* is the attitude to oneself," writes Maurer, "and the attitude to the neighbour's *syneidesis* is the attitude to the neighbour himself. When he deals with the strong and the weak in [Romans] Paul can thus use *pistis* instead of *syneidesis*."[11] The association of faith and conscience in Paul's thought is obviously noteworthy.

The rather obscure phrase in 1 Cor. 10, *dia ten syneidesin*, appears also in the thirteenth chapter of the epistle to the Romans, in the course of Paul's instructions about the relationship of Christians to the empire. Paul asserts here that Christians should recognize the authority that governing powers have over human beings by virtue of their divine ordination to restrain the wrongdoer. To do otherwise would incur the wrath and judgment of God for violating an appointed agent in the divine ordering of human life. "Therefore one must be subject, not only to avoid God's wrath but also for the sake of conscience" (Rom. 13^5). According to Maurer, Paul is alluding to the "responsible awareness that the ultimate foundations both of one's own being and also of the state are in God. Members of the community are to have neither a higher or lower estimation of the state than as a specific servant of God."[12] If Maurer is correct, Paul links conscience with both the ability and the obligation to make responsible judgments, i.e., to reason accountably about themselves and the world. The accountability that shapes one's powers of judgment in conscience, however, is not construed by Paul in terms of a direct link with God, an infallible and inextinguishable *vox dei* unrelated to the historical contours of the divine activity or one's participation in the community of faith. The believer stands before God, and responds to the divine activity, *in* the community and *through* all the relations of conscience.[13]

Both the relation to one's neighbor and accountability before God are implied in Paul's most intriguing and distinctive uses of *syneidesis* and its verbal equivalent, *synoida emauto*. He employs these terms six times to refer either to that which testifies to one's own thoughts and actions, or to render a judgment about the actions of others. Twice (1 Cor. 4[4] and 2 Cor. 1[12]) he speaks of the witness of his own conscience. In the first instance he states that he is aware of nothing that would count against his faithful stewardship of the mysteries of God; in the second he writes that his conscience affirms the fact that he and his colleagues have behaved with holiness and godly sincerity, as befits the grace of God.[14] In two other cases (1 Cor. 4[2] and 5[11]) Paul asserts that he and his helpers open themselves to the conscience of every person in sight of God, in order that each might judge concerning their labors on behalf of the gospel, so that what they are, knowing as they do the fear of God, may also be known by the others as it is known to God.

Finally, there are two occasions when Paul uses *syneidesis* in a similar fashion in Romans. The first comes in his celebrated and disputed remark in Rom. 2[15], when he states that while the Gentiles do not have the law, the work or labor of the law is written on their hearts,[15] and thus their conscience, i.e., their sense of relatedness and accountability to both creature and creator, will bear them witness and their conflicting thoughts will accuse or even excuse them on the day of judgment. The second occasion is at the beginning of the significant passage on the destiny of Israel in relation to the advent of the gospel, Rom. 9–11. Paul writes that his conscience testifies to the anguish in his heart due to the rupture between the body of Christ and the historic people of the covenant (Rom. 9[1]).

I would offer the following conclusions concerning Paul's many uses of the word *syneidesis*. First, when the apostle employs the term, he is referring to something more comprehensive and basic about human selfhood than just a subsequent bad conscience, i.e., the painful knowledge of past transgressions or the source of that knowledge. Those who argue for such a narrow range of meaning base their conclusions on the pericopes in 2 Cor. 8 and 10. However, when we look closely how the concept is used in these contexts, we see that Paul regards the conscience as something that can itself be weak and defiled, assailed and heavily burdened, although it does not necessarily have to be. How can something that is by definition a defilement or injury also be defiled or injured?

While a guilty conscience is certainly among conscience's possible dispositions, it does not exhaust the semantic scope of *syneidesis* in Paul's epistles. Much more than the painful knowledge of one's sins is implied even if we start with this definition, for it presupposes a tension between the painful knowledge of what one has done in the past *and* the acknowledgement of what one ought to have done. Those who restrict the meaning of conscience in Paul's writings must also account for its use in 2 Cor. 4^2 and 5^{11}, where he refers to the ability of conscience to make judgments concerning the faithfulness of others before God. These scholars attempt to account for this discrepancy by arguing that in these verses he uses the word with a radically different meaning, that of "mind" (*nous*) or "thoughts."[16] While such a shift in meaning cannot be ruled out, the fact that Paul is dealing here with the same kinds of issues that occupy the focus of concern in his other references to conscience suggests an underlying continuity of meaning.

Second, Paul forges a powerful instrument in the notion of conscience that enables him to deal imaginatively with the integrity and intentionality of human selfhood within the sphere of God's redemptive work in Christ. More specifically, he posits a reciprocal relationship between basic human awareness, knowledge, and accountability, on the one hand, and the practice of everyday life within the community of faith, on the other. In the words of Lehmann, "a Hebrew transformation of the Greek sense of conscience" occurs with Paul's adaptation of the term *syneidesis*, bringing its connotations of the human being as a rational being into the semantic orbit of the Hebrew understanding of the heart, *leb*, a word which names the responsive fulcrum of our humanity, where the Word of God addresses us in the midst of everyday life (and not at the boundaries of the modern subject in that esoteric realm known as "religion"). In Maurer's words, *syneidesis* names a type of *gnosis*, i.e., a way of knowing that "embraces in a totality the perception of a distinction between the facts, the acknowledgment and choice of divinely willed obligations, and self-evaluation."[17] Paul thus invests the Hellenistic notion of conscience with unprecedented breadth and scope as two traditions of inquiry converge around his innovative use of this term, each making a distinctive contribution to his discussion of the new humanity in Christ.

What occurs in Paul's adaptation of the notion of conscience is a transvaluation of Stendahl's "introspective conscience of the West"—in which a person only confronts herself in the polarity of conscience—into what may be properly termed a *theopolitical* conscience, combining without confusing the Hellenistic view of the human being as a thinking, rational being with the Hebraic emphasis on the address of the elusive, incomprehensible God to the heart, *leb*, of the human being who is situated within the covenant community.[18] Richard Hays similarly contends that Paul's hermeneutics is neither theocentric (as Stendahl holds) nor christocentric, but *ecclesiocentric*.[19] The apostle to the Gentiles reconfigures the idea of conscience in order to refer, quite unsystematically to be sure, to the sentience, motility, and intentionality that characterizes human life, and which the Hebrew Scriptures generally assign to the *leb*, the heart, as the performative fulcrum of human selfhood. This responsive and self-involving awareness employs the full range of discursive reasoning, but refracted through an emotionally powerful sense of accountability in the presence of God for one's thoughts and action. Because Paul also uses the word faith (*pistis*) in Rom. 14[1], when in a similar context he refers to conscience in 1 Cor. 8 and 10, we can discern an implicit correlation between these two crucial concepts in his writings, a correlation that later writers made explicit and developed further.

The term *syneidesis* also appears in three other places in the New Testament, where the tendencies established by Paul's creative use of the term emerge at a more explicit level. In the pastoral epistles (1 and 2 Timothy and Titus), the author refers to an intrinsic relationship between faith and a good or pure conscience: "This charge I commit to you, Timothy, my son, in accordance with the prophetic utterances which pointed to you, that inspired by them you may wage the good warfare, holding faith and a good conscience, which some have cast aside and thus made a shipwreck of their faith" (*hen tines aposameroi peri ten pistin evauagesan*, 1 Tim. 1[18–19]).

Maurer contends that in this context the reference is to more than merely an empty and blameless conscience or the pure and simple heart of Old Testament righteousness: "In all probability the author has in view the renewal of man by the new creation in faith, which embraces the whole life of the Christian."[20]

The theme of a good conscience also occurs in Hebrews and 1 Peter in relation to what appear to be baptismal formulas. In Hebrews the baptismal washing of the body is linked with the perfecting of the conscience, not through the external sacrificial system of the earthly temple but through the blood of Christ. In conscience, therefore, the whole person confronts the holiness of God in Christ (Heb. $9^{9, 14}$; $10^{2, 22}$; 13^{18}). In addition to the commentary on Romans 13^5 in 1 Peter 2^{19}, "for the sake of conscience of God" (*dia syneidesin theou*), 1 Peter also speaks of a clear conscience in relation to one's behavior in Christ, and of baptism as the appeal of the believer to God for a clear conscience through the resurrection of Christ (1 Peter $3^{16, 21}$). What is striking in these passages is the explicit connection of conscience with faith, and the understanding that one comes before God through the perfecting of conscience.

The apostle Paul's introduction of the notion of conscience into the New Testament canon and thus into subsequent theological reflection constitutes more than just a convenient biblical warrant for the use of this term by later theologians. By using the idea of *syneidesis* Paul has suggested (though admittedly it is little more than a suggestion) a seminal point of departure for attending to the theological concerns in the church, a conceptual fulcrum that pivots about the daily existence of believers in their relations with one another, with a world that God has judged and redeemed, and thus with and before this God. While the implications of the idea in the apostle's epistles remain to be developed by later writers, the kind of performative awareness and discursive reasoning invoked by conscience, shaped by a powerful sense of accountability for our actions at the core of our being, offers an imaginative framework for theological inquiry.

"My Conscience Is Captive to the Word of God"
Martin Luther on Conscience

In an essay on the question of Luther's fundamental conception of religion, Karl Holl concludes that, in the final analysis, "Luther's religion is a religion of conscience in the strictest senses of the word."[21] Holl's evaluation of Luther walks a fine line between description and caricature. It is accurate in that it correctly identifies the crucial role that conscience plays in Luther's theology. But it can also be misleading, as subsequent generations of modern scholars (including Holl) have consistently misinterpreted Luther's interpretation of conscience. When divorced from the context of late medieval scholasticism, Luther's doctrine of conscience is quickly distorted. However, when read within the social and intellectual horizon of his day, his position on conscience exhibits a large measure of continuity with the late medieval tradition. And where Luther moves beyond scholastic definitions of conscience, he usually has far more in common with Scripture than with the Enlightenment.

Luther is often celebrated (or vilified, depending on one's theological predispositions) as the liberator of conscience from the tyranny of institutional authorities, ecclesiastical and civil. According to this account, he elevates conscience as a religious principle equal in authority with the Bible, thus anticipating in significant ways the Enlightenment doctrine of the autonomy of the individual from all external authority and providing it with a religious foundation. Erik Erikson, for example, insists that "Luther's emphasis on the individual conscience prepared the way for the series of concepts of equality, representation and self-determination which became in successive revolutions and wars the foundation not of the dignity of some, but of the liberty of all." E. Harris Harbison argues that Luther regards Scripture and the privacy of one's conscience as the only legitimate authorities:

> A man alone in his room with God and God's Word, the Bible, like
> Luther in his tower room—this would be a picture of a Christian—not that
> of a man confessing his sins to a priest, traveling on a pilgrimage, or buying
> an indulgence to get his dead parents out of Purgatory. This was to be the
> heart of Protestant belief as it developed later: the Bible and a man's con-
> science are the channels through which God speaks to human beings, not
> the Roman Church and its sacraments.

This interpretation has also fueled Catholic charges that Luther inaugurates the modern tendency toward intellectual and moral subjectivism, an unfortunate development that quickly rent the unity of the Church and its apostolic witness, and rendered incoherent any claim it has to truth.[22]

However, when Luther's thoughts on the conscience are placed within their original social and intellectual milieu, Holl does correctly focus our attention on a pivotal concept in his theology. Luther rescues the idea of conscience, *conscientia, Gewissen*, from the margins of intellectual concern in the late medieval schools and places it at the leading edge of theological inquiry. Michael Baylor rightly observes that "the idea of conscience is... so central that virtually every attempt to deal with Luther's thought must deal, in some way, with his idea of conscience."[23] While his doctrine of conscience is not identical to that of Paul, Luther's use of the term creatively links soteriology and epistemology, faith and knowledge, in an effort to be faithful to the teachings of Scripture, particularly to Paul's epistles, and at the same time respond in timely ways to contemporary theological concerns. When viewed in this light, Luther is one of the foremost proponents of a theology of conscience in the history of Christian thought.

The intellectual context for Luther's revitalization of the idea of conscience was the consensus which existed between the two late medieval schools—the *via antiqua* and the *via moderna*—regarding the nature and function of conscience. According to Thomas Aquinas, Gabriel Biel, and William of Ockham, the term *conscientia* referred only to an exercise of the practical reason, that is, the application of knowledge in terms of general moral principles to individual cases regarding human activity, either in the past (consequent) or in the immediate future (antecedent). The term was also used on occasion to refer to the inference of moral maxims from foundational practical principles. Aquinas fixed this understanding of conscience in what he took to be its etymological roots: "*cum alio scientia*, i.e., knowledge applied to an individual case...[that is to say, the] application of knowledge or science to what we do."[24] With the exception of Ockham, who objected on philosophical grounds, the exercise of conscience was predicated on the *synteresis*, a faculty (Biel) or innate habit (Aquinas) of the mind which provided the individual with an infallible and inextinguishable knowledge of the first principles of moral reasoning.[25]

According to these theologians, the exercise of conscience was patterned after the practical syllogism, in which fundamental axioms supplied by reason or divine law provided the major premise and the particulars of a moral case served as the minor premise, and from which one was able to arrive at particular moral judgments. Aquinas, Ockham, and Biel agreed that conscience possessed an absolute negative authority, i.e., that a person should never violate the dictates of conscience. But conscience commanded only a relative positive authority, for the believer has an obligation to set aside and correct a conscience marred by remediable ignorance (Aquinas, Ockham, and Biel were divided about the virtue and merit of following a conscience that is invincibly in error). In addition, while all three recognized the affective dimension of conscience, this aspect was subordinated to the rational powers of the mind. Finally, conscience bore only an indirect theological significance in scholastic thought, obscuring the close relationship between faith and conscience which exists in the later New Testament writings. An individual thus stood in the presence of God through conscience only indirectly, that is, through the performance of particular actions within the moral universe established by God.[26]

According to Lehmann, the scholastic understanding of conscience was an important chapter in the story of the decline and fall of conscience. Focusing on the theology of Aquinas, he states that the schoolmen helped to bring about a domestication of the conscience:

> The ominous, sometimes even wildly terrifying fury of the guilty conscience has been tamed by a divine infusion of the rational soul which lightens the dark torment of negation and futility by an intrinsic power to distinguish between good and evil, and so either to defend or to accuse, to excuse or to cause remorse. The easy conscience has become the companion of the uneasy one...Originally conscience had but a single function and that was negative and unbearable. Now conscience has acquired a double function, a negative and a positive one, and has become bearable. Originally conscience was that in man which above all things else he could not endure. Now conscience can be lived with; the knowledge which a man has together with himself could be counted upon as still against him, but sometimes also—and this is the important change—as on his side.[27]

According to the medieval construction of conscience, the order of things is no longer seen as arbitrary, indifferent or even hostile, but as a stable and rational order. The conscience bears witness to this order insofar as it accuses or excuses particular acts which either violate or confirm this order; in addition, it binds the person to act in certain ways in the present or future with respect to the rational moral character of the world. By means of the domestication of conscience the pangs of guilt are mitigated by its positive function. Conscience, as the practical employment of the reason in particular cases, was suitably confined, in order that it might perform useful tasks within the given order of things.

According to Lehmann, it is Luther (along with John Calvin) who effectively counters the domestication of the Pauline revolution concerning the interchangeability of conscience and heart. "Luther and Calvin were too preoccupied with the pretensions and anarchies of human sinfulness and too at home in the humanistic tradition to perceive the full revolutionary impact of the Pauline revolution upon the subjugation of the conscience in these traditions to the tight alliance between divine wrath and human guilt. Yet each in his own way had perceived something of the ferment astir in the ethical predicament of man by reason of the bond between *conscience and koinonia*." In Lehmann's opinion, the Reformers had begun to realize, in spite of traditional concerns which often force them into intellectual detours, the humanizing character and function of conscience as the living bond between the reality and activity of God and the realization of what makes for truly human life in the world. Luther, "like Paul before him... broke across the frontier of the tragic conscience into a fresh sensitivity to the nexus of human responsibility in the intimate confrontation between God and man."[28] It thus falls principally to Luther, writes Lehmann, to confront the cultural domestication of knowledge and conduct with the liberating activity of Christ addressed to, and discerned by, the conscience.

A basic premise of Luther's doctrine of conscience is his disdain for the division between speculative and practical thought, and in particular for the priority of the former category in much of later medieval theology, a priority which he regards as demonically inspired. He therefore contends that

> True theology is practical, and its foundation is Christ, whose death is appropriated to us through faith...all those who do not agree with us and who do not share our teaching make theology speculative because they cannot free themselves from the notion that those who do good will be rewarded. This is not what was written, but rather "Whoso feareth the Lord, it shall go well with him at the last" (Ecclus. 1[13]). Accordingly speculative theology belongs to the devil in hell.[29]

Luther thus contends that true Christian theology is practical from start to finish, rejecting unprofitable speculation and vain, arrogant attempts to look upon the naked majesty of God with uncovered face.

Theology should instead concentrate on the merciful God who is disclosed in Christ and on our relationship in faith with the incarnate God:

> True Christian theology, as I often warn you, does not present God to us in
> His majesty...but Christ born of the Virgin as our Mediator and High
> Priest. Therefore when we are embattled against the Law, sin, and death in
> the presence of God, nothing is more dangerous than to stray into heaven
> with our idle speculations, there to investigate God in His incomprehensible
> power, wisdom, and majesty, to ask how He created the world and how He
> governs it. If you attempt to comprehend God in this way and want to
> make atonement to Him apart from Christ the Mediator, making your
> works, fasts, cowl, and tonsure the mediation between Him and yourself,
> you will inevitably fall...and in horrible despair lose God and everything...
> Therefore if you want to be safe and out of danger to your conscience and
> your salvation, put a check on this speculative spirit. Take hold of God as
> Scripture instructs you...[30]

In his early writings Luther largely accepts the account of conscience
developed by the two medieval schools. He views the *synteresis* and conscience according to the categories of Aristotelian reason, operating deduc-
tively according to the pattern of a practical syllogism. On the question of
the authority of conscience, Luther agrees with the scholastics with regard
to the absolute negative authority of conscience; however, he skirts the
question of an incorrigibly perplexed conscience by appealing to Paul's
statement in Rom. 14[23], that everything not done by faith is sin. To follow
even an invincibly erroneous conscience is sinful, he argues, since faith and
grace are absent.[31]

Luther is unique in scholastic theology, however, for the weight he
gives to the depth and strength of the emotive dimension of conscience, focusing in particular upon the guilty subsequent conscience. Baylor notes
that while the scholastics, by stressing the intellectual side of conscience,
refer to both a consequent and antecedent conscience, Luther is interested
almost exclusively in a consequent conscience that is consumed with guilt.[32]
His comments on the bed of sorrow in Psalm 40 (41) offer an example of
the stress that he places upon the affective element in the phenomenon of
conscience. While the scholastics are acquainted with the affective dimension of conscience, they deal almost exclusively with its rational import and
neglect for the most part its emotional component. Luther writes with regard to the powerful emotional aspect of conscience:

> "The bed of sorrow" is, in the first place, the conscience grieving over his
> sins, because it is in the conscience alone that the soul is at ease or troubled,
> through grace or guilt. [And since no pain exceeds that of conscience[33]],
> therefore it is the bed of sorrow in which the sinner is forced to lie after sin.
> And indeed it should be a bed for rest. But now because of sin it is a bed of

sorrow, for man cannot flee from his own conscience. Therefore it is a
bed. Yet he does not rest in it, therefore it is a bed of sorrow.[34]

Luther recognizes more than just the guilty conscience in this passage, noting that it ought to be a place of repose and assurance, but it is the guilty
conscience that dominates his early writings.

Luther introduces a new element into his early writings that does not
have a strict scholastic precedent. He proposes the unique configuration of
a double *synteresis*, the innate inclination of both the reason and the will to
know and choose the good. He refers to this double *synteresis* as the "tin-
der" (*fomes*) or "seed" (*semen*) of humanity's original inheritance from
Adam, retaining something of its initial integrity through the Fall and perpetuating in the individual a measure of conformity with God. According
to Luther,

> This *synteresis* in the will of man remains forever, for it wishes to be
> saved and to live well and beautifully; it does not desire, and hates to be
> damned, and thus the *synteresis* of the reason pleads inextinguishably for
> the best, the true, the right, and the just...this *synteresis* is a preservation, a
> remainder or a left-over portion of our nature in the corruption and faulti-
> ness of perdition. It is like a tinder, a seed, and the material of our future
> revival and the restoration of our nature through grace.[35]

The *synteresis* of the will does not comprise the whole will, but gives
to it an emotional witness outside of a person's control, creating a desire
for what is best for her. Luther is of the opinion, however, that this small
amount of conformity between God and the conscience has been thoroughly
disfigured by the corruptions of original sin, that even in the immediate
conclusions derived from the impetus of the *synteresis*, in the act of giving
assent to first moral principles (for example, when pagans know by virtue
of the *synteresis* that a powerful, invisible and good God exists and is to be
honored), there is error and sin (for they incorrectly conclude that the invisible, powerful and good God is Jupiter). Luther ridicules the scholastics
for believing that this almost imperceptible remnant of creation is able to
move a believer towards "an act of loving God above all things!"[36]

But in spite of the continuity with his scholastic heritage, a gradual and
significant transformation emerges in Luther's conception of conscience.
This transformation is signalled by the disappearance of all references to
the *synteresis* in his writings. Baylor interprets this change in terms of a
shift to a new object of concern for the conscience. In scholastic theology
the activity of conscience pertains exclusively to particular acts or to the

motivation for these acts. But Luther extends the scope of conscience to include a third and more vital object. In a sermon on the Tabernacle of Moses he draws an analogy between the commonly accepted concerns for the apprehensions of conscience with the outer court (external actions) and the sanctuary (internal motivations) of the tabernacle, but then he also argues that these concerns are not sufficient for true virtue and piety, since God is not satisfied with these works alone, variously motivated as they are by desire for reward or fear of punishment, and that depend upon humankind's own meager resources. Within the "holy of holies" conscience also makes a judgment about the self as a whole:

> Therefore, man must crawl here to grace and renounce himself. Here God has given us...the holy of holies. Here God has shown us Christ and promised that whoever believes in Christ and calls to Him, he will straightaway receive the Holy Spirit...And when the Spirit comes, He makes a clean, free, joyous, happy and willing heart, a heart that is always pious, seeks no rewards, fears no punishment, is only pious for the sake of piety or righteousness and does everything with joy; see, that is the truly good teaching to instruct the conscience and works: to go into the holy of holies. That is the last thing that a man on earth can do.[37]

Luther here definitively moves beyond the conception of conscience espoused by scholastic theology. He asserts that the testimony of conscience cannot be confined to particular actions and their relation to first moral principles, as its witness issues "a judgment of the same kind as God Himself—one which has as its object the person as a whole."[38]

Conscience thus receives in Luther's writings its own ontological status as a specific and independent power of the soul rather than as a habit or activity of a some other faculty. Its primary function is to make judgments about the person as a whole in conformity with God's judgments in Scripture, and for this reason he associates it with the heart (*cor*), spirit (*spiritus*), and even the soul (*anima*) of the human being. There are two senses in which Luther equates conscience with the heart and even with the whole conscious life of an individual. First, it is the source of the most powerful emotional experiences which comprise the basic affective contours of the soul. In addition, the witness of conscience is constituted by both cognitive and affective, rational and emotional elements, and thus can be placed in the center of the human person and identified with the soul and spirit as the unity of reason and will.[39]

The shift in the fundamental object of conscience occurs in concert with Luther's growing criticism of the role that an Aristotelian conception of practical reason plays in scholastic theology, a concept that he regards as ill-suited for the principal function of conscience. He is particularly critical of Aristotle's influence upon medieval thought that restricts the judgments of conscience to individual acts, for he holds that the Bible distinguishes between the righteousness of God—a divine judgment about the person as a whole prior to individual acts, which makes conscience the bearer of the individual before God—and the Aristotelian conception of human righteousness, which is a consequence of individual actions. The domestication of conscience in medieval theology effectively forestalls an accurate perception of the individual as God sees her, a judgment to which the Bible give testimony in the reconciling activity of God in Jesus Christ.[40] Luther distinguishes between his understanding of conscience and that of the scholastics in a crucial passage in his Romans commentary:

> Scholastic theologians did not know the nature of sin and forgiveness. For they reduced sin as well as righteousness to some very minute motion of the soul. They said, namely, that when the will is subject to *synteresis*, it is, only slightly to be sure, "inclined toward the good." And this tiny motion toward God (of which man is naturally capable) they imagine to be an act of loving God above everything! And now look at man as he actually is and see how his whole person [*totum hominem*] is full of these sinful desires (and how that little motion has no effect at all).[41]

As the faculty that renders a judgment about the self as a whole, conscience (when considered from the perspective before God, *coram deo*) is a type of battleground in the dialectic between the law and the gospel. When it grasps this dialectic rightly, conscience pronounces its verdict about the person as a whole in a way which mirrors the eschatological judgment of God. The conscience afflicted by the judgment of God's law experiences the consuming wrath of God and the horrors of punishment in hell, driving the soul inexorably to acknowledge that its condemnation is completely warranted. Even the saints are perpetually assailed by the tribulations of a conscience under the judgment of the divine law, writes Luther, for they concur with God's righteous condemnation of sinner:

> Hence the saints themselves never know that they perform and possess meritorious works, but they do all those things only that they might find mercy and escape judgment, praying for forgiveness with loud groaning rather than presumptuously looking for the crown...Because of their fear of judgment, their death and their sin are manifest with them, before

them, and in their consciences. They always judge themselves in fear, because they know that of themselves they cannot be righteous before God.
And thus they fear the judgment of God upon all their works.[42]

But the pangs of conscience, as important as they are for Luther, do
not constitute the final or proper work of God in those whom the divine
sovereignty has determined to save, for the fundamental purpose of conscience's perturbations is not despair, wrath, and condemnation. Rather,
"in order to humble the elect and teach them to trust in His mercy alone, to
lay aside every presumption of their own will and achievement, God permits them to be desperately afflicted and to be pursued by the devil, the
world, or the flesh, whom He Himself arouses against them." The crisis of
a guilty conscience thus forces us outside of ourselves and our own resources to find a sure foundation for the conscience. Hence the terrified
conscience reverberating with the accusations of the law has finally arrived
at the beginning of true and godly wisdom: "For from then His wrath is in
the heart of the penitent, because He causes His judgment to be preached,
because of which they tremble and cease to do evil, and also because of the
rumbling of an accusing conscience."[43]

The close link between faith and conscience in the New Testament thus
reemerges in Luther's theology, marking the site of the individual's relationship to God: "The 'place' is faith in the conscience, or the conscience in
faith. This is the place in which the good things of teachings, knowledge,
wisdom, understanding, and other constructions of good appearance are
built." Faith embraces both the guilty conscience, as the capacity of the believer to justify God's righteous judgment in the divine law about the self
as a whole, as well as the conscience which finds its consolation through
faith as the believer conforms herself in Christ to the merciful judgment of
God. Luther therefore states that "He who judges himself and confesses his
sin justifies God and affirms his truthfulness, because he is saying about
himself what God is saying about him." Baylor observes in this connection
that "The bad and good conscience are, in fact, the correlates in the conscience of Luther's fundamental conviction that the Christian is at once justified and a sinner (*simul iustus et peccator*)."[44]

In his Galatians lectures of 1531 Luther adapts the language of medieval bridal mysticism to help describe the conscience that finds sanctuary in
God's promise of mercy and solace through faith in Christ, stating that

in our conscience [the Law] is truly a devil, for in the slightest trial it cannot
encourage or comfort the conscience but does the very opposite, frightening

> and saddening it and depriving it of confidence in righteousness, of life, and
> of everything good...Therefore let the godly person learn that the Law and
> Christ are mutually contradictory and altogether incompatible. When Christ
> is present, the Law must not rule in any way but must retreat from the con-
> science and yield the bed to Christ alone, since this is too narrow to hold
> them both...Let Him rule alone in righteousness, safety, happiness, and
> life, so that the conscience may happily fall asleep in Christ, without any
> awareness of Law, sin, or death.

Only by clinging to Christ in faith does the guilty conscience find refuge
from its accusing thoughts under the law and a Defender who provides for
the soul in an exchange of properties—grace for sin and righteousness for
judgment. In this relationship there is peace for the person who turns to
Christ and says: "Christ has done enough for me. He is just. He is my defense. He has died for Me. He has made his righteousness my righteousness, and my sin His sin."[45]

In extending the judgment of conscience to the whole person, however, Luther makes a sharp distinction between the inner and the outer person, the former standing solely before God (*coram deo*) in conscience, and
the later in the historical sequence of particular acts, appearing only before
one's fellow human beings (*coram hominibus*).[46] Nothing which pertains
to the outer person, in his judgment, should be allowed to constrain the
conscience in its discernment of the divine judgment and mercy.[47] Luther,
in spite of all his disagreements with medieval scholastic theology, is unable
to break free from its dominant images of God and the atonement, which
were focused almost exclusively around the metaphor of the stern and demanding judge. He thus reinforces a conception of salvation as principally
a forensic event directed exclusively at individuals.[48] Luther's stress upon
the freedom of conscience from oppressive human laws, and finally from
divine law, is closely related to this understanding of God. The terrible
majesty and wrath of God, which is the overriding concern of the late medieval theology, must be satisfied, and so the liberation of conscience, constantly pursued by the divine wrath or mercy, takes precedence over a
semi-Pelagian conception of the will.

Luther's inability to completely break free from medieval conceptions
borders on the tragic. Baylor contends that "In crediting the conscience
with the capacity to have the person as its object, the whole man as he
stands before God, Luther...was beginning to add an important new dimension to the religious significance of the conscience, one that related the person to God with a new force and directness..."[49] Unfortunately, the dis-

tinction between the inner and outer person effectively thwarts the practical intent of Luther's understanding of conscience, making his contribution to the story of its liberation an ambiguous one. Ironically, by restricting the activity of conscience to judgments about the whole person *coram deo*, he eliminates it from consideration in the practice of day to day life *coram hominibus*. Luther severs the relationship of conscience with fellow believers that Paul had erected, and therefore undermines his own doctrine of the priesthood of all believers. In the final analysis, he extends and consolidates the medieval interiorization and individualization of faith, a process which began with the shift in the social location of the church following the "christianization" of the Roman empire.[50]

Bonhoeffer, ironically and perhaps unwittingly, makes explicit some of the consequences that accompany the rupture between the self *coram deo* and *coram hominibus*: "The Reformers' biblical faith in God had radically removed God from the world. The ground was thereby prepared for the efflorescence of the rational and empirical sciences, and while the natural scientists of the seventeenth and eighteenth centuries were still believing Christians, when faith in God was lost all that remained was a rationalized and mechanized world."[51] Furthermore, Luther's conception of the freedom of conscience, a liberty that he restricts to the inner person, provides one of the key elements which eventually coalesce into the liberal ideology of freedom, which is confined to an inner realm of the human subject and denied to the historical sphere of actions.[52] Luther's bifurcation of the person and the restriction of freedom to the inner self consequently sets the ideological stage for modernity's subjugation of conscience to the dominant interests of a market-driven culture.

The chapter on Luther's place in the narrative of the liberation of conscience, however, does have a positive side. In particular, the charge that Luther posits an introspective conscience, in which the soul deals only with itself as a final authority in religious matters, is simply wrong.[53] Luther insists that in the testimony of conscience the human being is above all, as Gerhard Ebeling puts it, "a hearer, someone who is seized, claimed and subject to judgment."[54] Whether Luther is referring to the activity of the Spirit working to undermine the self-righteousness and false sense of security of the easy conscience by means of the law, or of the comforting presence of God which persuades the conscience to set aside its own condemning witness, become blind to the law, and rest in union with Jesus Christ through faith, he always sees the conscience which correctly apprehends the self being preceded by God's activity, constantly forced outside of its own resources to trust in the promises of God's merciful word in the gospel.[55]

Contrary to both Catholic polemic and modern adulation, therefore, Luther does not regard the conscience as an autonomous reality, that is, as an organ of revelation or religious point of contact that has an independent authority equal to that of reason or Scripture. He never posits the conscience as a self-sufficient entity in a subjectivist or idealist fashion. At no time at the Diet of Worms does he appeal to the certainty of his conscience to justify his opinions, and he admits that, like anybody else, his conscience could be deceived. He invites anyone, in accordance with the basic scholastic position, to demonstrate that his conscience is in error and to correct it by proof of Scripture or evident reasoning. In short, there is no logical connection in his writings between his conviction that he has rightly interpreted Scripture and whatever certainty his own conscience might possess. He maintains that only in faith does conscience judge reliably about the whole person and render a decision which accurately reflects God's eschatological judgment about the self, and that the believer is obligated to set any other kind of conscience aside. He asserts that only the conscience that is "bound by the chains of Scripture and the holy Word"[56] has a sure foundation, and that one should only trust in the Bible and not in her own experience. According to Baylor, therefore,

> If Luther's assertions that his conscience might be in error, and that it was open to correction are to be taken as sincere—and there seems little reason to doubt them —then he was not essentially subjective or circular in his theology, and neither did he credit the conscience with any independent right to determine for itself what is religious truth. In brief, Luther's stand rested upon the same relative and negative authority which the scholastics had granted the conscience, not upon a new and positive right to profess that which a sense of certainty compels the conscience to accept as divine truth.[57]

In spite of his shortcomings, then, Luther does make an important contribution to the story of the liberation of conscience. He recovers something of conscience's theopolitical character, virtually neglected in medieval theology. Most importantly, he recovers the concern of conscience with the whole person, the human self considered in one's entirety, rather than restricting its witness to judgments concerning individual actions or the inference of moral axioms from first principles. This reconsideration of the entire person in conscience by Luther involves a renewed

understanding of the unity of will, reason, and affections in the human being claimed by God. Luther helps to uncover for subsequent generations,
as Calvin put it, the anthropological "treasure chest" in which Christian
faith is properly kept.[58]

The emergence of the modern world, with its "enlightened" outlook,
provides a new and challenging twist to the plot in the story of conscience.
In particular, the complex relationship between conscience and the chief artifact of the modern world, the human subject, which will be the focus of
the next chapter, requires careful consideration.

NOTES

[1]Poteat, *Polanyian Meditations*, 267.

[2]Robert L. Wilkin, "Conscientia in Ambrose's *de officiis* and in Stoic Ethics," paper
presented at Duke University, Durham, North Carolina, 27 September, 1985.

[3]Lehmann, *Ethics*, 327–28, 336.

[4]Some New Testament scholars argue that Paul was the first to introduce the idea of
conscience into Christian discourse through his controversy with the Corinthian "Gnostics," who supposedly used the term in ways that were consistent with its current usage in
the contemporary Hellenistic world. Robert Jewett, *Paul's Anthropological Terms: A
Study of Their Use in Conflict Settings* (Leiden: E. J. Brill, 1971), 436; Claude Anthony
Pierce, *Conscience in the New Testament* (London: SCM Press, Ltd., 1955), 99. However, as Hans-Joachim Eckstein rightly notes, this assertion confuses its chronological
appearance in the New Testament canon with it initial employment in Christian theology
and preaching. Hans-Joachim Eckstein, *Der Begriff Syneidesis bei Paulus: Eine neutestamentlich-exegetische Untersuchung zum 'Gewissensbegriff'* (Tübingen: J. C. B.
Mohr [Paul Siebeck], 1983), 319.

[5]*Theological Dictionary of the New Testament*, eds. Gerhard Kittel and Gerhard
Friedrich, s.v. "synoida, syneidesis," by Christian Maurer.

[6]For comprehensive treatments of the historical context informing Paul's use of the idea
of conscience, see W. D. Davies, "Conscience and Its Use in the New Testament," *Jewish
and Pauline Studies* (Philadelphia: Fortress Press, 1984), 243–50; Eckstein, *Der Begriff
Syneidesis*, 35–135; Jewett, *Paul's Anthropological Terms*, 402–21; Maurer, "synoida,
syneidesis,"; and Pierce, *Conscience*, 13–53.

[7]Davies, "Conscience," 243; Krister Stendahl, "The Apostle Paul and the Introspective
Conscience of the West," *Harvard Theological Review* 56 (July 1963): 199–215.

[8]David Daube, *Ancient Jewish Law* (Leiden: E. J. Brill, 1981), 123–29; Maurer, "synoida, syneidesis"; and Hans Walter Wolff, *Anthropology of the Old Testament*, 51–52, 54,
65.

[9]Plato *Apology* 21b; cf. Maurer, "synoida, syneidesis."

[10]Lehmann, *Ethics*, 328–30; Pierce, *Conscience*, 29–53; Eckstein, *Der Begriff Syneidesis*, 35–71; Maurer, "synoida, syneidesis."

[11]Maurer, "synoida, syneidesis."

[12]Maurer notes that "The first commentary on the passage [in Rom. 13[5]] in 1 Pt. 2[19], with its strange *dia syneidesin theou*, 'for the sake of co-knowledge with God', 'for the sake of consciousness of God', bears the same meaning." Maurer, "synoida, syneidesis."

[13]Eckstein, *Der Begriff Syneidesis*, 317.

[14]This witness of conscience corresponds to the self-examination of one's heart, *kardia*, in 1 John 3[19-22].

[15]In all likelihood an allusion to the prophesy of Jeremiah 31[33] regarding the Torah inscribed upon the heart, which is an aspect of the new covenant the God will establish with creation. See C. E. B. Cranfield, *A Critical and Exegetical Commentary on the Epistle to the Romans*, vol. 1 (Edinburgh: T. & T. Clark, 1975), 158–59.

[16]Davies, "Conscience," 250–54; Jewett, *Paul's Anthropological Terms*, 421–46, 458–60; Pierce, *Conscience*, 60–98.

[17]Lehmann, *Ethics*, 352; Maurer, "synoida, syneidesis." For a detailed discussion of the Hebrew word for heart, *leb*, as the inner fulcrum or core of the human being, encompassing a person's rational, volitional and affective qualities, see Hans Walter Wolff, *Anthropology of the Old Testament*, 40–58.

[18]The term *theopolitics* comes from Martin Buber. He defines it as "action of a public nature from the point of view of the tendency toward actualization of divine rulership," the realization of which he regards as "the Proton and Eschaton of Israel." Buber, *Kingship of God*, 3d ed., trans. Richard Scheimann (New York: Harper & Row, 1967), 57–58; cf. 140.

[19]"What Paul find in [the Old Testament] Scripture, above all else, is a prefiguration of the church as the people of God." Richard B. Hays, *Echoes of Scripture in the Letters of Paul* (New Haven, CN: Yale University Press, 1989), 86; cf. 84–87.

[20]Maurer, "synoida, syneidesis."

[21]Karl Holl, "Was verstand Luther unter Religion?" *Gesammelte Aufsätze zur Kirchengeschichte*, vol. 1 (Tübingen: J. C. B. Mohr, 1923), 35 (my translation).

[22]Erik H. Erikson, *Young Man Luther: A Study in Psycho-analysis and History* (New York: W. W. Norton, 1962), 231; E. Harris Harbison, *The Age of Reformation* (Ithaca, NY: Cornell University Press, 1955), 50, 52. Among the Catholics who contend against Luther from this perspective are Paul Hacker, *Das Ich im Glauben bei Martin Luther* (Graz: Styria Verlag, 1966), who contends that Luther's understanding of faith is flawed with the element of reflexivity, that is, where faith becomes its own justification; and Joseph Lortz, *The Reformation in Germany*, 2 vol., trans. Ronald Walls (London: Darton, Longman & Todd; New York: Herder and Herder, 1968), who argues throughout the two volumes that "Subjectivism was no accessory to Luther's make-up but a basic element." Lortz, *The Reformation in Germany*, 1: 458.

[23]Michael G. Baylor, *Action and Person: Conscience in Late Scholasticism and the Young Luther*, Studies in Medieval and Reformation Thought, vol. 20 (Leiden: E. J. Brill, 1977), 5–6.

[24]Thomas Aquinas, *Summa Theologica* 1a. 79. 13.

[25]It was St. Jerome, in an allegorical gloss of a prophecy of Ezekiel, who first identified the Greek *syneidesis* with what later became the medieval *synteresis*. Jerome characterized the *synteresis* as the unquenchable spark of the conscience, that most noble element of the soul which creates in humans an awareness of one's sinfulness when one is over-

come by evil desires, rage or the deceptive influence of reason. Baylor, *Action and Person*, 25–26.

[26]Baylor, *Action and Person*, 20–118, 171–72, 215.

[27]Lehmann, *Ethics*, 332.

[28]Lehmann, *Ethics*, 362–63.

[29]Martin Luther, *Luther's Works*, ed. and trans. Theodore G. Tappert, vol. 54: *Table Talk* (Philadelphia: Fortress Press, 1967), 22.

[30]Martin Luther, *Luther's Works*, ed. Jaroslav Pelikan, vol. 26: *Lectures on Galatians 1535: Chapters 1–4* (Saint Louis: Concordia Publishing House, 1963), 28–29. See also Arthur B. Holmes, *"Nos Extra Nos*: Luther's Understanding of the Self as Conscience," *The Drew Gateway* 53 (Fall 1982): 25–26.

[31]Baylor, *Action and Person*, 128–56.

[32]Baylor, *Action and Person*, 171–72.

[33]The translation quoted reads here: "It is not sorrow over the sorrow of conscience..." I have taken the liberty to substitute a modified form of Baylor's translation of this clause, for it renders the Latin *"Non enim est dolor super dolorem conscientiae"* more intelligible in this context. Baylor, *Action and Person*, 172 and note 36.

[34]Martin Luther, *Luther's Works*, ed. Hilton C. Oswald, vol. 10: *First Lectures on the Psalms I: Psalms 1–75* (Saint Louis: Concordia Publishing House, 1974), 191.

[35]As quoted in Baylor, *Action and Person*, 158.

[36]Martin Luther, *Luther's Works*, ed Hilton C. Oswald, vol.25: *Lectures on Romans: Glosses and Scholia* (Saint Louis: Concordia Publishing House, 1972), 157–58; *Lectures on Romans*, 262. See also Baylor, *Action and Person*, 140–41, 157–59, 168–69, 172–71.

[37]Martin Luther, "Sermon on the Threefold Good Life to Instruct the Conscience," as quoted by Baylor, *Action and Person*, 198–99.

[38]Baylor, *Action and Person*, 215.

[39]Baylor, *Action and Person*, 208.

[40]It is this act of rendering a judgment about the whole person according to God's righteous activity towards humanity which implicitly underlies Lehmann's critique of the medieval scholastic tradition as the domestication of conscience. The protracted reinteptetation of the nature and function of conscience in the Middle Ages represents a conspicuous departure from the biblical conceptions of conscience and its intrinsic connection to Christian faith itself. Conscience is no longer the unrestrained threat that it had been to the Hellenists, but its more direct function of involving the person in the transfigurative dynamics of God's reconciling activity in the world is also negated.

[41]Martin Luther, *Luther: Lectures on Romans*, trans. Wilhelm Pauck (Philadelphia: The Westminster Press, 1961), 129–30.

[42]Luther, *Lectures on Romans*, 277–78. "For the conscience to be under the law," states Holmes, "is for the whole person to be imprisoned under sin, death and the law." Holmes, *"Nos Extra Nos,"* 22. Luther asserts that the heart which complacently and mistakenly trusts in its own capacity to do meritorious works, thereby falsely considering itself righteous, is worse than the sufferings of a bad conscience. "To do this is to make the foundation of sand and to cast Christ aside...since Christ is the only foundation before all

good works; for by free grace He gives the foundation, the rest for the conscience, and the confidence of the heart, coming ahead of all our satisfaction and building." Luther, *Lectures on Romans*, 104 (n. 1).

[43]Luther, *Lectures on Romans*, 392; Martin Luther, *Luther's Works*, ed. Hilton C. Oswald, vol. 11: *First Lectures on the Psalms II: Psalms 76–126* (Saint Louis, Concordia Publishing House, 1976), 9. It is interesting to note that Luther makes use of the proverb which speaks of the fear of God as the beginning of wisdom (Prov. 1:7, 9:10) to illustrate the role of conscience in the biblical dialectic of law and gospel, whereas W. D. Davies uses it as evidence for the incommensurable gulf that exists between Hellenistic introspection and Hebraic theocentrism.

[44]Luther, *First Lectures on the Psalms II*, 93; Luther, *First Lectures on the Psalms I*, 238; Baylor, *Action and Person*, 231.

[45]Martin Luther, *Luther's Works*, ed. Jaroslav Pelikan, vol. 26: *Lectures on Galatians 1535: Chapters 1–4* (Saint Louis: Concordia Publishing House, 1963), 365f; Luther, *Lectures on Romans*, 188.

[46]See Martin Luther, "The Freedom of a Christian," *Three Treatises*, trans. W. A. Lambert (2d ed.; Philadelphia: Fortress Press, 1970), 277–316.

[47]Paul Althaus, *The Ethics of Martin Luther*, trans. Robert C. Schultz (Philadelphia: Fortress Press, 1972), 4–6, 61–62, 90, 109, 124, 126, 129, 130, 139, 149.

[48]The almost exclusive reliance upon forensic images in Western theology has been a long-standing criticism on the part of Eastern Orthodox theologians. See, for example, Alexander Schmemann, *Church, World, Mission: Reflections on Orthodoxy in the West* (Crestwood, NY: St. Vladimir's Seminary Press, 1979), 152.

[49]Baylor, *Action and Person*, 215.

[50]See Yoder, *The Priestly Kingdom*, 135–41.

[51]Dietrich Bonhoeffer, *Ethics*, ed. Eberhard Bethge (New York: Macmillan Publishing Co., Inc., 1955), 96. John Milbank adds: "Late-medieval nominalism, the protestant reformation and seventeenth-century Augustinianism…completely privatized, spiritualized, and transcendentalized the sacred, and concurrently reimagined nature, human action and society as a sphere of autonomous, sheerly formal power." Milbank, *Theology and Social Theory*, 1.

[52]See Herbert Marcuse, "A Study in Authority," *Studies in Critical Philosophy* (Boston: Beacon Press, 1973), 56–78.

[53]Stendahl, "The Apostle Paul," 220–25.

[54]Gerhard Ebeling, *Luther: An Introduction to his Thought*, trans. R. A. Wilson (Philadelphia: Fortress Press, 1970), 120; cf. 261–62. It is Ebeling who has developed in this century a theological conception of conscience in an intentional continuity with Luther's thought. See Gerhard Ebeling, "Theological Reflexions on Conscience," *Word and Faith*, trans. James W. Leitch (London: SCM Press Ltd., 1963), 407–23.

[55]Baylor cogently argues that while the conscience may be seen as the bearer of the person's relationship to God in Luther's theology, it is never viewed as a self-sufficient or self-contained entity: "Like the rest of man's capacities, the conscience needs a foundation which lies outside of itself." Baylor, *Action and Person*, 218; cf. 223, 236–37, 241. Holmes concurs with Baylor's judgment: "For Luther the conscience is never a neutral reality but is always the conscience already addressed and claimed. It is never free as its own Lord, as an autonomous agent in the presence of God. The conscience which is not in

Christ or the promise is already under the law." Holmes, *"Nos Extra Nos,"* 25; cf. 24, 26–28.

[56]Martin Luther, *Luther's Works*, ed. George W. Forell, vol. 32: *Career of the Reformer II* (Philadelphia: Fortress Press, 1958), 119.

[57]Baylor, *Action and Person*, 264. See Ebeling, *Luther*, 119; Paul Althaus, *The Theology of Martin Luther*, trans. Robert C. Schultz (Philadelphia: Fortress Press, 1966), 55; and Holmes, *"Nos Extra Nos,"* 25.

[58]John Calvin, *Institutes of the Christian Religion*, Library of Christian Classics, trans. Ford Lewis Battles, ed. John T. McNeill, vols 20 and 21 (Philadelphia: The Westminster Press, 1960), 3.2.12, 20: 558.

Chapter 3

THE STORY OF CONSCIENCE: II

"The Aboriginal Vicar of Christ"
John Henry Newman's Doctrine of Conscience

After the radical restructuring of categories that resuscitated the notion of conscience in the theology of the Reformers, a noticeable decline in its sense and significance occurs with the emergence of the modern world. As was the case during the Middle Ages, the term once again acquires a widely accepted definition wich unduly constricts its relation to the full range of concerns and issues addressed by theologians. The eclipse of conscience reaches its nadir in the pivotal writings of Immanuel Kant, whom Lehmann calls the primary architect of the decline of conscience. Kant strips conscience of its significance as that which forges the link between the production of the self and the order by which one's life is shaped and directed, and substitutes a conception of conscience as the autonomous internal voice of an external authority. Kant thus restores the tragic conscience as the awesome sense of duty that overshadows the positive function of conscience in the pure rationality of the moral law.[1]

Lehmann does not identify anyone during the modern era who contributes to the story of the liberation of conscience. However, I would suggest that John Henry Newman, a nineteenth century British theologian and bishop, offers a significant reevaluation of the character and significance of conscience. The story of the liberation and empowerment of conscience within the Christian tradition would be incomplete without Newman, who insists that conscience is "the essential principle and sanction of religion in the mind."[2] In a statement similar to the one Karl Holl makes of Luther, Bernard Reardon says that

> The basis...of Newman's whole position is that the very foundation
> of religion is conscience...Conscience is more indeed than the foundation of
> mere natural religion. In his own vivid phrase, it is "the aboriginal Vicar of
> Christ." Revelation itself has its primary authentication here. Once you rec-
> ognize the origin of conscience you are bound, Newman seems to say, to
> recognize its scope also. All Christian truth rests ultimately on conscience
> for its testimony and cannot be apprehended apart from it.[3]

Newman develops his doctrine of conscience in conjunction with what he calls the illative sense, the mode of reasoning which characterizes practical, moral, and personal judgments in general, and religious assent or faith in particular.[4] The principal difference between the illative sense and the strictly formal conceptions of scientific rationality which prevail in the modern era is best seen in terms of Newman's distinction between real and notional assent. Real assent is marked by its contingency and concreteness, practical certitude, and personal involvement and commitment, whereas notional assent is characterized by its abstract precision, purely conceptual nature, and the absence of any requirement for personal commitment. Newman speaks of the *totus homo*, the whole person, being involved in religious judgments, judgments which include the affective and volitional dimensions of human existence in conjunction with the active intellect.[5] By means of a culminating series of probable intellectual arguments (which are not necessarily syllogistic in form) that converge in conjunction with a person's affective and volitional powers, the illative sense rises to an unqualified assent and certitude that is individual and concrete, yet absolute in that only one conclusion is applicable for any one particular circumstance.

Newman's assertion that it would be as impossible for him to live without conscience and the certitude of real assent as it would be to exist without breathing reveals the inherently practical and performative character of this mode of reasoning.[6] Christian faith is therefore concerned with the course of human activity and with God as divine agent,[7] a personal, governing Sovereign in whom humans are personally interested. Reardon notes that Newman regards the core of life as action, which does not allow for the minute and precise reasonings and the apodictic certainty demanded by the Cartesian subject, but relies on assumptions which cannot be proved ultimately, but only embodied and acted upon by the whole person within the actual contours of history.[8] According to Jouett Powell,

Real apprehension or assent is dependent upon "moral experiences," that is, on personal formation or life history. One cannot arrive at real apprehensions second-hand by means of general ideas; one can only do so by means of lived experiences. Religious inquiry consists not only in matters of information but also in the way in which those matters come to have personal significance for the individual.[9]

Newman's understanding of conscience and the practical form of reasoning is indebted to both Joseph Butler and Samuel Taylor Coleridge. Newman himself characterizes the aim of the *Grammar* as being "of a practical character, such as that of Butler in his *Analogy*." J. Robinson believes that Butler and Newman can both be identified correctly, if somewhat ambiguously, by the term *practical*, for their common goal is to influence the overall conduct of individuals, hopefully to the end of conversion. Robinson also argues that the word practical describes their methodology, insofar as Butler and Newman take concrete human life as they find it, with the ways humans actually think and act, as the basis for discovering the natural modes of action and thought without disguising them behind an overlaid theoretical schema. Newman also follows Butler by grounding his argument for how one naturally gives real assent to the existence of God through conscience by way of its dual function as a moral sense and as a sense of duty.[10]

The influence of Coleridge is evident in Newman's assertion that the weakness of abstract reasoning in matters of religious assent is its impersonal quality, and that faith involves and invokes the entire self through a personal disposition and relation to God that is vitally grounded in the witness of conscience. As observed by Reardon, Coleridge likewise regards the conscience as the actual unity of reason and will, defining the human mind as "a mind capable of conscience," i.e., that sense of moral responsibility which is the prior condition and ground of consciousness. One is also related to God through the witness of conscience: "If you would have a good conscience, you must by all means have so much light, so much knowledge of the will of God, as may regulate you, and show you your way, may teach you how to do, and speak, and think, as in His presence."[11]

For both Coleridge and Newman, conscience cannot be equated with, nor broken down into, some more basic power(s) of the mind. Newman in particular clearly distinguishes (but does not separate) conscience from the related idea of the moral sense.[12] Conscience is thus a holistic concept, although it takes in the moral sense as its critical or rational office. The second and more significant element of the phenomena of conscience, "its primary and most authoritative aspect," is its sense of duty, encompassing both a judicial office and a magisterial dictate, i.e., the dictate of an authoritative monitor and the sanction of right conduct. This authoritative sanction and magisterial office pertains primarily to one's own self and actions, and indirectly to the actions of others in relation to the self. In its personal sense of obligation and responsibility conscience does not rest in itself, claims Newman,

> but vaguely reaches forward to something beyond self, and dimly discerns a sanction higher than self for its decisions, as is evidenced in that keen sense of obligation and responsibility which informs them. And hence it is that we are accustomed to speak of conscience as…voice, or the echo of a voice, imperative and constraining, like no other dictate in the whole of our experience.[13]

Conscience is also distinguished from moral sensibilities by the immediate and intimate bearing it has on human affections and emotions, evoking feelings of reverence and awe, hope and fear. Such emotions, Newman contends, always involve the recognition of a living, personal object as the focus of its concern. The theological nexus for conscience, a vivid awareness "which identifies the intimations of conscience with the reverberations or echoes (so to say) of an external admonition…a Supreme Ruler and Judge" is poignantly expressed by Newman in a passage from *A Grammar of Assent* that deserves to be quoted in its entirety:

> If, as is the case, we feel responsible, are ashamed, are frightened, at transgressing the voice of conscience, this implies that there is One to whom we are responsible, before whom we are ashamed, whose claim upon us we fear. If, on doing wrong, we feel the same tearful, broken-hearted sorrow which overwhelms us on hurting a mother; if, on doing right, we enjoy the same sunny serenity of mind, the same soothing, satisfactory delight which follows on our receiving praise from a father, we certainly have with us the image of some person, to whom our love and veneration look, towards whom we direct our pleadings, in whose anger we are troubled and waste away. These feelings in us are such as require for their exciting cause an intelligent being: we are not affectionate towards a stone, nor do we feel shame before a horse or a dog; we have no remorse or compunction on breaking mere human law: yet, so it is, conscience excites all these emotions, confusion, foreboding, self-condemnation; and on the other hand it sheds upon us a deep peace, a sense of security, a resignation, and a hope, which there is no sensible, no earthly object to elicit. "The wicked flees, when no one pursueth"; then why does he flee? whence his terror? Who is it that he sees in solitude, in darkness, in the hidden chambers of his heart?

If the cause of these emotions does not belong to this visible world, the Object to which his perception is directed must be Supernatural and Divine; and thus the phenomena of Conscience, as a dictate, avail to impress the imagination with the picture of a Supreme Governor, a Judge, holy, just, powerful, all-seeing, retributive, and is [sic] the creative principle of religion, as the Moral Sense is the principle of ethics.[14]

While Newman states that the testimony of conscience concerning the reality and holiness of God is so vivid that he could not imagine life apart from its witness, he also acknowledges that the decision to structure his discussion of Christian faith around conscience is due, at least in part, to the rhetorical judgment that he needs to begin with a phenomenon that is most widely accepted. He asserts that in the intimations of conscience there is a common and universal starting point for productive inquiry into the existence and character of God. Those who would deny the commonly held proverb that conscience is the voice of God so strive against the common acceptance of humankind that Newman feels there is no need to argue against those who are so obviously deficient in either religious sense or memory as to wholly attribute conscience's testimony to either an aesthetic sense or social teaching and association. Newman therefore begins his investigation into the truth of Christianity and its characteristic marks or evidences by stating that his warrant is the teaching of conscience and the moral sense. To do this he freely admits that he assumes the presence of God in the conscience, for he maintains that in matters of real assent, as contrasted with notional apprehension, a person cannot circumvent the concrete need to assume something.[15]

The task of discerning the identity of this Other to whom one senses the call to accountability in conscience falls to its critical or rational office, which Newman refers to as the moral sense. In the concrete testimony of conscience, however, the employment of the mind's rational powers in this office is extended beyond what is normally attributed to the mind's moral powers, that is, the determination of distinctions in the quality of actions and the obligation to act in particular ways. Conscience, as the natural connecting principle between creature and creator (thus making it the most authoritative channel of communication between God and humanity) teaches us not only that God is, it also provides, on the basis of its recurring reverberations, a real image of God and of the significant divine attributes as a medium of worship, as well as a natural rule of right and wrong that derives from God.[16]

One can detect a development in Newman's writings concerning what conscience is able to infer about God. In the Oxford sermons he says that conscience carries with it an implication of a relation between the soul and something distinct from the soul. He asserts that this exterior object of the mind's contemplation is characterized as being superior to the self, possessing an excellence and bearing a supreme authority that constitutes itself as a moral tribunal over the soul, and to whom obedience is due and sustained. "Hence...at once, we have the elements of a religious system; for what is Religion but the system of relations existing between us and a Supreme Power, claiming our habitual obedience." However, at this stage Newman held that Natural Religion, based upon the leading of conscience, gives little or no indication of the personal character of God, affording only an indirect argument for a Governor and Judge who is distinct from the moral system itself.[17]

In what is generally regarded as his most mature and philosophically sustained work, *A Grammar of Assent*, Newman shifts from his earlier position and maintains that the complex intimations of conscience do provide the mind with a distinct image of God's unity and personality, along with the requisite attributes, such that

> from the recurring instances in which conscience acts, forcing upon us importunately the mandate of a Superior, we have fresh and fresh evidence of a Sovereign Ruler, from whom those particular dictates which we experience proceed; so that...we may, by means of that induction from particular experiences of conscience, have as good a warrant for concluding the Ubiquitous Presence of One Supreme Master, as we have, from parallel experience of sense, for assenting to the fact of a multiform and vast world, material and mental.

From the sense of approbation or blame, pleasure or pain, that emerges from the activity of conscience, therefore, "lie the materials for the real apprehension of a Divine Sovereign and Judge."[18]

From this "creative principle of religion" he holds that even a child who is unhindered by the negative influences of prejudiced adults is able to see herself through conscience in the presence of God and thus to seek divine forbearance. Newman presents a long list of qualities that accompany the dictates of conscience. By means of this religious instinct the mind forms an image of an invisible and omnipotent Being and Personal Power with whom an individual is in immediate relation and in whom one can recognize a measure of goodwill toward herself. This image from conscience is of One who exercises a certain providence over the world, who knows and is able to change the heart, and who is always accessible to the prayers of a penitent supplicant. Furthermore, it is the image of a Personality who demands certain things, which the sense of moral approval acknowledges as indicating right and good, and thus it is an image of that Being who is truly good, thereby exciting in the individual hope and fear, gratitude and love for Itself. In addition, in and through this Personality imaged by the conscience as Lawgiver, all the qualities of goodness—truth, purity, justice, kindness, and so on—receive, through the moral law, their shape and character. In summary, Newman states:

> as [the child] can contemplate these qualities and their manifestations under the common name of goodness, he is prepared to think of them as indivisible, correlative, supplementary of each other in one and the same Personality, so that there is no aspect of goodness which God is not; and that the more, because the notion of a perfection embracing all possible excellences, both moral and intellectual, is especially congenial to the mind, and there are in fact intellectual attributes, as well as moral, included in the child's image of God, as represented above.[19]

Foremost among the many prominent inferences from conscience concerning the character of the divine unity and personality is the image of God as Judge, and to which is linked the concept of retributive justice. "We learn," contends Newman, "from [conscience's] informations to conceive of the Almighty, primarily, not as a God of Wisdom, of Knowledge, of Power, of Benevolence, but as a God of Judgment and Justice; as One who, not simply for the good of government, but as a good in itself, and as a principle of government, ordains that the offender should suffer for his offence." The image is of a Judges who is angry with us, threatening evil for our wrongdoing and burdening the conscientious mind, an inference that Newman feels is corroborated by the natural religions of primitive humans, providing ample evidence of an abiding sense of sin and of the need for a priestly atonement: "My true informant, my burdened conscience... pronounces without any misgiving that God exists:—and it pronounces too quite as surely that I am alienated from Him."[20]

Finally, in Newman's estimation, when the witness of conscience is properly apprehended, it not only functions in association with the illative sense, but it has an intrinsic relationship with the traditions and hierarchy of the Church. Newman makes the bold assertion that the authority of the teaching office of the Church, including that of the Pope, is founded upon the reverberations of the Divine Sovereign and Judge in conscience: "The championship of the moral law and of conscience is his *raison d'etre*."[21] He further contends that in conscience the priestly and prophetic functions of the Church are rooted: "Conscience is the aboriginal Vicar of Christ, a prophet in its informations, a monarch in its peremptoriness, a priest in its blessings and anathemas, and, even though the eternal priesthood through out the Church could cease to be, in it the sacerdotal principle would remain and would have a sway."[22] Newman also asserts that there is an inviolable integrity and foundational character to conscience such that, as in the medieval tradition, a person ought never to violate the dictates of conscience, even if—though only after intensive self-examination and prayer—it goes against the teachings of a Pope.

Newman is concerned, however, to demonstrate the need and desirability that conscience should have its proper context in what he calls the Supernatural Dispensations of Religion, primarily in the written Word, but also in the history, tradition, and magisterium of the Church. Newman states that it is a false distinction and antagonism which holds in many people's minds between dogmatic creed and vital religion. While he rejects any definition of faith which reposes in mere intellectual concepts, i.e., in notional assent, he also discards any understanding of Christian faith that does away with the necessary place which propositional truth has in the formation of real, religiously imaginative assent. As Ker notes, conscience and its imaging of God requires extrinsic help and clarification through revelation, and is deepened through devotion.[23] Notional assent to the dogmatic propositions of the creed is necessary, both personally and in corporate discourse, to denote the facts of a living, personal faith in language, so that the truths upon which the religious imagination is properly grounded can be adequately expressed and thus constitute the formative context for the witness of conscience. Propositions in the mode of dogmas set the object of devotion lucidly before those who love, fear, hope or trust God. Newman firmly believes that

> in religion the imagination and affections should always be under the control of reason. Theology may stand as a substantive science, though it be without the life of religion, but religion cannot maintain its ground at all without theology. Sentiment, whether imaginative or emotional, falls back upon the intellect for its stay, when sense cannot be called into exercise; and it is in this way that devotion falls back upon dogma.[24]

Newman's exposition of the idea of conscience has many elements that commend themselves. He clearly focuses upon conscience as the personal fulcrum of humankind's awareness of, and responsiveness to, the reality and activity of God, rather than as the practical employment of reason with respect to individual moral acts (Aquinas) or the authoritative and often oppressive voice of duty which compels one to obey the moral law (Kant). In contrast to the opposing emphases of Aquinas and Kant, Newman distinguishes, but does not separate, the two dimensions of the testimony of conscience: a rational or juridical office and a sense of duty, the later being an emotionally powerful perception of an authoritative sanction that communicates an acute sense of responsibility. Newman also connects the intimations of conscience to concrete, historical forms of life, action, and reasoning through the workings of the illative sense. The illative sense describes well, at least in part, the type of non-instrumental reasoning in which conscience engages: imaginative and pragmatic, but most of all, concrete and historical, oriented around human action.

On the negative side, Newman's account of conscience and the illative sense often fails to give adequate consideration of the social dimensions of human activity and discourse. By virtue of our retrospective advantage in the story of conscience we can recognize that many of the aspects which Newman attributes to the natural functioning of conscience and to natural religion, such as the insistence upon an intrinsic image of God as judge and supreme personal power and sovereign in the mind, are better attributed to the production of conscience that takes place within the intellectual and moral practices of the church. He does, however, recognize in a way that is unique for his time the contextual and historical framework of Christian thought in relation to everyday life. Newman is also keenly aware that theology is succinctly and irretrievably interwoven with practical concerns, i.e., with the shaping of human life and action in the presence of God. Unfortunately, while Newman is sensitive to the *historicity* of creaturely existence, he seldom takes the social and political dynamics of everyday life directly into account in his discussion of conscience. In particular, he seldom if ever deals explicitly with the *history* of nineteenth century England.[25]

But perhaps Newman's most significant contribution to the story of the liberation and empowerment of conscience, and in spite of inroads made by foundationalist categories, is the relationship he posits between conscience and the institutions, practices, and traditions of the church. In Newman's opinion the life of the church provides the necessary formative context for the witness of conscience, while the later establishes the internal dynamic and authorization for the life and ministry of the church, so that neither is prior to, or able to properly function without, the other. Moreover, his distinction between real and notional assent clearly articulates what Pietists were trying to say in their focus upon the believer's "inner life" and "personal commitment," but without divorcing these matters from her overall conduct or participation in the institutions and practices of the church. In short, Newman restores the relationship of conscience *coram hominibus* that Paul had established, and reunites it with the believer's standing *coram deo* within the body of Christ, on which Luther had placed great emphasis. While he unfortunately neglects the social and material relations that cannot be properly excluded from the reality and activity of conscience in its historical context, Newman does much to retrieve the humanizing vocation of conscience as the principal *raison d'etre* of theology in a culture intoxicated by the heady but illusory autonomy of "enlightened" reason.

Conscience in the Pedagogy of the Oppressed
Paulo Freire's Doctrine of Conscientization

In Lehmann's narration of the history of the decline and fall of conscience, Sigmund Freud plays the role of the chief architect of the fall of conscience, i.e., of the complete rejection of conscience as a significant reality and dynamic in human life. The father of psychoanalysis prematurely dismisses conscience as the residual, debilitating voice of the super-ego, "a neurotic manifestation arising from a hiatus between the instinctual drives of the organism and reality, as presented to the organism in its [social] environment." With Freud the pilgrimage of conscience has gone full circle in Western intellectual history, arriving back at the tragic and hostile conscience of the Greeks, only now it is deprived of its moral sense and significance, which he exchanges for a psychoanalytic role and function.[26]

Freud, however, does force theologians to reconsider the formative environment of conscience, and in particular its social and political context. Lehmann does not identify anyone on the contemporary scene who develops in detail this aspect of conscience as the performative fulcrum of human involvement in history. I wish to argue, however, that the Brazilian educator and social critic Paulo Freire helps to fill this void in my account of conscience as the *raison d'etre* of theological inquiry. While many theologians in the twentieth century have written on the topic of conscience, usually affording it a relatively minor role in the sub-discipline of theological ethics, few have assigned it the kind of role in theological inquiry that it has in Freire's writings. While he is not a theologian (although he notes that theological categories have played a pivotal role in the development of his pedagogical method), Freire's notion of conscientization has exerted a significant influence upon contemporary theology, particularly in Latin America.[27] Richard Schaull contends that "Paulo Freire's thought represents the response of a creative mind and sensitive conscience to the extraordinary misery and suffering of the oppressed around him." According to Arthur McGovern,

> Many of the changing attitudes within the Church in Latin America grew out of commitments on the part of many priests and religious to become more actively involved with the poor and to help them to become more conscious of their rights and dignity as human beings. While no single person can be credited with stimulating this change, the work and writings of Paulo Freire played a significant role both in influencing this new involvement and by providing ideas on "praxis" which would be come pivotal in the method of liberation theology.[28]

More than other factor, the need to confront and transform these oppressive, dehumanizing circumstances and their structural causes in his native Brazil led Freire to develop the pedagogical method of conscientization.

In order to understand the sense and significance of "conscientization,"[29] Freire states that one must begin with what the French refer to as *prise de conscience*, the activity of apprehending reality as a human subject whereby a person objectivizes or ad-mires (looks upon) a thing in order to be able to act intentionally upon it. He refers to this circumspective awareness as a spontaneous or intuitive phase of the apprehension of reality. As such, this spontaneous phase is an objectified perception of the world which is real but limited. This initial apprehension of the world must be seen as a limit-situation, an intentionally constituted mystification of reality which, if not perceived critically, will remain a realm of untested feasibility. In classical Greek thought such knowledge remains at the level of *doxa*, opinion. In order for this initial grasp of reality to move beyond *doxa* to the level of a task, one must embark upon a dialectical and phenomenological probing of the "ambience of reality," a process which constitutes a critical development of *prise de conscience*. In order to make progress one must take an epistemological stance and strive towards a further knowledge of action and reflection, with the goal of unveiling of the *logos* of reality.[30]

Freire states that the individual seeks through the process of conscient-ization to foster an awareness which is rooted in an active commitment to a world marked by radical historicity: "It means that men take on a role as subjects making the world, remaking the world; it asks men to fashion their existence out of the material that life offers them. The more they are con-scientized, the more they exist." Personal commitment leads to a renewed involvement in their historical circumstances, "a critical insertion into his-tory in order to create, to mould it. And when an oppressed individual sees that he is oppressed, if he does not set out to do something to trans-form the concrete oppressing reality, he is not historically committed, and thus he is not really conscientized."[31]

Such awareness is thus not merely an exercise in thought, as though thinking by itself could create reality. Freire speaks of this misconception as the danger of mythologizing the process of conscientization, something which empties it of historical content and dissolves the method into a sub-jectivistic idealism:

> Conscientization appeared to [the naive]...as a sort of Third Way which would allow them to escape miraculously from the problems of class conflict, creating through mutual understanding a world of peace and har-mony between oppressor and oppressed. When both were conscientized there would be neither oppressor nor oppressed, for all would love each other as brothers, and differences would be resolved through roundtable discussions—or over a good whiskey...
> Such mythologizing of conscientization...constitutes an obstacle rather than an aid to the liberation process.

Freire contends that this disfigurement distorts conscientization into a pana-cea and places it at the service of oppressors. Such a misunderstanding of conscientization also creates in many groups a reactionary error of me-chanical objectivism, thereby denying the very important role of conscious-ness in the transformation of oppressed reality, and negating the dialectical unity between consciousness and the world. Conscientization is critical re-flection upon the very conditions of existence in specific locations in order to transform them. The aim of this process is the emergence of a deepen-ing historical awareness, an attempt to grasp the significant dimensions of a people's contextual reality and its interactive components, and then to perceive these dimensions as causitive aspects of a totality, an exhaustive and oppressive structuring of the whole of reality.[32]

The most important aspect of the pedagogical process of conscientization is the centrality of *praxis*, the dialectical interrelation of action and reflection on the part of historical subjects, or as Freire refers to it, " a unity between practice and theory in which both are constructed, shaped and reshaped in constant movement from practice to theory, then back to a new practice." Freire is thus a significant figure in an intellectual tradition common to existentialism, Marxism, and pragmatism, a tradition which maintains that the paradigm of *praxis*—which modern thought has traditionally distinguished from and subordinated to *theoria*, that is, speculative thought—should be extended, in Richard Bernstein's words, "to the entire range of man's cognitive and practical life." Freire repudiates (at least to a certain degree) the dichotomy between humans as Cartesian subjects and the world; he strives to see them in their constant and historical interaction. Only through a liberating *praxis* can persons consciously and critically emerge from their oppressed status as objects, begin to engage the world, and assume the role of historical subjects, i.e., actors who meet in cooperative and dialogical action to name the world and thus to transform it.[33]

Authentic *praxis*, then, the critically reflective involvement of a people in the world in order to transform it (which is neither an eviscerating intellectualism nor an equally dehumanizing activism), is the source of knowledge and creative power, and becomes the *raison d'etre* of the oppressed. Through *praxis* they come to see themselves as persons prevented in the past from becoming fully human, and to learn why they have heretofore accepted an oppressive situation. As Bernstein observes, the critical issue ultimately turns on the question of who the human being is. Freire argues that human identity is produced through its historical *praxis*: "To exist, humanly, is to name the world, to change it. Once named, the world in turn reappears to the namers as a problem and requires of them a new naming." A properly "utopian" theology, he argues, begins with anthropology: "Just as the Word became flesh, so the Word can be approached only through man. Theology has to take as its starting point from anthropology."[34]

Because a pedagogy of conscientization takes humanity's historicity as its starting point, it involves an explicit social and political matrix, and thus invokes the need for a concrete historical commitment to a humanizing *praxis* on the part of those professing concern for the fate of the oppressed. Freire thus dismisses as mystifying illusion the idea of social and political neutrality, seeing it as an obstacle to a truly humanizing education and an impediment to the prophetic office of the church. For Freire there is no such thing as a neutral educational process. Either education strives to integrate human beings into the logic of the present system, or it will seek to engage them as historical subjects in the practice of freedom, so that men and women can deal critically and creatively with reality and discover how to participate in the transformation of the world.[35] Accordingly, a second danger to conscientization involves its methodization, i.e., the attempt to turn it into a purely methodological tool, thereby emptying it of all political content. Only as a social *praxis* with the aim of political education can conscientization function as a pedagogy for the oppressed in their struggle for liberation.[36]

In keeping with his focus on *praxis*, Freire rejects many (though unfortunately not all) of the traditional axioms of modern Western culture which underwrite liberal capitalism and its oppressive structures. The first of these axioms is the foundationalist conception of the individual. Freire asserts that while a person's existence is singular and unique, it cannot be isolated from other persons and made into the model of absolute meaning. "On the contrary, it is in the inter-subjectivity mediated by objectivity, that my existence makes sense." In a description of human life borrowed from Martin Buber, Freire contends that the "I" of the "I exist" does not come before, or exist apart from, the "We exist" of life in community, but is only realized in the corporate existence of humanity. The essence of humanity resides in the social, historical, yet fully personal existence which people create for themselves.[37]

Freire also criticizes what John Dewey appropriately terms the spectator theory of knowledge, according to which the knowing subject passively receives the objective reality as a pre-existing given that cannot be changed but to which a person must conform herself. This conception of knowledge functions as a material force for the maintenance of oppression, in order to establish and sustain this reality as unchanging and absolute in the consciousness of the oppressed, i.e., as a given and not as the product of human activity.[38] This definition of knowledge effectively precludes any construal of the world as a problem to be engaged by a liberating *praxis*. In opposition to this conception of knowledge Freire states that

> I cannot permit myself to become a mere spectator. On the contrary, I
> must demand my place in the process of change. So the dramatic tension
> between the past and the future, death and life, being and non-being, is no

longer a kind of dead-end for me; I can see it for what is really is: a permanent challenge to which I must respond. And my response can be none
other than my historical praxis—in other words, revolutionary praxis.[39]

Freire thus locates conscience within a historical (and thus political)
context—a context which, following the lead of Kant, has regularly been
denigrated by theologians, however unwittingly. The positioning of conscience within specific localities allows Latin American theologians to make
good use of the analytical tools of critical social theory. As a result, political *praxis* becomes the focus of conscience, wedded by way of the process
of conscientization to the contingencies of everyday life. Personal formation and communal transformation, both set within the dynamics of history,
emerge as leading concerns in Latin American theology.

Freire identifies two stages in the pedagogy of the oppressed. In the
first, the oppressed are enabled to remove the mythological veneer which
overlays their inherited perception of oppressive reality, and in the process
commit themselves to its structural transformation through a liberating
praxis. This stage is accomplished through an examination of a people's
"thematic universe" (which takes place as part of adult literacy programs),
i.e., an analysis of the existing patterns of life and discourse that discloses
the specific ways the people understand themselves in their engagement
with their social and physical world. The second and admittedly more utopian stage of conscientization occurs after the reality of oppression has
been transformed by means of a cultural confrontation of the culture of
domination, a process that he associates with the church's prophetic office.
At this level the pedagogy ceases to belong solely to the oppressed, but belongs to all in the process of permanent liberation. Conscientization is ultimately "a seizing of reality; and for that very reason, for the very utopian
strain that permeates it, we call it a reshaping of reality."[40]

Freire contrasts his pedagogical approach, a dialogical and problem-
posing process where teachers and students engage in a mutual effort to
critically apprehend reality, with the traditional and domesticating model
of education, which he refers to as "banking education." In the traditional
model, students are viewed as passive, empty minds into which the teacher,
who possesses the knowledge, "deposits" the correct information. Freire
contends that banking education not only anesthetizes human creativity, it
also maintains an inhibiting submersion of consciousness through the my-
thologization of reality—the concealing of certain facts which explain the
dehumanizing ways that the majority of the people in the world are forced

to live. Problem-posing education, by contrast, strives to name the concrete ways in which the oppressed confront and are confronted by forces of
domination, i.e., a constant unveiling and demythologizing of this oppressive reality that also authorizes a humanizing response to this world.[41]

In the second stage of conscientization, both leaders and the people are
reborn in a new knowledge and a new mode of action. "The more sophisticated knowledge of the leaders is remade in the empirical knowledge of the
people," Freire writes, "while the latter is refined by the former." He
warns against the tendency for educators to project the quality of absolute
ignorance on the people, and thus to adopt a self-defeating and contradic-
tory course of using the instruments of oppression—monologue, slogans,
communiqués, and all the other techniques of banking education—in order
to liberate the oppressed. This course treats the people, not as historical
Subjects moulding their own lives, but as objects to be manipulated and
robbed of their personhood. If a truly humanizing process of conscientization is to take place, the oppressed and the educators must be equally Subjects, co-investigators, who proceed upon a foundation of mutual trust and
accountable dialogue or intercommunication: "Dialogue, as the encounter
of men to 'name' the world, is a fundamental precondition for their true
humanization." An authentic pedagogy *of* the oppressed can only be forged
with the oppressed in a quest for mutual humanization, a quest marked by a
solidarity and a communion or fellowship between the oppressed and those
who seek to empower them in their struggle to regain their humanity.[42]

The event of Easter exemplifies the transformation that occurs on the
part of the coordinators and leaders within the process of conscientization.
The process demands an existential commitment of solidarity with the oppressed—an act of true love—that is characterized by conversion and a
new birth, so that both are mutually remade in the process: "The man who
doesn't make his Easter, in the sense of dying in order to be reborn, is no
real Christian." According to Freire,

> [T]he lust to possess, a sign of the necrophilic world-view, rejects the
> deeper meaning of the resurrection. Why should I be interested in rebirth if
> I hold in my hands, as objects to be possessed, the torn body and soul of
> the oppressed? I can only experience rebirth at the side of the oppressed by
> being born again, with them, in the process of liberation. I cannot turn such
> a rebirth into a means of owning the world, since it is essentially a means of
> transforming the world.[43]

The goal of the process of conscientization is the historical and onto-logical vocation of humanity, which Freire describes as the pursuit of be-coming more fully human or simply as humanization. He maintains that the banking form of education practiced by the status quo perpetuates the structures and institutions of oppression and denies humans their legitimate vocation because it inhibits creativity and domesticates the intentionality of conscience to create and mould their world. This domesticating and inhib-iting action is carried out by means of what Freire calls prescription, the imposition of the oppressor's consciousness of the world upon the con-sciousness of the oppressed, thus conforming the behavior of the oppressed to the patterns determined by the ruling classes. It is the great humanistic task of the oppressed not only to liberate themselves but to work toward the liberation of the oppressors from their false understanding and practice of humanity as well: "Only the power that springs from weakness of the oppressed will be sufficiently strong to free both."[44]

While he often vague regarding the contents of this humanizing voca-tion, Freire does state that the pedagogy of conscientization enables humans to enter the historical process as responsible subjects, people who meet in dialogical and cooperative action to name the world and thereby to trans-form it. Through the process of conscientization the marginalized come to understand the reality of oppression, not as a closed, immutable system, but as a limit-situation that has heretofore prevented them from becoming fully human, but also as a situation which can be changed through a liberating *praxis*. The oppressed come to see themselves as transformers of reality, to have confidence in themselves as they "cut the umbilical cord of magic and myth which binds them to the world of oppression," a confidence that is a necessary, though not sufficient, condition for their liberation. Thus, whatever else the vocation of humanity may entail, Freire characterizes hu-mans as beings who are fundamentally "more and more responsive and re-sponsible" for the "transformation of self and world."[45]

While Freire is not a professional theologian, theological categories, liturgical practices, and biblical narratives have strongly influenced the de-velopment of his approach to conscientization, especially his description of the historical and ontological vocation of humanity. He makes constant ref-erence to such theological notions as communion and fellowship, the vir-tues of faith, hope and love, the images of the new humanity and the new birth which brings forth the renewed creature, the necessity of conversion and the utopian hope of salvation, the faithful witness of the revolutionary to the historical task and struggle for liberation, the peace which comes in the solidarity of the oppressed in their common struggles for full humanity, and the stories of Exodus and Easter as master paradigms for the cultural action for liberation. His writings include a forceful critique of ecclesiastical institutions which serve to legitimate the oppressive structures of the status quo, and denounce false views of God that perpetuate oppression and foster a docile and fatalistic acceptance on the part of the people to the givenness of present reality. He advocates the kind of utopian theology, christology, and ecclesiology that leads to, and facilitates, cultural action for liberation.[46]

However, if it is apparent that Christian practices and discourses inform Freire's work with the oppressed, it is also equally clear that his pedagogical method lacks a context which can give definition and direction to the vocation of humanization. His theology, to be sure, has roots in the prophetic concern of the church for the redemption of humanity, and his utopian perspective has affinities with biblical eschatology. Unfortunately, he is also either unwilling or incapable of distinguishing the often subtle but always substantial differences between a Marxian revolutionary *praxis* for the continual transformation of the world and a biblical *praxis* ordered around the liberating activity of God in Jesus Christ.[47] The powerful realities of Exodus and Easter must first shape the Christian community in its practice of everyday life before it can consider how "to make its Easter" in the transformation of culture. Lash, in a concise yet insightful manner, sets forth both the similarities and differences between these two distinctive modes of pedagogy:

> Human identity is ever under threat, and ever under construction. The whole complex, conflictual, unstable process of human history is a matter of the production and destruction of the "personal." Christianity...at once discloses that this *is* the character of the process, serves as a "school for the production of the personal"—a school whose pedagogy is structured in suffering—and promises that process's eventual achievement.[48]

Missing from Freire's pedagogical method is a definitive communal context for discerning the contours of the historical vocation of humanization and cultural transformation which he posits as the aim of conscientization. When he does attempt to speak to this matter he often advances, quite unwittingly, the very tendencies he wishes to critique. For example, Freire does not question the rationalization of culture into autonomous spheres of value, which is a necessary (though not sufficient) condition of modern society's oppressive character. He also perpetuates, albeit inadvertently, many of the more subtle aspects of the Cartesian picture of the self as a self-possessing subject, and with it the impoverished and false notion that human beings, like discarnate gods, are able to construct the world according to their own desires and designs. Finally, Freire does not adequately come to terms with the complex and critical issue of power in connection with the practice of everyday life. For conscientization to be the focus of discipleship, the notion of humanity's historical and ontological vocation requires definition and content. In other words, what is implicit and often uncritical in his particular retelling of the biblical story needs to be made both explicit and self-critical by locating it within the church's distinctive practice of everyday life. By contextualizing conscientization within the church the requisite habits and relations are nurtured for a genuinely theopolitical mode of conscientization, one that is responsive to the Spirit of the triune God who is at work in history to redeem human life *from* its bondage and *for* its historical and ontological vocation.

In the final analysis, Freire has not only imbibed the intoxicating scientific spirits of Marxism's nineteenth century origins. He has also helped to create an illusory form of integralism which corrupts the traditional distinction between nature and grace, falling prey "to the 'theocratic' temptation of collapsing all secularity into a single, undifferentiated process of salvation or damnation."[49] He constantly claims to see the world as it "really is,"[50] and he continually tries to directly correlate the concrete conditions of oppressive society with the utopian vision that invests and empowers his critical analysis. In addition, this vision often falls prey to the very mythologizing tendencies he critiques in the hegemonic forces of modern and (post)modern society, placing the liberating dynamic of his pedagogical method in serious jeopardy. While Peter Berger's indictment of Freire, that he is guilty of philosophical error and political irony, does not adequately specify the inherent problems in his work,[51] his dialectical and utopian method is threatened by premature closure and thus is in danger of collapsing into a historicist mode of scientific positivism.

The Habits and Relations of Conscience
in the Story of Theology

Obviously we cannot glean a single unified theory or theology of conscience from this survey of four influential figures in the Christian tradition. But certain "family resemblances" do emerge when their writings are
carefully compared. Above all else, for each of these theologians the term
conscience designates what I have already referred to as self-involving
knowledge, producing a radically different sense of the self from that implicated in the Cartesian picture of human subjects "as spectators of a distanced spectacle, disembrangled from the moil and ruck of the world like
discarnate gods."[52] Hence those ideas which have obtained a privileged
status in the (post)modern world—knowing, doing, understanding, and reasoning—when repositioned within an account of conscience, acquire a
practical (craft-like) and performative (enacted in the practice of everyday
life) orientation.

All four writers would likely agree with Coleridge's assertion that
"conscience is the ground and antecedent of human (self)-consciousness...
[If] I was asked, 'How do you define the human mind?' the answer must at
least contain, if not consist of, the words, 'a mind capable of conscience'."
They would also in all probability concur with the sentiment of Luther, if
not with his expression, that true theology is thoroughly practical, its foundation is Christ, and all speculative theology belongs to the devil in hell.[53]
In other words, the practice or discipline of everyday life within the Christian community ultimately constitutes the *raison d'etre* of theology, pre-
cluding the abstract conceptualizing and monumental system building which
characterizes much of "scientific" theology, and which also functions as an
unwitting conspirator in (post)modernity's rationalization of existence.

As I have already noted, crucial shortcomings or omissions in the positions of these theologians need to be addressed with respect to the theological needs of the church in a (post)modern world, although each of them
also has something very valuable to contribute to the discussion as well.
We are now ready to take up these concerns in terms set forth by the theology of Paul Lehmann.

NOTES

[1]Lehmann, *Ethics*, 327–28, 336.

[2]John Henry Newman, *Fifteen Sermons Preached Before the University of Oxford* (London: Longmans, Green, and Co., 1900), 18.

[3]Bernard M. G. Reardon, *From Coleridge to Gore: A Century of Religious Thought in Britain* (London: Longman, 1971), 138–40. E. Gordon Rupp has traced some of the parallels he claims exist between Luther and Newman on the issues of conscience and authority in religious matters. E. Gordon Rupp, "Newman through Non-conformist Eyes," *Rediscovery of Newman: An Oxford Symposium*, eds. Sidney John Coulson and Arthur MacDonald Allchin (London: Sheed & Ward, 1967), 209.

[4]Henri Bremond notes this correlation: "The 'Grammar of Assent' has for its object to show us that the conscience is the only means of arriving at a religious knowledge of religious truths. The whole of this book is nothing but a long definition of the 'illative sense', and this 'illative sense' is the name taken by the conscience when in quest of religious truth." *The Mystery of Newman*, trans. H. C. Corrance (London: Williams and Norgate, 1907), 333.

[5]Newman writes: "Nothing surely have I insisted on more earnestly in *Essay on Assent*, than on the necessity of thoroughly subjecting abstract propositions to concrete. It is the experience of daily life that the power of religion is learnt...it is not by syllogisms or other logical processes that trustworthy conclusions are drawn, but by that minute, continuous, experimental reasoning, which shows badly on paper, but which drifts silently into an overwhelming cumulus of proof, and, when our start is true, brings us on to a true result." Charles Stephen Dessain and Thomas Gornall, S.J., eds., *The Letters and Diaries of John Henry Newman*, vol. 29 (Oxford: Clarendon Press, 1976), 116.

[6]John Henry Newman, *An Essay in Aid of a Grammar of Assent*, ed. Charles Frederick Harrold (New York: Longmans, Green and Co., 1947), 177; I. T. Ker, Introduction to *An Essay in Aid of a Grammar of Assent*, by John Henry Newman (Oxford: Claredon Press, 1985), xxx.

[7]Newman, *Oxford University Sermons*, 28. Newman elsewhere states that were it not for the voice speaking clearly in his conscience and heart, he would be an atheist, pantheist or polytheist in his considerations of the world. He acknowledges that this claim does not suffice for an argument in proof of the existence of God, but that, in the concrete contours of his own personal life it is what moves and enlightens him. He can thus say that he is as certain of God's existence as he is of his own, in effect it is "that great truth, of which my own being is so full." John Henry Newman, *Apologia Pro Vita Sua*, ed. Charles Frederick Harrold (New York: Longmans, Green and Co., 1947), 218–19.

[8]Reardon, *From Coleridge to Gore*, 132–36, 143.

[9]Powell contends that Newman's use of conscience as a moral sense—in Aristotle's terminology, *phronesis*—cannot be limited to "ethics," narrowly conceived. Rather, it is a hermeneutical sense related to the concrete matters of everyday life. Newman's discussion of the illative sense as the acquisition of such moral or personal judgment, built upon the development of the powers of conscience, spells out a mode of reasoning grounded in lived experiences and not in the abstractions of formal logic. In Powell's words, "Reason that exempts experience and practice is, therefore, inappropriate, illicitly formal, and negatively notional." "Newman on Faith and Doubt," 142–43.

[10]Newman, *Grammar*, 262; J. Robinson, "Newman's Use of Butler's Arguments," *The Downside Review* 76 (Spring 1958): 162, 172; Reardon, *From Coleridge to Gore*, 109–10, 139, 142–43.

[11]Reardon, *From Coleridge to Gore*, 134–35; Samuel Taylor Coleridge, *The Complete Works of Samuel Taylor Coleridge*, ed. William G. T. Shedd, vol. 1: *Aids to Reflection* (New York: Harper & Brothers, 1884), 185–86. For a detailed examination of the role of conscience in Coleridge's religious thought, see J. Robert Barth, S.J., *Coleridge and Christian Doctrine* (Cambridge: Harvard University Press, 1969), 27–31, 98–99, 109–10, and 114.

[12]Arthur Burton Calkins, "John Henry Newman on Conscience and the Magisterium," *The Downside Review* 87 (October 1969): 361–62; Ker, Introduction to *Grammar*, xxxi–xxxii. Ker notes that Newman had made the distinction between conscience and the moral sense strictly considered, as far back as 1832, thirty-eight years before the *Grammar* was first published.

[13]Newman, *Grammar*, 82.

[14]Newman, *Grammar*, 79, 83–84.

[15]Newman, *Grammar*, 92–93, 317.

[16]Newman, *Grammar*, 79–80, 88–89, 296; cf. John Henry Newman, *A Letter Addressed to His Grace the Duke Of Norfolk* (London: B. M. Pickering, 1895), 55–66.

[17]Newman, *Oxford University Sermons*, 19, 22–23. See also Ker, Introduction to *Grammar*, xxxi.

[18]Newman, *Grammar*, 49, 80.

[19]Newman, *Grammar*, 87.

[20]Newman, *Grammar*, 297, 302.

[21]"So indeed it is; did the Pope speak against Conscience in the true sense of the word, he would commit a suicidal act. He would be cutting the ground from under his feet. His very mission is to proclaim the moral law, and to protect and strengthen that 'Light which enlighteneth every man that cometh into the world'. On the law of conscience and its sacredness are founded both his authority in theory and his power in fact." Newman, *Letter to the Duke*, 60.

[22]Newman, *Letter to the Duke*, 57.

[23]Ker, Introduction to *Grammar*, xv. Newman writes in his famous letter to the Duke of Norfolk: "But the sense of right and wrong, which is the first element of religion, is so delicate, so fitful, so easily puzzled, obscured, perverted, so subtle in its argumentative methods, so impressible by education, so biassed by pride and passion, so unsteady in its flight, that, in the struggle for existence amid various exercises and triumphs of the human intellect, this sense is at once the highest of all teachers, yet the least luminous; and the Church, the Pope, the Hierarchy are, in the Divine purpose, the supply of an urgent need." Newman, *Letter to the Duke*, 60–61.

[24]Newman, *Grammar*, 92. Bremond observes that for Newman the dictates of conscience do not bring a person into direct or immediate relation with God, but are mediated, interpreted and discursively shaped by the traditions of the Church: "[B]y an inevitable association [Newman] immediately regards each of these commands or prohibitions [of conscience] as the infallible expression of the will of God in Three Persons, of the Incarnate Word. Thus each of the affirmations of his conscience is, if I may say so, charged with dogmas." Bremond, *The Mystery of Newman*, 333–34.

[25]This history has been examined in a variety of ways. An excellent historical survey of this period has been conducted by E. Thompson, *The Making of the English Working Class* (New York: Random House, 1963). The human significance of this history is addressed by Thomas Hardy in his novel, *Jude the Obscure*, ed. Patricia Ingham (New York: Oxford University Press, 1985).

[26]Lehmann, *Ethics*, 338–39, 342–43; cf. 327, 336–37.

[27]Robert McAfee Brown thus refers to Freire as a lay liberation theologian. Robert McAfee Brown, "The Roman Curia and Liberation Theology: The Second (and Final?) Round," *The Christian Century* 103 (June 4–11 1986): 553.

[28]Richard Schaull, Foreword to *Pedagogy of the Oppressed*, by Paulo Freire (New York: Continuum, 1982), 10; Arthur F. McGovern, *Marxism: An American Christian Perspective* (Maryknoll, NY: Orbis Books, 1980), 174.

[29]The Portuguese term that Freire uses, *conscientização*, had been variously translated into English as "conscientisation" and "conscientization." I will use the latter form as a standard spelling except when otherwise rendered in direct quotations.

[30]Paulo Freire, *Pedagogy of the Oppressed*, trans. Myra Bergman Ramos (New York: Continuum, 1982), 89, 92; Paulo Freire, "Conscientisation," *Cross Currents* 24 (Spring 1974): 24–25.

[31]Freire, "Conscientisation," 25.

[32]Paulo Freire, "Education, Liberation and the Church," *Study Encounter* 9 (1973): 3; *Pedagogy*, 95, 100–101.

[33]Freire, "Education, Liberation and the Church," 3; Richard J. Bernstein, *Praxis and Action: Contemporary Philosophies of Human Activity* (Philadelphia: University of Pennsylvania Press, 1971), 316.

[34]Freire, *Pedagogy*, 76, 92, 173–75; Bernstein, *Praxis and Action*, xiii; Freire, "Carta a un Joven Teologo," as quoted in Daniel S. Schipani, *Conscientization and Creativity: Paulo Freire and Christian Education* (Lanham, MD: University Press of America, 1984), 65.

[35]See Schaull, Foreword to *Pedagogy*, 15. This either/or is similar to Dewey's distinction between education as a function of society, and society as a function of education.

[36]Freire, "Education, Liberation and the Church," 4, 15; Malcolm L. Warford, *The Necessary Illusion: Church Culture and Educational Change*, (Phildadelphia: Pilgrim Press, 1976), 71–73.

[37]Freire, "Education, Liberation and the Church," 7–8; *Pedagogy*, 70

[38]According to Lentricchia, it was the early work of Herbert Marcuse which makes the connection between the celebration of the unquestioned status of the given inherent in a spectator theory of knowledge, such as in the philosophical movement of phenomenology,and totalitarian repression. Lentricchia, *Criticism and Social Change*, 5; cf. Herbert Marcuse, *Negations: Essays in Critical Theory* (Boston: Beacon Press, 1968), 43–87.

[39]Freire, "Education, Liberation and the Church," 7.

[40]Freire, *Pedagogy*, 40, 85–118; Schipani, *Creativity*, 1; Freire, "Conscientisation," 26–27.

[41]Freire, *Pedagogy*, 58–74.

[42]Freire, *Pedagogy*, 133, 183.

43Freire, *Pedagogy*, 35; "Conscientisation," 30; "Education, Liberation and the Church," 2.

44Freire, *Pedagogy*, 28; "Conscientisation," 26. Freire notes that the oppressed are often gripped by a paralyzing fear of freedom due to the ambiguity inherent in the situation of the oppression. He attributes this fear to the phenomenon whereby the oppressed "houses" or "hosts" the oppressor by means of an existential internalization of the prescriptive "givenness" of the structures of oppressive reality. When dominated by the fear of freedom the oppressed are prevented from appealing to or hearing the appeals of others, even to the appeals of their own consciences. *Pedagogy*, 12, 28, 31–33, 40, 61, 71, 73, 169.

45Schipani, *Creativity*, 159 (n. 27); Freire, *Pedagogy*, 20–21, 31, 34, 40, 55, 167–68, 175.

46Freire, *Pedagogy*, 33, 47–48, 72, 77–80, 127, 133, 142–43, 163, 169, 176–77; "Conscientisation," 26–31; "Education, Liberation and the Church," 1–2, 4–16.

47See Milbank's concise and insightful discussion of these similarities and differences, *Theology and Social Theory*, 177–205.

48Lash, *Theology on the Way to Emmaus*, 153.

49Lash, *Theology on the Way to Emmaus*, 67. For a critique of Freire's integralism, see Milbank, *Theology and Social Theory*, especially chapter eight, "Founding the Supernatural: Political and Liberation Theology in the Context of Modern Catholic Thought," 206–52.

50Freire, "Education, Liberation and the Church," 7.

51Peter Berger, "The False Consciousness of 'Consciousness-Raising'." *Worldview* 18 (January 1975): 33–38; also reprinted in *Mission Trends No. 4: Liberation Theologies in North America and Europe*, eds. Gerald H. Anderson and Thomas F. Stransky, C.S.P. (New York: Paulist Press, 1979), 96–110. Berger's critique is substantially flawed due to his failure to perceive correctly the central concern of Freire's thought. Berger concentrates on human consciousness abstracted from the central issue of *praxis*, i.e., of becoming and staying human in a world dominated by the dehumanizing forces of industrial capitalism and state socialism that work in collusion with the feudalistic structures of power that are still predominant in many parts of the developing world. The violation of indigenous spheres of consciousness, the legitimate object of Berger's concern, has long since been accomplished in the ceaseless advance in the political, economic and cultural hegemony of the industrialized world.

52Poteat, *Polanyian Meditations*, 267.

53Coleridge, *Aids to Reflection*, 185; Martin Luther, *Table Talk*, 22.

Chapter 4

LABORATORY OF THE LIVING WORD

The Dilemma of Conscience in (Post)Modern Culture

Perhaps the best way to think about the idea of conscience in this book is to see it as a name for the *radical* (root) of human selfhood, or in Lehmann's terms, "that delicate conjunction of the inner springs of human motivation and of human judgment" where God and human beings "have directly and insistently to do with one another. [Here] the aims and the direction, the motivations and the decisions, the instruments and the structures of human interrelatedness are forged into a pattern of response—a style of life." Put metaphorically, in conscience the fabric of human selfhood is woven on the loom of everyday life from the historically and socially trammeled threads of motivation and judgment. The particular and contingent ways that conscience is thus interwoven with the practice of everyday life ultimately "defines what man 'knows-in-relation-to-what', what kind of bond man is involved in and 'betwixt what two'."[1]

However, while this radical of selfhood makes it possible for us to participate in the divine activity for "a new and human future," conscience is not, in and of itself, a clear or certain interpreter of the will and ways of God. Beset by ambiguous generalizations which frustrate its human significance and diffuse its power to shape the practice of everyday life, it has no intrinsic resources of its own in order to discern the divine ordering of creation. In addition, the difficulties posed by conscience's inherently fragile nature are compounded by the abuse it has suffered in its pilgrimage through the history of Western thought. Worse yet, there is another and equally problematic aspect of the struggle to realize a more human ordering of life in the world. Conscience, which forms the epistemological and

ethical link between the practical context of everyday life and our performance within that context, is ensnared by the corruption of judgment and
motivation within the dominant mechanisms and disciplines of modern and
(post)modern society. As documented by the three great architects of radical anthropological doubt—Marx (whose concept of *falsches Bewusstsein,*
normally translated as "false consciousness," is rendered by Lehmann as a
negative or false conscience), Nietzsche and Freud—self-deception and illusion permeates the (post)modern context.[2] The practical convergence of
power and self-deception within this context invariably produces just such a
negative conscience.

This negative conscience is, as Michel Foucault might have put it, the
instrument and effect of a distinctive type of political anatomy, "a set of
material elements and techniques that serve as weapons, relays, communication routes and supports for the power and knowledge relations that invest human bodies and subjugate them by turning them into objects of
knowledge." The habits and relations produced within these networks of
knowledge and power usually mask the corruption of (post)modern culture, but these distortions have been unveiled, at least to a large extent by a
hermeneutics of suspicion (an exercise according to which, as Marx forcefully puts it, "the criticism of religion is the premise of all criticism").
When the question of conscience is considered from this standpoint, the issue is no longer whether it should still occupy the focus of our attention in
relation to the question of the practice of everyday life. As one of the defining characteristics of the (post)modern world, conscience is negating
what it is meant to affirm—shaping and directing the practice of everyday
life—and thus theology must seriously contend with this feature of contemporary human existence.[3]

Christian thought is thus confronted with a puzzling dilemma with regard to conscience. On the one hand, we must attend to conscience as the
locus of selfhood if our true humanity is to be realized in response to the
activity of God to make and keep human life human. On the other hand,
conscience is inherently fragile and tenuous, plus it has a history and a political anatomy which are antithetical to its humanizing function. And to
complicate matters further, conscience is often the bearer and source of debilitating guilt which paralyzes rather than productively empowers the
practice of everyday life. The question of conscience thus confronts Christian thought with the dilemma and the challenge of avoiding the twin pit-
falls of irrelevance and relativism in relation to the practice of everyday

life. As a result, theological inquiry, insofar as its human significance is concerned, stands or falls with the account it gives of conscience.[4]

What conscience requires, argues Lehmann, is contextual foundations that will shape and direct its performance as the place where "God and men have directly and insistently to do with one another."[5] The need for a humanizing context, or as Foucault would put it, an alternative political anatomy, is therefore the most pressing concern for a theology framed around conscience. The extent to which a liberating context for conscience can be identified will largely determine whether humans realize, on the one hand, those possibilities within everyday life that present themselves "in the providence of God," or continue to be captivated by the habits of self-deception and illusion embedded in the techniques, relays, communication routes, and material supports of (post)modernity, on the other.

Human judgment and motivation converge with the critical rationality of theological inquiry at the crossroads of conscience and context, investing the practice of everyday life with sense and coherence, and theological reflection with its intrinsic intelligibility and significance. It belongs to the office of theology, therefore, to identify the contextual foundations of conscience that comprise the habits and relations of discipleship, "the fabric that holds the Christian life together."[6] As I shall demonstrate in this chapter, Lehmann initiates a succinct and persuasive discussion of the context which conscience requires as the radical of humankind's participation in the mystery of God's purposed will for creation.

The Church as the Context for Conscience

The phenomenological starting point for examining the performative reality of conscience, and which is also the point of departure for theological reflection, is not the (post)modern artifact of the Cartesian ego, but the fact, faith and nature of the Christian community. The community of Word and Sacrament is, says Lehmann, the "proper milieu" for theology's deliberations, for only within the church are the ways of God and the ways of human beings concretely (i.e., historically and therefore productively) interrelated. The contextual character of this community cannot be determined, however, from the application of a general theory of contextualism to the church as a generic religious body, but it must be derived from the reality and social significance of the historical people of faith.

Lehmann looks to the self-understanding of the earliest gatherings of Christians in response to "their common involvement in the claims of Jesus Christ upon their way of looking at the world and of living" to locate the initial clues to the contextual basis of both the performance of conscience and the critical inquiries of theology. In particular, he states that the early church's understanding of itself as an eschatological fellowship provides him with the first and more important of these clues. "The people of God are...the people of the 'Age to Come', the people who are under a new covenant and hold membership in the true Israel. But so marked is the proleptic sense of reality in the New Testament that the 'inheritance of Christ' is viewed not only as a transforming membership in a brotherhood which is to be but also as the fruit and function the Spirit's operation here and now."[7]

Lehmann is not guilty of the genetic fallacy by appealing to the early church as the starting point for determining the formative context of conscience. As Hauerwas says in defence of Yoder's similar concern for the sense and direction of the New Testament church, "the form of the early church is normative for Christians, not because it was the early church but because what the early Christians believed is true." Neither does beginning with the eschatological hermeneutics of the early church preclude a developmental conception of doctrine and ethical insight. As Lash says in relation to the christological and trinitarian formulas of the church, "The new things which Christians wished to say could not be easily or quickly said. Great acts take time. It took four hundred years before what was eventually deemed satisfactory expression could be found for the conviction that, without jeopardy to the singleness of simpleness of God, God's *whole* self is given in begotten Son and breathed in outpoured Spirit." The growth of a healthy tradition, as Yoder rightly states,

> is like a vine: a story of constant interruption of organic growth in favor of pruning and a new chance for the roots. This renewed appeal to origins is not primitivism, nor an effort to recapture some pristine purity. It is rather a "looping back," a glance over the shoulder to enable a midcourse correction, a rediscovery of something from the past whose pertinence was not seen before, because only a new question or challenge enables us to see it speaking to us...*Ecclesia reformata semper reformanda* is not really a statement about the church. It is a statement about the earlier tradition's permanent accessibility, as witnessed to and normed by Scripture at its nucleus, but always

including more dimensions than the Bible itself contains, functioning as an instance of appeal as we call for renewed faithfulness and denounce renewed apostasy.[8]

The church's proleptic sense of history, and of the crucial role which it plays in that history, was informed by the memories and narrative traditions of the Old Testament. The awareness of having been called out (in the Septuagint, of being an *ecclesia*, a community that was "called out"), of entering into a covenant with God and of a redemptive relationship to all peoples, marks the history of the Hebrew people from Abraham to Second Isaiah. While Lehmann concedes that the scope of the covenant story and the complex of memories and traditions of Israel far exceed the semantic limitations of the terms and images used in the New Testament to describe them, he nonetheless insists that "This story describes the self-consciousness of the church as a *koinonia*, and explains how that self-consciousness unmistakably characterized the New Testament accounts of the earliest communities of Christians." In addition, the sense of *koinonia* within the story transforms the meaning of other technical terms and metaphors, especially *ecclesia* (assembly) and *soma* (body), so that together they refer to

a new 'fellowship-reality' between Jesus Christ and the believers, between the head of the body and its members. Just as there is no Messiah without his people, so there is no real presence of Jesus in history without or apart from the true people of God which as the work of the Holy Spirit is always at the same time a spiritual and a visible reality. It is this reality...whatever the word for it may be, which denotes the concrete result of God's specifically purposed activity in the world in Jesus Christ.[9]

The Christian *koinonia* is that "visible community, called together in the world, to be the vanguard of the presence of Christ in his purposed liberation (or, salvation) of all people for full participation in human fulfillment." What God is doing in the world to make and keep human life human becomes actual within the historical reality that is the *koinonia*. While Lehmann never (to my knowledge) explicitly uses the term sacrament to refer to the church, his interpretation of the role played by the Christian community within the mystery of the divine economy closely resembles the sacramental understanding of the church in *Lumen Gentium*, Vatican II's *Dogmatic Constitution on the Church*, according to which "the Church, in Christ, is in the nature of sacrament—a sign and instrument, that is, of communion with God and of unity among men."[10]

Lehmann emphasizes four aspects of the *koinonia* as the context of conscience. The first relates to the relations and habits that constitute the *koinonia* as the *"fellowship-creating reality* of Christ's presence in the world." The church plays a pivotal role in the redemptive activity of God in history as that through which the complex wisdom of God is manifested to the world, and as such is anchored in the very structure of God's creation and indwells the fulness of God's eternal purpose. The *koinonia*, in short, is the *antedonation* of God's humanizing presence in the world, inaugurating "the concrete practice of an order whose presupposition and condition is freedom, of law whose foundation and criterion is justice, and of the displacement of the love of power by the power of love in the societies of humankind."[11]

The significance of the *koinonia* for both conscience and theological reflection is seen in Lehmann's contention that there is no real presence of Jesus Christ in the world apart from this fellowship-creating reality. He observes that "as Jesus' life and ministry move on, the records implicitly or explicitly indicate an increasing identification of himself with the Messiah, who is unintelligible apart from the covenant community, the corporate structure of God's activity in the world." For it only is in the *koinonia* and due to the *koinonia* that humans are concretely and inescapably involved in God's humanizing activity. Abstract concepts such as the will of God make sense only within the context of the divine activity in Jesus Christ, which is both disclosed and discerned in and through the *koinonia*. The redemptive activity of God "does make a discernable difference in the world," writes Lehmann, "and the ongoing life of the *koinonia* is the context within which to come in sight of this difference."[12]

The inextricable link forged between the Messiah and the *koinonia* of the messianic community is fundamental for conscience, for not only does it pinpoint the historical context within which the production of the "personal" around the radical of selfhood in conscience takes place, it also locates this process within the trinitarian life of God, in which humans are not merely products, "we are also, in different ways...*cherished*."[13] The doctrine of the incarnation, classically articulated in the Chalcedonian formula, thus refers not only to Jesus' own individual humanity, but also incorporates "inconfusedly and inseparably" the community which he gathers about him, sustained by power of the Holy Spirit through history in his name. Humanity's participation in the divine activity is thus not extrinsic to who and what we are, but due to the *koinonia* coheres within the trinitarian relations of God as divine gift. Thus, wherever the redemptive presence and power of the Messiah manifests itself in the world, regardless of whether this occurs within the explicit institutional framework of the community of faith or not, the mystery of the divine economy shapes itself according to the corporate character of God's communion with the *koinonia*. God's creative and redemptive activity constitutes itself in terms of political solidarity, and thus of historical fellowship or communion, with the community of faith, and through this community, with the rest of the world. The relationship of Christ with the *koinonia* not only enacts the historical reality of human life in the everyday world, but also exhibits the contours and tendencies of God's own being and activity as the community of believers participates in the trinitarian life of God.

The significance of starting with the church for a theological account of the context of conscience cannot be overestimated. As Lehmann puts the matter in a discussion of the significance of the *filioque* clause in the creed, "it involves the question of whether 'history' or 'nature' is the key to the understanding of God's self-revelation in Christ," not merely with regard to the shaping of human life and activity in the world, but also with respect to the trinitarian economy of God's dealings with the world. By beginning with the social and historical reality of the church instead of a phenomenological analysis of human subjectivity, Lehmann posits conscience, and thus selfhood in all its relations, as a *social and historical performance* rather as a *transcendental referent* associated with the Cartesian ego. This starting point in turn situates human judgment and motivation, which form the conjunction of conscience, within this social and historical matrix, and opens them to critical scrutiny as historical *products*. In Lash's words, "The whole complex, conflictual, unstable process of human history is a matter of the production and destruction of the 'personal'. [And] Christianity...at once discloses that this *is* the character of the process, serves as a 'school for the production of the personal'—a school whose pedagogy is structured in suffering—and promises that process's eventual achievement."[14]

Lehmann further develops his understanding of the church as the corporate structure of God's messianic presence and activity in the world in terms of an eschatologically-oriented interpretation of the classical doctrine of election. The basis of the *koinonia*, from this vantage point, is the electing will of God, "God's purposed activity." The fundamental sense of this biblical motif, however, resides in "its sensitivity to 'a new order...already begun'." The effect of this sensitivity among God's people is significant, for "the conviction of divine election gave to the destiny of man a power over failure and pride which transformed life into a calling through which contingency became the instrument of an humanizing providence." Lash also draws attention to the biblical theme of election, stating that the sense of God's concern for all creation as that of a parent to a child "found focus in a people's recognition of election sustained in spite of waywardness... Eventually, in Christianity, the final intensification of this imagery finds creation finished in a human being ('*adam*), no longer wayward, the history of whose production transcribes in space and time the act of 'generation' that is God's own self." The crucial point is that with the doctrine of election (particularly as it highlights humanity's involvement in the creative and redemptive activity of God), the relation between the mystery and activity of God, on the one hand, and the human response of conscience within the messianic community, on the other, is focused upon the particularities and contingencies of history and its *telos* in the kingdom of God.[15]

According to Lehmann, the *koinonia*, the corporate structure of God's messianic activity in the world and the formative context of conscience, is primarily shaped and sustained though the church's liturgy. He maintains that the pattern of life nurtured in the *koinonia* as the communion of saints is principally a eucharistic achievement (and hence an implied sacramental understanding of the church): "To 'go to communion' is to engage in a twofold act: an act of receiving and of sharing. The celebration of the sacrament is the celebration of the miracle of authentic *transubstantiation*, 'which means', in [Luther's] unforgettably vivid phrase, 'through love being changed into each other.'" To communicate, in Lehmann's opinion, implies far more than Habermas's understanding of a life-world, "a culturally transmitted and linguistically organized stock of interpretive patterns." Communication within the *koinonia* cannot be limited to, nor grounded in, mere "linguisticality," but rather partakes of the New Testament and Elizabethan sense of the word, according to which a person actually exists only in relationships with others, and in which each shares of oneself with the other. Significantly, Lehmann uses the term transubstantiation to describe the production of selfhood within the corporate humanity of the eucharistic community.

> [W]ith his own inauguration of a new meal, a new sign and seal of a new
> community, [Jesus] was also inaugurating a new order of community of
> life. Contrary to existing political, social, and ecclesiastical authority and
> procedure, the community of the kingdom of God, the fellowship of be-

lievers in Him would be signed and sealed by the bread and the cup which
signified his presence in the community as one who serves.[16]

This intimacy of communication within the eucharistic community is
not a strictly human possibility, but requires a redemptive occasion and
foundation, i.e., grace. Lehmann, citing Luther's mystical description of
Christ's atoning work, asserts that the believers' fellowship with one other
is grounded upon the eucharistic presence of Christ, through which he
takes on the estate of the saints and strives with them against sin, evil and
death, while believers assume Christ's estate and dwell faithfully in his
righteousness, life and blessedness.[17] The eucharistic nature of Christ's
presence also discloses the *servant* character of the habits and relations that
exist within the *koinonia*:

> The atoning sacrifice of the sacrificial lamb has been dispensed with and
> displaced by one oblation, once-offered, one for all. The "sacrifice form,"
> if we may put it this way, has been superseded by the "servant-form"...It is
> the servant-presence of our Lord who unmasks the servant-disguises that
> we wear and throws us back upon [the] betrayal [of Judas]...You see, if we
> are not reconciled to one another, we can only wear a servant-mask.[18]

A second mark of the *koinonia*, says Lehmann, concerns the way believers make sense of the fellowship-creating reality of Christ's presence in
the world: "There is a 'line of revelation', a prophetic-apostolic line, which
is illumined in and to the fellowship by the Spirit. This line of divine revelation is the clue to the *koinonia*, the *ecclesiola in ecclesia*, the little church
within the church."[19] He specifies the content of this prophetic-apostolic
line of revelation in Scripture in terms of a running conversation between
the biblical narrative and the community. The activity of the Holy Spirit is
the presupposition and foundation of this dialogue that shapes the performative response of conscience to the mystery of God. The Spirit informs the
exercise of judgment within the *koinonia*, directing the practice of everyday life in accordance with basic motifs of the biblical narrative. The messianic community, therefore, is that point where the "prophetic-apostolic
witness and the *response* of the fellowship in the Spirit coincide."[20]

The interpretation of Scripture in the fellowship-reality of Christ is
therefore not limited to, nor is it primarily, a strictly intellectual apprehension of the being and will of God, "[f]or in the *koinonia*, and owing to the
koinonia, man is concretely and inescapably involved in what God is doing
in the world." Hence the stress for Lehmann falls upon the active, obedient, and liberating response of conscience to the divine activity, a response

in which "the conceptual is always instrumental to the concrete, and the concrete is never self-authenticating but always being fashioned by the dynamics of the self-authenticating activity of God in, with, and under the forms of man's humanity to man of which man's language speaks." Again Lash summarizes well Lehmann's position on this matter, arguing that "although the texts of the New Testament may be read, and read with profit, by anyone interested in Western culture and concerned for the human predicament, the fundamental form of the *Christian* interpretation of scripture is the life, activity and organization of the believing community." [21]

The *koinonia* is, moreover, a fellowship of diverse gifts: "There is no uniformity, no monotony in the *koinonia*. These diversities of gifts are themselves part of the Creator's purpose according to which Christ functions in the world."[22] These gifts are focused by, and grounded upon, the unity of the church in Christ, who is the head of the body, the heart of the *koinonia*. The diversity of gifts is seen as an enrichment of the church within the purposed activity of God, exhibiting the heterogeneity which marks the goodness of creation, a recognition of individual differences within the covenant community. The notions of reciprocity and reciprocal responsibility articulate both the distinctiveness and integrity of every individual, on the one hand, and the irreducible interrelatedness of selfhood that characterizes the corporate fabric of human existence in the *koinonia*, on the other.

The final aspect of, and also the goal and *esprit* of life in, the *koinonia* is the nurture of human maturity and wholeness, what Paul refers to as the "new humanity in Christ," and according to which "all of us [should] come to the measure of the full stature of Christ" (Ephesians 4[13]). Maturity and wholeness refer to the complete development of the human person as an individual and of all persons in their mutual relations, owing to their obedient response to, and involvement, in God's reconciling activity. "For Christianity," writes Lehmann,

> what is fundamentally human in human nature is the gift to man of the power to be and to fulfill himself in and through a relationship of dependence and self-giving toward God and toward his fellow man. Thus, maturity is self-acceptance through self-giving...Maturity is a constituent of human nature as well as an experience of human relatedness. It presupposes the sinfulness and brokenness of man as well as man's need and capacity for forgiveness and his experience of reconciliation. Maturity is always being achieved and in some sense already achieved. It is at once a gift and a power which came, as Christianity insists, from the relation of Jesus Christ

both to the Christian and to all men. This is the meaning of the New Testament claim that Jesus Christ is both Redeemer and he "in whom all things hold together," both prototype and bestower of the new humanity.[23]

The emphasis upon human maturity or wholeness cannot be generalized, but only practically exemplified in the *koinonia*, which Lehmann refers to as a *laboratory* of maturity, "the bearer in the world of the mystery (secret) and the transforming power of the divine activity, on the one hand, and, on the other, of the secret (mystery) and the 'stuff' of human maturity." The image of laboratory for the eucharistic community is revealing, particularly in light of the fact that its etymological roots, as well as those of "liturgy," are grounded in the idea of *labor*. Thus in the *koinonia* the activities and relations that comprise the labor of everyday life are concretely set forth, as "God sets up the conditions for human maturity and makes available to all men the power of human wholeness."[24]

According to Lehmann, "The thrust of the *koinonia* into the world means that all ordinary conduct is *socialized* rather than *universalized*, because in the *koinonia*, and this means in the ethical reality of Christian faith, the maturity and the humanity of man stand or fall together." He therefore rejects as misleading the commonly held assumption that "religious individualism is the characteristic stress and principal fruit of the Reformation." He contends, following the line of reasoning laid out by the church historian John T. McNeill, that "the fulcrum for the understanding of Christianity" is not the individual subject but the community of faith as the *communio sanctorum*, the communion of saints. This fulcrum gives rise in Reformation theology to the doctrine of priesthood of the believer, according to which the individual becomes in the *koinonia*, not her own priest, but a priest for her neighbor. The priesthood of all believers is ultimately "a congregationally derived priesthood."[25]

The fellowship of Christ and believers that forms the context of everyday life is therefore a *societal* rather than a *religious* entity, the later predicated on the mechanisms and knowledges of modernity's rationalization of life and the marginalization of "religion" to the "private realm" of the Cartesian ego. In keeping with this distinction, the emphasis in the eucharistic celebration rests on the societal rather than sacerdotal understanding of God's relation to the people of the covenant, as the basic sense of *leitourgein* and *leitourgia* in the New Testament is predominantly ethical rather than cultic. "Work and worship," Lehmann says, "are correlative forms of behavioral service to God. The laborer is the philological precursor of the worshiper."[26] The Eucharist is the liturgical presentation and celebration of a social-ethical reality, and apart from this reality the liturgy defeats itself by obscuring the dramatic presentation of God's redemptive presence in the world in Jesus Christ. The divine activity gives to the eucharistic liturgy its occasion and significance, and "the ethical reality of the *koinonia* gives to the celebration of the Eucharist its integrity."[27]

Individuality within the *koinonia* is thus more accurately described in terms of integrity rather than with liberal notions of freedom or autonomy. The integrity, i.e., maturity and wholeness, of the Christian is achieved *in and through* the interrelatedness of the communion of saints. Lehmann makes effective use of the Pauline image of the organic unity of the physical body to describe the reciprocity between integrity and interrelatedness:

> The contrast [in Eph. 4[13, 15, 16]] is between the full bodily growth of an adult and the incomplete physical development of an infant or boy...*Integrity in and through interrelatedness* characterizes bodily growth toward maturity...Just so, the interrelatedness between Christ, the head, and the several members of the fellowship of diverse gifts which is Christ's body is structured in the world in a pattern of integrity in and through interrelatedness. And participation in this pattern is at once the mark and the means of that organic vitality which carries forward toward wholeness, or maturity.[28]

The identification of the *koinonia* as the context of conscience raises important questions regarding the relation between the spiritual (or socio-ethical) and the empirical (or institutional) reality of the church. Lehmann argues that the spiritual or socio-ethical character of Christ's body, which as the work of the Holy Spirit issues from God's specifically purposed activity in the world in Jesus Christ, is intrinsically and inextricably linked with the empirical church, the visible *ekklesia*. Just as there is no real presence of Christ in history apart from the fellowship of the *koinonia*, apart from the historical continuity embodied in the institutions, traditions, and practices of the visible church there is no *koinonia*. The dynamic and dialectical relationship between the *koinonia* and the empirical reality of the church, says Lehmann, is deeply rooted in the biblical narrative:

> As the religious development of Israel tended toward a differentiation between the empirical reality of the covenant people and the hidden reality of the remnant, so in the New Testament a differentiation and tension may be noted between the hidden reality of the *koinonia* and the empirical reality of the church. The phenomenology of the situation is that there is a people whose "story" is the focal point of God's concrete activity in the world. But the dynamics and direction of God's activity are always toward bring-

ing to light, from the foundation and center of the "story" of his people, an actual foretaste of God's consummating purposes for them and for the world.[29]

"There is really no more satisfactory account of the dynamic and dialectical interrelations" between the *koinonia*, "the redeemed family of the Lord Christ," and the institutional reality of the church, "the pilgrim city of King Christ," says Lehmann, than Augustine's analysis of the two facets of the reality of the church in *The City of God*. Unfortunately, this historical dialectic evolved in the medieval church into the distinction between the invisible and the visible church, and the dialectical reciprocity between the two dimensions was gradually dissolved as the invisibility of the church was consigned to a realm beyond history. As a result, says Lehmann,

It is not difficult to understand that such a view of *invisibility* should have made room for and gradually succumbed to the identification of the "true" church with the *visible* church. Indeed, whenever the dialectic between the invisibility and the visibility of the church is weakened or lost sight of, a fateful consequence sooner or later follows. The attempt is made to affirm and safeguard the integrity of the church by so greatly stressing the invisibility of the church as to aggravate and accelerate the secularization of the visible church which has already begun with the weakened force of the dialectic between the two. It is a kind of vicious circle in which the more invisible the church becomes, the less it visibly becomes the church.[30]

Yoder also describes the breakdown of the dialectical relation between the *koinonia* and the empirical church which takes place at the beginning of the medieval period, but does so in terms of the reversal of ecclesiology and eschatology: "Before Constantine, one knew as a fact of everyday experience that there was a believing Christian community but one had to 'take it on faith' that God was governing history. After Constantine, one had to believe without seeing that there was a community of believers, within the larger nominally Christian mass, but one knew for a fact that God was in control of history...[for] it had become empirically evident in the person of the Christian ruler of the world." By the time of the Reformation, therefore, the New Testament's sense of the dialectical reality of the church was in urgent need of restoration in order to re-establish the dialectic which exists in the relationship between the church's empirical and spiritual dimensions, between the church as institution and the church as event. In the words of McNeill, "[t]he task of the reformer, then, was that of bringing the invisible to visibility again."[31]

Insofar as the dialectical relationship of the *koinonia* with the institutional reality of the church is concerned, then, Lehmann maintains that

> The hidden (*koinonia*) character of the church and the empirical (*ekklesia*) character of the church are dynamically and dialectically related in and through God's action in Christ, whose headship of the church makes the church at once the context and the custodian of the secret of the maturity of humanity...The *koinonia* is neither *identical* with the *visible* church nor *separable* from the visible church. *Ecclesiola in ecclesia*, the little church within the church, the leaven in the lump, the remnant in the midst of the covenant people, the *koinonia* in the world—this is the reality which is the starting point for the living of the Christian life.[32]

A Chalcedonian type relationship thus exists between the *koinonia* and the visible church, as they are to be neither confused nor separated. Instead they converge within the historical matrix of everyday life to form the context of conscience.

Lehmann warns, however, that one possibility must never be excluded, a possibility that "emerges precisely in the context and course of God's action in Christ in the fellowship of believers in the world." God's creative and redemptive activity in Jesus Christ, while disclosed in and through the *koinonia*, cannot be confined to, or exhausted by, what has been or is being done by God with respect to the community of faith. While bound in covenant *to* what has been accomplished in the church, God is not bound *by* it, so that God is free to work in the world as it pleases the divine will. "It may therefore always be possible," says Lehmann, "that the distinguishable, though inseparable, relation between the *koinonia* and the church may be strengthened, or corrected, or even set upon an entirely fresh track, by the unexpected eruption into visibility of the invisibility of God's purposed fellowship in Christ. If and when such a marginal possibility occurs, it can only be welcomed by those who belong to the *koinonia* anywhere."[33]

Lehmann's involvement in the ecumenical movement takes shape in terms of the dialectic between the *koinonia* and the empirical church. He states most emphatically that one can only welcome the contemporary efforts to relate "creatively the richness of the diversity of the one Church of Jesus Christ...toward the visible unity of the Body of Christ in the world." According to Lehmann, "The world cannot be expected either to hear or to heed a gospel of reconciliation committed to a Church which is itself unreconciled. And the Church cannot speak with healing power to a sick and sinful world if contention rules its heart and mind." However, he is critical of an uncritical identification of the unity of the church, which is always the work of the Holy Spirit as both gift and response, with the structural reunion of the churches, which can be the work of a cultural *Zeitgeist*, in which case "it would be the achievement of a Church which had come to regard faithfulness to the temper of the times as the primary clue to a faithful witness to the Church's Lord."[34]

The ecumenical movement thus brings out into the open basic assumptions concerning the essential nature of the church. The crucial distinction is between a conception of the church as primarily a sacerdotal institution, on the one hand, and as a societal alternative which is forged time and again upon the anvil of history by the power of the Holy Spirit, on the other. In the first instance the institutional reunion of the church assumes a precedence and primary importance in ecumenical activity. In the second case, structural issues, while not unimportant (for there is no *koinonia* apart from the empirical church, a stance that requires a serious consideration of its traditions, institutions, and practices), are not finally determinative of the unity of Christ's church on earth. When approached from a sacerdotal perspective, however, the relationship of the social witness of the church in the world to the structures of the empirical church are also vital, but consideration of these questions can be carried out independently. For Lehmann, faithfulness to the church's political vocation, "[its] identity in identification with what gives human shape to human life,"[35] is essential to its unity in the world, and this, rather than a preoccupation with structural uniformity, constitutes the criterion and goal of ecumenism. Questions pertaining to the visible unity of the church and its practice of everyday life cannot be faithfully separated in the dialectic that characterizes the historical reality of the church.[36] In short, ecumenical unity depends upon "the obedient involvement of the whole Church in every place, and of the Christian wherever he is, in, with, and under the world over which Jesus Christ is Lord."[37]

Conscience, Transfiguration, and the Politics of God

Through the conjunction of judgment and motivation in conscience humans develop an intellectual and behavioral sensitivity to God's activity in the world. This sensitivity, when realized, is the instrument and effect of the *koinonia*, the fellowship-creating reality of Christ's presence in the world. In the *koinonia* the eschatological patterns and practices of humanness in everyday life, characterized by the related notions of maturity and wholeness, become a historical reality through the work of the Holy Spirit, "the infinite communicability (as community) of the love that binds Father to Son."[38] Moreover, the divine activity, disclosed to the world in and through this eucharistic fellowship, is best defined in terms of the idea of *the politics of God*.[39] Lehmann, of course, realizes that certain connotations are associated with the concept of politics in modern Western thought which differ sharply from how he uses it: "The present adoption of the word 'politics' as applied to the activity of God has to do, not with...pragmatic and passing manifestations of political behavior, but with that to which the word 'politics' fundamentally and centrally refers. In this precise and basic sense, it is possible to say that God, if he is denotable by one phrase more characteristically than by another, is a 'politician'."[40]

According to Lehmann, the messianic politics of God creates and sustains the conditions for human maturity and wholeness within the fellowship of the *koinonia*: "For by [God's messianic] action God sets up and spells out in the world a community of life, in the context of which human maturity becomes both a possibility and a fact." And conversely, "The God whom in the *koinonia* we come to know as real, as the only God there is, the only God worth talking about, is not divided but one; and the God who is one is the God of politics."[41] The idea of the politics of God is derived from the combination of an Aristotelian *definition* and a biblical *description* of the divine activity. According to its Aristotelian definition, politics as human practice and as critical reflection upon practice attends to the historical possibilities for human existence as these are realized within the association of individuals in community. These associations are not extrinsic aspects of human existence, but are "the precondition for and the expression of the fulfillment of human life." Put another way, we are not "persons" prior to being members of a community. Jesus' well-documented concern for persons must not be confused with the "rugged individual" celebrated by modernity and crafted upon the artifact of the Cartesian subject, but is connected with the "redeemed individual...whose individuality is the by-product and the fruit of the fellowship of Christ's body, that is, of the *koinonia*." In short, politics names "the compound of justice, ordination and order that shapes, sustains and gives structure to the social matrix for the human practice of privacy and for the practice of humanness in community."[42]

Politics therefore refers to "activity, and reflection upon activity, which aims at and analyzes what it takes to make and to keep human life human in the world." Thus defined, politics is "the science, art, and practice of human community: i.e., of knowing, doing, and achieving what is required for relating and interrelating individuals and groups in the art of giving shape to a society fit for being human in." Lehmann observes that the phenomenological starting point for Aristotle's political theory is the *koinonia* of the *polis*, "the same word that markedly and specifically conveys the New Testament understanding of the phenomenological consequences of God's activity in Christ in the world." Lay theologian William Stringfellow summarizes nicely Lehmann's conception of politics in relationship to God's creative and liberating activity:

> Politics...refers comprehensively to the total configuration of relationships among humans and institutions and other principalities and the rest of created life in this world. Politics describes the work of the Word of God in this world for redemption and the impact of that effort of the Word of God upon the fallen existence of this world, including the fallen life of human beings and that of the powers that be. Politics points to the militance of the Word of God incarnate, which pioneers the politics of the Kingdom which is to come.[43]

Lehmann was among the first theologians to extend Aristotle's paradigm of political *praxis* to the entire range of dogmatic and ethical concerns in order to account for "the dynamic coinherence...of actions of God and actions of men." Theology is, according to this account, inquiry which "seeks to exhibit, in, with, and under, the activity of man, the formative and particular activity of God. It is this formative power of God, as He gives shape to the life and doings of man, that provides systematic theology with its specific content. The formative power of God...gives place to man and puts man in his place within a world of God's making."[44]

Two aspects of Lehmann's "Aristotelian definition of politics" need to be emphasized, each dealing with the question of who the human being is. First, as I noted above, the occasion and significance of everyday life, practiced in response to the creative and redemptive activity of God, provides the primary focus for theological inquiry. A consequence of this new focus for theology is that "faith...becomes a stance more central and sobering than creedal assent, liturgical repetition, or private belief or personal trust.

It becomes *involvement*, with heart and mind and soul and strength, in and with a formative way of looking at life and of living it." Faith, therefore, "is the involvement of man in the freedom of God to be God for man and in man. In this freedom all things are made new." Faith is always an act of obedience, and thus a performative activity. Hence "the risk of faith is the risk of obedience to what Jesus did and is still doing today. This is to invite men and women, in the power of their humanity for which He has set them free, to engage in the struggle for the liberation of any and all who are oppressed and enslaved; and thereby sharing in the saving risk of creating a new humanity." And finally, faith has no reality apart from the *koinonia*: "Participation in this [divine] disclosure and its human prospects [is] open to 'as many as received him' in a community of discernment and commitment whose dynamics and direction pointed toward the inclusion of all mankind."[45]

Second, realizing the maturity and wholeness characteristic of the new humanity in Christ is fundamentally a political task that cannot occur apart from the relations and habits of the Christian community. The nature and integrity of the mature individual is realized only within a social matrix that is "the precondition for and the expression of the fulfillment of human life."[46] The corporate structures and dynamics of human life—economic, moral, legal, cultural, political, scientific and, not least of all, ideological— are not incidental to what is essentially human, but intrinsic to the historical (which is to say, the political) vocation of human creatureliness. As Lash puts it, "there is no field of human endeavour and human enquiry—be it domestic, artistic, literary, social, scientific, economic or political—which lies outside the scope of the Christian project."[47]

Aristotle's account of what is required for the realization of human life in the *koinonia* diverges sharply from that of the Bible at the point of the normative content or description of politics. This divergence is rooted in the distinctive character of the biblical story and its formative images. The "fundamental sense of and significance of the politics of God," writes Lehmann, "takes intrinsically narrative form," so that the metaphors investing the biblical narrative imaginatively juxtapose without either confusing or divorcing the activity of God and the response of Christian discipleship. And inasmuch as "the formative biblical images which point to and describe the divine activity in the world are *political* images, both in the phenomenological and in the fundamental sense of the word," they provide the principal clue to the historical contours and dynamics of the divine activity. God chooses a people with whom to be in fellowship, redeems them from slavery and covenants with them in an everlasting commitment of reciprocity, provides for them a promised land, gives to them a law which spells out the directions of, and dangers to, the practice of everyday life within this covenant, and once in this land the Spirit of God raises up leaders, "judges," to administer this covenant life. "[A]nd then, under circumstances that are as fluid and complex as the policy is dubious—dubious to God as well as to the 'people'—God gives them a 'king'."[48]

Kingship thus becomes the focus of the politics of the covenant people, although it is a focus mired in ambiguity, for while "'kingship' becomes the bearer of the ancestral 'blessing' and the sign of the 'people's' redemption, of their deliverance and fulfillment in accordance with the promises and terms of the 'covenant'," the destiny and vocation of this people is also tied to the varying fortunes and often petty and self-centered concerns of the Davidic dynasty. Nevertheless, the primary focus in this litany of metaphors, and therefore of the biblical story which narrates the politics of God, lies in the image of the divine kingship, the all-embracing reign of God in the world. According to Martin Buber, the realization of the divine kingship is nothing less than "the beginning and the end (*das Proton und Eschaton*) of Israel." The preoccupation with the "complete kingly rule of God" in the life and faith of Israel, distinguished in its synchronic context by its historical and political character, contributes to the paradoxical character of Israel's distinctive understanding of theocracy. The theocratic paradox, seen "already in Gideon's refusal to rule, and more explicitly in the Sinai covenant and in the historically formative event and memory of the Exodus," manifests itself in humanity's desire and constant striving to be free from the domination of others, but not for the sake of individual autonomy, but for the sake of the highest bondage, that of covenant with God. "The existential depth of this paradox," says Buber, "is evident in this, that the highest bondage knows no pressure, that its implementation is uninterruptedly entrusted to the believing behavior of him who is bound, who under theocratic authority either strives toward a perfect fellowship in freedom, a kingdom of God, or under cover of this aspiration can succumb to an inert or wild disorder." The theocratic paradox thus constitutes the historical "stuff" of Israel's faith and tradition.[49]

The realization of the theocratic paradox in Israel's history culminates in a political crisis that brings with it what Buber refers to as the first "tremors of eschatology." These tremors are perceived in the conflict that

erupts between the advocates of monarchical unification and the proponents
of the traditional political ethos of exclusive divine kingship. This conflict
leads to a deeper and more significant crisis, says Lehmann, in which the
human king of Israel emerges as the Messiah of God, *meshiach JHWH*. As
a result, the crucial image of the politics of God, and the critical juncture
in the biblical narrative, "is the image of the Messiah. The 'tremors of eschatology' never cease their rumbling beneath the surface of Israel's historical and political life. From David's line he comes, the 'Anointed of God',
on an appointed 'day of the Lord'." The day of his coming, however, is
delayed time and again, "as 'exile' and 'captivity' and 'restoration' and 're-
volt and the wars of independence' lead the 'covenant-people' through vir-
tual abandonment of their hopes for his 'kingdom' to an abortive attempt to
'take it by force'."[50]

The fellowship-creating reality of the Christian *koinonia* is predicated
upon the church's confession that the Messiah, the inaugurator and consum-
mator of the kingship of God, has come in the person of Jesus of Nazareth.
In this person the power and pattern of God's eschatological rule, "the
'God-man' structure of reality" has broken in upon the present. Consequently, the inauguration of the messianic politics of God in the life, death,
resurrection and ascension of Jesus forms the center and criterion of life in
the *koinonia*, and in Christ the *koinonia* recognizes "the revelation of God
in and through whom all other apprehensions of God's activity are to be
criticized and comprehended."[51]

As implied in the church's confession of Jesus, eschatology plays a
crucial role within the messianic politics of God, where it has essentially
"to do with the connection between the *course* and the *consummation* of
human experience *in this world*." Lehmann terms "speculative and irrele-
vant" all eschatological thinking which is divorced from the social and historical activity of the divine politics in the present: "It makes no sense to
talk about the 'last things' apart from what is going on here and now. And
what is going on here and now...is primarily a matter of behavior, of what
God is doing in the world and of what in consequence man is involved in
[through the Holy Spirit], of what man is to do and can do." As a result,
the biblical images relating to the eschaton are almost exclusively political
images: "The kingdom of the world has become the kingdom of our Lord
and of his Christ, and he shall reign for ever and ever" (Revelation 11[15]).
Human politics and the eschatological tremors related to God's messianic
presence in Jesus Christ thus engage and mutually condition each other:

"Politics provide the terms and the structures by which the fulfillment of history invades and transforms the labyrinth of human involvement in history." The messianic fellowship of the *koinonia* offers to the world a sign and a foretaste "that God has always been and is contemporaneously doing what it takes to make and to keep human life human."[52] The vanguard of a new humanity, of maturity and wholeness, exists within the *koinonia*, making it possible to discern and set forth the truly human, an achievement that is not afforded by the negative conscience of modernity.

According to Lehmann, the paradigm for the convergence of politics and eschatology is the story of the transfiguration of Jesus (Mt. 17^{1-8}; Mk. 9^{2-8}; Lk. 9^{28-36}). Transfiguration names the fundamental ethos of the divine politics, and therefore of life lived under the liberating reign of God. It articulates the mystery of the messianic politics of God, thus exhibiting the tactical configuration of everyday life. In order to clarify what is signified by the concept of transfiguration, Lehmann develops a phenomenology of power (and of the forms of knowledge that accompany power) to describe the significant shifts that characterize the political matrix of all created life. A *transformation* of power signals a relatively straightforward exchange of one form of power for another, e.g., when nations use negotiations rather than military might to resolve their disputes, or when arbitration replaces a lockout or strike in labor relations. The *transvaluation* of power and knowledge involves a more radical shift, inverting an accepted value or sentiment in response to the unrelenting claim of humanness upon it. A classic example of transvaluation occurs in the teaching of Jesus when the love of one's enemy displaces hatred. Finally, a *transfiguration* of power (and therefore of knowledge) indicates an ingression of the "things that are not" (1 Cor. 1^{28-29}) into the present configuration of the world, a radicalization so urgent and dialectical that it signals that the practice of humanness in history has reached its divine-human moment of truth. Thus transfiguration, unlike the other two, is not strictly a historical possibility, but presupposes rather an eschatological event that breaks proleptically into history, where it is manifested by the *koinonia* as "the concrete practice of an order whose presupposition and condition is freedom, of law whose foundation and criterion is justice, and of the displacement of the love of power by the power of love in the society of humankind."[53]

The story of Jesus' transfiguration, located in the synoptic gospels between Peter's confession of Jesus' messianic status at Caesarea Philippi and the initial steps upon the path that were to lead to the confrontation with the

Jewish and Roman authorities at Jerusalem, becomes for Lehmann "the crucible of messianic identity, function, and destiny" in which "Jesus' relations to God and to man, to Israel and to the church, to principalities and powers and to new and fulfilling times and seasons of creativity and consummation, converge." So crucial is this event in the course of the narrative, states Lehmann, culminating in his arrest and death, that the transfiguration of Jesus in the company of Moses and Elijah

> occurs in the Synoptic accounts as a kind of dramatic mid-point between the imminent exposure—one might almost say, explosion—of the messianic secret and the imminence of a messianic exodus. It is as though the whole history of Israel had gone into a sudden inversion. The protracted journey from Exodus to Advent had suddenly come full circle in a prodromal crisis of Advent and Exodus.[54]

Under the incessant pressure of the politics of God in the person and community of Jesus, human politics undergoes an eschatological transfiguration as the presence and power of the future ruptures the temporal chain of cause and effect in everyday life (and especially of the effects of death), thereby liberating the practice of everyday life from the paralysis of the past. Due to the divine activity, therefore, "The Christian lives neither by his 'Adamic' past nor by his 'Christian' past, but by the future, of which his present is an exhilarating foretaste." In the transfiguration of Jesus the fulfillment of the Law and the prophets (testified by the presence of Moses and Elijah) is adumbrated in the messianic reign, for in this event

> The Maker, Sustainer, Redeemer and Fulfiller of heaven and earth, and of all things visible and invisible, has come awesomely and transformingly near the turmoil and travail of the human story: its sin and suffering, its exploitation and enmity, its promise and possibility, its forgiveness and fulfillment. And in the imminence of this divine presence and participation, a human presence and pioneer are released, with the power of a liberating and fulfilling lifestyle.[55]

As the foregoing discussion demonstrates, the doctrine of the Trinity is vital to the hermeneutics of messianic politics and therefore to the context which molds the performative reality of conscience. The politics of God finds form and direction, first, in the image and person of the Messiah, whom Christians confess in the man Jesus of Nazareth. In the life of this human being the world is confronted by "the revelation of God in and through whom all other apprehensions of God's activity are to be criticized and comprehended," and so in him the sense and significance of the divine politics are descriptively determined. Jesus Christ is the political center of the *koinonia*, or to switch images, the head of the body. The *koinonia*, however, does not exhaust or supplant the reality of Christ, for he is "the hidden center" of all things; in the words of Pascal, "Jesus Christ is the end of all, and the center to which all things tend. Whoever knows him knows the reason of everything." Christ is the "model," "prototype," "human presence and pioneer," and "image" according to which the maturity and wholeness of human life is being hammered out and hammered into being by the political dynamics of the divine activity.[56]

Susan Thistlethwaite, as well as others, strenuously objects to such "Christocentrism" in the Christian tradition due to its supposedly imperialistic and non-inclusive tendencies. There is no arguing that the image of Christ as head of the church has often been employed to illicitly serve such tendencies, but to state unequivocally that this must be the case distorts and corrupts the basic sense of the biblical story. As Lash notes in this regard,

> We call this man God's utterance, the Word made flesh. Does Jesus' flesh "contain" God's word in such a manner that, to hear the message which he is, we should close other books, block out all other sounds; consider him alone, in isolation? Or is it true even of *God's* Word that, as heard by us, it takes its meaning from the company it keeps?...God's utterance in Jesus, then, the message summarized in the second article of the Apostles' Creed, cannot be heard except in the context of the company that it originally kept: the company of Israel. But, since the message that is uttered there addresses all times and places, languages and cultures, hearing that Word requires the unending labour of its fresh interpretation into other contexts, other situations. There is no time or place, no culture and no circumstance, that does not form part of the company which God's Word keeps.[57]

The Christ of the New Testament is not a solitary Messiah, for his person and redemptive work are interwoven with the people and behavior of the messianic community, in whom lies a diversity of attributes and gifts which are not contained "within" him, and through his corporate body he relates to all people. Bonhoeffer probably put it best when he speaks in this regard about the *polyphony of life*: "God wants us to love him eternally with our whole hearts—not in such a way as to injure or weaken our earthly love, but to provide a kind of *cantus firmus* to which the other melodies of life provide the counterpoint." The image of the Messiah as the head or center of the *koinonia*, therefore, does not legitimate sexism, racism, tribalism, classism, nationalism, or any other form of exclusivism and hierarchy, but (in faithful company) exhibits the sense and direction which the politics of God gives to the diversity and integrity of individuals in the *koinonia*.[58]

The hidden premise of the trinitarian shape to the politics of God, and that which precludes any legitimation of "imperialistic Christocentrism," is the presence and activity of the Holy Spirit. There is in fact a continuous movement in a theology ordered around conscience between the second and third articles of the Apostles' Creed. Lehmann thus maintains that the reality of the church's fellowship does not exhaust or preclude the free activity of the Holy Spirit: "The same Spirit which informs the *koinonia* informs also the shaping of the new humanity in the world." Nevertheless, it is the Spirit who creates and sustains the fellowship-creating reality of Christ's presence and activity in the world, and illumines the prophetic and apostolic line of revelation that shapes life within the *koinonia*. But the Spirit's activity does not stop there, for "the general power of the Spirit provides the kind of theological and ethical substance and sobriety which intrinsically links the divine economy with human maturity and puts believers and unbelievers upon a common level of integrity about what the struggle for human maturity involves, and upon a common level of imaginative discernment about what the secret of maturity is."[59]

The awakening of an elemental piety is an essential dimension of the transfiguration of politics through the activity of the Holy Spirit. Piety, according to Lehmann, refers to that human response to God, compounded of reverence and thankfulness, which vivifies the political matrix of justice, ordination, and order. This matrix in turn shapes, sustains, and directs the practice of everyday life. The habits, relations, and institutions formed by this piety nurture the reciprocity of differences between individuals in a society—differences which should enrich rather than threaten the practice of humanness—towards the ends of maturity and wholeness. Piety also requires a political context, for when abstracted from the community of faith the *praxis pietatis* is privatized, a development that trivializes and, particularly in the modern era, reifies the genuine character of Christian piety: "Thus, piety and politics belong intrinsically and inseparably together... [for] piety apart from politics loses its integrity and converts into apostasy; whereas politics without piety subverts both its divine ordination and its ordering of humanness, perverts justice, and converts into idolatry."[60]

The political context of God's messianic activity, as noted previously, is realized in the *koinonia* of the church. In this community God provides a setting in which the eschatological possibility and power of human wholeness and maturity become a historical reality through the works of the Spirit. Lehmann describes the context of the *koinonia* as a *laboratory* of maturity in the world. Within the configuration of practices and relations that is realized in this laboratory "by the operative (real) presence and power of the Messiah-Redeemer in the midst of his people...[there is] the power to be and to stay human, that is, to attain wholeness or maturity. For maturity is the full development in a human being of the power to be truly and fully himself in being related to others who also have the power to be truly and fully themselves."[61]

Lehmann draws particular attention to the occasion and significance of the eucharistic celebration in the political laboratory of the *koinonia*. The social character of the *koinonia* as the political context of conscience is constituted in the liturgical celebration:

> The synoptic connection of the Lord's Supper with the messianic banquet supports this interpretation of the political character of the Supper. The celebration on the part of Jesus with his disciples was an anticipation of the coming banquet with the Messiah when the latter had assumed his role as earth's ruler. Christian faith affirms that the Messiah has already come in the life, death, resurrection, and ascension of Jesus of Nazareth and since his exaltation has already assumed his lordship over all things in heaven and in earth. Thus the Lord's Supper becomes a celebration both of Christ's sovereign presence and activity in and over the church and the world and an anticipation of the consummation of his work in the new heaven and the new earth and the new humanity.

Thus, says Lehmann, the socio-ethical or political character of the *koinonia* provides the Eucharist with its direction and integrity as the politics of God gives to the eucharistic liturgy its occasion and significance. To paraphrase Barth's imaginative construal of the relation between gospel and law,[62] the liturgical celebration is the necessary form of the messianic community, and the messianic politics of God comprises the irreducible content of the eucharistic celebration.

The emphasis on the Eucharist and its intrinsically political character specifies the primary social occasion through which the presence and activity of God shapes the fellowship of believers—the sharing of bread around the table in the manner of the family. The societal contours of this practice is further qualified by the servant form of Christ's atoning life and death, signified by, and communicated to, the *koinonia* by the eucharistic celebration. The involvement of the messianic community in the divine politics through its participation in the Eucharist, writes Lehmann, recreates time and again "a new order of community life" which lives and acts in a manner "[c]ontrary to existing political, social and ecclesiastical authority and procedure." The distribution of material goods such as bread within the household as charity or hospitality (rather than accumulating it as surplus to use as capital, as modern society does) signifies in an exemplary way the presence of a counter-society in the world. The stress upon the *koinonia* as a socio-political fellowship, which is at the same time a eucharistic achievement and a sign of God's creative and redemptive activity in the world, provides much-needed content to the formal images of the church as mystical communion, sacrament, witness, and servant.[63]

The description of faith as a believer's ecclesiocentric participation in the trinitarian presence and activity of God in the world, the identification of maturity and wholeness as the historical vocation of *koinonia*, and the reference to the social reciprocities that shape the process of wholeness and maturity, all help to set the context of conscience. However, this account is at this point incomplete, as it requires some concrete indication of how the *koinonia*, "the corporate structure of God's activity in the world," engages the disciplinary mechanisms, institutional structures, and relations of power (and of knowledge) that saturate the (post)modern world. It is to this critical facet of conscience's ecclesiocentric context that we now turn.

NOTES

[1]Lehmann, *Ethics*, 288, 316, 350, 354; "On Doing Theology," 233 (n. 10); "Messiah and Metaphor," 25–26; *Transfiguration*, 20, 47.

[2]Paul Ricoeur, "The Critique of Religion," 205–12.

[3]Michel Foucault, *Discipline and Punish: The Birth of the Prison*, trans. Alan Sheridan (New York: Random House, Inc., 1979), 28; Karl Marx, Introduction to "Contribution to Hegel's Philosophy of Right," *The Marx-Engels Reader*, ed. Robert C. Tucker, 2d ed. (New York: W. W. Horton & Company, 1978), 53; Lehmann, "On Doing Theology," 233 (n. 10); "Messiah and Metaphor," 25–27; *Transfiguration*, 283, 348 (n. 85).

[4]Lehmann, *Transfiguration*, 20; *Ethics*, 16, 327. Lehmann's assessment of conscience reminds one of Newman's observation that conscience, as the first element of religion, "is so delicate, so fitful, so easily puzzled, obscured, perverted, so subtle in its argumentative methods, so impressible by education, so biassed by pride and passion, so unsteady in its flight, that, in the struggle for existence amid various exercises and triumphs of the human intellect, this sense is at once the highest of all teachers, yet the least luminous." Newman, *Letter to the Duke*, 60–61.

[5]Lehmann, *Ethics*, 288.

[6]Lehmann, *Ethics*, 73; cf. Paul L. Lehmann, "The Context of Theological Inquiry," *Harvard Divinity School Bulletin* (1956–57): 65–67.

[7]Lehmann, *Ethics*, 14, 45–46; Paul L. Lehmann, "Black Theology and 'Christian' Theology," *Black Theology: A Documentary History, 1966–1979*, eds. Gayraud S. Wilmore and James H. Cone (Maryknoll, NY: Orbis Press, 1979), 148. Readers familiar with McClendon's work will recognize in Lehmann's point of departure the substance of the baptist vision: a "shared awareness of the present Christian community as the primitive community and the eschatological community." McClendon, *Ethics: Systematic Theology*, 31.

[8]Stanley Hauerwas, "A Christian Critique of Christian America," *Christian Existence Today: Essays on Church, World, and Living in Between* (Durham, NC: The Labyrinth Press, 1988), 189 (n. 34); Nicholas Lash, *Believing Three Ways in One God: A Reading of the Apostles' Creed* (Notre Dame, IN: University of Notre Dame Press, 1993), 28; Yoder, *The Priestly Kingdom*, 69–70.

[9]Lehmann, *Ethics*, 47. Greg Jones has elaborated on the principal character of the relations within the Christian *koinonia* in terms of the category of friendship, grounded in the friendship of God. L. Gregory Jones, *Transformed Judgment: Toward a Trinitarian Account of the Moral Life* (Notre Dame, IN: University of Notre Dame Press, 1990).

[10]Lehmann, *Transfiguration*, 168; Austin Flannery, O.P., ed., *Vatican Council II: The Conciliar and Post Conciliar Documents*, new rev. ed. (Northport, NY: Costello Publishing Company, 1992), 68–69.

[11]Lehmann, *Ethics*, 49; *Transfiguration*, 271. The reader should take care to note that three of the four characteristics of Pietism—experiential relationship with Christ, ethical maturity and a biblical mode of discourse—are contained within these four essential marks of the *koinonia*. The fourth mark of Pietism, viz., its counter-cultural dynamic, is also covered by Lehmann, but in another context.

[12]Lehmann, *Ethics*, 58, 112; cf. 47, 68, 72, 74, 80, 284. For an informative discussion of how the resurrection of Jesus is implicated in the historical difference that the redemptive activity of God makes in the world, see Christopher Morse, *The Logic of Promise in Moltmann's Theology* (Philadelphia: Fortress Press, 1979), 97–108.

[13]Lash, *Theology on the Way to Emmaus*, 164–65.

[14]Lehmann, *Ethics*, 110; Lash, *Theology on the Way to Emmaus*, 153. This account also locates theological inquiry, which attends critically and constructively to the performative relations between God and the messianic community, as a historical activity which is finally judged by the criterion of covenant faithfulness to God in history. The historical character of theology shall be addressed directly in chapter six.

[15]Lehmann, "The Formative Power of Particularity," 317; *Ethics*, 47, 95–96, cf. 49, 52; Lehmann, "Jesus Christ and Theological Symbolization," 17; Lash, *Believing Three Ways in One God*, 43.

[16]Lehmann, *Ethics*, 65; Jürgen Habermas, *The Theory of Communicative Action*, vol. 2, trans. Thomas McCarthy (Boston: Beacon Press, 1987), 124; Paul L. Lehmann, "Betrayal of the Real Presence," *The Princeton Seminary Bulletin* 49 (January 1956): 23. Lehmann addresses here the fourth mark of Pietism—its counter-societal dynamic.

[17]Lehmann, *Ethics*, 64–65.

[18]Lehmann, "Betrayal of the Real Presence," 23–25.

[19]Lehmann, *Ethics*, 50–51.

[20]Lehmann, *Ethics*, 51. According to Lehmann, the primary task of theology is to analyze and to set forth the terms of this running conversation between the Bible and the church. See chapter seven for an examination of the relation between canon and narrative.

[21]Lehmann, *Ethics*, 80, 248; Lash, *Theology on the Way to Emmaus*, 42.

[22]Lehmann, *Ethics*, 52. Again, note how the *koinonia* is involved in the messianic presence in the world, as the diversities of gifts form an integral aspect of the messianic presence of God in the world.

[23]Lehmann, *Ethics*, 16–17.

[24]Lehmann, *Ethics*, 101, 112, 131, 345.

[25]Lehmann, *Ethics*, 56, 63, 67; John T. McNeill, *Unitive Protestantism* (Richmond, VA: John Knox Press, 1964), 21–59.

[26]Lehmann, *Ethics*, 102; cf. *Theological Dictionary of the New Testament*, s.v. "leitourgeo, leitourgia," by Hermann Strathmann and Rudolf Meyer.

[27]Lehmann, *Ethics*, 103. In his critique of the sacerdotal or cultic understanding of the liturgy Lehmann is pursuing a long-standing criticism by both Protestantism and the Eastern church against the traditional Roman Catholic perception of grace as "a sacerdotal, quasi-physical power" rather than as "the renewing and enabling power of the divine forgiveness, concretely operative in the confrontation of a single human being of all men with the fact, as foretaste and prospect, of human wholeness or maturity in Jesus Christ." Lehmann notes that recent Roman Catholic theology has rejected this interpretation of grace in the Roman church. However, Lehmann insists that the issue is the radicality with which the relationship between God and humans is joined over the matters of sin, grace and renewal. "Radicality means that the test of whether grace is really understood as a divinely initiated gift and as personal is that it comes to man not merely as a power to aid in human renewal but as a transformed relationship which *is* human renewal." *Ethics*, 322–23. It would seem that prospects for the resolution of this question lie with how the relationship between what Lehmann refers to as the hidden and empirical dimensions of the church are understood, a question to which I shall shortly turn. For a presentation of the perspective of the Eastern church on this question, see John Meyendorff, *Christ in Eastern Christian Thought*, (Crestwood, NY: St. Vladimir's Seminary Press, 1975), 79, 115, 205.

[28]Lehmann, *Ethics*, 54–55.

[29]Lehmann, *Ethics*, 70.

[30]Lehmann, *Ethics*, 71

[31]Yoder, *The Priestly Kingdom*, 136–37; McNeill, *Unitive Protestantism*, 44.

[32]Lehmann, *Ethics*, 72. While he feels that the German Pietists drew too sharp a distinction between the 'little church' and the 'larger church', the phrase *ecclesiola in ecclesia* does enunciate for Lehmann the concern for the integrity of the historical relation between visible and spiritual facets of the church "as a fellowship of which Christ is the head and in which Christ is really present and at work in the world." *Ethics*, 50–51 (n. 1).

[33]Lehmann, *Ethics*, 72–73.

[34]Paul L. Lehmann, "Ecumenism and Church Union," *Realistic Reflections on Church Union*, ed. John MacQuarrie (Published privately for the Episcopal Church, 1967), 58; Paul Lehmann, "A Protestant Critique of Anglicanism," *Anglican Theological Review* 26 (July 1944): 151–52.

[35]Lehmann, "Ecumenism and Church Reunion," 63.

[36]Lehmann points to "the dangers to the integrity of [the church's] obedience inherent in structural unions. This is as true of churches in the so-called 'catholic traditions' as of the churches of the so-called 'protestant tradition'. The 'Great Schism' and the collapse of the *corpus christianium* should be sober warnings against confusing the catholicity of the church with global models of structural unification...*imperium, magisterium,* or corporation have been exposed by the record as singular temptations corruptive of the unity upon which authentic catholicity depends." "Ecumenism and Church Reunion," 61–62. A pre-occupation with structural reunion also discloses a procedural defect in a bureaucratic manner of conduct, and an ethical defect, such that ecumenism "seems more concerned with the Church in the act of saving itself, when the Lord of the Church has made readiness to lose oneself for the sake of obedience to Him and to the gospel a primary test of discipleship." "Ecumenism and Church Reunion," 62–63. Lehmann rightly concludes that "An undivided Church, therefore, is not as such the Church of the Holy Spirit." "A Protestant Critique of Anglicanism," 152.

[37]Paul L. Lehmann, *Ideology and Incarnation: A Contemporary Ecumenical Risk* (Geneva: The John Knox Association, 1962), 9.

[38]John Milbank, "The End of Dialogue," *Christian Uniqueness Reconsidered: The Myth of a Pluralistic Theology of Religions*, ed. Gavin D'Costa (Maryknoll, NY: Orbis Books, 1990), 188–89.

[39]Yoder, in an article entitled "The Hermeneutics of Peoplehood," develops many of the same hermeneutical motifs that I discuss in this and the ensuing chapters in terms of Lehmann's construal of the politics of God. Yoder, *The Priestly Kingdom*, 15–45.

[40]Lehmann, *Ethics*, 83.

[41]Lehmann, *Ethics*, 82–83, 98; cf. 345.

[42]Lehmann, *Ethics*, 58, 85; *Transfiguration*, 233. Lash rightly states in this regard that "human persons are not what we initially, privately, and 'inwardly' are, but what we may (perhaps) together hope and struggle to become." Lash, *Easter in Ordinary*, 86.

[43]Lehmann, *Ethics*, 85; Paul Lehmann, "Piety, Power, and Politics: Church and Ministry between Ratification and Resistance," *Journal of Theology for Southern Africa* 44 (September 1983): 58; Aristotle, *Politics* 1.2; 2.1.; William Stringfellow, *The Politics of Spirituality* (Philadelphia: The Westminster Press, 1984), 25–26.

[44]Lehmann, "On Doing Theology," 123, 130–31; cf. Bernstein, *Praxis and Action*, ix–xi, 316.

[45]Lehmann, *Transfiguration*, 84, emphasis mine; Lehmann, "Jesus Christ and Theological Symbolization," 22–23; Lehmann, "Black Theology and 'Christian' Theology," 151; Paul Lehmann, "A Christian Alternative to Natural Law," *Die moderne Demokratie und ihr Recht*, eds. Karl Dietrich Bracher et al., (Tübingen: J. C. B. Mohr, 1966), 534.

[46]Lehmann, *Ethics*, 85.

[47]Lash, *Theology on the Way to Emmaus*, 8.

[48]Lehmann, *Ethics*, 90–91, 95.

[49]Lehmann, *Ethics*, 91–94; Martin Buber, *Königtum Gottes*, 3d ed. (Heidelberg: Lambert Schneider, 1956), 118, quoted in Lehmann, *Ethics*, 93. The thesis which Buber and Lehmann have formulated has received critical conformation and elaboration by Norman Gottwald in his massive work, *The Tribes of Israel*. Gottwald contends that the political life of premonarchical Israel was unique in its socio-economic structures, for it displaced the hierarchical forms of life in Canaan in favor of a social structure that "organized its production, distribution, and consumption along essentially egalitarian lines." Norman K.

Gottwald, *The Tribes of Yahweh: A Sociology of the Religion of Liberated Israel, 1250–1050 B.C.E.* (Maryknoll, NY: Orbis Books, 1981), 326. However, as Brevard Childs has observed, Gottwald is often needlessly reductionistic in his analyses: "Certainly lying at the heart of Christian theology is the confession that God has brought into being a new reality which is different in kind from all immanental forces at work in history (Isa. 65:17; Rom. 4:17). With the widest possible variety of terminology—new creation, new birth, New Jerusalem, life in the Spirit—the Bible bears testimony to a divine activity which breaks into human society in countless unexpected ways. To claim [however] that these confessions are simply symbolic expressions of common social phenomena not only renders the uniquely biblical witness mute, but destroys the need for closely hearing the text on its verbal level." Brevard S. Childs, *Old Testament Theology in a Canonical Context* (Philadelphia: Fortress Press, 1986), 25. Milbank similarly criticizes Gottwald's methodological assumptions: "One can conclude that, as a *historian*, Gottwald rightly draws our attention to those dimensions of the Old Testament text which suggest the strong connection of religion with social arrangement in ancient Israel. But as a *sociologist* (or a sociologist/Marxist) he makes the incredible discovery that for a certain brief moment, not traceable in the texts, the ancient Israelites arrived at Kantian insights: they distinguished morality from custom, ritual, and religion, and already realized that theological representations, while not 'operationable' like empirical concepts, still had a regulative function, giving a certain 'onlook towards *praxis*'." Milbank, *Theology and Social Theory*, 113.

[50]Lehmann, *Ethics*, 94. Brevard Childs has rightly argued that the proto-apocalyptic (i.e., Jeremiah, Ezekiel, Zechariah 1–8, Joel, Isaiah 24–27, 40–55) and apocalyptic (Isaiah 56–66, Zechariah 9–14, and of course, Daniel) writings of the Old Testament represent both an extension and consolidation of the prophetic tradition, but also a radicalization of "the prophetic oracles of judgment and salvation." Brevard S. Childs, *Biblical Theology of the Old and New Testaments: Theological Reflection on the Christian Bible* (Minneapolis: Fortress Press, 1992), 184 85. Hauerwas, affirming the insights of both Lehmann and Childs, contends in an article appropriately entitled "The Church as God's New Language" that "Apocalyptic does not deny the continuation of the history of creation but rather reminds us it is historical exactly because it has an end." Stanley Hauerwas, "The Church as God's New Language," *Christian Existence Today,* 51.

[51]Lehmann, *Transfiguration*, 91, 279; *Ethics*, 89; cf. 94, 105.

[52]Paul L. Lehmann, "Evanston: Problems and Prospects," *Theology Today* 11 (July 1954): 149; *Ethics*, 101; cf. 117–18, 121–22; "Evanston," 149.

[53]Paul Lehmann, "The Metaphorical Reciprocity Between Theology and Law," *The Journal of Law and Religion* 3 (1985): 187; Lehmann, *Transfiguration* 73–78, 271; cf. Paul Lehmann, "The Politics of Easter," *Dialog* 19 (Winter 1980): 38.

[54]Lehmann, Transfiguration, 81–82.

[55]Lehmann, *Ethics*, 123; *Transfiguration*, 13, 83.

[56]Lehmann, "A Christian Alternative to Natural Law," 534; Paul Lehmann, "The Trinity of God," *Union Seminary Quarterly Review* 21 (November 1965): 44; "Jesus Christ and Theological Symbolization," 13–14; "Formative Power of Particularity," 308; *Ethics*, 17, 52, 89, 97, 99, 105, 349; *Transfiguration*, 20, 80.

[57]Susan Brooks Thistlethwaite, *Metaphors for the Contemporary Church* (New York: The Pilgrim Press, 1983), 93–100; Lash, *Believing Three Ways in One God*, 68–69.

[58]Bonhoeffer, *Letters and Papers from Prison*, 30; cf. Lehmann, *Transfiguration*, 87–88.

[59]Lehmann, "On Doing Theology," 135; *Ethics*, 158–59.

[60]Lehmann, "The Politics of Easter," 37; *Transfiguration*, 233–34.

[61]Lehmann, *Ethics*, 98, 101, 131, 344–45.

[62]Lehmann, *Ethics*, 100, 103; Karl Barth, "Gospel and Law," *Community, State, and Church*, (Gloucester, MA: Peter Smith, 1968), 80.

[63]Lehmann, "Betrayal of the Real Presence," 23; Milbank, *Theology and Social Theory*, 35; Dulles, *Models of the Church*, 39–108.

Chapter 5

THE HERMENEUTICS
OF THE POLITICS OF GOD

Power and the Age of Anxiety

The realization of human maturity and wholeness via the politics of God, says Lehmann, has historically been a traumatic process compounded of deliverance and fulfillment. And within this risk-filled venture into the political dynamics of the divine activity, the question of power—the types, purposes, and relations of power vested in the structures and mechanisms of everyday existence, and therefore the relation of power to knowledge—emerges as perhaps the single most crucial issue in a viable account of conscience. Through conscience we come "to discern in, with, and under the concrete course of human events the presence and power of God at work, giving shape to human life...the steady pressure upon the shape of things to come of the sovereign, freeing, and fulfilling purpose and power of God."[1] Due to the performative conjunction of human judgment and motivation in conscience, framed historically by the messianic politics of God, the church participates in, contributes to, and calls into question, social networks of power and knowledge. But discernment in such matters cannot be acquired abstractly, but only within the actual (i.e., diachronic and synchronic) configurations of power. It is therefore necessary that we address the historical confrontation of the divine activity with the mechanisms and institutions of contemporary society—the hermeneutics of the politics of God understood as a distinctive grasp of how to deal with the world.

Lehmann never addresses the question of power abstractly, but always in terms of "the fundamental sense and significance of the politics of God" as it is articulated by the metaphoric contours of the biblical story. This story of Scripture "concerns God's ways with men and centers upon his will and purpose for men in the world and upon the conflict between his will and theirs." According to this narrative, God does not intend to be a solitary deity, "to be himself by himself." Rather there is on God's part a fundamental "will to fellowship" with "a people of God's own possession" (1 Peter 2[9]), "a longing for companionship with man," which grounds and orients God's creative activity. "The people of God whom God thus wills are the 'people of the covenant'. For their sakes, and for their destiny, God makes the world, upholds and governs it."[2]

But God's will to fellowship with humankind is disrupted by the later's inability to resist the great temptation to be like God, *eritis sicut Deus* (Gen. 3[5], Latin Vulgate), initiating the "great rebellion, the sinful act wherein the attempt is made to reconstitute the terms of the covenant, the terms on which the world has been made." This temptation is characterized by "the will to power," a form of life which displaces God's will to fellowship and, as a consequence, deprives humankind of the mystery and source of its humanity: "What was a gift has now become a quest in which man seeks what he does not know and knows what he does not seek. Refusing to trust the risk of trust, man has become the creature of the backward look [oriented to the past rather than the future] at the end of which only questions lurk and mystery is filled up with foreboding rather than fulfillment." As a result, the present age is not one of maturity but, in the words of W. H. Auden, "the age of anxiety."[3]

Juxtaposed to the "paradox of the great defection" is God's steadfast will to fellowship, but now in the form of "the paradox of the great denouement," in which fulfillment, the realization of maturity and wholeness, becomes a movement toward eschatological consummation via messianic deliverance. Confronted with humanity's distortion and disruption of the goodness of creation, purposed toward the aim of fellowship with God and with the neighbor, God has judged this "original sin," found it wanting, and initiates in history the work of redemption, i.e., the consummation of the divine will to fellowship by means of the reconciling activity of the messianic politics of God. Lehmann writes:

> Creation : sin—judgment : redemption! These are the twin anvils upon which the humanity of man is being hammered out and hammered into being...A divinely willed order of life, in which all created things are instru-

mental to the possibility and the power given to man—through fellowship with God—to be himself in being related to his fellow man, has been inverted by the will to power by which man subdues his environment, including his "brother," to the will to be himself by himself. Over against, and working against, this inverted order is a divinely renewed order of life in which the will to power has been transformed into the power to will what God wills by the power of God's Messiah.[4]

The biblical image of a dead stump in the wilderness, "from whose unproductive and utterly unpromising decay a tiny shoot may be observed," illumines the juxtaposition of these two great paradoxes. A messianic sign emerges in the fellowship-creating reality of the *koinonia* like the green shoot in the decaying stump, so that in the midst of the disrupted human community the politics of God "sets up and spells out a community of life" in which the habits and relations of the new humanity become both "a possibility and a fact," and in which "the secret and the experience of maturity are being expressed and achieved against that time when 'God will be everything to everyone'" (1 Cor. 15^{28}). God's winnowing aside of the present society shattered by the will to power is thus prefigured in the messianic community. The eucharistic liturgy is the dramatic presentation of this process, with the primary focus upon the crucifixion as the historical catharsis and eschatological catalyst of the new humanity:

> The penultimate chapter of the biblical story is the story of the eucharistic community in the world. Here is a *laboratory of maturity* in which, by the operative (real) presence and power of the Messiah-Redeemer in the midst of his people, and through them of all people, the will to power is broken and displaced by the power to will what God wills. The power to will what God wills is the power to be what man has been created and purposed to be. It is the power to be and to stay human, that is, to attain wholeness and maturity...The Christian *koinonia* is the foretaste and the sign in the world that God has always been and is contemporaneously doing what it takes to make and to keep human life human.[5]

The messianic *koinonia*, constituted in and through the eucharistic celebration, thus lies at the heart of Lehmann's analysis of the power struggle between God's will to fellowship, on one hand, and humankind's will to power, "a continual striving for increased control and more precise determination of ourselves and the world, that is *never* subordinated to any other concern," i.e., the desire and the effort "to reconstitute the terms of the covenant, the terms on which the world has been made," on the other. With the image of God's will to fellowship, Lehmann assigns fundamental significance to history, as once again an emphasis upon the election of God as the basis of the divine activity in the world is strongly implied in his narration of the biblical story. His stress upon the gracious priority of the divine will is seen in a response to James Cone's assertion that "God cannot be God" unless the creature is liberated. Lehmann counters by stating that "putting it this way involves Cone in an imprecision as regards the gospel ...The gospel is that God *refuses* to be God without being reconciled to man and in this empowerment man is to be reconciled to his fellowman."[6]

Lehmann analyzes the dynamics of power and knowledge set forth in the biblical story in terms of what he contends is the most pivotal social phenomenon of contemporary society—the modern revolution. While he does not use Barth's terminology, Lehmann regards the complex phenomenon of revolution as a "secular parable of truth."[7] Lehmann does refer to revolution as "the lifestyle of truth," i.e., "nearer to what God is doing in the world" than the authority exercised by the Establishment, for in light of the distortions of will to power on the part of the status quo "the dynamics of human reality as originally designed have been profoundly challenged by a counterthrust of power that confuses freedom with enslavement and counterfeits enslavement as freedom." Biblical politics, he writes, should see in the modern phenomenon of revolution an eschatological indication of the messianic transfiguration of politics and therefore as the bearers of a righteousness not of their own making. Nevertheless, as Bernstein notes, we need to recall "how easily a demand for absolute humanism and human emancipation can turn into its opposite—absolute totalitarianism. Radicalism, not simply as a professed intellectual ideal but as actual political practice, is double-edged. It can and has at times ended in destroying the basic ideals professed by the most thoroughgoing radicals." Consequently, while revolution may be the lifestyle of truth due to its passion for humanization, its revolutionary promise is invariably negated by its revolutionary fate, which is (in Hannah Arendt's poignant depiction) that of "devouring its own children."[8]

This tragic outcome may be attributed to the revolutionary's own dependence on the disruptions of the will to power, and as a consequence revolution is unable to give human shape to the freedom that allows us to become and stay human in the world. At one time, says Lehmann, Marxism-Leninism showed great promise as the bearer of revolutionary ferment: "Despite the stresses and strain of power, of heresy and schism within the communist movement, and despite the technological alterations in the power struggle, the Marxist-Leninist account of the impact of power upon revolutionary promise and passion is still the point from which to take our bearings in the revolutionary situation in which we live." Nevertheless, Marxism-Leninism also radicalized and intensified the ambiguity of the will to power, resulting in a debilitating crisis of authority that ultimately led to its downfall.[9]

It is the inherent ambiguity in the will to power that haunts the revolutionary's frustrated struggle to give human shape to the practice of everyday life, and also gives rise to a crisis of authority. "The ambiguity of power," says Lehmann, "is its drive to absolutize itself because it cannot validate itself." Due to its inability to redeem its knowledge of social relations and thus its exercise of power in these relations, the only recourse left to the will to power is to extend and consolidate its control over these relations. And therein lies the weakness of the will to power, for "of itself it cannot make room for the freedom that being and staying human in the world take." Thus the perennial crisis of authority that plagues the injustice and oppression of established power, resulting from the inherent ambiguity of the will to power—the always radical and usually unbearable tension between the promise of a new beginning and the inability to realize that promise—also imperils the revolutionary promise by revolutionary fate. If the purpose of the messianic context is to enable conscience to respond redemptively to the habits and relations of power and knowledge in a (post)modern world, it must deal concretely with the question of humanity's will to power, and realize through its involvement in the messianic politics a radically different configuration of power and knowledge, or more precisely, it must aspire to the *transfiguration of power* which will communicate to the church "the power to will what God wills."[10]

Lehmann observes that the etymology of the Latin term *auctoritas* can be traced to the root *augere*, and therefore the question of authority principally entails "what it takes to enlarge or increase what has been started."[11] Authority, therefore, relates to that place (whether personal or corporate) where social relations and structures of power converge with the rules of law and the offices and exercise of sovereignty. This convergence in turn establishes either a creative or destructive link between the promise for everyday existence implicit in the origins and legitimacy of authority, on the one hand, and the prospects for realizing that promise, on the other. The critical relationship between those forces which initially produce the relations of authority and the on-going dynamics of that authority poses the

question of whether the exercise of power can point beyond itself to a
source that supplies the purposes which shape its exercise. "The dynamics
of power are such," Lehmann contends, "that whenever the exercise of
power becomes detached from the authentic purposes of power, a crisis of
self-evidence arises." The modern nation-state, as the dominant site of the
convergence of law, sovereignty, and power, occupies the focus of the will
to power's struggle for legitimacy, a struggle that manifests itself in both
established structures of power and the success or failure of revolutions to
actualize their redemptive passion and aspirations. Within this moral environment, responsibility for nurturing habits and relations that adequately
sustain the practice of everyday life becomes the measure of authority.[12]

Lehmann thus suggests that the authority required to make and to keep
human life human in this world is a complex phenomenon which weaves
together more fundamental elements. The bearer of authority must bring
the power networks investing particular institutions and practices together
with the specific ends toward which power is directed (thus shaping its exercise), and from which the promise and prospect of power is derived.
The church, for its part, needs to consider how it is to account for the syn-
thetic character of authority by virtue of its participation in the mystery of
God's will to fellowship, so that "the corporate structure of God's activity
in the world" can imaginatively engage the institutions, interests, and techniques of a world firmly grounded in the will to power.

The failure to account for the political nature of authority unites Clark
Pinnock, Edward Farley, and to a somewhat lesser extent Jeffrey Stout, in
their otherwise disparate attempts to locate the either lamented or desired
"collapse of authority" with the rise of the modern world in strictly intellectual rather than in political terms. In their debate over the authority of
Scripture, which takes place around the idea of "the Scripture principle,"
Farley and Pinnock each neglect one of the two facets in the relationship
between the spiritual and the empirical reality of the church, thus perpetuating the medieval church's error of separating the invisible and the visible
within the economy of salvation. Farley, in his desire to be rid of all so-
called "external authorities," loses sight of the institutional or empirical aspect (the rules of law and the offices and exercise of sovereignty) that is required in any intelligible account of authority. Pinnock, always mindful of
the position that the Bible has occupied in the history of the church, obscures the inherently socio-ethical character of authority (the particular so-

cial relations and structures of power), which is not secured by abstract principles but by the style of life nurtured within the *koinonia*. Both theologians demonstrate in their views on authority that they are deeply rooted in the political configurations of modernity, and therefore overlook the historical location of the community whose existence is authorized by, and whose pattern of activity co-authors, the biblical story.[13]

The ambiguity that characterizes the will to power, leading to its crisis of authority, is further defined by the problems posed by the use of violence in the revolutionary struggle against the institutionalized violence of established patterns of conduct in the modern nation-state. The question of violence also draws attention to the apocalyptic tremors inherent in all human activity as the messianic activity of God adumbrates the eschatological transfiguration of politics. Violence, Lehmann argues, is the *ultima ratio* that distinguishes between a revolutionary future and a revolutionary fate, for "the crucial question posed is whether revolutionary passion and purpose are foredoomed by the violent seizure of power to their own undoing, or whether the sociological reality of violence points to an authentic revolutionary alternative to violence, adequate to the social reality of power and to the struggle for liberation from oppression and for the freedom to be human in the world." Violence thus marks the impasse created by the will to power between the practice of everyday life and the existing mechanisms and relations of power in the modern nation-state. This impasse initially tempts the revolutionary with the premature seizure of power, then moves to an obsession with the power seized, and ultimately with "the ideological self-justification to which...revolutionaries are no less vulnerable than are existing authorities." As William Stringfellow so forcefully puts it, there is "an inherent inefficacy in classical revolution because of the reliance upon the very same moral authority as the regime or system which it threatens to overthrow and succeed—death."[14]

The weakness of the will to power, states Lehmann, is "that of itself it cannot make room for the freedom that being and staying human in the world takes." Power, held captive by the will to power, cannot serve the liberating purposes for which it is created and toward which it is to be directed. Pure power, regardless of its source or structure, cannot justify itself, regardless of whether it is exercised by established authorities or by revolutionaries opposing the abuses of the Establishment. In order for power to fulfill its intended role an elemental piety is needed, "the compound of reverence and thankfulness that forms and transforms the reciprocity between creaturehood and creativity, in privacy and in society, into the possibility and the power of fulfilling human freedom and joy." Piety shapes the performative response of conscience according to the messianic politics of God, confronting the weakness of the will to power with the power to will what God wills, "the power to be what man was created and purposed to be...the power to be and to stay human, that is, to attain wholeness or maturity," the power which is made perfect in weakness (2 Cor. 12⁹). Lehmann thus claims that "The sovereignty that undergirds freedom had to make its way against a power of resistance pervasively masquerading as strength...as demonic substitution of the power that shows itself as strength for the power that is made perfect in weakness." In the community of Jesus, conscience responds to the redemptive presence of God and thus in terms of that style of life through which the exercise of power is liberated "from the ambiguity of its own dominion."[15]

According to the account of his trial before Pilate in the Fourth Gospel (John 18³³–19¹⁶), Jesus demonstrates by word and deed that the only legitimate authority that power has is the authority of truth, i.e., the fundamental, *theandric* reciprocity between the purposes intrinsic to God's creative and redemptive activity, on the one hand, and the sense and direction of human life lived in obedience to the divine activity, on the other. This reciprocity is paradigmatically grasped in God's self-disclosing activity as Father through the Son, and humankind's filial relation with the Father and with each other in the Son. The intrinsic relationship between power, authority, and truth is manifested in the character of Jesus' "kingly" reign, which in turn exhibits the paradox and tension of the divine theocracy in the story of the Old Testament that culminates in the figure of the Messiah. As Lehmann says, "the question whether kingship is instrumental to power whose authority lies elsewhere, or whether the authority of power is intrinsic to kingship was exactly the ambiguity of kingship that Old Testament experience and memory had carried as far as the purposes of God himself ...And when the monarchy was institutionally launched, the tension between the will of the people and the will of God was unmistakable."[16]

According to the sentiments of the crowd at Jesus' trial, the king is axiomatically the bearer of the authority of power, as exemplified by the behavior of Pilate in his encounter with Jesus: "Do you not know that I have the authority to release you, and authority to crucify you?" (John 19¹⁰). With the inauguration of Jesus' messianic reign, however, ultimate purposes and penultimate authority conjoin, as his ministry marks the ingression into the world of an eschatological power reality, i.e., the transfigurative reciprocity between God's activity and fellowship with humankind, and humanity's communion with God and with each other. With this radically distinct form of power the self-justification of the will to power is judged, found wanting, and condemned by the advent of the messianic reign and the authority of truth. This authority is not Jesus' own merely as the occupant of the messianic office, but it is a penultimate authority, that is, it derives from his filiation with the Father and the divine purposes investing this filial relationship.

In his analysis of the structures, habits, and relations of power as these are ordered around the phenomena of the modern revolution, Lehmann has spelled out many of the possibilities for the historical convergence of piety and power within the *koinonia*. However, we should proceed cautiously at this point, for in Lehmann's account the church tends to fade as the lens that critically focuses the redemptive activity of God in a world marked by revolutionary ferment, and into which the *koinonia* is drawn as the community of justice and reconciliation to be the messianic sign and foretaste of the eschatological kingdom. It sometimes appears as though Lehmann sees the phenomenon of revolution itself, rather than the reality of the church in situations of revolution, assuming the role of the context for God's redemptive activity. Were such a hermeneutical shift allowed to take place, it would render the community of faith epiphenomenal in that the church would be required to take its primary cues from the constellation of factors that give rise to revolutions rather than from their own eucharistic understanding of the God who is at work in all kinds of human struggles to provide signs of the wholeness and maturity which are the products of the messianic kingdom.

Politics, Confrontation, and Transfiguration

According to Lehmann, the liberation of power from the ambiguity of its own dominion is both a freedom *from* the confusion of power and truth, which is the effect of the messianic politics of confrontation, and a freedom *for* the practice of everyday life, which involves the politics of transfiguration proper. The character of the messianic confrontation of the will to power is signified by the code words *submission* and *silence*. These code words do not imply that obedience to God is to be confused with the acceptance of the status quo, but rather indicate the nature of the confrontation of the weakness of power by a power made perfect in weakness, thus identifying the boundary and the threshold where "the dynamics of revolutionary passion, promise, and struggle are liberated from self-destruction and shaped instead for a new and divinely appointed order of human affairs in which time and space are ordered so as to make room for freedom." It is finally a matter of the *transfiguration* of, not the surrender to, power.[17]

Within this divine-human ordering of reality, "experienced whenever and wherever time gives shape to space, people to processes, and providence to history,"[18] the exercise of power and the truth regarding the human shape of life are neither confused nor separated. Legitimate authority, in other words, does not exercise power which is alien to its truth. The failure of Marxism-Leninism is that it did not, and indeed could not, account for the ambiguity of power that both arises from, and culminates in, an eviscerating crisis of authority. If the revolutionary's exercise of power is not marked by the style of life which it advocates as its goal, but uses the same moral authority as does the established power—i.e., death, which is ultimately the source of the will to power—then revolutionary promise and passion will always give way to revolutionary fate. Any exercise of power foreign to the truth of God's kingdom, a power which is made perfect in weakness, suffers from the debilitating crisis of authority and is doomed to failure. There is no provisional use of the moral authority of death that does not inevitably become the normative authority.

Therefore, at the threshold of the transfiguration of human politics, the power to attain human wholeness, a power which is made perfect in weakness, consistently refuses the exercise of the will to power that is exposed as weakness due to the inability to acquire a humanizing authority. Lehmann, citing Barth's analysis of Paul's exhortation to the Christians in Rome to be subject to the governing authorities, contends that the practice of love for the neighbor in obedient response to the messianic politics of God permits the code word *submission* to serve as an indication of the freedom that must finally shape and direct everyday life:

> Love exalts the humanity of the neighbor above the cause that proclaims its
> advent, and transfigures the passion of revolution so that its promises may

in truth be born...Thus *submission* to existing authorities is not the confusion of obedience to God with the acceptance of the status quo. It is the
confrontation of the weakness of power with the power of weakness. In
this confrontation the fear of [divine] retribution has been overruled by conscience, that is, the discernment that obedience to God and the practice of
love for the neighbor are the twin safeguards against the fury by which revolution begins to devour itself.[19]

Submission in this context, according to Lehmann, is a form of negative obedience (amounting to indifference) in response to God's ordination
of the state for a humanizing purpose (Rom. 13[1]). The refusal to resist
against the state forestalls the destructiveness to any human endeavor that
results from what Friedrich Nietzsche calls *ressentiment*—the sickly response of those for whom the will to power has been frustrated by the noble or master class, resulting in the inversion of the later's healthy values
into their opposite and manifesting itself in the sentiments of hatred, re-
venge, jealousy, and envy. Submission, however, is more directly determined by the positive obedience of one's obligation to love the neighbor,
"which admits of no exceptions, including the exception of the state."[20]
From the dialectic signified by the code word submission, human maturity
and wholeness stand through the discerning conscience at the threshold of
the messianic transfiguration of politics within the institutions and disciplinary techniques of the modern and (post)modern worlds.

In like manner the code word *silence* signals the confrontation of the
truth of the messianic reign of Jesus and his followers with the falsehood of
the will to power. Lehmann says of the confrontation between Jesus and
Pilate: "Unlike Socrates, who had to be reminded by his jailor to stop talking so that the hemlock might take its unimpeded course, Jesus does not say
a word. The recognition of the Presence, whose power liberates as it binds
and binds as it liberates, cannot be assisted by speaking." The type of commitment required for the realization of human maturity and wholeness involves "an affirmation of, and involvement in, the messianic reality, dynamics and direction of the truth," an affirmation and involvement which is
radically incommensurate with the self-deceptive conduct of the will to
power. "So," concludes Lehmann,

the code word uncovered by this paradigm of a politics of confrontation is:
Silence! The silence of Jesus is the sign that the end is the beginning of a
new and humanizing order of human affairs (*novus ordo saeculorum*). The
boundary between confrontation and crucifixion, between the acceptance
and the rejection of an unconditional commitment to Jesus' messianic life-

style, comes into view whenever and wherever the passion for freedom and new beginning and a new order of human affairs has been paralyzed by a dehumanizing conflict between power and truth. When power crucifies truth, it signals to all the world that it has come to its effective end. When truth confronts the power to crucify with the power of silence, it passes beyond the rhetoric of liberation and signals to all the world the appointed rightness in a revolutionary lifestyle that only silence can express.[21]

Together with *submission*, the code word of *silence* indicates the moment of obedient waiting in the power of weakness as the politics of confrontation stands in the human story at the threshold of the politics of transfiguration, in which both submission and silence are vindicated as the lifestyle of truth in conscience by the power of the resurrection.

The unity of power and truth is a crucial aspect of the messianic politics of God as it confronts the hegemony of (post)modern society. The code word *submission* points to a counter-hegemonic style of life which does not surrender its sense and significance to the reactionary tendencies of *ressentiment*. The code word *silence* identifies the response of the messianic community to the insistence of (post)modern culture that humans account for their lives only in terms of its ideological illusions and mystifications. Unfortunately, Lehmann often leaves these dynamics at an abstract level, neglecting to give an indication of how they are realized in the contours and directions of everyday life. In particular, he fails to set forth the historical content and dynamics of power according to the messianic politics of God, which by his own account inheres in the socio-ethical fellowship of the *koinonia*, "the corporate structure of God's activity in the world."[22] What happens when the power made perfect in weakness confronts the weakness of the will to power within the structures and mechanisms of (post)modern society? How does the power of weakness confront the dehumanizing tendencies of (post)modern culture—nationalism, racism, classism, sexism, militarism, multiculturalism, and civil religion? Apart from the life of the church, theology has no critical lens with which to focus the response of conscience to these questions, thereby negating much of Lehmann's incisive analysis of the hermeneutics of the divine politics.

Jesus' confrontation of the dominant social order of his (and our) day discloses the threshold of the messianic transfiguration of politics—"the unveiling of the hidden destiny of revolution in the miraculous inversion of its dynamics from self-justifying self-destruction to the concrete practice of an order whose presupposition and condition is freedom, of law whose foundation and criterion is justice, and of the displacement of the love of power by the power of love in the societies of humankind." Transfiguration signals the radical reversal of priorities that comprises the crucial difference between the will to power and the power to will what God wills, i.e., communion with God and with the whole of the created order. The words identifying the political reversal in which accountability becomes the measure of authority, service of neighbor takes precedence over status, and persons over power,[23] are *freedom*, which is the presupposition and condition of order, and *justice*, which is the foundation and criterion of law.

In the context of the politics of God and the movement toward integrity and wholeness in and through interrelatedness, freedom is an essential characteristic of the growth toward maturity. For Lehmann, "freedom" does not refer to the spontaneous exercise of autonomous personal power on the part of the Cartesian subject (a conception that presupposes the politics of liberal capitalism). In some respects, he advocates what Luther calls the freedom of conscience, the source of which he expresses in the rather cryptic formulation, "the power of a presence that liberates as it binds and binds as it liberates."[24] Freedom, in other words, is the freedom in covenant of an obedient response to the redemptive activity of God, which takes the form of love for God and the neighbor. In this respect, "freedom is a way of being in the truth, and the truth is the reality in relation to which, as gift and response, all created things are free." A radical permissiveness is thus intrinsic to God's creative and redemptive activity which declares "to every creature according to its kind: 'You may be who or what you are! Be, then, who or what you are'!" When it is situated within the context of the politics of God, freedom is neither a license for anarchy that gives to raw power *de facto* sovereignty, nor a capriciousness which is devoid of order, purpose and direction. Rather, contends Lehmann,

> this radical permissiveness makes ultimate purposes the measure of penultimate possibilities and policies, and gratitude the secret of the human sense of things in privacy and in community. On its positive side, freedom is the experience of this givenness of things as good, i.e., as foretaste and avenue of fulfillment for every creature according to its kind…amidst the whole panorama of the divine economy…On its negative side, freedom is the experience of the givenness of things as a liberating limit, within which every creature according to its kind finds the fulfilling direction and order of its own time, in the world of time and space and things and people. Thus there is a paradox of being free and being bound, of liberation and limitation, that ordains freedom as the presupposition and condition of order and order as the practice of freedom.[25]

Freedom, the opportunity for every creature to discover who and what it is
in the fellowship of creation, has become a historical possibility within the
divine economy of redemption proleptically embodied in the *koinonia*.

The meaning of the ideas of righteousness and justice also undergoes a
messianic transfiguration in the context of the laboratory of the *koinonia*.
They refer not to an abstract ethical norm or principle such as the contemporary standard of fairness, or its classical predecessor, the *suum cuique*,[26]
but to the redemptive fellowship of God's activity in the world in and
through the messianic community. In Scripture, the ideas of righteousness
and justice refer to God's way of being true to the purposes for which humans were created and covenanted, and towards which God's eschatological
presence and power is drawing creation. The transfiguration of justice
shapes and directs power and knowledge according to God's will to fellowship, and thus serves the end of reconciliation. As a consequence, reconciliation becomes both the presupposition and the goal of justice, or the words
of Lehmann, "Reconciliation without justice is empty; justice without reconciliation is blind."[27]   Righteousness becomes a human quality neither
through *impartation* or *imputation*, but through *participation* in the eschatological righteousness of God.

Within the context of the politics of God, then, *justice* refers to the reciprocal relations of accountability that shape and direct the diversity of
creation and covenant, a reciprocity that cannot be achieved either through
hierarchical or egalitarian social orders. Lehmann contends that "it has
become ominously evident that neither hierarchical nor egalitarian social,
economic, cultural, and political structures are capable of furthering the
freedom which being human in this world takes. Neither is able to bring
personal and social reciprocity and mobility under the discipline of a foundational justice." The many attempts in liberal capitalist societies to elimi-
nate hierarchy and its self-justifying, self-serving exercise and corruption
of knowledge and power through an egalitarian conversion have been concretely exposed as a self-deceptive mask for the subordination or reifica-
tion of all individuals to material things and interests: "The world which
the egalitarian individual set out to conquer and to make new now binds
him fast in a prison of his own making."[28]

Lehmann argues that all references to *equality* in contemporary social
analysis should be stripped of its mythic underpinnings in the Cartesian
subject, and reconceived as *heterogeneity*, which refers to what he calls the

nominal parameter of social differentiation, i.e., a grouping of individuals with no inherent rank or order, such as gender, race, religious affiliation, and occupation. In similar fashion, *hierarchy* needs to be redefined in terms of *inequality*, i.e., the graduated parameter which differentiates between persons in terms of concrete ranks of status and order: wealth, income, power, and education.[29] According to Lehmann, these two parameters form the basic structural patterns of social differentiation, and therefore the issue at hand concerns the nature of the humanizing relation between heterogeneity and inequality. In what ways, he asks, can the diversity that enriches rather than threatens the practice of everyday life be shaped and directed by habits and relations which avoid the twin perils of modern and (post)modern thought—the reifying tendencies of liberal egalitarianism, on the one hand, and the propensity for heterogeneity to transform themselves into class boundaries (as in the case sexism and racism), on the other—so that in the end accountability can be the measure of authority, freedom can be the criterion of order, service of neighbor can have precedence over status, and the person rather than power (usually in the form of surplus value) can serve as the focus of our labor?

Lehmann states that the threshold of humanness between heterogeneity and inequality, i.e., that "primordial rightness or fitness of things that is expressed the creation of the world and the destiny of a human people through whose story all people are sustained and fulfilled in the trust and openness, the caring and the responsiveness [which is] the human side of the righteousness of God," is disclosed as the "practice of reciprocal responsibility." In the messianic community rank and status are sundered from "a heteronomous and self-justifying privilege and claimed for the reduction of inequality through enlarging heterogeneity." Authority, when considered from this standpoint, embodies the compound of power and purpose that contributes to the increase and enhancement of differences among members of the community under the discipline of a foundational justice. Within the context of the *koinonia*, justice thus pertains to "the reciprocity of differences in creaturehood and creativity, experienced as enrichment rather than as a threat."[30]

Within the radical reconfiguration of priorities by the politics of God, the concepts of order and law serve functional rather than normative roles. Order, as embodied in social relations, institutions, and structures, is instrumental to the freedom which becoming and staying human requires, "the enabling possibility, pattern, and power through which the lifetime of

creatures in one time and place and culture and society may be so lived, not
only so as not to destroy the possibility of other times and places and cultures and societies, but so as to make one's own and given time and space
and culture and society make room for freedom." However, if order is
given priority over freedom, rather than subsisting in the practice of freedom, then "that society has embarked upon a politics, ethics, and lifestyle
of self-justification." In the same manner, law, as an important mode of
human rationality, fulfills a functional role towards the ends of justice,
which is the foundation and criterion of law. The moral force of law in
the Bible is vested in God's dealings with the community of faith, setting
forth the social context in which law operates: "The quintessence of the
Decalogue is the indicative reality whose direction and boundaries are defined in covenantal, that is, personal terms through commandment form.
The reality is God's presence in the midst of his people as help and salvation." Law, when considered strictly as a mode of human reasoning, is incapable of bearing by itself the reconciling weight required as the norm
and ground of justice. It can only reflect the particular commitments (in
Newman's terms, the real assent) which are always and necessarily presupposed in the contingencies of everyday life, and which concretely shape and
direct (and too often, distort) the reciprocity between human life and accountable life.[31]

The effect of the transfiguration of politics on the practice of everyday
life is brought to a climax in a shift in the relationship between power and
violence. Lehmann primarily assesses this shift, not in moral, legal, or sociological terms, but as an apocalyptic phenomenon. At the apocalyptic
threshold the reality and significance of violence undergo a double transfiguration. At the level of revolutionary politics, violence is discerned as a
sign that the present course of humanity's political activity has come upon
its apocalyptic moment of truth and point of no return. At the level of biblical politics, violence is exposed as the *ultima ratio* of a fallen world, rest-
ing upon the primal crime of the will to power, "a world already lost, in
the act of being displaced by a new and human world already on the way.
In short, the apocalyptic significance of violence is the talisman of its transfiguration." At the threshold of violence in both its systemic and counter-
systemic forms, the conscience which is the instrument and effect of the divine activity "discerns an accelerating tempo, which carries the sociological
reality and inevitability of violence in a world of power beyond all estab-

lished patterns and structures toward the concreteness of a new thing that God is about to do in the midst of his people, and for the sake of the world which has reconciled to him in Jesus Christ." The redemptive politics of God shatters both the vicious circularity of violence and its self-deceptive justification, inaugurating an alternative style of life that is realized through the power of God's Messiah, who transfigures the will to power into the power to will what God wills, "the power to be and to stay human …to attain wholeness or maturity."[32]

At that point where revolutionary and messianic politics converge, "violence is always a risk but can never become a policy or program."[33] The question of whether Christians should participate in the violence of this world of politics—be it systemic violence, "violence that converted risk into calculated policy," or countersystemic violence, "violence as a calculated risk always threatened by conversion into policy"—now becomes the question of the church's redemptive presence as "the vanguard of the presence of Christ in his purposed liberation (or, salvation) of all people for full participation in human fulfillment" in situations that are determined by the moral force of death and violence. In this context, says Lehmann, the question of Christian involvement or non-involvement in acts of violence is not the primary concern of the church (hence its potential as risk), and yet such involvement is regarded as antithetical to what is its principal concern —a messianic style of life which embodies the habits and relations of the new humanity before a world that is literally sick unto death (and therefore violence can never become policy).[34]

In his discussion of the messianic politics of transfiguration, Lehmann dislodges the concepts of freedom, justice, order, and law from their entanglements in the corruptions of Enlightenment and reasserts their sense and direction with reference to the mystery of God's gracious activity on our behalf. Unfortunately, his analysis is impaired by the shift in focus from the church to the modern phenomenon of revolution. Had he discussed, for example, how piety, power, and politics converge within the habits and relations of the *koinonia* as the historical fellowship of reconciliation and justice within revolutionary situations, his claim that "righteousness is the test case of covenantal obedience and the key to justice purposed for reconciliation"[35] would have acquired much needed historical content and direction. Lehmann discusses the social relations shaped by the practice of a foundational justice according to the messianic politics of God largely on a con-

ceptual level, apart from the practices and relations of power and knowledge of the church within the contingencies and particularities of history.

Ironically, Lehmann makes allowances in his doctrine of the *koinonia*
for just such an account of the transfiguration of politics. In *Ethics in a
Christian Context* he maintains that in the *koinonia*, where we are "through
love changed into each other," the historical significance of the fellowship-
creating reality of Christ's presence in the world is achieved through "the
rejection of preferential differentiation and its displacement by organic in-
terrelational differentiation. We are what we are in and through God's action in Christ, bringing our authentic humanity to pass through authentic
belonging." The laboratory of human maturity which is the *koinonia* provides the kinds of paradigmatic social practices for nurturing these types of
habits and relations within and over against the disciplinary mechanisms of
a late capitalist social order. The sacraments, as Yoder has demonstrated,
are themselves exemplary social processes that reconfigure the sense and
direction of human existence. The necessity of pastoral roles, recognized
in Scripture among the gifts given by the Spirit to the people of the age to
come, is severed from their perennial connection with wealth and privilege. As Milbank says, "The real point of necessity for hierarchy...is the
transitive relationship of education, where an unavoidable non-reciprocity
nonetheless works towards its own cancellation."[36]

The linking of education with the function of the laboratory of faith is
not accidental, for as Hauerwas notes, the essential purpose of any community, and especially the Christian community, is educational in the sense of
nurturing a particular style of life. Lash likewise contends that "Christianity is perhaps best seen as an *educative* project," created by God to be "a
kind of school the purpose of whose pedagogy is to foster the conditions in
which dependence might be relearned as friendship; conditions in which the
comprehensive taming of chaos by loving order, of conflict by tranquility,
of discord by harmony, might be instantiated and proclaimed." To this
end, Milbank suggests, "the project of the Church is the establishment of a
new, universal society, a new *civitas*, in which these intimate relationships
are paradigmatic: a community in which we relate primarily to the neighbour, and every neighbour is mother, brother, sister, spouse." And, as
Elisabeth Schüssler Fiorenza argues, "the 'new family' of Jesus...recog-
nizes sisters, brothers, and mothers, but no fathers in the community of
disciples, since [God] alone is their father." The Eucharist, in the context

of this educative project, is no longer a sacerdotal rite but an act of economic ethics. Yoder notes that "bread *is* daily sustenance. Bread eaten together *is* economic sharing. Not merely symbolically, but in actual fact, it extends to a wider circle the economic solidarity that normally obtained in the family. When, in most of his post-Resurrection appearances, Jesus takes the role of the family head distributing bread (and fish) around his table, he projects into the post-Passion world the common purse of the wandering disciple band whose members had left their prior economic bases to join his movement."[37]

A lack of concreteness also impoverishes Lehmann's discussion of freedom. Historical specificity could have been secured had he discussed how, as we are bound together in the covenant community with the living God, we are freed for the practice of humanness, i.e., the fullest possible development and expression of our individual gifts in and through the fellowship-creating reality of the *koinonia*. How is it in circumstances such as those encountered in a (post)modern world that God's presence and power in Christ binds us through covenant for liberation and liberates us for life in the covenant? Authentic freedom is discovered *in*, as well as being the product *of*, the messianic presence and power of God who binds human beings together within a *eucharistic political anatomy*, an anatomy that relativizes all other commitments and all other involvements, and liberates us *from* reified social structures and relations and *for* humanness. In this anatomical context, says Hauerwas, "freedom literally comes by having our self-absorption challenged by the needs of another."[38] Furthermore, had Lehmann not shifted the focus of his account of the context of conscience away from the church and toward the secular parable of revolution, his assessment of the question of violence would transpose what can be a rather confusing statement into an affirmation of the church's redemptive presence as "the vanguard of the presence of Christ in his purposed liberation (or, salvation) of all people for full participation in human fulfillment"[39] in situations of systemic and/or counter-systemic violence.

Power in the Age of Maturity

In *The Transfiguration of Politics*, Lehmann makes an important observation that pertains directly to the question of the context that shapes and directs conscience as the radical of human selfhood. He asserts that "The responsibility for the *determination* of priorities is a *theological* one. The responsibility for the *identification* of the priorities is a *historical* one." As we have seen, the question of power is a principal concern in any account of the context of conscience, and therefore plays a leading role in forming the general contours of a theology that is attentive to the practice of everyday life. The next step in this account must be to demonstrate with respect to the question of power how the theological determination and the historical identification of priorities can neither be divorced from, nor confused with, each other in a theology which attends to the particularity and contingency of human existence. The relation between these two dimensions is dialectical, as "they mutually inform, enable, correct and enlighten each other."[40] Moreover, this demonstration can be accomplished within the theological framework which Lehmann constructs.

According to Lehmann, two conditions are fundamental to this framework. The first pertains to the human reality and meaning of God's self-disclosing activity in the world as narrated in Scripture and set forth in the doctrines of incarnation, atonement, redemption, and reconciliation. "The second condition," he continues, "is the insistence upon the *concreteness* of theological conception and analysis." The deep and abiding concern for concreteness permeates Lehmann's theology, constituting in his opinion the formative power of Christian thought. He deals several times with the issue of concreteness in terms of the controversy between Bonhoeffer and Barth over Barth's alleged "revelational positivism," and contends that they share much more in common with each other on this matter than either of them realized.[41] Yet it is with the concern for concreteness that the Neo-Reformation perspective of Barth, Bonhoeffer, and Lehmann, in a most untimely and ironic fashion, falls short of its own expectations.

As I have already stated, a problematic shift in focus in Lehmann's theology from the *koinonia* to the modern revolution deprives his account of the context of conscience of its concreteness and, subsequently, of its formative power. The convergence of piety, power, and politics at the heart of his account lacks a historical occasion, precisely because the theological and historical tasks remain strangely disjointed. This is particularly the case in *The Transfiguration of Politics*, for while he does offer in this work an insightful typology of contemporary revolutions, thus attending to the historical office of a theology of conscience, he neglects the crucial role of the *koinonia* as the principal *locus* and the sole *focus* of the eschatological transfiguration of politics and the practice of a politics of transfiguration, thereby slighting, most ironically, the theological task. The role of the messianic community in the formative concreteness that authorizes theological inquiry, emphasized by Lehmann in his other writings, remains curiously beneath the surface of this text for the most part, emerging only occasionally, and by all appearances as an afterthought rather than as "the foretaste and the sign in the world that God has always been and is contemporaneously doing what it takes to make and to keep human life human."[42]

More specifically, Lehmann fails to indicate how the formative structures, traditions and liturgical practices of the church lend historical shape and direction to the reciprocities of human maturity and wholeness that characterize the diversity of creaturehood and creativity, and for which justice and freedom are the measure of law and order. Where else but in the *koinonia* can a theology of the politics of God concretely specify the nature of a humanizing authority in social situations of self-justifying tyranny and inhuman oppression? Is there any other actual focus apart from the community of Word and Sacrament for inquiring into the historical character of the reconciliation which is the effect of God's activity in Jesus Christ? Where else but in the eucharistic community do the social, historical, and the eschatological dimensions of "the transfigured people of God," who are "the vanguard of a new and fulfilling human order in the world," come focally into view as "a sign of the new humanity which is coming to be in the world in which Jesus Christ lived and died, over which he rules as Lord against the day of his coming"?[43]

Nevertheless, Lehmann refers on occasion to something which could help to overcome the bifurcation that robs his work of the requisite concreteness, a hermeneutical standpoint which fits readily within the theological framework of the eucharistic community and the messianic politics of God. He states that God has chosen what the world regards as folly, "mere nothings," and "the ingression of 'things that are not' into the 'things that are'," in order to bring about the justice which marks the transfiguration of politics. In particular, he refers to the poor as "the test case of the practice of justice in human society" and as "the bearers of the battle between freedom and order, justice and law, humanization and dehumanization, true and false piety, in the world."[44] Were Lehmann to complete the contextualization of the *koinonia* as the ethos of Christian conscience in terms of the social location of the poor and dispossessed, the concreteness for which he constantly strives would have a historical occasion to go along with its theological authorization in the electing will of God.

Lehmann generally explores the theological implications of the preferential option for the poor and dispossessed in terms of Bonhoeffer's famous exhortation "to see the great events of world history from below, from the perspective of the outcast, the suspects, the maltreated, the powerless, the oppressed, the reviled—in short, from the perspective of those who suffer," and has revised his description of the politics of God accordingly. Yet in spite of his readiness to affirm that "theology today must begin with the wretched of the earth," and for the North American context in particular, "must, from the beginning and throughout, take account, in its talk about Jesus Christ, or about God, or about sin and salvation, of the concrete realities of black experience," he seems reticent to commit himself and the reality of the *koinonia* to this standpoint, stating that the theologian must always keep in mind the distance and tentativeness "with which the self-disclosure of God—in election and incarnation, in crucifixion and resurrection, in a new humanity and a new creation on their way to fulfillment—lends itself to theological description and conceptualization." While this note of caution and humility must never be forgotten, Lehmann overlooks another observation he once made that pertains to the preferential option for the poor, an observation which serves well the catalytic function he believes that theology should play as the "guardian of the human" in the life of the *koinonia*. At one point he says that "The life-style of a Christian is marked by righteousness compounded with freedom, both anchored in a divine election. Far from closing up and closing off the life of the believer, election radically opens it up. This happens because contingent happenings and policies, motivations and goals are liberated from the necessity of demonstrating their own ultimacy." It is this freedom to live justly, which is rooted in the divine election, that enables the church to affirm the significance of "contingent happenings and policies, motivations and goals," and warrants the recognition of the social location of the marginalized and oppressed, who surely are the "mere nothings" and "the things that are not" in this world.[45]

The preferential option for the poor and dispossessed, based upon the electing will of God and realized in the messianic presence and power of Jesus, need not be grounded in a problematic "epistemological" or "hermeneutical privilege of the poor,"[46] indeed, it cannot be coherently rooted there, dependent as such notions are on the myth of the Cartesian ego and the surreptitious privileging of a liberal capitalist political order. Cornel West correctly points out that theology must take account of these marginal voices and peoples, not because they have a monopoly on truth, "though there is much to learn from marginal peoples...but rather because the historical development of the structural societal mechanisms, such as class exploitation, state repression, patriarchy, and racism, reproduce and reinforce such marginality." Lash suggests that "a 'preferential option for the poor'...is *not* to be construed as an option in favour of powerlessness, an option against the possession and use of power. It is an option, which, in the light of hope sprung from the memory of the Crucified, equips us with a criterion of discrimination concerning the forms and uses of power."[47]

The preferential option for the oppressed is therefore not a hermeneutical principle but a *eucharistic indication* of the sense and direction of God's redemptive activity in Jesus Christ in a (post)modern world, a *leitmotif* of the biblical story that signals to the contemporary world "the advent of the Messiah, the ingression of the 'new age' upon the 'old age', the proleptic inauguration of the kingdom of God." This option places the church, as the laboratory of conscience, squarely within the relations and structures of power which invest (post)modern society, marking the point in the *koinonia* where piety, power, and politics actually converge within the practice of everyday life. The corruption of everyday life by reified modes of social and cultural production—life created for fellowship with God and the neighbor—sets the historical stage on which the power made perfect in weakness confronts the weakness of the will to power and issues in a politics of confrontation. Within the *koinonia* of the messianic community God offers the world a range of possibilities for confronting the social stratification that characterizes a (post)modern world, "forc[ing] to the light hidden directions and dispositions that would otherwise never come to view, and thus make the conflicts of goals and interests between people a *public* affair."[48] And as a consequence of that confrontation, God opens up concrete possibilities for exhibiting the habits and relations that comprise the politics of the new humanity. In short, the preferential option for the poor and dispossessed makes explicit the dialectical relationship between the theological and historical determination of priorities, a relationship that can only be discerned by the mature conscience forged on the anvil which is the fellowship-creating mystery of the *koinonia*.

To his credit, Lehmann is aware of how often the preferential option for the poor has been brushed aside in the history of Christian thought. He maintains, nevertheless, that "This view has been the sign of the obedience of faith at least since the Lord and Giver of life began to make dry bones come alive [Ezekiel 37], to shatter the stranglehold of death in the power of the Resurrection, and to confront the spirits in prison, as a prelude to his own assumption of all authority and power at the right hand of God, angels and authorities and powers having been made subject to him." It is a hopeful sign, then, when he argues that the early church's celebration of Easter as a political feast is apostolically warranted from precisely this viewpoint:

> The view from below is the view from the perspective of those who suffer. In the light of this perspective, what really matters is "to know Christ, to experience the power of his resurrection, and to share his sufferings, in growing conformity with his death, if only (one) may finally arrive at the resurrection from the dead" (Phil. 3^{10-11}). The power of Christ's resurrection is the power to live in this life prepared for death and free from the fear of death. It is the power to live in this life without taking this life for granted, or making any of the values and achievements of this life the measure of its meaning and purpose. The power of Christ's resurrection is the power to live in this life with a lively and liberating confidence that God's new world is the warrant for and confirmation of hope, and is already under way in all those struggles in which we are called to share his sufferings in conformity with his death. To share Christ's sufferings is to stand with and for all in this life who are without opportunity, without power, and without hope, and to make their cause and claims one's own.[49]

NOTES

[1]Lehmann, *Ethics*, 99; *Transfiguration*, 47, 234.

[2]Lehmann, *Ethics*, 95; "The Tri-Unity of God," 36. Lehmann reiterates here Barth's description of the creative activity of God as the external basis of God's intention to covenant with Israel and the church, and conversely, sees the covenant as the internal basis of creation. See Barth, *Church Dogmatics*, 3.1: 94–329.

[3]Lehmann, *Ethics*, 95–97; W. H. Auden, *The Age of Anxiety* (New York: Random House, 1947), 23–24.

[4]Lehmann, *Ethics*, 97. Lehmann here alludes to, but does not develop, the notion of the usurpation of humankind's environment, which includes the humanity of the neighbor, in the quest for the will to power. The reality of domination and exploitation looms in the background of such a position as the historical actualization of the *eritis sicut Deus* in which "the attempt is made to reconstitute the terms of the covenant…on which the world has been made." *Ethics*, 95–96.

[5]Lehmann, *Ethics*, 95–96, 101–103, 160; "Jesus Christ and Theological Symbolization," 15, 17, 22, 23.

[6]Rouse, *Knowledge and Power*, 261f; Lehmann, *Ethics*, 95–96; "Black Theology and 'Christian' Theology," 150.

[7]See George Hunsinger, "Epilogue: Secular Parables of Truth," *How to Read Karl Barth: The Shape of His Theology* (New York: Oxford University Press, 1991), 234–80. Contrary to many on the current scene, I would disagree with those who insist that we live in a "post-revolutionary" era, but would argue that (at least for the time being) the revolutionary movements in both the "First" and the "Two-Thirds" worlds have adopted somewhat less confrontational strategies, perhaps due to their fragmentation in an increasingly transcultural (and therefore rationalized) social order. With increased fragmentation, however, comes both heightened instability and unpredictability.

[8]Lehmann, *Transfiguration*, 5, 24, 46, 261; Bernstein, *Praxis and Action*, 80–81; Hannah Arendt, *On Revolution* (New York: Viking Press, 1947), 42.

[9]Lehmann, *Transfiguration*, 28, 39; cf. 103.

[10]Lehmann, *Transfiguration*, 15, 23, 32; *Ethics*, 97. 101.

[11]Lehmann, *Transfiguration*, 15. According to *Harper's Latin Dictionary*, *auctoritas* is derived from *auctor*, "he that brings about the existence of an object, or promotes the increase and prosperity of it, whether he first originates it, or by his efforts gives permanence or continuance to it." *Auctor* in turn is derived from the verb, *augeo*, "to increase, to nourish (Orig. to produce, bring forth that not already in existence; in which significance only the derivative auctor is now found." *Harper's Latin Dictionary: A New Latin Dictionary*, ed. E. A. Andrews, s.v. "*auctor*," "*auctoritas*," and "*augeo*."

[12]Lehmann, *Transfiguration*, 52; Paul Lehmann, "The Commandments and the Common Life," *Interpretation* 34 (October 1980): 343–44.

[13]Edward Farley, *Ecclesial Reflection* (Philadelphia: Fortress Press, 1982), 107–68; Clark H. Pinnock, *The Scripture Principle* (San Francisco: Harper & Row, 1984), 3–82; Jeffrey Stout, *The Flight from Authority*, 25–92.

[14]Lehmann, *Transfiguration*, 260–61; William Stringfellow, *An Ethic for Christians and Other Aliens in a Strange Land*, (Waco, TX: Word Books, 1973), 123.

[15]Lehmann, *Transfiguration*, 32, 46, 233; "The Politics of Easter," 38–39.

[16]Lehmann, *Transfiguration*, 50–53.

[17]Lehmann, *Transfiguration*, 236, 282.

[18]Lehmann, *Transfiguration*, 279.

[19]Lehmann, *Transfiguration*, 47; Karl Barth, *The Epistle to the Romans*, trans. Edwyn C. Hoskyns, 6th ed. (London: Oxford University Press, 1933), 475–502.

[20]Friedrich Nietzsche, "The Antichrist," *The Portable Nietzsche*. trans. Walter Kaufmann (New York: Penquin Books, 1954), 588, 593; Lehmann, *Transfiguration*, 38.

[21]Lehmann, *Transfiguration*, 64–66.

[22]Lehmann, *Ethics*, 58.

[23]Lehmann, *Transfiguration*, 271; "The Commandments and the Common Life," 344; Paul Lehmann, "Harvey Cox, Martin Luther and a Macro-Sociological Appropriation of the Decalogue," *Sociological Analysis* 45 (Summer 1984): 88.

[24]Lehmann, *Transfiguration*, 32; cf. 15, 64, 122, 279, 282. For Luther, freedom of conscience is the freedom *coram deo* from the righteous judgment of God that delivers us *from* self-interest in the achievements which will merit our salvation by works and *for* service to the neighbor, and to which human law should add nothing that will burden it. According to Lehmann, freedom of conscience is the liberating power of an obedient response to and involvement in the antedonation of human maturity and wholeness in the messianic community. The crucial difference between Luther and Lehmann involves a shift from a forensic context, concerned primarily with the "inner" person, to a socio-political matrix, involving the whole person in relation to God and the neighbor.

[25]Lehmann, *Transfiguration*, 241–42.

[26]Cicero, *De Finibus* 5. 23. 65; John Rawls, *A Theory of Justice* (Cambridge: Harvard University Press, 1971).

[27]Lehmann, *Transfiguration*, 87–88; "Metaphorical Reciprocity between Theology and Law," 189. This formulation is an adaptation of Kant's aphorism concerning the relationship between concepts, and percepts, ideas and sensations in finite human experience: "*Gedanken ohne Inhalt sind leer, Anschauungen ohne Begriffe sind blind*" Immanuel Kant, *Kritik der reinen Vernuft* (Riga: Johann Friedrich Hartknoch, 1781), 77. The stress upon reconciliation as the goal and abiding purpose of justice has been a constant emphasis for Lehmann, as evidenced by the publication of his doctoral dissertation, "A Critical Comparison of the Doctrine of Justification in the Theologies of Albrecht Ritschl and Karl Barth," (Ph.D. dissertation, Union [NY] Theological Seminary, 1936) under the title *Forgiveness: Decisive Issue in Protestant Thought* (New York: Harper & Brothers, 1940). See also Lehmann, "Law as a Function of Forgiveness," *Oklahoma Law Review* 12 (February 1959): 102–12.

[28]Lehmann, "The Commandments and the Common Life," 347, 350.

[29]Lehmann takes these terms from Peter Blau, *Inequality and Heterogeneity: A Primitive Theory of Social Structures* (New York: The Free Press, 1977).

[30]Lehmann, *Transfiguration*, 233, 258; "The Commandments and the Common Life," 353; "Cox, Luther, Decalogue," 88–90.

[31]Lehmann, *Transfiguration*, 242–43, 258; "A Christian Alternative to Natural Law," 531.

[32]Lehmann, *Transfiguration*, 262; *Ethics*, 101.

[33]Lehmann, *Transfiguration*, 267. Lehmann seems to be recalling in his apocalyptic perspective on violence a distinction which Luther draws between the "proper work" (*opus proprium*) and "alien work" (*opus alienum*) of God in the realization of the divine economy of salvation, in which the alien work always aims to realize the proper, i.e., redemptive work of God. See Althaus, *The Theology of Martin Luther*, 120, 168, 171–72, 258, 279–80.

[34]Lehmann, *Transfiguration*, 56–57, 168. The principal concern of the church is, as Hauerwas says, to be the church, i.e., the vanguard of the city of God. While some regard Lehmann's position on violence as incompatible with the pacifism they regard as essential

to the gospel, it is at greater odds with traditional conceptions of just war theory, for the latter is, in the final analysis, a policy statement.

[35]Lehmann, "The Metaphorical Reciprocity Between Theology and Law," 187.

[36]Lehmann, *Ethics*, 66; John H. Yoder, "Sacrament as Social Process: Christ the Transformer of Culture," *Theology Today* 48 (April 1991): 31–44; Milbank, *Theology and Social Theory*, 199.

[37]Hauerwas, *After Christendom?*, 42; Lash, *Believing Three Ways in One God*, 21, 54; Milbank, *Theology and Social Theory*, 228; Elisabeth Schüssler Fiorenza, "A Discipleship of Equals: Ekklesial Democracy and Patriarchy in Biblical Perspective," *A Democratic Catholic Church: The Reconstruction of Roman Catholicism*, eds. Eugene C. Bianchi and Rosemary Radford Ruether (New York: The Crossroad Publishing Co., 1992), 27; Yoder, "Sacrament as Social Process." 37.

[38]Hauerwas, *After Christendom?*, 54.

[39]Lehmann, *Transfiguration*, 168.

[40]Lehmann, *Transfiguration*, 155; Lash, *Theology on the Way to Emmaus*, 80.

[41]Lehmann, "Black Theology and 'Christian' Theology," 145; "The Formative Power of Particularity," 312; Paul L. Lehmann, "The Concreteness of Theology: Reflections on the Conversation Between Barth and Bonhoeffer," *Footnotes to a Theology: The Karl Barth Colloquium of 1972*, ed. Martin Rumscheidt (Waterloo, Ontario: The Corporation for the Publication of Academic Studies in Religion in Canada, 1974), 53–76; "Karl Barth, Theologian of Permanent Revolution," *Union Seminary Quarterly Review* 28 (Fall 1972): 73–74; "On Doing Theology," 129–30 Cf. Bonhoeffer, *Letters and Papers from Prison*, 280, 286, 329.

[42]Lehmann, *Transfiguration*, 103–226; *Ethics*, 101.

[43]Lehmann, *Transfiguration*, 287; *Ethics*, 152.

[44]Lehmann, *Transfiguration*, pp. 68–69, 76, 258.

[45]Bonhoeffer, *Letters and Papers from Prison*, 17; Lehmann, "The Concreteness of Theology," 62; "Black Theology and 'Christian' Theology," 146, 148; "On Doing Theology," 136; "Jesus Christ and Theological Symbolization," 21.

[46]See, for example, Lee Cormie, "The Hermeneutical Privilege of the Oppressed: Liberation Theologies, Biblical Faith, and Marxist Sociology of Knowledge," *The Catholic Theological Society of America: Proceedings of the Thirty-Third Annual Convention* 33 (June 1978): 155–81.

[47]Cornel West, "The Politics of American Neo-Pragmatism," *Post-Analytic Philosophy*, eds. John Rajchman and Cornel West (New York: Columbia University Press, 1985), 270–71; Lash, *Theology on the Way to Emmaus*, 193–94.

[48]Lehmann, *Ethics*, 112; Rowan Williams, "Postmodern Theology and the Judgment of the World," *Postmodern Theology: Christian Faith in a Pluralist World*, ed. Frederic B. Burnham (San Francisco: Harper & Row, 1989), 96.

[49]Lehmann, "The Politics of Easter," 42–43.

Chapter 6

LANGUAGE, TRUTH, AND POWER

The "The-Anthropological" Focus of Theology

"The Christian community," says Lehmann, "lives always in the present out its past and fully open to the future. This is why the materials of theology are compounded of tradition and experimentation. Indeed, it is precisely those elements of tradition which exhibit great openness, in their own present, to the future, which guide theology in the exercise of its own contemporary responsibility."[1] Lehmann's understanding of theological inquiry offers an imaginative approach to the interaction between the continuity embodied in the Christian tradition, on the one hand, and on the other, the kind of innovation which is needed to come to terms with a world which is struggling (and failing) to come of age. The *koinonia* of the Christian community provides the laboratory where this synthesis of tradition and experimentation takes place, shaping the consciences of those whose humanity is vested in its habits and relations.

As I noted previously, Lehmann's method extends Aristotle's paradigm of *praxis* "to the entire range of man's cognitive and practical life." He therefore ties theological reflection to what he terms the parabolic juxtaposition of the ways of God and the ways of humanity. "Sensitive to every mode of human knowledge and experience," he writes,

> systematic theology seeks to exhibit, in, with, and under, the activity of man, the formative and particular activity of God. It is this formative power of God, as He gives shape to the life and doings of man, that provides systematic theology with its specific content. The formative power of God which gives place to man and puts man in his place within a world of God's making also gives to the doing of theology its...occasion and significance.

Lehmann thus prescribes an anthropological (or as Karl Barth phrases it, a *the-anthropological*) focus for theological inquiry. He contends, however, that the ways of God and of human beings cannot be correlated either in a systematic or *ad hoc* fashion, as revisionist and postliberal theologians attempt to do, but only metaphorically exhibited within the church: "God's providential ordering of human affairs can be discerned only in broken configurations of events, not in uni-linear traditions. Accordingly, obedience can never be literal but is necessarily paradigmatic." In Scripture, the paradigm for this obedience is the "Fatherhood" of God, but as Lash warns us, "before we take this name and use it to weave comforting patterns of speculation concerning the 'domestic' character of the relationship between human beings and the mystery of God, we need to remind ourselves of the context which is paradigmatic for all descriptions of ourselves as 'sons' and 'daughters' of him whom we call 'Father'. That context...is Gethsemane and Calvary. That is where we learn what it is truthfully to stand in filial relation to the mystery of God."[2]

Simply put, since theology is not solely the doctrine of God, but the doctrine of the commerce and communication between God and humankind (or as Lehmann puts it time and again, "what God is doing to make and to keep human life human"), Barth rightly contends that had the nineteenth century kept in mind that humanity's dealings with God are founded upon the divine favor towards humankind, such an anthropological focus for theology would not only be possible but in many ways expedient. The methodological point of departure for such "the-anthropology," Barth concludes (and Lehmann concurs), would be the third article of the Apostles' Creed, that is, a theology which sets out from the activity of the Holy Spirit: "Everything which needs to be said, considered, and believed about God the Father and God the Son in an understanding of the first and second articles might be shown and illuminated in its foundations through God the Holy Spirit, the *vinculum pacis inter Patrem et Filium*. The entire work of God for his creatures, for, in, and with human beings, might be made visible in terms of its one teleology." Coincidentally, at one point Barth explicitly links the activity of the Spirit in the church with the reality of conscience: "Schleiermacher and his whole school would have been right to assume that there is a God-consciousness immanent in human self-consciousness if only they had not overlooked its nongivenness, its pure futurity, and if only they had described it as conscience, i.e., as the Word of God which does not belong to human self-consciousness but is *entrusted* to it."[3]

It is important to note that this "humanization" of the theological must be distinguished from a "divinizing" of the human that fails to discriminate between what God does to shape and interpret what is human, and what humans make of themselves and of the world in their most noble efforts. Without the intellectual and moral skills of the Christian tradition that permit us to make this distinction, the ministry of the Holy Spirit will be idolatrously confused with the potential and activity of whatever *Zeitgeist* is popular. Identifying the forms of the Spirit's presence with human potential and activity as such, as Lash notes, "obscures the difference between the world and God, mistakes the sign and promise for the reality, and thereby leads us disastrously to misread our circumstances and responsibilities...the 'gifts of the spirit', gifts of community and relationship, forgiveness and life-giving, are at least as much a matter of promise, of prospect, and of the task that is laid upon us, as they are a matter of past achievement or present reality."[4] A *the-anthropological* theology, consequently, presupposes an *ecclesiocentric* methodology.

Theology that is ordered in this fashion attends to the historical relation (a relation that is metaphorically articulated both diachronically and synchronically) between the mystery of the divine initiative in creation and redemption, and the human response to that initiative within the church. Lehmann argues that theology secures its paradigmatic occasion in the messianic politics of God, and therefore it finds its *raison d'être* in the question of who the human being is, i.e., the question of the self. As a result, all theological inquiry is oriented toward the "reality of a transformed human being and a transformed humanity owing to the specific action of God in Jesus Christ, an action and transformation of which the reality of the Christian *koinonia* is a foretaste." The dialectical movement between the self-disclosing activity of God in Jesus Christ that creates, sustains, and consummates the human conditions whereby God's revelation is apprehended and under which humans freely and obediently live, on the one hand, and the human response of obedient freedom, on the other, displaces for theological reflection "the schizoid spectre of an abyss between metaphysics and epistemology, between a theory of reality and a theory of knowledge and its possibilities" which "has haunted Cartesian and post-Cartesian habits of mind."[5] In short, the everyday realities of human existence, rather than modern theology's traditional foundations in epistemology (or theoretical hermeneutics) and metaphysics (or ontology), provide the methodological warrants for the discipline of theology.

From its anthropological point of departure, theology seeks to provide "a contextual account of the divine activity" that addresses in a self-critical manner the concrete and dialectical relations between God's self-disclosing activity in Word and Spirit, and the obedient response of conscience on the part of the messianic community. According to Lehmann, therefore,

> [t]here is the accent upon the historical self-disclosure of God in revelatory instruction and action, apprehended in and confirmed by the historical destiny of a particular people. There is the accent upon a pivotal center of meaning and fulfillment in an historical person who bears in himself and in his action among his people and their contemporaries, the secret of personal, community and cosmic existence and fulfillment. Christ, in another New Testament phrase, is "the wisdom of God" and "the power of God." There is the accent upon the participation of a community of faith in the historical activity of God and in the redemptive disclosure of human and cosmic meaning and consummation. And there is the accent upon the possibility and the power to live responsibly and to make sense out of life until the days of our years shall be filled up with all the fullness of God.[6]

With reference to the messianic occasion for theological reflection, Lehmann argues that "A theology of the incarnation affirms that the presence of Jesus of Nazareth in the human story opens up a way of perceiving the world of time and space and things that gives primacy and priority to the human sense and significance of what is going on. In the jargon of the Schools, a theology of the incarnation alters the priorities in the possibility and the order of inquiry. The science of 'human things' takes precedence over the sciences of knowing and of being; in short, anthropology is the clue to, and the criterion of, epistemology and ontology (or metaphysics)." He elaborates on the significance of the paradigmatic occasion for theology by amending Ludwig Feuerbach's axiom that all theology is anthropology to read: "All theology is anthropology as a reflex of Christology." When modified in this way, Feuerbach's inversion of Hegel is also an inversion of Calvin's fundamental theological maxim that "Nearly all the wisdom we possess, that is to say, true and sound wisdom, consists of two parts: the knowledge of God and of ourselves. But while joined by many bonds, which one precedes and brings forth the other is not easy to discern."[7]

Theology, on this account, primarily concerns itself with "the dynamic co-inherence (Calvin) of actions of God and actions of men," actions which are always concrete and particular, include all types and conditions of everyday life, and ultimately refer "to a self-identifying self-disclosure of God which claims and elicits a human response of obedience and results in a human experience of freedom." Through conscience, christology and anthropology are dialectically bound together within the messianic community through the nurture of a distinctive style of life: "The knowledge of God and the knowledge of ourselves are thus reciprocally and revelationally joined; and the point of intersection, at which the point of no return is disclosed as the moment of truth, is Jesus of Nazareth."[8]

Lehmann insists that a theology that is faithful to its messianic referent and impetus must deal "at one and the same time" with two distinct but interrelated dimensions. These dimensions thus constitute the fundamental conditions for theological inquiry. The first, which he terms the referential dimension, pertains to theology's distinctive content, "the human reality and meaning of God's self-disclosing activity in the world as described in the Bible and expressed in the central doctrines of incarnation, atonement, redemption, and reconciliation." According to Lehmann, "It is the office of theology to provide the critical weapons wherewith faith 'tests the spirits' [1 John 4[1]] in the warfare which is always at hand and on that line of battle where the peripheral and the central problems of human knowledge are discerned and distinguished." The referential dimension of theology thus deals with that point "where the line between God's humanizing activity and man's dehumanizing action is being drawn, and where the frontiers of human wholeness are being extended," where "the boundary on which the issue of the humanity or inhumanity of man to man must be fought through, and the direction of God's activity must be sighted again."[9]

The distinctive office of theology, therefore, is "to analyze and work out the terms of the running conversation" between the messianic community and the biblical story, for it is this story that juxtaposes both diachronically and synchronically the ways of God and our ways. The church's conversation with the Bible, however, is in the final analysis much more than simply talking, for as Lash reminds us, "the fundamental form of the *Christian* interpretation of scripture is the life, activity and organization of the believing community." The task of the theologian is thus to bring intellectual skills acquired through disciplined study to the "grammatical" relation which the discourses of the church must have with the performative reasoning of conscience. According to David Burrell, the grammatical role of theology is neither to reinforce nor to supplant the "college of attitudes, aphorisms and generalizations which coalesces into something best described as [the Judaeo-Christian] picture of God," but "to exercise critical watch over it, now unraveling confusions and inconsistencies that arise from it, now checking it with *praxis* to offset its stereotypical drift, now challenging it as a lazy simplification. So a grammatical inquiry makes its impact on...life indirectly, by an ongoing critique of the conceptions which mediate life to us, thereby guiding our attitudes toward it as well as our participation in it." Brian Wicker helps unravel the complex and rather abstract nature of the grammatical relationship between theology and the parabolic juxtaposition of God's ways with those of humankind when he states that "Metaphor...raises questions that only analogy...can answer, while conversely analogy can only answer questions that are raised in metaphorical form."[10]

The second dimension of theological inquiry, which is dialectically related to the first, pertains to "the ethos and the options posed by the human situation in which systematic theology must work," that is, "the insistence upon the concreteness of theological conception and analysis." This second aspect, which Lehmann calls the phenomenological dimension of the theological task, analyzes the concrete situation in relation to which theology functions as critical inquiry. In keeping with an ecclesiocentric method, this aspect of the theological task principally attends to the historical (and thus sacramental) reality of the Christian community. The church lives in the concrete situation of the present on the basis of its particular and contingent existence as a community of memory. And while many in the (post)modern world have yet to come to terms with this aspect of everyday life, the particularity and contingency of human life in the present can no more be extricated from the phenomenological dimension of theology than they can from the referential. It is solely as a historical community, constituted in the present by its eucharistic memory, that the church (or any group of people, for that matter) can be open to a world that only has a future by virtue of the messianic politics of God. In the words of Johann Baptist Metz, "memory...is the means by which reason [can] become practical as freedom." Conscience, as the radical of selfhood and its performative reasoning, is rooted in the memory of a particular community. Moreover, writes Rowan Williams,

> the self's transcendence is in its memory, precisely in its recollection *now* of another reality, a past reality, both distinct from and part of the present situation. Memory affirms that the present situation has a context; it, like the self, is part of a continuity, it is "made" and so it is not immutable. By learning that situations have wider contexts, we learn a measure of freedom or detachment from (or transcendence of) the limits of the present. Things may be otherwise; change occurs...When the power of given present facts

is challenged as we come to see the present situation as the issue of contingent processes and choices, we gain resources for new decision, and openness to new stages of process. We learn to act and to hope. Memory…can be the ground of hope, and there is no authentic hope without memory.

Consequently, those elements of the tradition that allow conscience to display the same openness to the future "guide theology in the exercise of its contemporary responsibility."[11]

The phenomenological dimension of theology, therefore, takes into account the nature of the messianic community as both an institutional entity extended through space and time, and a political fellowship ordered by its conception of goods and the good. As a social institution, the church has a twofold character. With respect to its existence as the community of Word and Sacrament, the institutional church embodies the practices which give the community of faith it recognizable historical form. As such, the fact and nature of the church constitutes the "proper milieu" for the critical inquiry of systematic theology. It is also as an institutional reality that the church participates in the structures and disciplinary mechanisms of the larger society, realities that are intrinsic to human existence in a (post)-modern world but which are also inherently ambiguous. But theology must also deal with the spiritual reality of the church as the *koinonia*, i.e., the eucharistic achievement of a particular form of communion among human beings and with the rest of creation, brought about by the presence and power of God's messianic politics and interwoven dialectically with its institutional structures. In every respect, therefore, the phenomenological dimension of Christian theology lies uniquely "in its historical-political character," from which comes the concreteness of its formative power.[12]

It is in the dialectical relationship between these two conditions that theology exhibits "the congruence of faithfulness with concreteness in dealing with 'the great deeds done by God'." Hence theological inquiry always strives to manifest the dialectical interrelation between Word, Spirit and the *koinonia* in reference to God's self-disclosing activity in Jesus Christ and to God's shaping of the community of believers in Word and Sacrament. The referential dimension, for its part, guards theology from taking its primary cues from the phenomenological aspect. But Word, Spirit and community are "also always quite concretely phenomenological, in the sense expressed in the celebrated description of the Church as there 'wherever we see the Word of God purely preached and heard and the sacraments administered according to Christ's institution'." The fatal error for the theologian, therefore, would be either to *identify* the politics of God with the practices of the church, or to *separate* them. Thus they belong together, juxtaposed "inconfusedly and inseparably" in the mystery of God, a juxtaposition which, as Herbert McCabe puts it, "is nothing other than the triune life of God projected onto our history, or enacted sacramentally in our history, so that it becomes story." As Lehmann puts it, "theology tries to express the dynamics of divine initiative and human response through a dialectic of analysis and criticism which inter-relates the referential and the phenomenological factors in the doing of theology."[13]

Three traits characterize the interaction between the referential and phenomenological dimensions. The first pertains to theology's *confessional* status. Theology "is involved from the first in a commitment to the truth and life-giving power of the referent to which its context points. Such theology confesses what it knows; it does not confess where it does not know …[Theology is] committed to that which *in concreto* elicits its response." A second mark is its *dialogical* character, for theology seeks to express and explicate its referent in open encounter with other perspectives and referents. Based upon the tacit premise of the continuing activity of the Holy Spirit, "[a] dialogical confessionalism…recognizes that the ultimate test of its humanizing responsibility may well be its hospitality to what it can learn about the genuinely human from other perspectives which do not claim to be what they are not (i.e., which do not claim to be theological)." Finally, theology is to exercise a *catalytic* function. This trait specifies theology's critical function as it presses its own confessional occasion and integrity in an ongoing effort to expose the limitations of other perspectives and disciplines in service to what is genuinely human, "that is, what is the truth and the life." When approached in this manner,

> a catalytic theology becomes the "guardian of the human"…because it re-
> fuses either to subordinate the human to its own confession or to exclude,
> from any identification of the human, the self-disclosing initiative of the
> particular referent which has shaped its own content and setting. Theologi-
> cal criticism and theological self-criticism are thus inseparable. To this ex-
> tent, a *catalytic* theology is a *prophetic* theology whose function is and re-
> mains that of a *creative iconoclasm*. A creative iconoclasm in the doing of
> theology is always prepared for the collapse of its own idols as it exhibits
> the idolatry in other perspectives.[14]

To take seriously an anthropological point of departure for theological inquiry, says Lehmann, one must never lose sight of the interrelation of the referential and the phenomenological dimensions. In the North American context, this dialectic means that "the integrity of dogmatics today requires that at whatsoever point one begins the exploration of Christian doctrine, a 'Christian' theology must, from the beginning and throughout, take account, in its talk about Jesus Christ, or about God, or about sin and salvation, of the concrete realities of black experience." Only as the church fosters a mutual accountability between African- and Euro-Americans in the practice of everyday life can they "be honest about the sociological reality which reminds them at once of their own vulnerability to ideological distortion and of the wisdom of the dogmatic tradition which reserves omniscience for God alone. Only as black theologians and white theologians together take primary account of the concrete realities of black experience, can they reciprocally correct one another in the truth and grace that in Jesus Christ *are* the reality of the human condition."[15]

If theology is to foster mutual accountability between African- and Euro-Americans, it cannot be embarrassed by either the presence of "ideology" in its criticisms and analyses, nor by the implications of this presence. "On the contrary," Lehmann writes,

> theology welcomes [ideology's] involvement in a dynamic theatre of reality and in a point of view. Such an involvement serves, on the one hand, as a limitation which prevents theology from oracular pretensions, and on the other, as a liberation of theology to take unlimited account both of the responses of reason to the knowledge of faith and of the critical function of the reason in clarifying and correcting the relations between the knowledge of faith and non-theological knowledge about man and the world.[16]

To risk the ideological factor, then, is to recognize that interest and purpose are always present and operative in all human discourse and inquiry. Power and knowledge can no longer be seen as extrinsically related; as Rouse puts it, "power itself becomes the mark of knowledge."[17] The crucial question at this point, therefore, is "whose power, which knowledge?"

According to Lehmann, Marx was among the first to grasp the significance of ideology as "a functional type of thinking which exhibits the corruption of reason by interest," and therefore to document "the concrete functioning of this corruption in the social relations and social processes of contemporary society." When the term ideology is used to describe the thinking of those who either embrace or resign themselves to the relations of power that presently determine the possibilities for everyday life, it may be defined as "the self-justifying defense and expansion of existing power

through a subtle and pervasive invasion of the people's consciousness in order to achieve an identification between the happiness of the people and the
security guaranteed by the very power that seeks to justify itself." Nevertheless, says Lehmann, the meaning of "ideology" may be transposed into
an instrument of the struggle to realize human maturity and wholeness
within concrete networks of power "by changing the function of ideology
from an unconscious to a conscious instrument of power in the social struggle to overcome the alienation of man." The power of an ideology, in contrast to an ideology of power, "is the power of a humanizing vision to
shape values and of values to shape the organization of a social order in
which time and space make room for the freedom that being human takes."
Here all "truth" functions ideologically (that is, politically), "it exerts its
power in and through *ad hoc* critical alterations of established patterns and
structures."[18] Truth, in other words, subsists as a *performative* utterance.

The anthropological emphasis of Lehmann's ecclesiocentric theology
also influences his construal of the relation between theological inquiry and
the (post)modern academy. He discusses this relation in terms of an extra-
ecclesial ecumenism focused on the question of the human being. Theology's dialogical confessionalism, he suggests, can play an important role in
the academy, opening up kerygmatic opportunities that arise from disciplined reflection on the church's involvement in the mystery of God for
seeking out the sense and direction of human life. As such, Christian participation in the deliberations of the academy is predicated upon our conviction that "Jesus Christ is in some sense at the center of the restless curi-
osity, conceptuality, and criticism through which man tries to understand
and to apprehend both the mystery of his experience and his experience of
mystery." This understanding of theology in the context of the (post)mod-
ern university, however, implies that the modern conception of academic
inquiry—value-free, disinterested, universal knowledge—can no longer assume its accustomed cultural status. As Richard Rorty has observed, the
Age of Enlightenment, like the Age of Faith, is beyond recovery, and its
quest for a universal language which expresses Nature's own "vocabulary"
will likely remain unrequited.[19]

If theology is to attend truthfully to the complex relationship between
the referential and the phenomenological dimensions of everyday life from
the standpoint of the *koinonia*, it can no longer divide its sub-disciplines—
philosophical theology, dogmatics, and theological ethics (or fundamental,
systematic, and practical theology)—into autonomous spheres of inquiry.

Within the context of the politics of God, says Lehmann, "dogmatics and ethics become distinguishable perspectives of a systematic whole." Christian ethics, when divorced from the dogmatic tradition of the church, is stripped of its behavioral significance and power, and surrenders to either moral relativism or irrelevance. And therefore, apart from the church's account of its "'common knowledge of the Son of God', of God's revealed behavior," spelled out in terms of the correspondence between its unique language about God with the parabolic juxtaposition of the ways of God and of humankind attested in Scripture, theology empties its phenomenological aspect of concrete significance, and rips asunder the reciprocity of word and deed in the performative reasoning of conscience. Conversely, when "the concern of theology with and for dogma" is not accompanied by ethical analysis and criticism, it "becomes an end in itself and hardens into dogmatism." Therefore, when dogmaticians do not regularly concern themselves with "an account of the transformation of the concrete stuff of behavior, i.e., the circumstances, the motivations, and the structures of action, owing to the concrete, personal, and purposeful activity of God," they obscure rather than expresses the dynamics of the divine activity. Theological reflection once again renders inert the performative interrelation of word and deed in the practice of everyday life, this time with respect to its referential dimension.[20]

Stanley Hauerwas is therefore correct when he states that "If theological convictions are meant to construe the world—that is, if they have the character of practical discourse—then ethics is involved at the beginning, not the end, of theology. Theological discourse is distorted when portrayed as a kind of primitive metaphysics—a view all too common among Protestants as well as Catholics." Dogmatics and ethics share a common concern—in Lehmann's words, "a divinely renewed order of life in which the will to power has been transformed into the power to will what God wills by the power of God's Messiah"—and therefore a common framework for inquiry. The politics of God thus gives to dogmatics a trinitarian focus and to ethics a trinitarian foundation. Together they seek to exhibit "the order by which goodness is the fruit of truth, and forge a creative link between confession and responsibility, between the concern for dogma and the concern about ethics."[21]

The ongoing life of the church, and especially its worship, orders the complex relations between dogmatics and ethics in keeping with the ancient rule of faith—*lex orandi, lex credendi.* Lehmann notes that there is an "intrinsic semantic connection between liturgy and ethics...in the messianic community of the New Testament," because "Life in the *koinonia* requires both liturgical and theological nourishment." Not only does the eucharistic life of the church give to the *koinonia* its sense and direction, it also forms the architechtonic structure of dogmatic and ethical reflection. Theology is therefore a complex task in which the disciplines of dogmatics and ethics, working both synchronically and diachronically, endeavor to make explicit in the context of the eucharistic community the *poetics* of everyday life. The performance of life within the *koinonia*, in turn, is the product of the contingent relationship between God's transfiguration of politics and the church's politics of transfiguration. The liturgy thus forms the political core of the "science of 'human things'" that "takes precedence over the sciences of knowing and of being" in a theology of the incarnation, and therefore forms the imaginative basis of both ethical and dogmatic inquiry.[22]

The emphasis on the "science of 'human things'" also reconfigures the idea of *revelation* (and with it the form and content of philosophical theology) from a special type of "religious knowledge" (viewed either as a disembodied system of beliefs or universal facet of human consciousness, and correlated with an epistemologically defined concept of faith), into a political category bound "inconfusedly and inseparably" to the believing community and its style of everyday life. Lehmann thus routinely refers to the revelation of God in Christ in terms of the "redemptive" or "humanizing activity of God," "God's messianic activity or politics," "the politics of God," and "what God is doing in the world to make and to keep human life *human*." Moreover, due to this reconfiguration, revelation can no longer be regarded, as Lash has observed, as "an event of which an adequate account can be given independently of and prior to an account of the human recognition of that event as revelatory. Christian faith is, as recognition, a constitutive element in the event of revelation. And Christian faith has a history. It follows...that it makes no sense to speak of 'preserving' revelation, but only of continuing its history, which is the history of faith."[23]

When theological inquiry—ethical, philosophical, and dogmatic—is linked to the particularities and contingencies of history in the way that Lehmann has done it, it subsists in the post-critical dialectic between human history and the politics of God, relies on the performative reasoning of conscience, and is formed by the practice of everyday life as it takes place in the *koinonia*. The fundamental conditions under which theology is to be done are now historical and political rather than epistemological or onto-

logical, due to the focus upon the inextricable interrelation of the phenomenological and the referential dimensions of theology. In order to complete
this move, however, we must examine the philosophical assumptions that
inform this account of theology.

A Pragmatic Construal of Theology

It should not come as a surprise that the account of theological inquiry
that I am developing here, carried out in the social and intellectual environment of North America, bears the marks of that environment. In particular, this account appropriates in distinctive ways the style of reasoning
commonly identified with the pragmatic movement. This movement, begun by Charles Peirce in the later half of the nineteenth century and elaborated by William James, George Mead, and John Dewey in the first half of
this century, is now represented by the works of Richard Bernstein, W. V.
Quine, Richard Rorty, and Cornel West, to name just a few of the scholars
who are the principal heirs of pragmatism's intellectual legacy. Theology's
appropriation of the insights of pragmatism, however, must always be done
self-critically, in ways that remain faithful to its trinitarian focus and foundation, as Thomas Aquinas appropriated the lessons taught by Aristotle
within the overall context of the Christian tradition in the thirteenth century. The crucial issue concerning theology's engagement with the pragmatic tradition is ultimately the question of *which community*—the church
or the modern nation-state—and *whose politics*—the politics of God or of
liberal capitalism—most truthfully juxtaposes the ways of humankind with
the incomprehensible and irreducible mystery of our existence. The principal aim of this engagement will be to combine and integrate a pragmatic
definition of theological inquiry with a trinitarian *description* of its messianic occasion and significance.

Perhaps pragmatism's most important contribution to contemporary
philosophy, writes Cornel West, is that it "dethroned epistemology as the
highest priority of modern thought in favor of ethics: not the professional
discipline of ethics but the search for desirable and realizable historical
possibilities in the present." West's emphasis on "the search for desirable
and realizable historical possibilities in the present," when correlated with

Lehmann's understanding of ethics as "a *descriptive* discipline...providing an account of the transformation of the concrete stuff of behavior, i.e., the circumstances, the motivations, and the structures of action, owing to the concrete, personal, and purposeful activity of God," supplies our first clue to the direction which a pragmatic definition and a trinitarian description of theology will ultimately take.[24]

Lehmann acknowledges his own indebtedness to the pragmatic tradition in an analysis of James's ethical account of religion. He quotes with approval James's revolutionary account of truth as "the name of whatever proves itself to be good in the way of belief, and good, too, for definite, assignable reasons," a view which suggests that truth is inseparable from its practical context. Lehmann also accepts James's assertion that "all our theories are *instrumental*, are mental modes of *adaption* to reality, rather than revelations or gnostic answers to some divinely instituted world-enigma." Consequently, in spite of significant shortcomings, Lehmann commends James for providing "an instrumental vehicle for an interpretation of ethics which seeks to understand and shape behavior in terms of the dynamics and the pattern of the politics of God."[25]

Lehmann also shares Dewey's criticism of the spectator theory of knowledge. This picture of knowledge, West rightly notes, is vested in "the controlling notions of modern thought: *the primacy of the subject and the preeminence of representation*."[26] Such notions acritically depend on ocular metaphors, i.e., the Cartesian picture of the human subject as a disinterested and disembodied spectator of the world, and culminate in a conception of the site of knowledge—mind and/or language—as a "mirror" which is to "reflect" accurately what is "given" to it as its object. The function of this mirror is to produce a conceptual "picture" of that object. Embedded in the Cartesian picture of the human subject and knowledge is the assumption of an identity or *ratio* between the place of knowledge and the world, between the vocabulary of the mind (or of a certain type of discourse) and nature's own vocabulary. This gnostic identity is actually constituted by the tacit imposition of the particular knower's social location and practices as the mirror that "depicts" reality, or rather, which *produces* reality according to its own material and cultural interests and goals.

The illusion of gnostic identity further invests the search for a universally valid method of inquiry or first philosophy with its cultural authority, perpetrating "the myth that rationality consists in being constrained by rule. According to this...myth, the life of reason is not the life of Socratic conversation but an illuminated state of consciousness in which one never needs to ask if one has exhausted the possible descriptions of, or explanations for, the situation. One simply arrives at true beliefs by obeying mechanical procedures." Rorty refers to this peculiar compulsion of modern thought as the "urge to substitute *theoria* for *phronesis*," i.e., the replacement of conversation, inquiry, and deliberation with the promulgation of a fundamental scientific method or first philosophy. Wolfhart Pannenberg exemplifies this quest for a normative, "scientific" method among theologians. His self-professed objective is "to reach a new self-understanding of science in general which will provide the basis for a new ordering of scientific disciplines and their methods," particularly with reference to the legitimation of theology within the modern university.[27]

Lehmann readily concurs with the pragmatist's critique of the spectator theory of knowledge and the urge to ground theology in a universally valid scientific method, fundamental theology, or first philosophy. "The conditions under which theology is done," he writes, "lie beyond such good and evil, beyond the 'given' upon which knowledge is imposed and the 'knowledge' which somehow mirrors the 'given' which is presupposed by it." These conditions, he argues, "are neither discernable nor describable …in terms of the subject-object or self-world relation. This relation has haunted Cartesian and post-Cartesian habits of minds with the schizoid spectre of an abyss between metaphysics and epistemology, between a theory of reality and a theory of knowledge and its possibilities." Theologians must therefore "learn to write theology in a way that denies that theology can be systematic."[28]

Modernity's foolish investment in an illusion can be attributed, at least in part, to the very real need for something to bear the normative burden of articulating the relation and reciprocity between the responsible life and human life. This is a burden, however, that rationality *per se* cannot bear, no matter whether it is defined as fundamental, cognitive, or ethical discourse. Rorty rightly observes that "our culture clings, more than ever, to the hope of the Enlightenment, the hope that drove Kant to make philosophy formal and rigorous and professional. We hope that by formulating the *right* conceptions of reason, of science, of thought, of knowledge, of morality, the conceptions which express their *essence*, we shall have a shield against irrationalist resentment and hatred. Pragmatists tell us that this hope is vain."[29] The most reliable indications of the relation between everyday life and human maturity do not lie in a set of precepts about what constitutes essential reasonableness among human beings, regardless of their place or time in history.

The reciprocity between the practice of everyday life in the present and the goal or *telos* of that practice can only be exhibited through the complex interactions between the referential and phenomenological dimensions of inquiry. The conception of knowledge in this process is therefore not invested in "the metaphors of vision, correspondence, mapping, picturing, and representation," but as MacIntyre points out, "is rather of mind as activity, of mind as engaging with the natural and social world in such activities as identification, reidentification, collecting, separating, classifying, and naming in all this by touching, grasping, pointing, breaking down, building up, calling to, answering to, and so on." The activity of knowing aims, in other words, at exhibiting, consolidating, and extending the complex relationships between the one who knows and that which is known. This construal of knowledge or understanding, Rouse adds, "is thus not a conceptualization of the world but a performative grasp of how to cope with it." The function of knowledge, Lehmann says, "is evidently to get things thus directly acted on, or thus directly introduced into life. Thus, the old dualism between something known from the 'inside' and from the 'outside', between consciousness and its object, has been overcome."[30]

Lehmann's conception of inquiry and knowledge is predicated upon what James refers to as the *complementarity* or the *adaptability* of mind to the world, a capacity that is realized in and through the practice of everyday life rather than upon an *identity* founded upon ocular metaphors and the Cartesian picture of the human subject. Rorty rightly states that "On this view, the activity of uttering sentences is one of the things people do in order to cope with their environment." The emphasis upon agency also clarifies the assertion, made by many in recent years, that the figure of the artisan or the laborer, rather than the spectator or observer, is a more appropriate way of picturing the human self and the intellectual and moral skills she needs to relate to others. Thus in the natural sciences one should now take seriously the etymological roots of the *labor*atory, and in the study of liturgy one cannot avoid the common etymology in Greek between worship and work.[31]

For Lehmann, the pragmatist's emphasis upon agency with respect to the activity of mind corresponds to the biblical stress upon the "*heart* [that] knows by a kind of sensitivity at once central and total [and] which marks the person as a whole; this relational knowledge involves man as a doer in a behavioral response to a God whose claim upon him is the foundation of his humanity." This kind of sensitivity can never be reduced to a set of logical or metaphysical precepts, for it is ultimately *poetic*, i.e., the ability to know how to go on and go further, which, as MacIntyre rightly puts it, "is the badge of elementary linguistic-competence." And, says Lehmann, when the notion of conscience is brought into the semantic orbit of the Hebrew understanding of the heart by the apostle Paul, theology discovers that it has as much in common with art as it has with metaphysics, for art

> is the province of sensitivity both to nature and to man where what is concretely and fundamentally human is continually taking shape and being reshaped. Since ethics is concerned with the human shape of reality, it continues to depend upon art for the nourishment of sensitivity to light and shade, to form and configuration; and...to nourish art with the human substance of its creativity. The biblical context within which conscience acquires its ethical integrity is confirmed in artistic creativity.[32]

From the standpoint of a pragmatic definition of theology, then, there is no real dichotomy between *saving-knowledge* and *scientific knowledge*, between *faith-knowledge* and *truth-knowledge*, or between *value-judgments* and *judgments of fact*. Lehmann argues that "theology involves both inquiring knowledge and answering knowledge, both the critical reason and the responding reason. The knowledge of the truth with which theological inquiry deals is a compound both of intellectual knowledge and the knowledge of faith." He further contends that such distinctions, artifacts of post-Reformation habits of mind, miss "altogether what the Reformers were presupposing when they managed so lively a connection between theology and faith." Insofar as a pragmatist approach to knowledge is concerned, says Rorty, "there is no epistemological difference between truth about what ought to be and truth about what is, nor any metaphysical difference between facts and values, nor any methodological difference between morality and science."[33]

The pragmatist, Rorty asserts, also discounts "the traditional distinctions between reason and desire, reason and appetite, reason and will." With his focus on the radical of human responsiveness under the category of conscience, "that delicate conjunction of the inner springs of human motivation and of human judgment informed by the divine activity in a single, decisive, and free act of obedience," Lehmann likewise draws attention to the performative unity of reason with the volitional and affective aspects of human agency. In conscience critical reason and responding reason con-

verge to form the fulcrum of our engagement in history, and owing to our
membership in the fellowship-creating reality of the *koinonia*, of our involvement in "the dynamics of divine initiative and human response."
Lehmann thus avoids the dilemma of the modern rationalization of existence into separate categories, according to which, as Milbank puts it, "aesthetics may now validate the unethical, religion the unaesthetic, politics the
nonreligious, and so forth."[34]

Theological inquiry thus consists of discerning and describing of "the
dialectical reality and movement whereby the self-disclosing activity of
God in his revelation in Jesus Christ creates, continues, and fulfills the human conditions required for its own apprehension, and for the free obedience by which man lives under these conditions." Accordingly, the mode
of reasoning in theological inquiry, writes Lehmann, "is *responsive* not *reflexive*. Theology is not concerned with reason in the act of thinking about
itself, about the structure of the mind, or about the laws of thought. Theology is concerned instead with reason in the act of responding to a limiting
condition of a quite particular kind." This condition, he continues, is "the
self-disclosing initiative of God, as the *Subject* (not the *Object*) of theology,
and the intrinsic character of theology as response to God's initiative." The
correlative notion of faith, now rooted in conscience, involves "the whole
person of the believer in what God in Jesus Christ had unmistakably been
pleased to do, and was doing."[35]

It is the need to cope with the world rather than to copy it through
conceptual representations, and more specifically, the need to *respond* to
God's gracious initiative and redemptive activity rather than to *reflect*
God's "being," which keys the pragmatist approach to human discourse and
critical inquiry, to which the language of faith and theological reflection
belong in a world created for fellowship with God and between all creatures. The *purpose* of theology, therefore, is not to *mirror* reality, but to
respond to the divine activity, to participate fully in the messianic politics
of God. Lehmann typically refers to the teleological aspect of reflection as
its catalytic function, for the ability to engage in conversation, to conduct
critical inquiry and to participate in concrete acts of communication, shapes
and consolidates all the other activities of individual and communal life.
Thought and discourse thus engage the world and respond in obedient freedom to God's redemptive presence and power through the concerns and
celebrations of everyday life, and thus "from the coherence of practices,

roles, and equipment to which [they] belong." As such, thought is always concretely situated, historically rooted, and political in character.[36]

Such a position implies that those who wish to talk of some sort of realism may do so, but in terms of political rather than philosophical (i.e., epistemological or metaphysical) realism. Lehmann states that such realism must be carefully distinguished from the negative conscience produced by a *Realpolitik*, which Pilate exemplifies in his encounter with Jesus:

> The confrontation between Jesus and Pilate underscores the great gulf between *political realism* and *Realpolitik*. *Realpolitik* is politics with the accent upon the primacy of power over truth. *Political realism* is politics with the accent upon the primacy of truth over power. *Realpolitik* increasingly succumbs to the temptation of confusing immediate goals and gains with ultimate outcomes and options and seeks validation by increasingly dubious authority. *Political realism*, on the other hand, involves an increasing struggle against the temptation to overcome irrelevance through premature ventures to close the gap between the ultimate and the immediate, thus overdrawing on the truth in its power. Ever and again, the successors of Jesus have sought to convert the moment of truth exposed by his presence into a blend of political realism and power politics (Caesaro-papism, theocracy, sectarian withdrawal) that seeks to effect the triumph of Jesus over the 'Prince of this world' in this world. Meanwhile, the successors of Pilate follow him in opting for the view that the state can have no interest in truth, i.e., in radical reality. In so doing, they convert the moment of truth exposed by Jesus into a politics of power that disregards the real and exalts the possible as necessary.

Apart from a politically conceived form of realism, however, the church "seems ineluctably to leave the level of simple and direct comprehension of religious experience behind, and to lose itself in a labyrinth of inquiry which mistakes abstraction for profundity, and systematic precision and coherence for the poetic and pragmatic wisdom by which men make their daily choices and ultimately live and die."[37]

Lehmann thus defines theology as an inherently practical mode of inquiry rather than as a speculative or reflexive endeavor. He regards the distinction between the practical and the speculative uses of reason as ultimately misleading, and alludes to it as an ideological component of the negative conscience. However, as Lehmann himself concedes when he states that "Clearly, this [perspective] changes the approach to and interpretation of the problem of truth," for many the most problematic aspect of pragmatism in general is its position on this problem. If, as Rorty argues, "it is the vocabulary of practise rather than of theory, of action rather than contemplation, in which one can say something useful about truth," or as Lehmann says, "*truth*...is a word used in a political sense, not in a theoretical sense," I need to supply an account of truth which does not reduce it to the instrumental expediency that betrays *Realpolitik*.[38]

The Living Word of Truth

According to Lehmann, "truth" properly refers neither to a Platonic essence or eternal form governing the relations between thought and the world, nor to a set of protocols defining what legitimately constitutes the value of a particular statement. The word truth, therefore, is neither some *thing* nor a property of something (even of a proposition), but is an effect that most directly and significantly refers to the mystery and redemptive activity of God. Lehmann takes his primary clue for this conception of truth from the Fourth Gospel: "The 'Truth' of which the Fourth Gospel speaks is not an intellectual formulation but a specific kind of activity of God," denoting "the behavioral dependability or faithfulness of God." Lehmann further contends that

> It is not too much to say that truth, in the Fourth Gospel generally...is a word used in a political sense, not in a theoretical sense. It is a *participatory*, not a *speculative* word. It expresses a movement and a relation in which men are caught up and involved. It does not refer to a fundamental seeing into the being and reason underlying and shadowed in all that exists and is experienced. The range, depth, and import of this distinction are marked by the way in which the Gospel of John associates *truth* with *life* and with *faith*. Truth refers to the fundamental relation between God and the world, according to which God is distinct from the world, yet involved in it in a personal way.[39]

The concept of truth, in other words, finally refers to "the incisive indicative of God's activity" in the "fundamental and ultimately inescapable" reciprocity between "humanity's filial and human, human and filial participation" in the mystery of God, and not to the Enlightenment myth that rationality consists in being constrained by a precept that regulates the identity between the vocabulary of the mind (or that other foundational locus for the organon of knowledge, language) and the vocabulary of the world. Lehmann thus functions confessionally when he says that truth, "i.e., radical reality" is comprehended in the assertion that "Jesus is the truth! He is the truth primally and primarily in a political sense; consequently and correlatively in a theoretical or philosophical sense."[40]

If truth is primarily used in reference to God's characteristic way of being God in Jesus Christ, then the activities of *doing the truth* and *telling the truth* find in "the incarnation…an Archimedian point on which to stand and from which to move the earth." The notion of doing the truth is taken from the Fourth Gospel (John 3[21]), and is defined by Lehmann as "an act of obedience…through which God may be clearly seen as the source, support and seal of meaningful behavior." To do the truth means "to be what one is in the context of the Truth." Doing the truth is thus tied to the practice of freedom as "a way of being in the truth, and the truth is the reality in relation to which, as gift and response, all created things are free."[41]

Lehmann elaborates on the notion of doing the truth by noting the encounter of truth with the social realities of power and authority in the confrontation of Jesus with Pilate in the narrative of the Fourth Gospel:

> Pilate is unable, either by conviction or by role, to exhibit the unity of truth and power and authority. When power is divorced from truth, authority loses its integrity. When truth is divorced from power, the exercise of power is doomed to self-defeat because power can function only under the spurious authority of self-justification and falsehood.
>
> Jesus, on the other hand, affirms, both by conviction and by role, that the only authority power has is the authority of truth.

The convergence of truth with power and authority, which always occurs within a determinate social setting, undergirds Lehmann's contention that revolution is the lifestyle of truth insofar as the revolutionary shares with Jesus a "common sensitivity to the boundary between the realism of a politics of the power of truth and the pseudo-realism of a politics whose power has lost its claim to truth. The confrontation between Jesus and Pilate underscores the great gulf between *political realism* and *Realpolitik*." Hence to do the truth is to live according to a "divinely renewed order of life in which the will to power has been transformed into the power to will what God wills by the power of God's Messiah."[42]

Only when one recognizes, as Hauerwas puts it, that "all questions of truth and falsity are political," can theologians adequately address "consequently and correlatively in a theoretical or philosophical sense" the matter of speaking the truth. The Cartesian picture of truthfulness, built upon "the metaphors of vision, correspondence, mapping, picturing, and representation," is thus called into question. These metaphors falsely justify (and are, in a vicious turn of circular reasoning, justified by) the presumption that "truth" names the gnostic protocols that comprehend the identity in the difference between the human organon of knowledge (either the Cartesian conception of the mind or the neo-Cartesian notion of language-as-such, the later invariably cast in the singular) and the world. Juxtaposed to this dubious picture of how human discourse and the world of necessity interact is Lehmann's account, according to which truth has to do with the *human* significance and import of what is the case. To speak the truth, in the words of Bonhoeffer, is to speak the *right* or *living word*, an act which "is as much alive as life itself."[43]

Bonhoeffer's understanding of the living or human word, according to Lehmann, makes explicit "the verbal expression of the full complexity and totality of the existing, concrete situation." It is this word "which makes it possible for human beings to be open *for* one another and *to* one another. In so far as the *right* word, or the living word, is instrumental to such an openness of human beings to each other, telling the truth is ethically real." It is the *human* factor in the everyday relations that only exist in and between communities, that is, not merely the factual but "the significant in the factual," which gives to the complex matter of telling the truth its sense and direction. Accordingly, it is the responsibility of theology "to show that the *human* in us all can be rightly discerned and adhered to only in and through the reality of a climate of trust established by the divine humanity of Jesus Christ and the new humanity, however incipient, of all men in Christ." In concert with Bonhoeffer, Lehmann asserts that conformity to the truth cannot be regulated by rules or concepts, for "'God is no general principle, but the Living One who has set me down in a living situation and demands my obedience'...It is the fact that God became incarnate in Jesus Christ, as this fact is spelled out by a theology of messianism, which requires...that the diverse relationships in which men find themselves be taken seriously as bearers of ethical reality and significance."[44]

Lehmann's discussion of the question of truth resembles in certain respects James's definition of the true as "the name of whatever proves itself to be good in the way of belief, and good, too, for definite, assignable reasons." This definition calls into question the modern bifurcation of knowing and doing, as well as its dichotomy between reason and passion, between epistemology and teleology. Lehmann specifically contends against the reified separation between knowledge and purpose in the process of critical inquiry, "the sure persuasion that truth and goodness can be pursued in their own right, independent of desire and interest." He contrasts the modern distinction between truth and goodness with the position affirmed in the *Book of Order of the Presbyterian Church (USA)*, that "truth is in order to goodness; and the great touchstone of truth, its tendency to promote holiness...that there is an inseparable connection between faith and practice, truth and duty. Otherwise it would be of no consequence either to discover truth, or to embrace it." Truth in order to goodness, and thus to maturity in the practice of everyday life, refers to the living word that "is as much alive as life itself."[45]

The performative coordination of truth and goodness embodies a paradigmatic shift in the way we conceive of the relationship of the mind to the practice of everyday life. When we make a truth-claim, we are not drawing a picture of some aspect of the world (though one could invoke this metaphor, so long as she recognizes that it will have the aesthetic character of a portrait rather than a photograph, with all that is entailed in such an artifact) but forming a judgment about the particular circumstances and conditions in which we live, all the while striving to realize our existence in the historical and political fabric of the created order in response to the Spirit of life. But as MacIntyre notes,

> it is important to remember that the presupposed conception of mind is not Cartesian. It is rather of mind as activity, of mind as engaging with the natural and social world in such activities as identification, reidentification, collecting, separating, classifying, and naming in all this by touching, grasping, pointing, breaking down, building up, calling to, answering to, and so on. The mind is adequate with objects insofar as the expectations which it frames on the basis of these activities are not liable to disappointment and remembering which it engages in enables it to return and recover what it had encountered previously, whether the objects themselves are still present or not...falsity is recognized retrospectively as a past inadequacy when the discrepancy between the beliefs of an earlier stage of tradition of enquiry are contrasted with the world of things and persons as it has come to be understood at some later stage. So correspondence or lack of it becomes a feature of developing complex conceptions of truth.

According to Lehmann, when a theologian makes these judgments, she "exhibits the order by which *goodness* is the fruit of *truth*, and forges a creative link between confession and responsibility, between the concern for dogma and the concern about ethics."[46]

In place of speaking about truth as a speculative correspondence between the mind's vocabulary and the vocabulary of the world, Lehmann alludes to a practical congruity, a certain practical fitness or appropriateness, similar to the skills which an artisan develops to use her tools properly, to describe the complex relationship that exists in the course of everyday life between mind and world. God's gift of truth and life in the messianic politics of Jesus, he writes, is congruent with the gift of faith and knowledge through our involvement in the "truth-life syndrome" of a distinctly disciplined style of life, a congruity that cannot be theoretically prescribed with precision, but only is realized in the contingency and particularity which characterizes the performative relationships of everyday life.[47] "Truth," therefore, alludes to the practical congruity of conscience as the members of the community of faith respond in the course of day-to-day existence to the politics of God. Or, if we wish to preserve the terminology of correspondence with respect to the question of truth, it refers to the faithful *co-responding* of the church to the gracious initiative and continuing faithfulness of God's creative and redemptive activity.

According to this account, then, human thought and language do not provide us with nonindexical pictures of objects. Rather, in an almost infinite number of ways, they attend to, consolidate, and extend our real—i.e., historical, social, bodily—relations with the world of which we are a part and to which we are inextricably bound. Lehmann notes in this regard that most persons "are aware that the problem of telling the truth actually does vary according to the relationships in which we find ourselves. In the relations between parents and children, between husband and wife, between friends and friends, between teacher and student, between friend and enemy—in all of these relationships the truth in words varies." In the formative context of conscience, the *koinonia*, these relationships are configured according to the contours and directions of messianic politics of God. Lehmann thus speaks of the *koinonia* as a laboratory of the living word in which "a continuing experiment is going on in the concrete reality and possibility of man's interrelatedness and openness for man."[48]

Consistent with pragmatism's conception of truth, Lehmann contends that the imagery and concepts associated with theological inquiry have an intrinsically instrumental or functional character. In MacIntyre's words,

> The mind, being informed as a result of its engagement with objects, is informed by both images which are or are not adequate—for the mind's purposes—re-presentations of particular objects or sorts of objects and by concepts which are or are not adequate re-presentations of the forms in terms of which objects are grasped and classified. Representation is not as such pic-

turing, but re-presentations. Pictures are only one mode of re-presenting, and their adequacy or inadequacy in functioning as such is always relative to some specific purpose of mind.

Lehmann therefore argues that "the conceptual is always instrumental to the concrete, and the concrete is never self-authenticating but always being fashioned by the dynamics of the self-authenticating activity of God in, with, and under the forms of man's humanity to man of which man's language speaks." In other words, theology, as a second-order activity in the realm of "knowing," serves the communication[49] of faithful modes of life within the church, shaping in concrete ways the character and direction of our relations with God and our neighbors. And conscience, when guided by the "two grand rules of 'right reason' and 'Scripture'," names "the exercise of judgment sensitized by an imaginative grasp of the divine-human involvement in the doing of what it takes to make and to keep human life human."[50] Assertions of truth ultimately function according to the contextual indications of the sense and direction of everyday life lived in the presence and power of the creator and redeemer of life.

The sense of Lehmann's provocative statement that "All truth, not least the truth that sets people free for being human in the world, functions ideologically, i.e., it exerts its power in and through *ad hoc* critical alterations of established patterns and structures," is grounded in this context. He calls these patterns of life *ad hoc* because "contingent happenings and policies, motivations and goals are liberated from the necessity of demonstrating their own ultimacy" by the mystery of divine election. The assertion of truth, which is the culmination of an activity called judging, is never divorced from its particular context, that is, from a sustained consideration of issues of social roles, purpose, desire, motivation, and goals. Truth-claims therefore function in an *ad hoc* manner, exhibiting the timely and timeful interaction between the pattern of actions on the part of a distinct community and its members, on one hand, and the things of this world, on the other. Telling the truth thus renders explicit some aspects of a community's engagement with the world while tacitly relying on others (and for this reason the community needs a self-critical methodology that takes into account the ideological factor).[51]

It follows from this conception of truth, as Lash observes, that "the 'problem' of ideology arises, not from the fact that our ideas are social products, but from our 'forgetfulness' of this fact." Ideological conflicts with respect to the truth-claims of Christians (or those of anyone else, for that matter), therefore, cannot be resolved at the grammatical level of theological inquiry: "The Christian must prove the truth, i.e., the reality and power, the this-sidedness of his believing in practice...That correspondence eludes theoretical demonstration. It can, however, be practically, imperfectly, partially and provisionally *shown* by the character and quality of Christian engagement in patterns of action and suffering, praise and endurance, that refuse to short-cut the quest by the erection of conceptual or institutional absolutes."[52]

In light of the role that ideology plays in all forms of discourse, attention is again focused upon conscience, for it is only through the performative conjunction of reason and motivation that we are engaged concretely—historically and thus politically—in the ideological functioning of truth. As a result, truth also functions *teleologically*, and thus for the church it has an eschatological referent which proleptically intrudes upon present circumstances. It is due to this future referent that humans are involved in the "truth-life syndrome" of God's messianic politics. In the power of this coming kingdom, Christians are free to risk involvement in the configurations, policies, and ideologies of contemporary society and culture, in the freedom that is the product of the righteousness of God's messianic politics. And therefore the "ultimately prevailing values and norms, howsoever diverse they may be, manifest their truth and relevance to what is already there in their power to direct and to sustain social interaction in freedom and order, by nurturing the discernment of what is coming to be as 'the significant-in-the-factual' response to what is."[53] Conversely, falsehood, error, and illusion are characteristics of hypocrisy, i.e., of a lifestyle which stands opposed to that of the truth which initiates, sustains, and consummates human maturity and wholeness.

The notion of reference also functions differently in Lehmann's discussion of truth. A Cartesian approach which maintains that thoughts and words mirror or picture the world loses the metaphorical sense of reference as "pointing" to something. Such an ahistorical and disembodied approach attempts to argue that a person in some literal fashion "gesticulates with words."[54] Lehmann juxtaposes to this speculative theory of reference what might best be called a performative doctrine of reference, which is realized through the coherence of practices, relations, and style of life that are embodied in, and bodied forth by, the messianic politics of the church. For example, with respect to the word God, he argues that in the context of biblical politics, the word *God* acquires a specific and humanizing referentiality. The word *God* refers to him who, in the power of the future that is coming to be, picks up the humanizing pieces of the past and makes a humane and humanizing present. Thus the human meaning of reality is a compound of this divine pressure upon the dynamics and the shape of things, experienced as the moment of truth and the point of no return; and its *metaphorical* description and communication.[55]

It is due solely to this context that the most disputed word in the vocabulary of the church, *God*, "properly refers to the Father of Jesus Christ, and with him and through him of all 'who in his great mercy (have been given) new birth into a living hope by the resurrection of Jesus Christ from the dead' (1 Peter 1[3])." A performative account of reference is predicated on the association in the Gospel of John of *truth* with *life* and with *faith*, and particularly on the *filial* relation between the divine mystery and the adventure of human existence,

> according to which God is distinct from the world, yet involved in it in a personal way. He brings the world to pass and to pass away. He sustains, renews, and fulfills the world in its coming to pass and in its passing away. He is the Giver of life and the shaper of purposes that guarantee to *life* an ultimacy that death cannot claim; to *hope* a certainty that what is coming to be is a surer sign of life's meaning than what is; and to *faith* the assurance that it makes sense to trust what faith knows in this life about this life and about the life of the world to come.[56]

Theology cannot ultimately tell us whether such references to God make good sense (nor can any other form of human inquiry), for the believer refers to God in the particularity and contingency of her existence, not through words-as-such, but through conscience, where "the aims and the direction, the motivations and the decisions, the instruments and the structures of human interrelatedness are forged into a pattern of response —*a style of life*." But as Lash notes, "there is a sense, however obscure and indirect, in which a disciplined attention to linguistic usage can *show* us something of the character of the objects of our discourse (and therefore, possibly, something of the character of our relationship to God)."[57] In the next chapter, therefore, we shall attend to this "grammatical" relationship between the performative reasoning of conscience and the doctrinal protocols of the church.

NOTES

[1]Lehmann, "On Doing Theology," 132–33. Lehmann here implicitly affirms what Lash makes explicit in an examination of tradition and authority, which is that the effort to preserve the tradition untouched, and the attempt to do theology "from scratch," as it were, are both impossible. Lash, *Theology on the Way to Emmaus*, 53–58.

[2]Bernstein, *Praxis and Action*, 316; Karl Barth, *Evangelische Theologie im 19. Jahrhundert, Theologische Studien*, eds. Karl Barth and Max Geiger, vol. 49 (Zurich: Evangelischer Verlag Ag. Zollikon, 1957), 3, 16; Lehmann, "On Doing Theology," 130–32; *Ideology and Incarnation*, 6; Lash, *Theology on the Way to Emmaus*, 14. Lash's admonition about the domestic character of God is equally applicable to the metaphorical description of God in feminine imagery. I shall deal with the question of inclusive language in more detail in the next chapter.

[3]Karl Barth, "Concluding Unscientific Postscript on Schleiermacher," *The Theology of Schleiermacher*, ed. Dietrich Ritschl (Grand Rapids, MI: William B. Eerdmans Publishing Company, 1982), 278; Karl Barth, *Ethics*, ed. Dietrich Braun (New York: The Seabury Press, 1981), 481.

[4]Lehmann, "On Doing Theology," 134; *Ethics*, 112, 322–24; Lash, *Easter in Ordinary*, 268.

[5]Lehmann, *Ethics*, 17, 84; *Transfiguration*, 230–31; "On Doing Theology," 123, 126.

[6]Lehmann, "The Context of Theological Inquiry," 71.

[7]Ludwig Feuerbach, *Principles of the Philosophy of the Future*, trans. Manfred H. Vogel (Indianapolis: Bobbs-Merrill, 1966; Indianapolis: Hackett Publishing Company, 1986); Calvin, *Institutes*, 1.1.1, 20:35; Lehmann, *Transfiguration*, 230–31. "As Calvin read the Bible amidst the ferment and fomentation of his days," says Lehmann, "he reports his conviction that the discernment of wisdom involved a movement from the Scriptures to the knowledge of God in Christ without disallowing the possibility of setting out from the knowledge of human things. Beginning with 'the knowledge of ourselves', as Feuerbach did, does not necessarily exclude a livelier appropriation of Scripture, as Feuerbach appears to have done."

[8]Lehmann, "On Doing Theology," 123; *Transfiguration*, 232.

[9]Lehmann, "The Context of Theological Inquiry," 65, 67; *Ethics*, 147, 349; "On Doing Theology," 132f; "Black Theology and 'Christian' Theology," 145.

[10]Lehmann, *Ethics*, 29; Lash, *Theology on the Way to Emmaus*, 43; David B. Burrell, CSC, *Aquinas: God and Action* (Notre Dame, IN: University of Notre Dame Press, 1979), 178; Brian Wicker, *The Story-Shaped World: Fiction and Metaphysics: Some Variations on a Theme* (Notre Dame, IN: University of Notre Dame Press, 1975), 27. I shall deal with the roles that metaphor, narrative, and dogma play in theology more fully in the next chapter.

[11]Lehmann, "On Doing Theology," 133; Johann Baptist Metz, *Faith in History and Society: Toward a Practical Fundamental Theology*, trans. David Smith (New York: The Seabury Press, 1980), 195; Rowan Williams, *Resurrection: Interpreting the Easter Gospel* (New York: The Pilgrim Press, 1982), 30–31.

[12]Lehmann, *Ethics*, 70, 92, 84–86, 153; "Black Theology and 'Christian' Theology," 145; "The Formative Power of Particularity," 312.

[13]Lehmann, "On Doing Theology," 132f; "Black Theology and 'Christian' Theology," 145, 148; Herbert McCabe, OP, *God Matters* (London: Geoffrey Chapman, 1987), 48.

[14]Lehmann, "On Doing Theology," 135–36.

[15]Lehmann, "Black Theology and 'Christian Theology," 148. This focus on black theology is not exclusive, but opens up a dialogue with other groups who have been systematically excluded from modernity's "conversation."

[16]Lehmann, "The Context of Theological Inquiry," 69–70.

[17]Rouse, *Knowledge and Power*, 19.

[18]Lehmann, *Ideology and Incarnation*, 21, 22; *Transfiguration*, 132, 278.

[19]Lehmann, "Jesus Christ and Theological Symbolization," 13; cf. Paul Lehmann, *Christianity and Community* (Chapel Hill, NC: The Committee on Convocations and Lectures of the University of North Carolina at Chapel Hill); "Truth is in Order to Goodness," *Theology Today* 6 (October 1949): 348–60; *Your Freedom is in Trouble* (New York: National Student Council of the YMCA and YWCA, 1954); *Ideology and Incarnation*; and "Messiah and Metaphor." Richard Rorty, "Pragmatism, Relativism, Irrationalism," *Consequences of Pragmatism*, (Minneapolis: University of Minnesota Press, 1982), 171, 175.

[20]Lehmann, "On Doing Theology," 132–34; *Ethics*, 14, 103–104, 271–72; "The Metaphorical Reciprocity Between Theology and Law," 181.

[21]Stanley Hauerwas, The *Peaceable Kingdom: A Primer in Christian Ethics* (Notre Dame, IN: University of Notre Dame Press, 1983), 54; Lehmann, "On Doing Theology," 136; *Ethics*, 97.

[22]Lehmann, *Ethics*, 102–103; "Piety, Power, and Politics," 58; *Transfiguration*, 230. As MacIntyre notes, the *poetic* is not the sole property of the poet, but names that which enables every language-user, by virtue of those habits and relations that are inherently a part of a particular community and tradition, "to know how to go on and to go further." MacIntyre, *Whose Justice? Which Rationality?*, 382.

[23]Lash, *Theology on the Way to Emmaus*, 53.

[24]West, *Prophesy Deliverance!*, 21; Lehmann, *Ethics*, 14.

[25]Lehmann, *Ethics*, 193, 199, 202; William James, *Pragmatism* (New York: Longmans, Green and Co., 1908), 76, 194.

[26]Dewey, *The Quest for Certainty*, 23; West, *Prophesy Deliverance!*, 51.

[27]Rorty, "Pragmatism, Relativism, Irrationalism," 164; Pannenberg, *Theology and the Philosophy of Science*, 4. See also Theodor Adorno, *Against Epistemology: A Metacritique*; Bernstein, *Praxis and Action*; and Lamb, *Solidarity with Victims*, 33–37, 73–75.

[28]Lehmann, "On Doing Theology," 123; cf.*Ethics*, 192–200; Hauerwas, *After Christendom?*, 182.

[29]Lehmann, "A Christian Alternative to Natural Law," 522, 530–31; "On Doing Theology," 122; *Ideology and Incarnation*, 24. Rorty, "Pragmatism, Relativism, Irrationalism," 171–72.

[30]Rorty, "Pragmatism, Relativism, Irrationalism," 164; MacIntyre, *Whose Justice? Which Rationality?*, p.356; Rouse, *Knowledge and Power*, 63; Lehmann, *Ethics*, 192–93.

[31]Lehmann, *Ethics*, 102, 194, 199; William James, *The Meaning of Truth* (New York: Longmans, Green and Co., 1909), 184–86; James, *Pragmatism*, 194; Bernstein, *Praxis and Action*, 219; Rorty, Consequences of Pragmatism, xviii–xix; Rorty, "Pragmatism,

Relativism, Irrationalism," 162–63; Rouse, *Knowledge and Power*, 23. Hauerwas spells out the practical import of this alternative picture of human existence in his delightful discussion of "How We Lay Bricks and Make Disciples," *After Christendom?*, 93–111.

[32]Lehmann, *Ethics*, 352–53; MacIntyre, *Whose Justice? Which Rationality?*, 382; Paul L. Lehmann, "Integrity of Heart: A Comment upon the Preceding Paper," *Ecumenical Dialogue at Harvard: The Roman Catholic-Protestant Colloquium*, eds. Samuel H. Miller and G. Ernest Wright (Cambridge: Harvard University Press, Belknap Press, 1964), 279.

[33]Lehmann, "The Context of Theological Inquiry," 67; "The Formative Power of Particularity," 310; Rorty, "Pragmatism, Relativism, Irrationalism," 163.

[34]Rorty, "Pragmatism, Relativism, Irrationalism," 164; Lehmann, *Ethics*, 316; "On Doing Theology," 133; Milbank, "The End of Dialogue," 181.

[35]Lehmann, "On Doing Theology," 124, 130; "The Formative Power of Particularity," 310.

[36]Lehmann, "On Doing Theology," 136; "The Tri-unity of God," 48; "Jesus Christ and Theological Symbolization," 15, 22, 23; Rouse, *Knowledge and Power*, 60.

[37]Lehmann, *Transfiguration*, 56–58, 274; "The Context of Theological Inquiry, 64.

[38]Lehmann, "Messiah and Metaphor," 25–27; *Ideology and Incarnation*, 21–23; "The Formative Power of Particularity," 309–10; *Ethics*, 193; *Transfiguration*, 53; Rorty, "Pragmatism, Relativism, Irrationalism," 162.

[39]Lehmann, *Ethics*, 159–60; *Transfiguration*, 53–54.

[40]Lehmann, *Ethics*, 160; *Transfiguration*, 54, 57.

[41]Lehmann, *Ideology and Incarnation*, 27; "On Doing Theology," 119; *Ethics*, 159; *Transfiguration*, 242.

[42]Lehmann, *Transfiguration*, 5, 24, 55–56; *Ethics*, 97.

[43]Hauerwas, *After Christendom?*, 24; Rorty, "Pragmatism, Relativism, Irrationalism," 164; Lehmann, *Ethics*, 129; Bonhoeffer, *Ethics*, 364–65.

[44]Lehmann, *Ethics*, 130–31; "The Commandments and the Common Life," 347, 355; Bonhoeffer, *Ethics*, 69, 364.

[45]James, *Pragmatism*, 76; *The Constitution of the Presbyterian Church (U.S.A.): Part II: Book of Order* (New York: The Office of the General Assembly of the Presbyterian Church (U.S.A.), 1981), G–1.0304; Lehmann, "Truth is Order to Goodness," 348, 350; *Ethics*, 321; Bonhoeffer, *Ethics*, 365. Incidentally, Lehmann states that this affirmation on the part of Presbyterians represents one of Calvinism's "brighter moments of faithfulness to Calvin."

[46]MacIntyre, *Whose Justice? Which Rationality?*, 356–57; Lehmann, "On Doing Theology," 136, my emphasis.

[47]Lehmann, *Transfiguration*, 54; "Black Theology and 'Christian' Theology," 145. Cf. "A Christian Alternative to Natural Law," 539; "On Doing Theology," 128; and especially "The Tri-unity of God," 41.

[48]Lehmann, *Ethics*, 130–31.

[49]As I noted in chapter four, the sense of the term communication within the *koinonia* cannot be limited to, nor grounded in, mere "linguisticality," but rather partakes of the New Testament and Elizabethan sense of the word, according to which a person actually exists only in relationships with others, and in which each shares of herself with the other.

⁵⁰MacIntyre, *Whose Justice? Which Rationality?*, 356–57; Lehmann, *Ethics*, 248, 316.

⁵¹Lehmann, *Transfiguration*, 278; "Jesus Christ and Theological Symbolization," 17, 20–21; "The Context of Theological Inquiry," 69–70.

⁵²Lash, *Theology on the Way to Emmaus*, 116, 136.

⁵³Lehmann, *Transfiguration*, 54; "The Commandments and the Common Life," 352.

⁵⁴Ludwig Wittgenstein, *Culture and Value*, trans. Peter Winch (Chicago: The University of Chicago Press, 1980), 85e.

⁵⁵Lehmann, *Transfiguration*, 234.

⁵⁶Lehmann, *Transfiguration*, 53–54.

⁵⁷Lehmann, *Ethics*, 288; Lash, *Theology on the Way to Emmaus*, 113.

Chapter 7

POETICS OF THE THEOLOGICAL

The liberating sense and power of conscience, writes Lehmann, ultimately reside in "contextual foundations and parabolic directives." The paradigmatic forms of Jewish and Christian discourse, in other words, are not founded on pictorial representations of either "external" objects or "internal" structures of human subjectivity, nor are they grounded in some type of rule. Rather they rely on the communicative power of metaphor and narrative, embedded within the patterns of activity fostered in the *koinonia*. As such, Lash reminds us, these forms are

> autobiographical both in the sense that they are "self-involving"…and in the sense that, as self-involving, they situate the speaker (or the group for which he or she is a spokesman) in a particular cultural, historical tradition: "My father was a wandering Aramean." Christians are tellers of a tale, narrators of a story which we tell as our story, as a story in which we acknowledge ourselves to be participants. The Christian creeds are abbreviated statements of a story which, as the autobiography of the narrators and of the Christ "in whom" they seek to tell their story, is a *particular* story and which yet, as the story of the origin, course and destiny of the world, purports to express what is *universally* the case.[1]

Nevertheless, while these paradigmatic forms are both irreducible and basic, as the products of particular communities and cultures they are especially susceptible to ideological distortion and idolatrous self-justification. As a result, "countervailing influences" are required "to discipline and purify faith's tendency to construct a significance which, *as* constructed, is at best distorted and, at worst, illusory."[2] The rectitude of doctrine, when construed as grammatical reflection on actual performance, constitutes one of the principal ways the Christian community has traditionally disciplined its all-too-human tendency toward distortion and illusion. However, the performative relationships between metaphor, narrative, and doctrine cannot be adequately conceived in abstraction from each other or from the historical contingency which marks the practice of everyday life within the *koinonia*. The intelligibility and coherence of conscience does not reside solely with metaphor, narrative, or doctrine, as they are the product of their performative interrelation within the eucharistic community. In this chapter, therefore, I shall attend to these three components of Christian discourse *and* to their coherence in the patterns of everyday life and the institutional forms that comprise the community of faith.

The Metaphorical Directives of the Politics of God

Lehmann's discussion of the metaphorical intentionalities[3] of Scripture begins with "The scriptural preoccupation with a God who speaks, who is known in and through 'his Word'." He argues that this biblical *leitmotif* should not be read anthropomorphically, for it pertains to "a power of imaginative apprehension which rejects definition but does not forswear description as man's way of responding to and reflecting upon what God is doing in the world." Hence the fundamental sense and direction of Scripture is rooted in parabolic description. As such, the humanizing activity of the messianic politics of God, juxtaposed metaphorically to our own labors, opens up a hermeneutical option that is congruent with "the hermeneutical surmise at the frontier of [modernity's] radical doubt." The practice of everyday life within the Christian community, and the identity of Christianity, is thus a matter of the historical production of the *koinonia*, in the power of the Spirit, through the metaphorical trajectories of Scripture.[4]

According to Lehmann, "Christian apperception, Christian sensibility, and a Christian way of thinking...do not interpret the goings-on in the world of time and space and things 'off the pages of the Bible', as it were. Nor do they interpret the Bible 'off the pages' of the daily goings-on in the world of time and space and things. There is a more appropriate hermeneutical option." He states that "the notable achievement of the Higher Criticism of the Scriptures is its liberation of biblical images from the debilitating dominion of textual literalism and for the metaphorical understanding and interpretation of the *locus de Scriptura sacra*." This *locus*, he adds, always included "both the canon of Scripture and the dogmatic tradition and, at least until Schleiermacher at the beginning of the nineteenth century, was the starting point for all responsible theological thinking and interpretation." The enduring fruit of the liberation of Scripture's metaphoric images has to do with the fact that they have been set "free from their confinement by the text, free for the literary and historical context in which biblical imagination could give pointed expression to what God is doing in the world." Lehmann therefore strives to move away from a *constantive* hermeneutics, according to which the text in some mysterious way "contains" meaning, and toward a *performative* account of meaning, according to which the sense and direction of the Bible's images and stories is inextricably bound to the "company" they keep within the contingencies of everyday life, i.e., within the configuration of practices, social roles, and purposes which forms the context for conscience.[5]

According to Lehmann, Barth's principal contribution to theology has to do with the way he "delivered theological language and conceptuality from bondage to propositional logic and joined them once again to poetry," that is, to the metaphorical exploration of the content and meaning of the language of dogmatics. Lehmann characterizes Barth's recovery of the poetic sensibility of theology as a "knowledgeable and zealous theological attempt to liberate orthodoxy from orthodox literalism." To borrow a term from Burrell, Barth helps theology re-establish the "grammatical" relationship between biblical metaphor and metaphysical analogy, and thus between art and knowledge, between the parabolic imagery of Scripture and the dogmatic traditions of the church. This relationship also, in Hauerwas's words, frees theological inquiry from "The very idea of systematic theology [which] was a result of a church with hegemonic power that belied the very substance that made it church to begin with."[6]

In order to explore the performative frontier which Barth's insights open up with respect to the interpretation of Scripture, Lehmann relies on the long-standing tradition of non-literal or figurative interpretation of texts which the church inherited from the early Fathers. In this tradition "Christian theologians drew particularly upon hermeneutical practices long familiar in rabbinic Judaism and from the Stoic interpretation of Homer." He specifically appeals to Origen's distinction between the literal and the spiritual sense of Scripture, and also to Augustine's insistence that Scripture is to be interpreted tropically. Augustine in particular distinguishes between simple tropes, which relate to the resemblance of properties, and metaphors, which pertain to the resemblance of relations. "Accordingly," says Lehmann, "the paradigmatic interpretation of certain New Testament passages...is tropic in character," and as such must be positioned within the metaphorical intentionalities of "an incarnational hermeneutics."[7]

Metaphor (or parabolic imagery, as Lehmann also refers to it) offers an imaginative description of what is otherwise incommensurate—the ways of God and the ways of humankind. He argues that "the parabolic image, far from being a 'blind alley', is the image which more precisely than any other juxtaposes 'inconfusedly (and) inseparably' the ways of God and the ways of man. The formative biblical images partake of this parabolic power. Consequently, they are the stuff of authentic reflection upon and description of the activity of God." When regarded from the standpoint of the *koinonia*, "the human meaning of reality is a compound of divine pressure upon the dynamics and the shape of things, experienced as the moment of truth and the point of no return; *and* its metaphorical description and communication." The parabolic image thus articulates the divine-human relationship which is realized in the historical context of the *koinonia*. The figurative tendencies of metaphor "break open the break-through of the divine presence and pressure upon the shape of things to come." As a result, says Lehmann, "these images point precisely to 'the realness of God' and the responsiveness of man of which the knowledge of faith is comprised."[8]

We should note in passing Lehmann's use of the Chalcedonian definition of the two natures and the one person of Christ to elaborate upon the communicative power of the parabolic image. Metaphor, unlike analogy and simile, does not lead the imagination to what is judged to be the truth by means of drawing comparisons. He thus claims, quite ironically, that

> metaphor is a deliberate lie which contains the truth not as solution, but in solution. It is now the explanation by means of an exploded diagram. This is the way of analogy: we start by allowing that the two things being compared are not the same but resemble each other, and then go on by a kind of parsing of the parts, as means of illustrating the nature of the whole. The metaphor deals simultaneously with the things in themselves and in their union, demanding that we assemble even as we dissemble—that we pursue unity through a willing duplicity with the facts. The analogy illustrates, the metaphor illuminates.

Another way of distinguishing between the communicative power of metaphor and analogy, states Lehmann, is that "the experience of metaphor...

can be thought of as an answer to the child-styled conundrum, 'When is a comparison not a comparison?' Answer: 'When it is a metaphor!'"[9]

The parabolic image, therefore, is not a comparison of two subjects, nor can it be reduced either to a more fundamental (and thus analogical) conception of God's being and activity or (as is the habit of most theologians since the time of Schleiermacher) to some universal facet of human consciousness or existence which can be explored apart from participation in the *koinonia*. In other words, the two terms of a metaphor cannot be divorced from their particular juxtaposition. Metaphor is "that process of identification which catches the truth by allowing the lie…by considering diverse elements not separately but together…" The interpretive tension of metaphor, imaginatively juxtaposing the ways of God and the ways of humanity in the context of a single utterance, is the distinctive mark of parabolic imagery. The Bible's metaphorical images do not draw comparisons within the commonplace, but simultaneously make use of, and depart from, accustomed frames of reference from the standpoint of messianic politics, which in turn is disclosed in and through the *koinonia*: "So on the frontier where we are trying to get beyond the '*cache-montre*' of the '*conscience-fasse*' where there is this running dialogue between faith and doubt, God juxtaposes to the mystery of our own incognito, the mystery of His."[10]

In her important study of the role of metaphor in religious language, Janet Soskice affirms and amplifies Lehmann's account of Scripture's parabolic imagery, arguing that metaphor has a unique cognitive ability to generate new perspectives. She emphasizes three aspects in a general theory of metaphor. First, she maintains that the meaning of a metaphor is "the consequence of the interanimation of words in a complete utterance." In particular, Soskice distinguishes between the tenor of a metaphor, its underlying subject, and its linguistic vehicle. The distinction between tenor and vehicle, however, must not be construed as a separation of two distinct subjects which are somehow compared, contrasted or otherwise treated in a bifurcated manner, but as a tensive unity and an imaginative strain that "conjointly depict and illumine." To state the matter concisely, "the metaphor is the product of the whole."[11]

Second, Soskice contends that each metaphor involves two or more different networks of associated meaning that ground the imaginative tension between its tenor and vehicle. A metaphor, in other words, invokes multiple interpretive models which constitute the associative networks of its imagery: "We might consider the associative network of a term as its place-

ment in a semantic field where the 'value' of the term is fixed not simply
by the terms for which it might be exchanged...but also by the entities of
which the term would customarily be predicated." The performative context of models and networks of meaning helps to distinguish between the
designations of "literal" and "metaphorical" with respect to their communicative value. She says that "what we call 'literal' usage is accustomed usage
and that metaphorical usages...begin their careers outside the standard lexi-
con." This distinction between "literal" as customary speech and "metaphor" as innovative and even counter-hegemonic discourse secures her
claim that metaphors are not comparisons containing two distinct subjects
or positing two meanings or truth-values, one "literally false" and the other
"metaphorically true." The metaphor "suggests a community of relations"
within the context of a complete utterance, and thus it cannot be reduced to
its more "literal" or customary components. In other words, the supposition that metaphor is either a linguistic ornament or a substitution for what
can be satisfactorily understood through some type of "literal" comparison
does not hold up to scrutiny.[12]

Finally, says Soskice, the meaning of a metaphor is that of a complete
utterance as concretely employed by a particular speaker in a determinate
context. This context, moreover, is inextricably related to an interpretive
community and a tradition of inquiry which provide the descriptive vocabulary and communal authority by which individual experiences articulated
by metaphor are assessed: "Community is essential because each speaker is
a member of a particular community of interest, which provides the context for his referential claims. A great part of our referential activity depends on what Putnam has called a 'division of linguistic labour', that is,
we rely on authoritative members of our community to ground referring
expressions."[13]

Soskice identifies in her study of metaphor many of the formal components of the imagery contained in Scripture. In particular, her assertion
that metaphor is a linguistic device which interanimates through juxtaposition the tenor and vehicle of a parabolic image in a unique and irreducible
manner ("inconfusedly and inseparably") specifies the distinctive semiotic
structure of the Bible's parabolic imagery, as does her claim that metaphorical utterances invoke both particular associative networks and models
of meaning, and an interpretive community and tradition. It is the performative content of concrete historical networks, however, that is ultimately
at stake in any meaningful discussion of metaphor.

According to Lehmann, the question of human existence in a (post)-modern world is tied to the search for the essential or root metaphor. He claims that there are two basic paradigms for realizing the sense and direction of everyday life, and these are sharply juxtaposed through their respective metaphorical networks. One paradigm is enunciated via the messianic metaphor around the two "adams"—Adam and Christ—and the other heuristically centered on the philosophy of Jean-Paul Sartre and the metaphorical tendencies of its Cartesian anthropology. The question of human existence in a world desperately trying to come of age is "whether man is a rebel, or free; whether man by free self-affirmation can go it alone without God, without guilt, without neighbor or whether in his knowledge of good and evil, the image of Christ is the healing link between man's origin and his destiny." With respect to this fundamental juxtaposition, Lehmann argues that

> the Adam-Christ model provides a prototypical discussion, or prototypical presentation of a structure of interpretation, of inquiry, of self-understanding, of motivation in which man ever and again, is brought back to the damning option: to have a world of his own making, or to receive a world whose fulfilling destiny is intrinsic to its origin and whose origin is ever and again discovered as a gift available to all who participate with responsible i.e., (responding) creativity in the world's appointed purposes.

And thus we return again to a primary characteristic of the formative biblical images, that they are paradigmatically political metaphors, with the *koinonia* of the church and the modern nation-state as the two communities in which the truth-falsehood dilemma of these essential metaphors continually confronts us.[14]

Nevertheless, there are two points of contention between Lehmann and Soskice that help distinguish the respective emphases of their accounts of metaphor and theological inquiry. The first has to do with what one can say about the reality and activity of God by means of metaphor. Soskice restricts rather severely what can be said of God, and argues that metaphorical language such as the claim that "'God is spirit'...denominates rather than describes God, or more precisely, it denominates the source of thousands of experiences which Jews and Christians have spoken of, using the descriptive language at their disposal as the working of the spirit, and which they take to be God." By contrast, Lehmann contends that far more can be said with metaphor than Soskice would allow. He makes in this regard a crucial distinction between definition and description, which has no parallel in Soskice's book, but which enables the biblical metaphors to express much about the character of the messianic utterance of God. As a result, Lehmann agrees with Soskice that our language cannot in any way capture the mystery of God, that is, it cannot *define* the divine nature. But the parabolic imagery of Scripture does authorize us to *describe* in appropriate ways the self disclosing, self-communication of the triune God, thus liberating the biblical images from the biblical text and permitting us to go on and go further on the basis of the associative networks of meaning that Soskice rightly identifies as one of the characteristic marks of metaphor. For Lehmann, the primary network of signification for metaphorically describing the creative and redemptive activity of God is the realm of politics, and thus the political context of the biblical story acts as the paradigmatic network for articulating the messianic metaphor, to which all other types of images are related in the *koinonia*.

We must not forget, however, that these images are products of a traumatic process which, as Lehmann notes, consists of "a movement toward consummation via deliverance. To the paradox of the great defection has been juxtaposed the paradox of the great denouement. Creation : sin— judgment : redemption! These are the twin anvils upon which the humanity of man is being hammered out and hammered into being." Unless we call to mind the political context from which the metaphors of the biblical narrative initially emerged, says Lash,

> we too easily forget that these images, and the stories in which they occur— within the complex history of conflict and clarification which is the history of the Jewish and Christian people—were usually produced in criticism of inhuman (and hence "ungodly") practices. God is *not* a king or father as other kings and fathers are; he, unlike all other shepherds, is the *good* shepherd; unlike other judges, God judges justly, and so on. In other words, it is only through the redemptive transformation of our human practices that we can acquire some sense of what the truth of these images might be when used as metaphors for our relation to the unknown God.[15]

The second point of contention between Lehmann and Soskice is related to the first, and has to do with Soskice's latent Cartesianism. It seems likely that Soskice does not distinguish between definition and description in her otherwise powerful account of metaphor because she continues to rely on the imagery of depicting reality, of mapping and picturing the world, thus perpetuating the (post)modern metaphor for knowledge as that mental bridge which establishes a dependable relation between the *external* world and the experience of the *knowing* subject. Thus her project continues to depend, albeit unwittingly, on those ocular metaphors, particularly that of the disinterested, disembodied spectator, which have traditionally informed modern anthropology. From the standpoint of Lehmann, on the other hand, the point of language is not to *picture* a world external to an uninvolved and disembodied spectator, but to act as a catalyst for our bodily engagement with a reality to which we are inextricably linked, providing form and direction to our everyday lives in obedient response to its creator, redeemer, and sustainer. According to Lehmann, therefore, it is *behavior* and not an abstract concept of "language" that is "the parabolic bearer of a new humanity."[16] What Soskice refers to as networks or models of meaning associated with the contextual use of metaphor might more accurately be spoken of as networks or patterns of activity that function as paradigmatic (and hence sacramental) indications of the mystery and grace of God's activity in the world.

Moreover, the point of my criticism regarding Soskice's assertion that the principal function of language is to "depict" the world is not that she believes that our representations are in some way privileged or that "the terms of a mature science mirror the world in an unrevisable fashion." It is rather the controlling influence of the ocular imagery that prescribes how language normatively functions in the world to which I object. To say that language gives us "descriptions of...external reality," and that "our statements provide an 'epistemic access'...to the world," as Soskice does,[17] unwittingly perpetuates the misconception that the "problems of knowledge are...problems of *engineering*—of how the little person [lurking somewhere in my head] might make contact, build bridges, with the 'outside' world."[18] It is not the claim that some descriptions might be privileged or unrevisable that entangle her position within this imagery, nor is enough for her to disavow this claim in order to avoid its dubious assumptions.

Lehmann states that the power of the biblical story to save relies upon "the metaphorical indication of the correspondence between the biblical and the human meaning of politics." Because the biblical metaphors and their associative networks are not separate entities but are presented to us as interwoven threads of the fabric which is the comprehensive biblical story, he refers to Scripture as "'a well of living water', i.e., an inexhaustible reservoir of the formative images in terms of which the humanization of life may be both conceptually and behaviorally exhibited." However, as Lash has already reminded us, the interaction between the biblical metaphors and the narratives of Scripture works in both directions. Lehmann, referring to modern developments in biblical studies, notes that

> in the providence of God and the confusion of men, a whole find of stuff, artifactual and literally, has recently been come upon which promises to deliver us all from the hegemony of J. D. E. and P. and put right with the stubborn historicity of the semitic way of apprehending. This way assigns priority to the function of STORY in the search for the essential metaphor. Story is not what Plato said it was, though not unrelated to it. Story is what you tell from one generation to another about the wonderful works of God; story is the way you tell the truth by lying; story is the way you lie not for truth's sake, but at the service of truth.
>
> Now the messianic metaphor comes to us by story...pinpointed at the crucial point of identification of God with man in such a way that man identifies himself. This self-identifying, self-communication of God frees man for the self-identifying freedom, in Auden-Cox language, "To name every what in his world."[19]

In order to follow the logic embedded in the relationship between metaphor and story, then, we need to look at how the category of narrative properly functions in theology.

The Narrative Configuration of the Politics of God

The fundamental sense and direction of the biblical metaphors which point to the messianic politics of God take intrinsically narrative form. Narrative, Lehmann contends, is the form of discourse in Scripture which spells out the contours and dynamics of the eschatological transfiguration of politics, and therefore indicates the way in which human maturity and wholeness are historically realized through the conscience that is formed by, and sensitive to, the redemptive activity of God. Consequently, both the messianic dynamics of reality and the everyday life of the *koinonia* that is the parabolic bearer of these dynamics only become concretely human in terms of "an experienced story of covenant, exodus, advent, crucifixion, and parousia."[20]

While Lehmann does not offer a detailed analysis of how narrative properly functions in theology, one finds in his writings some clues that offer significant insights into the role of the category of story in theological inquiry. He does state that "At the profoundest level, the capstone of a theory of social structures, as of an adequately integrative cultural context, is the reciprocity between sociological reality and a saving story." A saving story is a narrative that "offers insights and language, and through these a power of symbolization and structuralization through which the tension, and ultimately the conflict, between gratitude and power in social interaction are overcome in a social order that is instrumental to the freedom that being human takes." The biblical story, in short, is "the narration in the power of language and of social cohesion of what it takes to be and to stay human in the world."[21]

Story, simply put, shapes and directs the practice of everyday life. Alluding to the narrative format of the politics of God, Lehmann argues that

> The word story...refers to the way in which one generation tells another how the future shapes the present out of the past; how destiny draws heritage into the human reality and meaning of experience, which is always a compound of happening, hope, and remembrance; how promise and disillusionment, celebration and suffering, joy and pain, forgiveness and guilt, renewal and failure, transfigure the human condition and are transfigured in it. In this way "the wonderful works of God" are made known both to those who believe in him and to those who no longer believe in him; both to those who are afar off and to those who are nigh.[22]

According to this account of narrative, story functions not as a category or principle of transcendental consciousness, but as the *historically* necessary mode of discourse which sustains a particular community and its individual members through time. Moreover, as Greg Jones has observed, "It is certainly true that there is a narrative quality to human life that is morally significant. But that is not the primary claim Christians are concerned to make. It is rather that the biblical *narrative* seeks to incorporate all people into God's narrative."[23]

"Consequently," states Lehmann, "at the center—where the action is—story is the mode of experience of a presence in the present whose power liberates as it binds and binds as it liberates." In short, narrative constitutes "the verbal form of freedom—i.e., what it takes to be and to stay human in the world—and that which shapes the content of freedom," a sign that the experience of the messianic power and presence in history "has changed a way of thinking, and that a way of thinking has changed experience." Only through the power of a liberating story does character interact with circumstance to offer the possibility that a form of life could achieve what it takes to realize within history the eschatological contours of human maturity and wholeness. The biblical narratives focus the meaning of human life around the presence and power of the future disclosed within the *koinonia* as the historical convergence of creation and consummation, such that the promise and prospect of the age to come are displayed in the political dynamics of the present.[24]

According to Lehmann, the primary *leitmotif* of the biblical story centers upon the confrontation between the creative intentions of God, exhibited in terms of the divine will to fellowship, and the rebellion and resistance of humanity, narrated in terms of the disobedience and distortion of the will to power. The narrative reaches its apogee in the advent of the Messiah and the messianic community, where the principal motif moves through the great twin paradoxes of creation : sin and judgment : redemption, and toward the goal of human maturity and wholeness. Lehmann describes these two paradoxes of the biblical story as the "twin anvils" upon which the maturity and wholeness of human life in the present age are being hammered out and hammered into the image of Christ by the political dynamics of the divine activity.[25] Robert Alter summarizes the dialectical tension embedded in this story:

> The ancient Hebrew writers...seek through the process of narrative realization to reveal the enactment of God's purposes in historical events. This enactment, however, is continuously complicated by a perception of two, approximately parallel, dialectical tensions. One is a tension between the divine plan and the disorderly character of actual historical events, or, to translate this opposition into specifically biblical terms, between the divine promise and its ostensible failure to be fulfilled; the other is a tension between God's will, His providential guidance, and human freedom, the refractory nature of man.[26]

At stake in the biblical story are the divine and human realities of power in history. The reality and significance of power, Lehmann writes, are focused by this narrative upon the faithfulness and righteousness of God's activity in the world and therefore upon humankind's response to the divine politics. He states that the prophets and Jesus advance righteousness as the test case of covenantal obedience and the key to the justice which is purposed by God for reconciliation. The ideas of righteousness and justice are interchangeable terms in the biblical story, each expressing "God's way of being true to the purposes for which human life and human living were covenanted." Justice, states Lehmann,

> is the critical link between the power of responsibility and the responsibility
> of power because justice is the righteousness of God in action, setting right
> what is not right in the world. In doing so, the praxis of justice exposes the
> human reality of enmity as the point of entry for the healing of the alienation
> which reconciliation is purposed to overcome. Reconciliation is the presup-
> position and purpose of justice. Justice is the direction finder of the way to
> reconciliation.[27]

"Justice" thus stands as the code word denoting the convergence of the
biblical story with the human story, and in like manner "reconciliation" denotes the purpose which shapes and directs the story of the divine will to
fellowship as God first confronts and then transfigures the will to power.
Lehmann offers a concise summary of the fundamentally political matrix
of the biblical narrative:

> The Christian or messianic story documents its "saving reality and power"
> in a paradigmatic movement from a politics of confrontation to a politics of
> transfiguration whose code words are: *submission*, *silence*, and *transfigura-*
> *tion* itself. These code words identify the boundaries toward which and
> within which the dynamics of revolutionary passion, promise, and struggle
> are liberated from self-destruction and shaped instead for a new and divinely
> appointed order of human affairs in which time and space are ordered so as
> to make room for freedom.[28]

A comparison of Lehmann's interpretation of the biblical story with
Michael Goldberg's critical introduction to narrative theology brings out
some interesting similarities and contrasts. According to the categories developed by Goldberg, Lehmann takes a paradigmatic approach to the story
embodied in Scripture and narrated by the *koinonia* and its practice of everyday life. This approach maintains that the biblical stories "claim not only
to *be true* accounts of what has happened in the past, but they also claim the
capacity to *ring true* to common aspects of human experience, thus being
paradigms of our existence which can sustain and transform that existence
now and in the future."[29]

In Lehmann's case, the paradigmatic status of the biblical stories operates on two levels. First, there is the fundamental tenor of the overall biblical story, described previously as the historical dialectic between God's
will to fellowship and humankind's will to power. But in addition, certain
images, such as that of the messianic shoot which emerges from the stump
of Jesse (Isaiah 11[1-10]), or Jesus' transfiguration, function paradigmatically
within the biblical story to help frame its general contours. Lehmann, who
asserts that Thomas Kuhn's observations about scientific paradigms extend

into the realm of politics insofar as in both politics and science "perspectives and commitments are as decisive as data when it comes to seeing the world and acting toward it," thus advances a *performative* understanding of how paradigms function in the messianic politics of God: "In exegesis, a paradigm expresses an achievement in the making as regards a way of looking at life and of living it."[30] The biblical story is therefore not a completed work, but "an achievement in the making" within the eucharistic community, whose life and behavior embodies and bodies forth that story in the practice of everyday life.

However, Lehmann does not subscribe to Goldberg's assertion that the truth of a narrative is tied to its ability to depict or represent reality. The point is not to abstractly picture the world but to help shape and direct a community's engagement with the world, and thus narratives can function in a variety of ways. All types of literary endeavor, including historiographical works, are socially significant activities or forms of behavior which are governed to a considerable extent by controlling, often competing, goals and interests. Consequently, the theological focus to the use of narrative categories revolves about the historical articulation of everyday life rather than the speculative depiction of reality. The question of truth, by this account, must attend to "the full complexity and totality of the existing, concrete situation" and express the living or human word which "is instrumental to...an openness of human beings to each other..."[31] The shaping of conscience within the context of the *koinonia* in response to the humanizing activity of God in the world thus requires considerable literary flexibility in order to re-present the apostolic witness in a manner that is not only historically accurate but also historically significant.

There is a problematic (though not insurmountable) aspect to the use of a narrative approach to the interpretation of the Bible. Lehmann notes the collapse in the modern era of the naive literalism that characterized the traditional understanding of the church concerning the factual core of the apostolic witness of Scripture, a core that forms the basis of a narrative appropriation of the Bible by the community of faith.[32] However, he distinguishes the naive literalism that marks the apostolic dimension of Christian thought from a crude literalism, that is, from an insistence that there is "a one-to-one correlation between the empirically verifiable data concerning Jesus of Nazareth and the messianic convictions and associations which clustered about Him," (a claim, moreover, which Scripture never makes for itself). He proposes that a reestablishment of the naive literalism of the early church is required in order to recover the apostolic dimension of the biblical story. The naiveté Lehmann suggests is neither a return to primitivism nor an abdication to vulgar literalism, for he understands that "the substance and the prospects of a naive literalism...can be neither pursued or pressed in disregard of the data and the canons of historical evidence." Lehmann's naive literalism resembles what Paul Ricoeur calls "second naiveté," i.e., an autobiographical reading of the biblical narratives that is carried out in, through, and beyond critical methods.[33]

However, Lehmann's account of naive literalism is not identical to the approach of Ricoeur, for he seeks to recover in a contemporary context what David Steinmetz has argued is the superiority of precritical exegesis, that is, "a hermeneutical theory [that] is capable of sober and disciplined application and avoids the Scylla of extreme subjectivism, on the one hand, and the Charybdis of historical positivism, on the other."[34] As such, naive literalism or second naiveté goes beyond Ricoeur and strives for what could be paradoxically termed a post-critical naiveté. This type of naiveté, embodying "the one critical surrender of the neutral to the personal in the arcanum of historical investigation and verification," would allow the apostolic witness to the biblical story to challenge the illusions of privileged objectivity and neutrality (which is almost always tied to some type of Cartesian anthropology) on the part of the scientist presumption of modernity and its reified narrative of human existence, thereby exposing its mystifications, mechanisms, and illusions.[35] For all of its merits, Ricoeur's understanding of second naiveté is still tied to Enlightenment anthropology and thus it lacks the kind of critical traction which is needed to confront the unwarranted assumptions of (post)modern rationality.

It is the apostolic content of theology which distinguishes Lehmann's post-critical naiveté from that of Ricoeur, and determines how the Scriptures shape and direct the life and conduct of the church. The apostolic character of theology, and therefore of the biblical story, is firmly tied to the *canonical* authority of Scripture, which presupposes a performative understanding of the canon and the canonical process. Lehmann does not restrict the term canon to the collection of books in the Christian Bible or to the process in the history of the church which resulted in the formation of that collection. Instead, he maintains that both the formation and recognition of the canon on the part of the church indicates a monumental decision by the community of faith regarding the Bible's authority.

The existence and historical significance of the canon, Lehmann says, testifies to a dialectical conversation that has occurred throughout history between the authority of the Scriptures within the institutions and traditions of the church, on the one hand, and the life of the church as the performative acknowledgement of, and response to, that authority in history. Due to its decision about the canon, the church avoids what he terms an acute dilemma. "On the one hand," says Lehmann, "the Canon means an avoidance of the absolutization of the Scriptures. One cannot go to the text—as text —for guidance. The Canon means that one goes to the text in the context of the faith and life of the church."[36] The attempt to bypass the community of faith as the necessary context for interpreting the Bible, particularly as the community is shaped in and through its liturgy, is an ill-fated effort to make the Scriptures into "a photoelectric instrument for discerning the mind and will of God."[37] Lehmann contends that the relationship between Christian faith and the biblical text is too complex to posit the simple and unmediated derivation of contemporary faith from the Scriptures. He argues that

> the reality and activity of God, the shaping of a community of faith in consequence of the divine activity, the apprehension of the divine activity and the historical life and destiny of the community of faith—all are involved in the simple act of taking up the Bible to read. To ignore these considerations is to ignore the crucial question of the possibility and validity of theological knowledge...to court a greater risk than that of theological abstraction.[38]

The fact that there was a struggle over the canon implies that the church needed (and still needs) to carefully consider the sense in which the biblical story marks the point of departure for the life of faith. "Had the authority of the Scriptures been self-evident," Lehmann argues, "the Canon would have been self-evident. To consult the Scriptures as one would consult an oracle (or to modernize the allusion, a telephone directory) is a procedure inadequate both to the catechetical and to the anti-heretical responsibilities of the church."[39] Thus the "prophetic-apostolic line of revelation" which initiates the biblical story is not only illumined *to* the *koinonia* by the Holy Spirit. This story is also only illumined *in* and *through* the fellowship of the community of faith.

In addition to avoiding the absolutization of Scripture, however, the decision about the canon on the part of the church also avoids the absolutization of tradition, for the canon stands as a constant reminder that the life and mind of the church are not of themselves normative for the faith of the church. Rather, says Lehmann, it was the genius of the Reformation to point out that the presence of the canon alludes to a delicate balance between the Scriptures and the believing community. This performative balance, in marked contrast to the one-sided position of verbal inerrancy posited by Protestant Orthodoxy, sees the entire canonical process itself as the work of the Holy Spirit within the eucharistic community of faith. Therefore, "as members of the church, believers encounter the Scriptures and find themselves in a continuous conversation with the Scriptures," a conversation which, as I stated earlier, is more than mere talk. Lehmann's approach to the canon and the canonical process thus highlights the reciprocity between institution (the canonical Scriptures of the church) and event (the contemporary interpretation of these texts in the life of the community that produced them, under the guidance of the Holy Spirit) that also characterizes the relations between the spiritual and empirical dimensions of the church, a process which Lehmann describes as "the dialectical interrelation between Word, Spirit, and community of believers."[40]

With his construal of the categories of narrative and canon, Lehmann has once again placed the life of the church in a crucial position with regard to theological inquiry. The pivotal role of the church is exemplified by the way he regards the messianic community as a dialectical movement within the canonical process. The story of the *koinonia*, the story of the eucharistic community in the world, is thus the penultimate chapter of the biblical story. The story of "the life, activity and organization of the believing community" narrates the mystery of God's redemptive activity in the world, so that the story of the church is at the same time the story of the Trinity. As a result, neither the messianic politics of God nor the biblical story is intelligible nor actual apart from their enactment in history through the *koinonia*, "the corporate structure of God's activity in the world." And as such the life and conduct of the church is the parabolic bearer (or sacrament) of the human maturity and wholeness set forth by the biblical story, making the community of faith the concrete foretaste and sign of the future consummation of the new humanity promised by that story. Reciprocally, the biblical story as the pedagogical form of the Holy Spirit's activity in the church also encompasses the dialectical interrelation between the spiritual reality of the church, on the one hand, and its historical institutions, on the other.[41]

Since neither the Bible nor the intellectual traditions of the church can do without the other, and the church cannot long live or live faithfully without them, we shall conclude this chapter by developing further the idea that a "grammatical" relation properly exists between them. The doctrines of the church—its dogma—thus play an indispensable role in informing the practice of everyday life in faithfulness to the messianic politics of God.

The Dogmatic Grammar of the Politics of God

Lehmann maintains that "doctrine is an inescapable instrument both of the clear articulation of the faith and the guidance of the faithful," and therefore "the rectitude of doctrine, i.e., orthodoxy, is a primary task and duty of the Church." So crucial are this task and duty Lehmann calls dogma "that which one generation is not prepared to take responsibility that the next generation should be without." He thus concurs with Barth that dogma is the self-examination of the church with respect to its teaching and preaching about God. However, he also states that dogma ought not to be regarded in and of itself as the norm of faith, noting that "the peril to which the dogmatic mode exposes the knowledge of faith is that dogma becomes the norm of faith rather than the faithful instrument by which what faith knows may be interpreted and communicated." As a result, "doctrinal statements have tended to define the limits rather than to indicate the freedom of the divine initiative and man's confessional response to it. And faith itself has functioned as an ideology rather than as the power by which man's fundamental loyalties and his imaginative and critical judgments are shaped." Too often in the history of doctrine, he concludes, "the dynamics of the divine activity are obscured rather than expressed."[42]

The doctrine of the Trinity exemplifies Lehmann's understanding of the place and function of dogma within the context of the *koinonia*. In particular, he contends that the church's affirmation of the Trinity as "revealed doctrine" is "an authentic impulse of its intellectual obedience." He rejects, however, a pictorial or propositionalist reading of this dogma, insisting that "'revealed doctrine' is not, as the church has so often mistakenly asserted or alleged, a doctrine whose words and sentences are identical with God's self-identifying self-communication."[43] Put otherwise, doctrines are not depictions of God or of anything else (including so-called pre-thematic religious experience, without which liberal and revisionist theologians have little or nothing to say), although this has often been the prevailing conception of doctrine within the Christian tradition, including much of (post)-modern theology. This construal of doctrine falls victim to the fallacy that Christian faith consists in a series of nonindexical beliefs or propositions which somehow *mirror* a metaphysical or moral order (which exists either within or over against the Cartesian subject). This misconception either ignores or is unaware of the grammatical relationship between the biblical imagination and intellectual inquiry that shapes and directs the contextual *articulation* of conscience and the liberating obedience of faith.

Lehmann's understanding of doctrine thus appears, at least initially, to have much in common with postliberal construals of religion and doctrine that have attracted considerable attention in recent years. Advocated by the late Hans Frei, Paul Holmer, Theodore Jennings, George Lindbeck, Ronald Thiemann, and Charles Wood,[44] postliberal theologians argue that religion in general, and religious doctrine in particular, primarily exercise a regulative or rule-like function. Lindbeck, for example, maintains that "religions resemble languages together with their correlative forms of life and are thus similar to cultures (insofar as these are understood semiotically as reality and value systems---that is, as idioms for the construing of reality and the living of life.)" He asserts that theologians should regard a religion and its teachings as though it were a distinct culture, and thus "As interlocked systems of construable signs...a context within which social events, behaviors, institutions, and processes may be intelligibly described."[45]

Lindbeck and other postliberal theologians often compare doctrine to a conception of linguistic competence that is acquired through a process of enculturation within a given culture and/or linguistic framework. Most of these theologians trace this conception of religious doctrine back to Ludwig Wittgenstein's reflections on "language-games" and "forms of life," and in particular to a terse, almost cryptic observation he makes in *Philosophical Investigations*: "Grammar tells what kind of object anything is. (Theology as grammar.)"[46] However, a regulative construal of doctrine begs the questions of how rules actually function in the course of everyday life, bypassing the historical process in and through which members of particular communities and cultures acquire and employ the skills which concretely make up these "competencies." One thus has good reason to suspect that postliberal theology is of a piece with the Enlightenment obsession with the essence of rationality and knowledge. The appeal to rules in order to define the essential nature of doctrine only brings us back to the need to describe in historical (and thus in narrative) terms how rules have variously functioned in particular contexts, i.e., back to the "genealogy" of rules.

Postliberal theologians who advocate a regulative conception of doctrine have been seduced by the modern fallacy that the norms of reasonableness, goodness, and knowledge consist in the mind being constrained by a non-indexical set of rules. Poteat, in a powerful critique of Noam Chomsky's implicit Cartesianism that also applies to the work of Lindbeck and the other postliberal theologians, states that this conception of language (and therefore of culture) "abstracts linguistic *competence* from the concrete setting of actual linguistic performance. In [this] model, man, in the twinkling of an abstraction, ceases to be an actual speaker and becomes an abstract, competent, worldless 'operator' of this rule-governed but open grammar. In short, man becomes strictly inconceivable." MacIntyre makes a similar point, asserting that there is no such thing as *a* language-as-such, much less a generic "language-as-such." Simply put, only particular languages-in-use actually exist.[47] The attempt to reduce the poetics of Christian identity (insofar as doctrine functions in relation to that identity) to an explicit set of rules, patterned after reified conceptions of human language and discourse, is symptomatic of the adherence to the Cartesian myth of "rationality by rule-constraint."

Liberal and postliberal conceptions of doctrine persist, as Lehmann puts it, "when theology says too little, [for the] biblical description of God's exercise of his naming function in the freedom to name himself is transposed into a dogma of communication. The result is that the *name* of God is displaced by the *names for God* proposed by man in exercising the freedom of his naming function. The language of communication becomes the language of theology, absorbs the language of faith, and God dies 'the death of a thousand qualifications'." Lehmann counters by asserting that the grammatical character of rules, precepts, laws, etc., whether ethical or cognitive in orientation, is instrumental and not normative. Doctrines and moral principles within the *koinonia* do not function principally as intellectual constraints upon an otherwise unencumbered subject, but as contextual indications of the parameters, dimensions and relations within which "the freedom to be human happens."[48] Such discourse, therefore, is finally descriptive and not definitional, indicative and not preceptual, performative and not constative.

Within the realm of ethics, laws and rules, whether construed as positive or natural, can never be the norm or criterion of action with reference

to the will of God. "In short," says Lehmann, "what God requires is mean-
ingless apart from the dynamics of the divine activity, and the dynamics of
the divine activity define the context within which 'all this commandment'
is to 'be righteousness for us' [Deuteronomy 6:25], indeed, is to be carefully done." On this point Lehmann takes Luther and Calvin to task failing
to follow up on their position concerning Christian liberty, as they too fall
back upon a preceptual reading of the law, allowing "the pre-Reformation
tradition on the matter to overshadow the creative rediscovery of the Bible
which had propelled the Reformers on their reforming way." The flaw intrinsic to a preceptual reading of ethical law is that human reason, when
divorced from a particular intellectual and moral context, cannot bear the
normative weight assigned to it. A rule-based construal of reason is thus
unable to direct and shape in conscience the performative relation between
responsible life and human life. For Lehmann, reason does not function as
the foundation and norm for this relation, but as an instrumental or grammatical catalyst for its realization. As a result, law does not mirror, map,
copy or represent a timeless moral order. Rowan Williams argues in this
regard that "By affirming that all 'meaning', every assertion about the significance of life and reality, must be judged by reference to a brief succes-
sion of contingent events in Palestine, Christianity—almost without realizing it—closed off the path to a 'timeless truth'." Regulative discourse
serves, rather, to make explicit various aspects of our concrete (i.e., contingent) relations with a timely (and finally for the church, an eschatological) moral orderer.[49]

Regulative forms of discourse, insofar as Christian faith is concerned,
are intelligible only in the context of "a pattern of relationships, freely offered and freely taken up in election and covenant, in calling and commitment to the foundational, liberating, and fulfilling purposes for which the
world was purposed. In that context, law [expresses] the dynamics and the
direction of the divine will toward the boundaries of freely accepted limits
within which the practice of humanness [is] certain to become 'a thing of
beauty and a joy forever'." It is a long-standing misinterpretation of the
Old Testament meaning of righteousness, that "an absolute idea of righteousness" or "an absolute ethical norm" exists, thanks to "an ingrained
habit in Western thought." Rather, "righteousness is a relational term that
refers to the social reciprocities in which man acts, which actually function
in a directional way, and at the same time in very diverse ways."[50]

Within the context of these reciprocities and in response to the fellow-ship-creating reality of the *koinonia* between Christ and the community of believers, "Law orders human relations by exposing crucial danger spots affecting human relations and also indicates the direction of humanization. Human relations always veer toward the boundary on which the issue of the humanity or the inhumanity of man to man must be fought through, and the direction of God's activity must be sighted again. Law has the function of exposing this boundary and in that sense is instrumental to the divine activity." As McClendon puts it, the commandments "forbid those social ruptures—murder, adultery, theft, and false witness (i.e., perjury)—that would destroy a people's solidarity with one another." Consequently, the overriding purpose of law in the context of the divine activity is forgiveness and reconciliation, for apart from reconciliation the historical ordering of social relations designated as righteousness or justice is blind. Law, in Lehmann's terms, "is the instrumentality which makes reconciliation either a fiction or a human bond," and which therefore binds together the biblical sense of justice and love.[51]

According to Lehmann, the dogmatic tradition of the church also functions in an instrumental or grammatical fashion, as evidenced by the trinitarian dogma of the church—a vital component in the doctrinal *regula fidei* of the messianic community. The *koinonia* "can only be faithful to its messianic occasion and character upon a trinitarian foundation. This foundation is none other than he who, as the Lord's Anointed (Messiah) is 'of one substance (*homoousion*) with the Father', whose Spirit, proceeding from the Father and the Son (*filioque*), is 'the Lord and Giver of life; who with the Father and the Son together is worshipped and glorified'." In Lehmann's estimation the fundamental issue in the doctrine of the tri-unity of God, is "the recognition of and the response to the historic Christ as the disclosure and bearer of the divine economy." A descriptive or performative congruence exists between the self-disclosing, self-communication of the name of God to which the biblical story bears witness, on the one hand, and the life, activity, and institutions of the church which are shaped and directed by the doctrine of the Trinity, on the other. This doctrine articulates the "dynamic initiative of God's sovereign freedom over and towards all that is not God. This initiative is at once sustaining and transforming of the faith and life, the language and thought of the community shaped by response to it. This initiative also sustains and transforms the environment of cosmos and culture in which this community takes shape." The historical occasion for the disclosure of the divine mystery is Jesus of Nazareth, "through whom the God of Abraham, Isaac, and Jacob and the God who is Father, Son, and Spirit belong descriptively together."[52]

"The persistence of a trinitarian habit of mind in Christian theology," Lehmann says, is thus due to the divine and human significance of Christ, for in him

> a self-disclosing action of God occurred which generated a response of commitment and conviction in those whom Jesus of Nazareth drew around him in a community of faith and discipleship. This action of God was received as a saving action, in the light of which the language, images and memories of Old Testament piety and experience acquired a transformed and transforming dimension of meaning. In Jesus of Nazareth, the self-identifying self-communication of God had come among men with the force of a particular and concrete fulfillment. From this center of renewal, a radical shift of perspective and function opened up a new way of looking at life as well as of living it.[53]

This soteriological occasion gives rise to the intrinsic congruence between the divine activity in history and the church's affirmation of God as triune, the later providing a "'principle of intelligibility'...and a 'moral and spiritual release' whereby ultimate reality, as well as life in this world, could be understood and responsibly lived." According to the trinitarian form of the divine activity,

> the structure and the destiny of the world and of human life in the world were at once full of movement and of meaning. It made sense, in the context of such an economy, to be a human being; and to be a human being meant to be on the way toward the new humanity to be consummated in the "second Adam" and the "second Advent." Once it has been established and understood that the structure and destiny of the world are directed toward this new humanity, the way is open for the exploration of what its achievement and consummation in Christ involve...At the same time...the foundation [is laid] for an understanding of the nature and activity of the Holy Spirit in relation to the Father and the Son, thereby explaining the power by which this new humanity was being achieved and could be achieved.[54]

Lehmann lists three constraints that form the historical parameters of the doctrine of the Trinity. The first is the canonical dialogue conducted within the church, "the intrinsic relationship between Scripture and Tradition [which]...became the source and the norm of the life and thought of the Church." From the standpoint of this relationship, there are always two limits within which the freedom of theology for its tasks occurs.

One limit is set by a due regard for the response to Scripture exhibited by the language and thought of the church in the past. The other limit is set by a due regard for the language and thought of the church in the present. Orthodoxy is, and can be, creative to the degree to which it is open and sensitive to the pressures of the language and thought of the present upon it. Otherwise, the congruence between its own language and thought and the language and events of the Scriptures is corrupted by apostasy. The contemporaneity of theology is, and can be, creative to the degree to which it is open and sensitive to the pressures of the past upon it. Otherwise, the congruence between its own language and thought and the language and events of the Scriptures is corrupted by heresy.

The performative relation between doctrine and Scripture, a relation that functions both diachronically and synchronically, invests the biblical metaphors and stories with their contextual intelligibility. Lehmann thus maintains that patristic thought, when read descriptively rather than as conceptual definitions, and located within the ongoing life and activity of the church, "is nearer to us than we have allowed ourselves to suppose."[55]

Two other constraints have historically influenced the development of the doctrine of the divine tri-unity. One has to do with what Lehmann calls the religious and cultural pressure (i.e., the story) of Hebrew monotheism and messianism. This pressure pertains to the question of the relation of Jesus of Nazareth's appearance as savior to the God of Abraham, the God of Isaac and the God of Jacob, who acts in history to save the covenant people of Israel. "At stake," says Lehmann, "were the righteousness, or justice, and the faithfulness of God. Translated into a broader idiom, Jesus of Nazareth had called into question, *die Richtigkeit der Stetigkeiten*, the integrity and dependability of the stabilities." The other constraint relates to the pressure (and the story) of Western forms of rationality and politics (concepts which, as I have argued, must be considered together): "The problem posed by the rational and political structures for dealing with change in nature and society was fundamentally the problem of the relation of the savior to the human and cosmic conditions of salvation. Translated into a broader idiom, Jesus of Nazareth had called into question previous ways of dealing with the pervasive persistence of contingency, of giving meaningful and institutional shape to it."[56]

The church's effort to deal with the last two constraints converge with particular force upon the doctrine of the Trinity:

The soteriological reality uncovered by and in Jesus of Nazareth seemed, to the community of faith and life which he inaugurated, exactly designed to give fulfilling meaning to the problems of constancy and contingency, so basic to man's life in the world, by bringing these very problems into the orbit of God's self-identifying self-communication. What the church found in the Scriptures was a language and a context of meaning which offered a profound and original way of making sense both of God's revelation and of the human condition. Here was a way of identifying God by name and of discovering in that identification a creative matrix of consummation within which the constant and contingent factors in nature, history, and personal life could acquire a structure of meaning and responsibility.

Starting with Hebrew culture and tradition, then, the doctrine of the divine tri-unity exhibits and expresses both intra- and extra-trinitarian relations of God, thus making "room for God's self-revelation in his activity and for the transformation of the human condition by reason of this activity."[57]

With its christological focus in the story of Jesus of Nazareth, the doctrine of the Trinity describes rather than regulates the relations within "God's own activity of self-identifying self-communication," set forth in response to the soteriological occasion and significance of the biblical confession regarding the righteousness and faithfulness of God. "According to this description," says Lehmann,

> the function of the relation of the Father to the Son is the function of origination, of sustaining purpose, of consummation; the function of the relation of the Son to the Father is one of mediation, of reconciliation, of order and authority; the function of the relation of the Spirit to the Father and the Son is one of power, of participation and transformation. In the language and context of the Scriptures, the names by which God is identified and the relations and functions to which those names refer are congruent with God's own activity of self-identifying self-communication.

Within this matrix, Lehmann concludes, "it is the name of Jesus which binds together the God of Abraham, Isaac and Jacob who disclosed his name to Moses and the God who is worshipped and obeyed in the church, who highly exalted Jesus, 'and bestowed on him the name which is above every name'."[58]

With respect to the rational and political constraints of Western culture on the doctrine of the Trinity, Lehmann contends that "The language and context of 'substance' and 'hypostases', of 'nature' and 'persons', were also designed to make room for God's self-revelation in his activity and for the transformation of the human condition by reason of this activity."[59] The shift in terminology does not indicate a shift in theological content, but represents a "creative attempt of theological translation," for "it is precisely for the sake of the God who saves that the translation from the name-language of the Scriptures to the language of tri-unity was attempted."[60]

This reference to the concept of translation in this context, however, must be read grammatically and not as an attempt to supplant the imagery or narratives of Scripture with either classical or modern metaphysics. It is "a disastrous error," contends McCabe, to conclude that when patristic and medieval theologians "took over with delight the instruments of Greek classical and post-classical thought and used and developed their logic and their language, they were therefore thinking in the way that, say, Plato or Aristotle thought." Lash rightly states that these theologians "well knew that they were bending familiar notions, metaphorically, to strange new uses." MacIntyre accurately describes the metaphorical extension (and consequently also the distention) of classical thought that occurs within the *poetics* of Christian theological inquiry. "The possibility to which every tradition is always open," he writes,

> is that the time and place may come, when and where those who live their lives in and through the language-in-use which gives expression to it may encounter another alien tradition with its own very different language-in-use and may discover that while in some area of greater or lesser importance they cannot comprehend it within the terms of reference set by their own beliefs, their own history, and their own language-in-use, it provides a standpoint from which once they have acquired its language-in-use as a second first language, the limitations, incoherences, and poverty of resources of their own beliefs can be identified, characterized, and explained in a way not possible from within their own tradition.

In short, it may be that "by the standards of one's own tradition the standpoint of the other tradition offers superior resources for understanding the problems and issues which confront one's own tradition."[61]

With respect to the Christian tradition's innovative use of classical Western thought to relate the savior to the human and cosmic conditions of salvation, Lehmann states that it makes "all the difference in the world" whether the church confesses that the Son is of one substance (*homoousion*) or of like substance (*homoiousion*) with God: "The difference is between a world the Redeemer and the Creator of which are one and the same God and a world with at least two gods, one who creates, the other who redeems. It is the difference between a world in which men have been redeemed, set upon a new and living way, in the *same* world, and redemption in a world *toto caelo* other than the one in which men have been set down and, even after the incarnation of the Word, continue to live.[62]

In similar fashion, the *filioque* clause in the Creed, says Lehmann, addresses the relation of the Holy Spirit to the other two members of the Trinity, and of the triune God to creation. At stake here is the critical question of "whether 'history' or 'nature' is the key to the understanding of God's self-revelation in Christ; and if history, whether there are in actual history signs of redemption which 'are not merely extensions of human wisdom or human virtue (or even human power) but are the consequence of a radical break-through of the divine spirit through human self-sufficiency'." The *filioque* juxtaposes the sense and direction of history to the messianic activity of God, and reciprocally, the mystery of God to the intelligibility of history. In other words, the *filioque* clause helps make explicit the narratability of history and thus the shape and significance of human existence within this story, thereby providing "[a] radically new and unclassical account of the structure and content of experience [which] is a perennial need and enterprise of human culture. To respond to such a need and enterprise, equipped with the language and context of the Scriptures and of tri-unity, is the continuing and catalytic function of theology." The doctrine of the Trinity thus provides "the 'logos of power' in terms of which Christianity effectively displaced the attempt of Graeco-Roman classicism to adapt the Augustan experiment in 'creative politics' to the changing circumstances of life in this world, and thus to make the world 'safe for civilization'." In crafting the doctrine of the Trinity out of the materials of classical European culture, the church achieved "a new context of apprehension and behavior within which the whole process and complexity of human inquiry and conduct made intelligible and behavioral sense."[63]

The construal of the doctrine of the Trinity as the church's logos of power illustrates the shift of focus for dogma from the regulative categories of epistemology and metaphysics (or ontology) to the descriptive grammar of history and politics, and once again accentuates the intrinsic role that the church plays within the history of the divine economy as "God's new language," exhibiting through its everyday practices (which in turn are informed by its liturgy and dogmatic teachings) the historical shape and direction of the messianic politics of God. As Rowan Williams puts it, when "God 'utters' the life of Jesus, he 'speaks' an event, a human history; and so he enters the fabric not merely of human verbal or conceptual exchange but of human society, community, making it the *commixtio et communio Dei et hominis*...of human language in the fullest sense of the word, a shared 'form of life'." Classical orthodoxy, therefore, is properly read, not as a series of intellectual abstractions based on Hellenistic philosophy, the acceptance of which comprising the norm or rule of Christian identity, but as an intrinsic dimension to what Matthew Lamb describes as "subversive memories linked to eschatological and apocalyptic expectations of the coming reign of God." Consequently, writes Lehmann, "dogma—far from identifying an arbitrary limitation imposed upon thought and action—identifies, nourishes, and sustains what it takes foundationally and focally to be and to stay human in the world."[64]

Consistent with an instrumental account of doctrine, Lehmann always keeps together the economic Trinity—the creative and redemptive disclosure of God's activity in history—and the ontological or immanent Trinity. We should note in passing that the distinction between the economic and the ontological Trinity is derived from the Aristotelian distinction between *theoria* and *praxis*, between "contemplation" and "practical activity," which made its way relatively early into the vocabulary of Christian theology. Lehmann holds this distinction at arm's length, as it often culminates in the "metaphysical and liturgical sterility" which characterizes much of the church's dogmatic reflections. Doctrinal sterility is symptomatic of the theological temptation to say too much, i.e., to transpose the biblical *description* of the self-disclosing economy of God into the speculative fallacy of *definition*, resulting in the displacement of the *name* of God with the *nature* of God. In this substitution of the divine nature for the name of God, the speculative definition of God's "being" for the historical description of the divine activity substitutes classical metaphysics for biblical politics and thus negates the political and historical character of the messianic activity of God "without which theology lacks both content and context."[65]

To be sure, classical metaphysics are involved in the creedal formulations concerning the mystery and activity of God. What must be kept in mind regarding the use of Western categories of thought, however, is that "Nicaea was not led to define this [trinitarian] dogma out of a 'hunger for metaphysics'."[66] According to Lehmann, "The decisive question in such a situation is always whether or not a 'metaphysical surrender' has occurred. The significance of a theology of messianism is exactly this, that the faithfulness of its response to the context and dynamics of the activity of God not only excludes such a surrender but sooner or later makes it possible for theology to effect the...transvaluation of culture and politics." What occurs in the trinitarian description of God's activity is the performative reconfiguration of the language of classical culture, resulting in "a radical transvaluation of the context, meaning, and direction of life in this world, and accordingly, of human behavior."[67]

Apart from its instrumental character as conscience's logos of power within the *koinonia*, says Lehmann, the doctrine of the Trinity quickly becomes confused with the arithmetic involved in the coordination of the three persons of the Trinity with the unity of the divine substance, thereby depriving "the dynamics of 'God with us', of 'God for us', of the humanization of God for the sake of the humanization of man...of their mythopoetic power to give meaning to and to transform what is human."[68] Put in another way, speculative thought illicitly transposes the poetics of biblical politics into transcendental mathematics. Yet there is serious question as to whether arithmetic has ever been the primary sense of the numerical imagery with reference to God in either the Jewish or Christian tradition. Buber, to cite one example, observes that "The vital basis of monotheistic faith is after all not established by counting how many gods there may be... It is the exclusiveness which permeates the relationship of faith." And Pinchas Lapide, a Jewish scholar known for his involvement in the Jewish-Christian dialogue, states that

> the difference between gods and the One God is indeed not some not kind of difference in number—a more miserable misunderstanding there could hardly be—but rather a difference in essence. It concerns a definition not of reckoning but rather of inner content; we are concerned not with arithmetic but rather with the heart of religion, for "one" is not so much a quantitative concept as a qualitative one. Two or more cannot be absolute. Two or more also cannot be timeless and eternal. If there are two or more, there can be no concept of omnipotence...[T]hus monotheism also becomes an indispensable presupposition of a mono-ethics.[69]

Indeed, apart from the assumptions of Cartesian anthropology, especially the idea that the primary function of language is to depict reality, misconceptions regarding number with reference to God's three-in-oneness are deprived of any intelligible context. However, when situated within the poetics of everyday life and informed by the performative anthropology of conscience, "the trinitarian achievement of the church links the mystery and the meaning of the reality and activity of God revealed in Christ so as to guarantee signs of redemption in the world in which God became incarnate and the Holy Spirit is at work." In the *koinonia*, where "God sets up and spells out in the world a community of life, in the context of which human maturity becomes both a possibility and a fact," the "naming function and significance of 'tri-unity' as a descriptive sign of the self-naming of God in revelation" provides "signs of redemption in the world" marking "the advent of the Messiah, the ingression of the 'new age' upon the 'old age', the proleptic inauguration of the kingdom of God."[70]

The complex question of the patriarchal language which dominates the imagery of the Trinity exhibits the performative character of the relations between metaphor, narrative, and doctrine. Indeed, only out of the poetic compound of tradition and experimentation that Lehmann claims for theology can the church go on and go further in this matter to "live [faithfully] in the present...and fully open to the future." The problem which is at the heart of this important debate over inclusive language is nicely summed up for us by Lash when he notes that "the nuclear form of...our faith, our trust, is—in the Christian tradition—the declaration that the mystery of which we seek to speak, the mystery that has become part of the truth and texture of our history, in the form of a servant, is least inappropriately addressed as 'Father'." Feminist critiques of patriarchy, in one sense, only deepen the church's awareness of how inappropriate the metaphor of father is, particularly in view of the company the church has kept since the third century. As a result of these and related critiques, the church once again confronts a dogmatic and ethical boundary where "the issue of the humanity or the inhumanity of *man* to *man* must be fought through, and the direction of God's activity must be sighted again."[71]

As recent debates, there are no easy solutions to the problem of inclusive language. Much of the difficulty can be attributed to the inherent ambiguity in any reference to the mystery of God. The Christian tradition, together with Judaism, has generally held that, as Buber puts it, "The relation to a human being is the proper metaphor for the relation to God." However, this affirmation has always been made in association with an even more fundamental confession, viz., that God is an incomprehensible and irreducible mystery, and therefore eludes our categorical grasp. God, simply put, has no proper name. Consequently, the divine mystery can only be *defined* in negative terms, that is, in terms of what God is not. The metaphorical *description* of God thus always stands under the apophatic sign of the *via negativa*.[72]

Furthermore, there is also a sense in which metaphorical descriptions of God involve their own form of negation. As I noted earlier, Lash helps us to see that the images for God in Scripture "and the stories in which they occur—within the complex history of conflict and clarification which is the history of the Jewish and Christian people—were usually produced in criticism of inhuman (and hence 'ungodly') practices." The particular circumstances of their production would thus appear to implicate metaphorical imagery for God in a second type of *via negativa*, only in this case the negation involves a political critique of oppressive society. Embedded within the parabolic affirmations about God in Scripture is a tacit negation: God is not a king or father as other kings and fathers are; God is not like all other shepherds or other judges. "In other words," says Lash, "it is only through the redemptive transformation of our human practices that we can acquire some sense of what the truth of these images might be when used as metaphors for our relation to the unknown God."[73]

This double negation does not mean that all human speech about God is ultimately devoid of positive content. According to Karl Rahner, there is "an 'unknowing', centered on itself and the unknown, which when compared with knowledge is not a pure negation...but a positive characteristic of a relationship between one subject and another." As Buber reminds us in his discussion of the difference between the two basic words that humans utter, "I-It" and "I-Thou," all genuinely *human* relations are founded upon a form of "unknowing" which eludes the grasp of categorical knowledge. And so Lash asserts that getting to know other people better

> is not simply, or even primarily, a matter of "comprehending" them, of subjecting them to procedures of cognitive explanation and control. Persons are not problems to be solved. Indeed, the *closer* we are to people, and the better we understand them, the more they evade our cognitive "grasp" and the greater the difficulty that we experience in giving adequate expression to our understanding. Other people become, in their measure, "mysterious," not insofar as we *fail* to understand them, but rather in so far as, in lovingly relating to them, we succeed in doing so.[74]

A descriptive rather than prescriptive understanding of "theology as grammar" cannot resolve by itself the difficult question of inclusive language, but it can help give sense and direction to the debate. In this respect the church's trinitarian logos of power also functions, as Lash puts it, as "a set of protocols against idolatry." The purpose of such protocols, according to Lehmann, is to help the church avoid saying either too much or too little with respect to God, or as Lash says, to rightly distinguish between telling the story differently (which we can and must do in new times and places) and telling a different story. In this particular case, many of those who advocate innovative and non-patriarchal images for God, and especially for God as "Mother," surrender to the temptation to say too little. However, as Lehmann notes, "when theology says too little, the biblical description of God's exercise of his naming function in the freedom to name himself is transposed into a dogma of communication. The result is that the *name* of God is displaced by the *names for God* proposed by man in exercising the freedom of his naming function. The language of communication becomes the language of theology, absorbs the language of faith, and God dies 'the death of a thousand qualifications'."[75]

The exchange of the patriarchal name *of* God with more inclusive names *for* God takes both a naive and a sophisticated form. The naive form is wed to the consumer-oriented individualism which determines so much of (post)modern existence, and which religious sociologist Robert Bellah aptly refers to as "Sheilaism" after a young woman named Sheila for whom the only authority is "my own little voice." Sheilaism exposes the self-deception endemic to the Enlightenment tradition, viz., that each of us is free to write our own story and thus to name our own gods, fashioned to serve our self-determined ends. The more sophisticated form of the theological temptation to say too little with respect to the name of God is represented by the theologies of Sallie McFague and Brian Wren. In ways that are both ironic and tragic, given the genuine *pathos* out of which both of them write, McFague and Wren transvalue the personal imagery that, according to the tradition, is "least inappropriate" for God into a cipher for the subject's will to power, thus confusing the ways of God with those projects we enlightened and "scientific" peoples continually undertake to name ourselves, that is, to determine and control our own lives and the world we inhabit. In this particular case, the empowerment of women within the disciplinary habits of (post)modernity (which has traditionally only empowered men) is the goal, a very noble form of idolatry, to be sure, but idolatry none the less. Ultimately, while both the naive and the sophisticated forms proceed with the best of intentions, they not only ignore the grammatical relationship that theological inquiry has with the metaphorical and narrative motifs of Scripture and liturgy, they also unwittingly convert the propriety of personal metaphors with reference to God into the idolatrous extension and consolidation of instrumental rationality.[76]

The grammatical responsibility of the theologian, as I have already stated, is "to exercise critical watch over [the church's language], now unraveling confusions and inconsistencies that arise from it, now checking it with *praxis* to offset its stereotypical drift, now challenging it as a lazy simplification." In the case of inclusive theologies which say too little, the stereotypical drift is implicit within the parenting image of either "father" or "mother." Lash rightly cautions us that

> before we take this [image] and use it to weave comforting patterns of spec-
> ulation concerning the "domestic" character of the relationship between hu-
> man beings and the mystery of God, we need to remind ourselves of the
> context which is paradigmatic for all description of ourselves as "sons" and
> "daughters" of him whom we call "Father." That context...is Gethsemane
> and Calvary. That is where we learn what it is truthfully to stand in filial re-
> lation to the mystery of God.

And thus, as Rowan Williams rightly notes, "The cry to God as Father in the New Testament is not a calm acknowledgement of a universal truth about God's abstract 'fatherhood', it is the child's cry out of the nightmare. It is the cry of outrage, fear, shrinking away, when faced with the horror of the world." Nevertheless, he continues, this cry is "not simply or exclusively protest, but trust as well. 'Abba, Father, all things are possible to thee' (Mark 14[36])."[77]

On the other hand, the tendency of those who rigorously defend the male imagery of the Trinity is to say too much, as Donald Bloesch does, for example, when he contends that "the Trinitarian names are ontological symbols based on divine revelation rather than personal metaphors." While Bloesch is right to reject a liberal or revisionist view of doctrine, viz., that all religious language are but symbolic expressions of a special dimension of experience or transcendental possibility for human existence as such, he nonetheless transposes the *biblical description* of God's messi-anic politics into an *ontological definition* of the divine being, thus displac-ing the *name* of God with the *nature* of God. The temptation to say too much is ultimately a (vain) attempt to capture the divine mystery within our categorical forms of knowledge, i.e., to transform God from a *Thou* into an *It*.[78]

Not only does the temptation to say too much neglect the two-fold *via negativa* of the tradition, it also fails to take due note of the "maternal" character of God's "fatherhood" in Scripture. In an extraordinarily pro-found meditation on the meaning of the doctrine of the Trinity, Lash notes that the history of creation is imaged in the New Testament as the painful process of giving birth (Romans 8[15–17, 22–23, 26, 29]; John 16[21–22]; cp. Genesis 3[14–19], Isaiah 26[17]). The world, accordingly, is depicted as God's wayward "child." This process of creation comes to completion in a human being, an *adam*, who is no longer wayward, "the history of whose production transcribes in space and time the act of 'generation' that is God's own self. If Jesus of Nazareth may properly be called 'the first-born among many brethren', then human being and, perhaps, all of creaturely existence, is brought within the very life of God." When God thus makes the world "parentally," writes Lash, "the outcome of present suffering (Jesus' passion and the disciples' 'sorrow') will be the achievement of the birth of humankind, the finishing of God's creative work." He argues that "the strong and central Jewish doctrine of the endlessly generous fidelity of God (one form of which is the Jewish, and then the Christian, doctrine of God's fatherhood) is, in the trinitarian development of Christianity, radicalized in the direction of a maternal understanding of how the Creator in due time brings the world to birth through the laborious bearing of her Son in love."[79]

Obviously, these few comments do not resolve this very difficult issue, and there are other factors which complicate the matter that I have not even considered, including the traditional imaging of the church, as John XXIII puts it, as *Mater et Magistra*, mother and teacher. In this regard the existence of the church as an alternative *civitas* in the world, says Milbank, is inextricably linked with "the ever-renewed transmission of the signs of love and the bringing to birth of new members from the womb of baptism. (Mother Church is mediated by real female generation, unlike the 'mother earth' of the *polis*.)" It is apparent, however, that the search for more inclusive imagery to describe our relationship to the unknown God takes on radically different proportions depending on whether or not it is conducted within the constraints of trinitarian theology, and especially on whether these images deal adequately with the manifold relationships of origin in God. And yet such are the complications and constraints which are part of the burden that theological inquiry of *historical* necessity must bear within the contingencies of everyday life. Not only does the compound of tradition and experimentation preclude both *ex nihilo* innovation and a fixed index of meaning, it also does not allow us to exempt ourselves from the need to account for the labor of the Spirit within the one body of Christ, an accounting which is, in Lash's words, "the fundamental form of the Christian interpretation of scripture."[80]

NOTES

[1]Lehmann, *Ethics*, 347; Lash, *Theology on the Way to Emmaus*, 29.

[2]Lash, *Theology on the Way to Emmaus*, 103.

[3]I have borrowed the notion of metaphorical intentionality from Poteat, who uses it to argue convincingly that "our language has the sinews of our bodies which had them first; that its grammar, syntax, meaning, and metaphorical and semantical intentionality are pre-formed in the 'grammar', 'syntax', 'meaning', and 'metaphorical' and 'semantical' intentionality of our prelingual mindbodily being which are their conditions." Poteat, *Polanyian Meditations*, 187.

[4]Lehmann, *Ethics*, 89; "Messiah and Metaphor," 28.

[5]Lehmann, *Transfiguration*, 230; "The Metaphorical Reciprocity Between Theology and Law," 181; *Ethics*, 90. I am indebted to Lash for the difference between the "container" and the "company" theories of meaning. Lash, *Believing Three Ways in One God*, 11–12.

[6]Paul Lehmann, "The Ant and the Emperor," *How Karl Barth Changed My Mind*, ed. Donald K. McKim (Grand Rapids, MI: William B. Eerdmans Publishing Company, 1986), 41; Hauerwas, *After Christendom?*, 19.

[7]Lehmann, *Transfiguration*, 231–32. We see here Lehmann's warrants for using the image of transfiguration as the decisive metaphorical indication of the messianic politics of God.

[8]Lehmann, *Ethics*, 87 (n.2), 90; *Transfiguration*, 234–35.

[9]Lehmann, "Messiah and Metaphor," 29. Lehmann relies extensively in this discussion of metaphor upon unpublished work by Edward Lueders, especially his paper entitled "The Need for An essential Metaphor: The Lie We Can Believe."

[10]Lehmann, "Messiah and Metaphor," 29.

[11]Janet Martin Soskice, *Metaphor and Religious Language* (Oxford: Oxford University Press, Clarendon Press, 1985), 45–46, 66.

[12]Soskice, *Metaphor and Religious Language*, 24–38, 45–46, 50, 66, 83, 95.

[13]Soskice, *Metaphor and Religious Language*, 53, 149.

[14]Lehmann, "Messiah and Metaphor, 31; *Ethics*, 90.

[15]Soskice, *Metaphor and Religious Language*, 154; Lehmann, *Ethics*, 90, 97; Lash, *Easter in Ordinary*, 276.

[16]Soskice, *Metaphor and Religious Language*, 120, 131–36; Lehmann, *Ethics*, 154.

[17]Soskice, *Metaphor and Religious Language*, 120, 132, 136.

[18]Lash, *Easter in Ordinary*, 69.

[19]Lehmann, *Transfiguration*, 236; *Ethics*, 316; "Messiah and Metaphor," 30.

[20]Lehmann, *Ethics*, 95, 154; "Deliverance and Fulfillment," 389; *Transfiguration*, 80.

[21]Lehmann, *Transfiguration*, 10, 248.

[22]Lehmann, *Transfiguration*, 7; cf. "On Doing Theology," 132–33.

[23]See the influential article of Stephen Crites, "The Narrative Quality of Experience," *Journal of the American Academy of Religion* 39 (September 1971): 291–311; L. Gregory Jones, "Alasdair MacIntyre on Narrative, Community, and the Moral Life," *Modern Theology* 4 (October 1987): 67, cited in Hauerwas, *Christian Existence Today*, 65.

[24]Lehmann, *Transfiguration*, 8, 10, 24.

[25]Lehmann, *Ethics*, 97, 99, 349.

[26]Robert Alter, *The Art of Biblical Narrative* (New York: Basic Books, Inc., 1981), 33. Cf. Walter Brueggemann, *Genesis* (Atlanta: John Knox Press, 1982), 8–9, and Lehmann, "The Tri-unity of God," 45–48.

[27]Lehmann, "The Metaphorical Reciprocity Between Theology and Law," 188–89.

[28]Lehmann, Transfiguration, 236.

[29]Michael Goldberg, *Theology and Narrative: A Critical Introduction* (Nashville: Abingdon, 1981), 37–38.

[30]Lehmann, *Transfiguration*, 231–32, 288.

[31]Goldberg, *Theology and Narrative*, 214–26; Lehmann, *Ethics*, 130.

[32]Lehmann, "The Formative Power of Particularity," 313–16; cf. "The Ant and the Emperor," 43. This collapse has been exhaustively documented by Hans Frei, *The Eclipse of the Biblical Narrative: A Study in Eighteenth and Nineteenth Century Hermeneutics* (New Haven: Yale University Press, 1974). See also Hans Frei, "The 'Literal Reading' of Biblical Narrative in the Christian Tradition: Does It Stretch or Will It Break?", *The Bible and the Narrative Tradition*, ed. Frank McConnell (New York: Oxford University Press, 1986), 36–77.

[33]Lehmann, "The Formative Power of Particularity," 314–15; Ricoeur, *The Symbolism of Evil*, 350–52.

[34]David C. Steinmetz, "The Superiority of Precritical Exegesis," *Theology Today* 37 (April 1980): 37–38 Steinmetz's article may also be found in Donald K. McKim, ed. *A Guide to Contemporary Hermeneutics* (Grand Rapids, MI: William B. Eerdmans Publishing Company, 1986), 65–77.

[35]Lehmann, "The Formative Power of Particularity," 317.

[36]Lehmann, *Ethics*, 29.

[37]Lehmann, *Ethics*, 27.

[38]Lehmann, *Ethics*, 26.

[39]Lehmann, *Ethics*, 29.

[40]Lehmann, *Ethics*, 26; "On Doing Theology," 133.

[41]Lash, *Theology on the Way to Emmaus*, 42; Lehmann, *Ethics*, 31–32, 47, 58, 68, 70, 95–101, 154.

[42]Lehmann, *Ideology and Incarnation*, 13, 24; "The Metaphorical Reciprocity Between Theology and Law," 181; "On Doing Theology," 122; *Ethics*, 104; Barth, *Church Dogmatics*, 1.1, 33.

[43]Lehmann, "The Tri-unity of God," 42–43.

[44]Hans W. Frei, *Types of Christian Theology*, ed. George Hunsinger and William C. Placher, (New Haven, CT: Yale University Press, 1992); Paul L. Holmer, *The Grammar of Faith* (San Francisco: Harper & Row, 1978); Theodore W. Jennings, *Beyond Theism: A Grammar of God-Language* (New York: Oxford University Press, 1985); Ronald F. Thiemann, *Constructing a Public Theology: The Church in a Pluralistic Culture* (Louisville, KY: Westminster/John Knox Press, 1991); and Charles M. Wood, *Vision and Discernment: An Orientation in Theological Study* (Atlanta: Scholars Press, 1985).

[45]Lindbeck, *The Nature of Doctrine*, 18, 115.

[46]Ludwig Wittgenstein, *Philosophical Investigations*, trans. G. E. M. Anscombe, 3d ed. (New York: Macmillan Publishing Co., 1958), 116e.

[47]Poteat, *Polanyian Meditations*, 179; MacIntyre, *Whose Justice? Which Rationality?*, 373–84.

[48]Lehmann, "The Tri-unity of God," 38; *Ethics*, 146; "Cox, Luther, Decalogue," 90; cf. "The Commandments and the Common Life," 354.

[49]Lehmann, *Ethics*,, 78; "A Christian Alternative to Natural Law," 522, 525–26, 531–32; Williams, *The Wound of Knowledge*, 1.

[50]Lehmann, *Transfiguration*, 87–88.

[51]Lehmann, *Ethics*, 146–47; "The Metaphorical Reciprocity Between Theology and Law," 188–89; "Law as a Function of Forgiveness," 110–11; McClendon, *Ethics*, 180.

[52]Lehmann, *Ethics*, 107, 111; "The Tri-unity of God," 41–42.

[53]Lehmann, "The Tri-unity of God," 44.

[54]Lehmann, "The Tri-unity of God," 45; *Ethics*, 106–107.

[55]Lehmann, "The Tri-unity of God," 40–41.

[56]Lehmann, "The Tri-unity of God," 45–46.

[57]Lehmann, "The Tri-unity of God," 46; *Ethics*, 108.

[58]Lehmann, "The Tri-unity of God," 46–47.

[59]Lehmann, "The Tri-unity of God," 47.

[60]Lehmann, "The Tri-unity of God," 47.

[61]McCabe, *God Matters*, 43; Lash, *Believing Three Ways in One God*, 39; MacIntyre, *Whose Justice? Which Rationality?*, 387–88. Many philosophers of science have taken note of the metaphoric quality of theoretical discourse. According to one of these philosophers, Ernan McMullin, "The language of theoretical explanation is of a quite special sort. It is open-ended and ever capable of further development. It is metaphoric in the sense in which poetry...is metaphoric, not because it uses explicit analogy or because it is imprecise, but because it has resources of suggestion that are the most immediate testimony of its ontological worth." Ernan McMullin, "The Case for Scientific Realism," *Scientific Realism*, ed. Jarrett Leplin (Berkeley: University of California Press), 36, cited in Rouse, *Knowledge and Power*, 148–49.

[62]Lehmann, *Ethics*, 108.

[63]Lehmann, *Ethics*, 110–11; "The Tri-unity of God," 48; Lash, *Theology on the Way to Emmaus*, 72–73; cf. Charles Cochrane, *Christianity and Classical Culture* (New York: Oxford University Press, 1940), 157–58, 361–62, 436–37, 450–51, 480–90.

[64]Hauerwas, "The Church as God's New Language," *Christian Existence Today,* 51; Williams, *The Wound of Knowledge*, 32; Lamb, *Solidarity with Victims*, xiv; cf. 110–11; Lehmann, "The Ant and the Emperor," 40.

[65]Lehmann, *Ethics*, 108; "The Tri-unity of God," 37–38 See also Jürgen Moltmann's helpful discussion of this Aristotelian distinction in the tradition of Christian theology, formulated both to preserve the freedom of God over creation and to express the purity of the church's doxological adoration of God. Jürgen Moltmann, *The Trinity and the Kingdom*, trans. Margaret Kohl (San Francisco: Harper & Row, 1981), 151–61.

[66]Bernhard Lohse, *A Short History of Christian Doctrine*, trans. F. Ernest Stoeffler (Philadelphia: Fortress Press, 1966), 7. The quote is by Werner Elert, "Die Kirche und ihre Dogmengeschichte," *Der Ausgang der altkirchelichen Christologie*, eds. Wilhelm Maurer and Elisabeth Bergstrasser (Berlin: Lutherisches Verlaghaus, 1957), 323.

[67]Lehmann, *Ethics*, 111–12 (n. 3).

[68]Lehmann, *Ideology and Incarnation*, 24; "The Ant and the Emperor," 41.

[69]Buber, *Königtum Gottes*, 76–77, quoted in Lehmann, *Ethics*, 92; Pinchas Lapide and Jürgen Moltmann, *Jewish Monotheism and Christian Trinitarian Doctrine*, trans. Leonard Swidler (Philadelphia: Fortress Press, 1981), 30.

[70]Lehmann, *Ethics*, 98, 112; "The Tri-unity of God," 42.

[71]Lash, *Theology on the Way to Emmaus*, 14; Lehmann, *Ethics*, 147, my emphasis. Note in this connection the irony embedded in Lehmann's own habits of speech, which were bequeathed to him by a patriarchal culture.

[72]Martin Buber, *I and Thou*, trans. Walter Kaufmann (New York: Charles Scribner's Sons, 1970), 151.

[73]Lash, *Easter in Ordinary*, 276.

[74]Karl Rahner, "The Concept of Mystery in Catholic Theology," *Theological Investigations*, vol. 4, trans. Kevin Smyth (Baltimore: Helicon Press, 1966), 41; Lash, *Easter in Ordinary*, 236.

[75]Lash, *Easter in Ordinary*, 257–66; *Theology on the Way to Emmaus*, 30, 44, 183.

[76]Robert Bellah et al., *Habits of the Heart* (New York: Harper & Row, 1986), 221; Sallie McFague, *Models of God: Theology for an Ecological, Nuclear Age* (Philadelphia: Fortress Press, 1987); Brian Wren, *What Language Shall I Borrow?* (London: SCM Press, Ltd., 1989).

[77]Burrell, *Aquinas*, 178; Lash, *Theology on the Way to Emmaus*, 14; Williams, *The Wound of Knowledge*, 12.

[78]Donald G. Bloesch, *The Battle for the Trinity: The Debate over Inclusive God-Language* (Ann Arbor, MI: Vine Books, 1985), 36; cf. also Charles H. Talbert, "The Church and Inclusive Language for God?", *Perspectives in Religious Studies* 19 (Winter 1992): 421–39.

[79]Lash, *Believing Three Ways in One God*, 43–47.

[80]Milbank, *Theology and Social Theory*, 403; Lash, *Theology on the Way to Emmaus*, 90.

CONCLUSION

In the course of a discussion about the biblical shape and direction of the messianic politics of God, Lehmann offers a concise definition of a paradigm as it applies to the interpretation of Scripture. "In exegesis," writes Lehmann, "a paradigm expresses an achievement in the making as regards a way of looking at life and of living it."[1] In a similar fashion, Lehmann offers to the church a *theological paradigm* which expresses a *eucharistic achievement in the making* as regards a way of looking at life and of living it. This paradigm provides a grammatical framework for the everyday life of the church in response to the sense and direction of God's messianic initiative in history. The practice of everyday life, when understood as a eucharistic achievement in the making, requires constant reassessment in terms of the church's primary accountability to its messianic occasion and humanizing vocation. In conclusion, then, I shall set forth briefly what I take to be the theologically significant aspects of this particular way of looking at life and of living it.

1. *The performance of conscience and the historical production of believers.* The selection of conscience as methodological linchpin serves to focus theological inquiry in general on the production of the human being as a historical actor or agent, and more specifically on humanity's participation in the creative and redemptive activity of God in and through the person and community of Christ. The word conscience is in this respect a curious one, possessing even in its construction something of a hybrid character. Perhaps this is because with this term, a linguistic artifact derived from the Greek (*syneidesis*) and Latin (*conscientia*), I am attempting to account for what is otherwise neglected in (post)modern descriptions of the human being—the self's historical involvement with that which it knows.

As I noted in the second chapter, there is no cognate term for conscience in ancient Hebrew, for in that way of looking at life and of living it
the activity of knowing was inseparable from one's overall relationship
with what is known; in David Daube's words, there was a "previous self-
understoodness" in this regard.[2] According to the Hebraic sense of the
word, then, to know someone or something is to be intimately involved
with that person or object in some respect. When Scripture states that
Adam knew his wife Eve, it meant (among other things) that they had sex-
ual relations; in the Old Testament, to know God is to live as God lives, to
indwell the divine economy of salvation, to share in God's conscience
(Genesis 4[1, 25]; Jeremiah 22[15–16]). Moreover, the act of communicating,
which means in part (but only in part) to talk with another person, is a performative act which exemplifies the complex character of the personal involvement invested in the activity of knowing.

The Hebrew word that names this "pivotal personal center of man's total response to the dynamics, direction, and personal thrust of the divine
claim upon him," is *leb*, the heart, which "knows by a kind of sensitivity at
once central and total [and] which marks the person as a whole; this relational knowledge involves man as a doer in a behavioral response to a God
whose claim upon him is the foundation of his humanity."[3] The word conscience, when correlated with this conception of the heart, serves as a rhetorical bridge that allows us to move away from the Cartesian picture of
the human being as a disinterested and disembodied spectator (the principal
activity of which is the nonindexical generation of mental representations),
and toward the biblical description of the human being as a historical agent
whose activities and identity are the product of her response of obedience
to the politics of God.

2. *The ecclesiocentric context of conscience.* In keeping with their
original Pietism, Baptists have long affirmed the deeply personal and ethically rigorous character of Christian faith. The personal relationship to
Christ and the demand of ethical maturity or wholeness are two of the primary characteristics of Pietism in general. What has also been regularly
neglected in Baptist life and thought is the ecclesiocentric matrix of the biblical anthropology and piety. The *koinonia* of the church, the fellowship
creating reality of Christ with believers, is, as Lehmann observes, "the corporate structure of God's activity in the world." The individualistic thrust
of Baptist Pietism needs to be set aside in favor of the political context of
the messianic community, for "Individuals are 'saved' into the *koinonia*,

not one by one!" The integrity and maturity of the individual is only realized within the church through the reciprocity of diverse gifts and roles.
Authentic Christian piety, the sense of gratitude and reverence that shapes
"the reciprocity between creaturehood and creativity...into the possibility
and the power of fulfilling human freedom and joy,"[4] emerges only within
the messianic community. It is solely within the eucharistic structure of the
koinonia that the priesthood of all believers—the priestly role of the believer for the neighbor, apart from which there is no personal relationship
with Christ—becomes a historical reality.

Lehmann correctly points to the role played by the church's liturgical
practices in shaping the type of disciplined piety which life in the (post)-
modern world demands, at one point describing the fellowship of Christ
with his people as an eucharistic achievement, "the miracle of authentic
transubstantiation...through love being changed into each other." As a result, the roles played by tradition and dogma in the practice of everyday
life need not be seen as a threat to the historic fidelity of Baptists to biblical
authority (a recurring fear for which there is some historical justification)
but as that without which the authority of Scripture is only a pious self-
deception. The everyday life of the church is also the site for realizing a
humanizing authority in which the extremes of relativism and authoritari-
anism are rejected for that set of practices in terms of which "power, law,
and sovereignty, in their separateness and inseparability, converge...[upon]
an authority that binds as it liberates and liberates as it binds."[5] Such humanizing authority must take into account the dialectical character of the
koinonia as both a spiritual and an institutional reality, and attend to both
the life of the local community (the traditional Baptist emphasis in ecclesiology) and the catholic unity of the church (traditionally neglected by Baptists, again attributable to experiences which make their truncated doctrine
of the church intelligible, if not justifiable).

3. *The political character of the divine activity.* In a passage which
could have been written specifically with Baptists in mind, Lehmann warns
of "an unholy and unhealthy rhythm" between dogmatism and pietism that
is indicative of "the pathological immaturity that frustrates the body of
Christ as a *koinonia* in the world." Dogmatism in this context refers to the
rigid and enervating scholasticism that constantly seeks to impose upon the
church comprehensive and precise doctrinal statements as a precondition of
fellowship. Pietism, again in this context, refers to the privatization of
spirituality, which Scripture maintains can only be nurtured within the

messianic fellowship of the church.[6] Neither dogmatism nor pietism is able to provide the practice of everyday life with the shape and direction it requires to fulfill the church's sacramental vocation in the world.

The vacillation between dogmatism—which can take the form of a preoccupation with classical dogma or with the more contemporary concerns of ontology, phenomenology, epistemology, or hermeneutics—and privatized spirituality is symptomatic of the church's failure to attend to the political context of the gospel and to its own role in the messianic presence and activity of God in the world. Thus the intersection of motivation and judgment in conscience does not simply make explicit the concrete unity of piety and reason in this context, but it also emphasizes the formative relationship that exists between piety and politics within the *koinonia*. Piety apart from politics loses its eucharistic integrity and dissolves into a self-glorifying apostasy, while politics apart from piety has no foundation, neglects its divine ordination and the messianic events which define the just ordering of human life, which is its *telos*, and thus converts into a self-serving idolatry.[7] The ecclesiocentric conjunction of piety and politics is thus a necessary historical condition of the Christian *koinonia*.

4. *Piety, politics, and the will to fellowship.* The conjunction of piety and politics within the messianic community intersects in turn with the historical configurations of knowledge and power in a (post)modern culture. Consequently, theology must attend to the role of the church in the messianic confrontation and transfiguration of these configurations. In its account of the politics of God the church cannot lose sight of the dialectical unity between the phenomenological and the referential dimensions of theology. These dimensions correspond to the dialectical relations between Word, Spirit, and the community of faith, but they only come into view when the *koinonia* (which embodies the dialectical unity of Word, Spirit, and community of faith as both a visible and a spiritual entity) remains the focus of the account of conscience and the cite where piety and politics intersect with the structures and relations of knowledge and power.

With respect to the phenomenological dimension, theologians need to account for the configurations of power that govern the social habits and relations in those social contexts where Baptists are located. Lehmann rightly observes that "Social involvement and social criticism have been and are intrinsic to the doing of theology in a Christian context. The roots of this connection and tension between involvement and criticism lie deep in Israel's prophetic tradition and in Jesus' personal exemplification in word and deed of his prophetic heritage." For Baptists in the southern part of the United States, this account should begin with what Will Campbell calls the creation of the "redneck" by the ruling aristocracy of the Old South. The distinctive patterns of racism, sexism, and militarism that comprise everyday life in America can be traced in good measure to the emergence of marginalized whites in the South both before and after the Civil War.[8] But if this contextualized account of knowledge and power is to avoid collapsing into yet another sociological analysis of religion, that is, if it is to be concerned with the *messianic* transfiguration of the will to power by the power to will what God wills, the will to human fellowship and accountability, then the referential dimension of Christian theology must not be divorced from this social setting.

5. *Theological method.* With reference to methodology, I am proposing a messianic variant of what Cornel West calls dialectical historicism.[9] This term draws attention to the performative reciprocity between the phenomenological and referential dimensions of theology. Christian theology is historicist insofar as truth functions ideologically, i.e., in historically vested institutions and practices. Theology is also a form of dialectical historicism insofar as the truth which functions ideologically refers solely to the self-disclosing activity of God in history in the person and eucharistic community of Jesus Christ. The classical doctrines of the church—Christology, eccesiology, soteriology, pneumatology, etc.—are therefore inextricably interwoven into the story of the messianic community's involvement in the politics of God.

For example, in this study I highlighted Lehmann's understanding of the doctrine of election as an essential aspect of the politics of God. This doctrine, when read in this context, offers a poetic description of the self-determination of God in Jesus Christ for covenant solidarity with the people of God, and through them with the rest of the world. The doctrine of election thus identifies the eucharistic communion of the church as the context which provides the content and directions for such notions as justice, mercy, freedom, and love. In turn these notions focus attention on the new political reality emerging from Jesus' life and death, particularly in connection with his social location among the poor and dispossessed of Israel, and therefore from God's vindication of this way of life and this style of power in resurrection, ascension, and Pentecost. In concert with eschatology, the doctrine of election binds together the creative and redemptive purposes of God in history, framing the church's engagement with the world and the political character of the maturity and wholeness that marks the inauguration of the new humanity in Jesus Christ. A crucial element of this doctrine is the evangelical option for the poor, which provides a concrete focus for integrating the phenomenological and referential aspects of the messianic transfiguration of politics within the life of the church.

6. *The grammatical function of theology.* The role of theological reflection—philosophical theology, dogmatics, and theological ethics—needs to be carefully and critically reconceived from a historicist standpoint. In no sense should it be defined, as Charles Woods does, "as a critical inquiry into the validity of the Christian witness." Such a definition simply perpetrates the errors of Protestant liberalism exposed by Ludwig Feuerbach and analyzed with great clarity by Eberhard Jüngel.[10] The very idea of validating the Christian witness is incoherent, for the creature cannot validate the Creator. The church can only communicate the story of the divine will to fellowship in the practice of everyday life, and thereby extend the invitation of the story's leading character to follow him in his community.

Lash is correct when he contends that "It is no business of the...theologian to seek to verify religious truth-claims." The correspondence of the messianic story to the harsh, complex, conflictual, unstable, and irreducible story of creation "eludes theoretical demonstration. It can, however, be practically, imperfectly, partially and provisionally *shown* by the character and quality of Christian engagement in patterns of action and suffering, praise and endurance, that refuse to short-cut the quest by the erection of conceptual or institutional absolutes."[11] Theology thus seeks to impress upon the eucharistic community its accountability to the messianic content and character of its heritage and destiny. In short, theological inquiry, by responding to questions which can only be raised by the metaphorical intentionalities of the biblical story embodied in, and bodied forth by, the messianic community, properly attends to the historical (and thus sacramental) vocation of the church as the corporate structure of God's presence and activity in the world. As such, theology is not merely *Wissenschaft,* that is, science- or knowledge-craft, but *Ge-wissenschaft,* conscience- or performance-craft.

7. *The discipline of discourse in theological inquiry.* The grammatical ambiguity of the phrase "the discipline of discourse" is deliberate, requiring that we read it both as a genitive and as a possessive. This ambiguity makes explicit the essential role which language plays in the practice of everyday life, but also how language is itself disciplined with the messianic

community to fit its performative contours. Theological grammar begins with a pragmatist construal of human discourse as a type of activity, and thus as a material force which collaborates with other kinds of behavior to articulate distinctive patterns of conduct and styles of power. Accordingly, Christian doctrine forms the church's logos of power, and more specifically, the logos of the messianic transfiguration of power. This logos in turn is vested in the metaphorical intentionalities of Scripture and thus in the practical configurations invoked by the Bible's parabolic imagery. These parables and practices juxtapose the mystery and grace of God's activity in the world with the ways of humankind. Finally, the intelligibility and coherence of these images, and with them the discipline of discourse in theology in general, are secured in the narrative contours and direction of Scripture, for the categories of story and canon are the paradigmatic forms of the church's identity and participation in the creative and redemptive activity of God. Thus, as Lehmann maintains, "the penultimate chapter of the biblical story is the story of the eucharistic community in the world."[12] The *koinonia* must constantly attend to this story and canon if it is to faithfully account for its presence and activity in the world.

One final word is in order. I have argued that the theological heritage of Baptists can best be shaped and directed when it is explicitly tied to the political contours and content of the corporate structure of God's activity in the world, i.e., the church. In this century leaders such as Clarence Jordan, Walter Rauschenbusch, and Martin Luther King, Jr., struggled heroically to communicate this heritage in ways that were both faithful to the biblical story and pertinent to their place and role in history. In some respects they succeeded, in others they fell short, in still others they either neglected, or were ill-equipped to attend to, crucial issues and questions.

Unfortunately, probably the most dubious aspect of the Baptist legacy is the inaccessibility of its ecclesial institutions and intellectual traditions. When you spend most of your time and energy insisting that you neither have nor need such things to be Christian, as Baptists have regularly done for decades, while at the same time tacitly relying on a particular set of institutionalized habits and relations in order to make such statements, it is virtually impossible to address shortcomings in these matters in an coherent fashion. It is at this point that Lehmann's theology provides the kind of grammatical framework which may enable Baptists to discuss these issues in a consistent and intelligible manner. Critically appropriated, this account of theological inquiry provides the church with many of the discursive tools it needs to attend to the context of conscience, so that the practice of everyday life in the *koinonia* might disclose the mystery of God's creative and redemptive presence in history.

To the degree that the church is faithful to its eucharistic vocation, therefore, it prefigures the rejoicing of creation at the revelation of the daughters and sons of God (Rom. 8[19–24]). In its faithfulness to Christ, the *koinonia* "tells the world what is the world's own calling and destiny, not by announcing either a utopian or a realistic goal to be imposed on the whole society, but by pioneering a paradigmatic demonstration of both the power and the practices that define the shape of restored humanity. The confessing people of God is the new world on its way."[13] In a fitting summation of this vocation John Milbank writes: "Even today, in the midst of the self-torturing circle of secular reason, there can open to view again a series with which it is in no continuity: the emanation of harmonious difference, the exodus of new generations, the path of peaceful flight..."[14]

NOTES

[1]Lehmann, *Transfiguration*, 288.

[2]Daube, *Ancient Jewish Law*, 123–24.

[3]Lehmann, *Ethics*, 316, 353.

[4]Lehmann, *Ethics*, 57f; *Transfiguration*, 233.

[5]Lehmann, *Ethics*, 65; *Transfiguration*, 15.

[6]Lehmann, Ethics, 55; "The Politics of Easter," 37.

[7]Lehmann, *Transfiguration*, 233–34.

[8]Paul Lehmann, "Christian Theology in a World of Revolution," *Openings for Marxist-Christian Dialogue*, ed. Thomas W. Ogletree. (Nashville: Abingdon Press, 1968), 101; Will D. Campbell, "The World of the Redneck," *Katallagete* 5 (Spring 1974): 34–40. See also James W. Silver, *Confederate Morale and Church Propaganda* (Tuscaloosa, AL: Confederate Publishing Co., 1957); and H. Shelton Smith, *In His Image, But...: Racism in Southern Religion*, 1780–1910 (Durham, NC: Duke University Press, 1972).

[9]West, *Prophesy Deliverance!*, 19.

[10]Wood, *Vision and Discernment*, 22; Jüngel, *God as the Mystery of the World*, 105–52.

[11]Lash, *Theology on the Way to Emmaus*, 113, 116.

[12]Lehmann, *Ethics*, 101.

[13]Yoder, "Sacrament as Social Process," 44.

[14]Milbank, *Theology and Social Theory*, 434.

BIBLIOGRAPHY

Abendroth, Emerson I., ed. *Religious Studies in Higher Education*. Philadelphia: The Division of Higher Education of the United Presbyterian Church, 1967.

Adorno, Theodor. *Negative Dialectics*. Translated by E. B. Ashton. New York: Continuum Publishing Company, 1973.

Alter, Robert. *The Art of Biblical Narrative*. New York: Basic Books, Inc., 1981.

Althaus, Paul. *The Ethics of Martin Luther*. Translated by Robert C. Schultz. Philadelphia: Fortress Press, 1972.

_____. *The Theology of Martin Luther*. Translated by Robert C. Schultz. Philadelphia: Fortress Press, 1966.

Anderson, Gerald H., and Stransky, Thomas F., C.S.P., eds. *Mission Trends No. 4: Liberation Theologies in North America and Europe*. New York: Paulist Press, 1979.

Ansbro, John J. *Martin Luther King, Jr.: The Making of a Mind*. Maryknoll, NY: Orbis Books, 1982.

Arendt, Hannah. *On Revolution*. New York: Viking Press, 1947.

Auden, W. H. *The Age of Anxiety*. New York: Random House, 1947.

_____. *Collected Longer Poems*. New York: Random House, 1969.

Ayer, Alfred Jules. *Language, Truth and Logic*. 2nd edition. New York: Dover Publications, Inc. 1952.

Barth, J. Robert. *Coleridge and Christian Doctrine*. Cambridge: Harvard University Press, 1969.

Barth, Karl. *Church Dogmatics*. Edited by G. W. Bromiley and T. F. Torrance. Vol. 1: *The Doctrine of the Word of God*. Vol. 2: *The Doctrine of God*. Vol. 3: *The Doctrine of Creation*. Vol. 4: *The Doctrine of Reconciliation*. Edinburgh: T. & T. Clark, 1936–1969.

_____. *Community, State, and Church: Three Essays*. Introduction by Will Herberg. Gloucester, MA: Peter Smith, 1968.

_____. *The Epistle to the Romans*. Translated by Edwyn C. Hoskyns. 6th edition. London: Oxford University Press, 1933.

_____. *Ethics*. Edited by Dietrich Braun. New York: The Seabury Press, 1981.

_____. *Evangelische Theologie im 19. Jahrhundert. Theologische Studien*. Edited by Karl Barth and Max Geiger. Vol. 49. Zurich: Evangelischer Verlag Ag. Zollikon, 1957.

_____. *The Theology of Schleiermacher*. Edited by Dietrich Ritschl. Grand Rapids, MI: William B. Eerdmans Publishing Company, 1982.

The Basic Works of Aristotle. Edited by Richard McKeon. New York: Random House, 1941.

Baylor, Michael G. *Action and Person: Conscience in Late Scholasticism and the Young Luther.* Studies in Medieval and Reformation Thought. Vol. 20. Leiden: E. J. Brill, 1977.

Bellah, Robert, et al., *Habits of the Heart.* New York: Harper & Row, 1986.

Berger, Peter. "The False Consciousness of 'Consciousness-Raising'." *Worldview* 18 (January 1975): 33–38.

Bernstein, Richard J. *Praxis and Action: Contemporary Philosophies of Human Activity.* Philadelphia: University of Pennsylvania Press, 1971.

Bianchi, Eugene C., and Ruether, Rosemary Radford, eds. *A Democratic Catholic Church: The Reconstruction of Roman Catholicism.* New York: The Crossroad Publishing Co., 1992.

Bieler, Andre. *The Social Humanism of Calvin.* Translated by Paul T. Fuhrmann. Richmond: John Knox Press, 1964.

Blau, Peter. *Inequality and Heterogeneity: A Primitive Theory of Social Structures.* New York: The Free Press, 1977.

Bloesch, Donald G. *The Battle for the Trinity: The Debate over Inclusive God-Language.* Ann Arbor, MI: Vine Books, 1985.

Bloom, Harold. *The American Religion: The Emergence of the Post-Christian Nation.* New York: Simon & Schuster, 1992.

Boesak, Allan. *Coming in out of the Wilderness: A Comparative Interpretation of the Ethics of Martin Luther King, Jr. and Malcolm X.* Kampen: J. H. Kok, 1976.

_____. *Farewell to Innocence: A Socio-Ethical Study on Black Theology and Power.* Maryknoll, NY: Orbis Books, 1977.

Boff, Clodovis, O.S.M. *Theology and Praxis: Epistemological Foundations.* Translated by Robert R. Barr. Maryknoll, New York: Orbis Books, 1987.

Bonhoeffer, Dietrich. *Ethics.* Edited by Eberhard Bethege. New York: Macmillan Publishing Company, 1955.

_____. *Letters and Papers from Prison.* Translated by R. H. Fuller, John Bowden, et al. Enlarged edition. New York: Macmillan Publishing Company, 1971.

Bracher, Karl Dietrich; Dawson, Christopher; Geiger, Willi; and Smend, Rudolf, eds. *Die moderne Demokratie und ihr Recht.* Tübingen: J. C. B. Mohr, 1966.

Bremond, Henri. *The Mystery of Newman.* Translated by H. C. Corrance. London: Williams and Norgate, 1907.

Brown, Robert McAfee. "The Roman Curia and Liberation Theology: The Second (and Final?) Round." *The Christian Century* 103 (June 4–11 1986): 553–554.

Bruegemann, Walter. *Genesis.* Atlanta: John Knox Press, 1982.

Buber, Martin. *Kingship of God.* 3d edition. Translated by Richard Scheimann. New York: Harper & Row, 1967.

Burrell, David B., CSC. *Aquinas: God and Action.* Notre Dame, IN: University of Notre Dame Press, 1979.

Burnham, Frederic B., ed. *Postmodern Theology: Christian Faith in a Pluralist World.* San Francisco: Harper & Row, 1989.

Burke, Kenneth. *Attitudes Toward History.* 3d edition. Berkeley: University of California Press, 1984.

Calkins, Arthur Burton. "John Henry Newman on Conscience and the Magisterium." *The Downside Review* 87 (October 1969): 358–369.

Calvin, John. *Institutes of the Christian Religion. Library of Christian Classics.* Translated by Ford Lewis Battles, edited by John T. McNeill. Vols 20 and 21. Philadelphia: The Westminster Press, 1960.

Campbell, Will D. "The World of the Redneck." *Katallagete* 5 (Spring 1974): 34–40.

Capra, Fritjof. *The Turning Point.* New York: Simon and Schuster, 1982.

Cauthen, Kenneth. *The Impact of American Religious Liberalism.* 2nd edition. Washington: University Press of America, 1983.

Childs, Brevard S. *Old Testament Theology in a Canonical Context.* Philadelphia: Fortress Press, 1986.

Clarke, William Newton. *Systematic Theology.* 18th edition. New York: Charles Scribner's Sons, 1909.

Cobb, John B. "Two Types of Postmodernism: Deconstruction and Process." *Theology Today* 48 (July 1990): 149–158.

Cochrane, Charles Norris. *Christianity and Classical Culture.* New York: Oxford University Press, 1940.

Coleridge, Samuel Taylor. *The Complete Works of Samuel Taylor Coleridge.* Edited by William G. T. Shedd. Vol. 1: *Aids to Reflection.* New York: Harper & Brothers, 1884.

The Collected Dialogues of Plato. Edited by Edith Hamilton and Hunington Cairns. Princeton: Princeton University Press, 1961.

Commager, Henry Steele. *The Empire of Reason: How Europe Imagined and America Realized the Enlightenment.* Garden City, NY: Anchor Press/Doubleday, 1977.

Comte, Auguste. *Cours de philosophie positive.* Paris: Ballière. 1864.

Cone, James H. *Martin & Malcolm & America: A Dream or a Nightmare.* Maryknoll, NY: Orbis Books, 1991.

Conner, Walter T. *The Gospel of Redemption.* Nashville: Broadman Press, 1945.

Cormie, Lee. "The Hermeneutical Privilege of the Oppressed: Liberation Theologies, Biblical Faith, and Marxist Sociology of Knowledge." *The Catholic Theological Society of America: Proceedings of the Thirty Third Annual Convention* 33 (June 1978): 155–181.

Cox, Harvey. *Religion in the Secular City: Toward a Postmodern Theology.* New York: Simon and Schuster, 1984.

Cranfield, C. E. B. *A Critical and Exegetical Commentary on the Epistle to the Romans.* 2 vols. Edinburgh: T & T. Clark, 1975.

Crites, Stephen. "The Narrative Quality of Experience." *Journal of the American Academy of Religion* 39 (September 1971): 291–311.

Curran, Charles E., and McCormick, Richard A., eds. *Readings in Moral Theology No. 4: The Use of Scripture in Moral Theology.* New York: Paulist Press, 1984.

D'Costa, Gavin, ed. *Christian Uniqueness Reconsidered: The Myth of a Pluraistic Theology of Religions.* Maryknoll, NY: Orbis Books, 1990.

Daube, David. *Ancient Jewish Law.* Leiden: E. J. Brill, 1981.

Davies, W. D. *Jewish and Pauline Studies.* Philadelphia: Fortress Press, 1984.

De Certeau, Michel. *The Practice of Everyday Life*, trans. Steven F. Rendall. Berkeley: The University of California Press, 1984.

Dessain, Charles Stephen, ed. *The Letters and Diaries of John Henry Newman.* 31 vols. Oxford: Clarendon Press, 1961–1980.

Dreyfus, Hubert L., and Rabinow, Paul. *Michel Foucault: Beyond Structuralism and Hermeneutics*, 2nd edition. Chicago: The University of Chicago Press, 1983.

Duff, Nancy J. *Humanization and the Politics of God: The Koinonia Ethics of Paul Lehmann*. Grand Rapids, MI: Wm. B. Eerdmans Publishing Co., 1992.

Dulles, Avery, S. J. *Models of the Church*. Garden City, NY: Image Books, 1974.

Ebeling, Gerhard. *Luther: An Introduction to his Thought*. Translated by R. A. Wilson. Philadelphia: Fortress Press, 1970.

_____. *Word and Faith*. Translated by James W. Leitch. London: SCM Press, Ltd., 1963.

Eckstein, Hans-Joachim. *Der Begriff Syneidesis bei Paulus: Eine neutestamentlich-exegetische Untersuchung zum 'Gewissensbegriff'*. Tübingen: J. C. B. Mohr (Paul Siebeck), 1983.

Encyclopedia of Religion in the South. Edited by Samuel S. Hill. Macon, GA: Mercer University Press, 1984.

Erikson, Erik H. *Young Man Luther: A Study in Psycho-analysis and History*. New York: W. W. Norton, 1962.

Farley, Edward. *Ecclesial Reflection*. Philadelphia: Fortress Press, 1982.

Flannery, Austin, O.P., ed. *Vatican Council II: The Conciliar and Post Conciliar Documents*. Newly revised edition. Northport, NY: Costello Publishing Company, 1992.

Foucault, Michel. *Discipline and Punish: The Birth of the Prison*. Translated by Alan Sheridan. New York: Random House, Inc., 1979.

_____. *Power/Knowledge*. Edited by Colin Gordon. New York: Pantheon Books, 1980.

Frei, Hans. *The Eclipse of the Biblical Narrative: A Study in Eighteenth and Nineteenth Century Hermeneutics*. New Haven: Yale University Press, 1974.

Freire, Paulo. "Conscientisation." *Cross Currents* 24 (Spring 1974): 23–31.

_____. "Education, Liberation and the Church." *Study Encounter* 9 (1973): 1–16.

_____. *Pedagogy of the Oppressed*. Translated by Myra Bergman Ramos. Foreward by Richard Schaull. New York: Continuum, 1982.

Feuerbach, Ludwig. *Principles of the Philosophy of the Future*. Translated by Manfred H. Vogel. Indianapolis: Bobbs-Merrill, 1966; Indianapolis: Hackett Publishing Company, 1986.

Gilson, Etienne. *The Spirit of Medieval Philosophy*. Translated by A. H. C. Downes. New York: Charles Scribner's Sons, 1936, 1940.

Giurlanda, Paul. *Faith and Knowledge*. Lanham, MD: University Press of America, 1987.

Gottwald, Norman K. *The Tribes of Yahweh: A Sociology of the Religion of Liberated Israel*, 1250–1050 B.C.E. Maryknoll, NY: Orbis Books, 1981.

Graham, W. Fred. *The Constructive Revolutionary: John Calvin and his Socio-Economic Impact*. Richmond: John Knox Press, 1971.

Gramsci, Antonio. *Selections from the Prison Notebooks*. Translated and edited by Quintin Hoare and Geoffrey Nowell Smith. London: Lawrence and Wishart, 1971.

Griffin, David Ray, and Smith, Huston. *Primordial Truth and Postmodern Theology*. Albany, NY: State University of New York Press, 1989.

Gutierrez, Gustavo. *The Power of the Poor in History*. Translated by Robert R. Barr. Maryknoll, NY: Orbis Books, 1983.

Habermas, Jürgen. *Knowledge and Human Interests*. Translated by Jeremy J. Shapiro. Boston: Beacon Press, 1971.

_____. *The Theory of Communicative Action*. Translated by Thomas McCarthy. 2 vols. Boston: Beacon Press, 1984, 1987.

Hacker, Paul. *Das Ich im Glauben bei Martin Luther*. Graz: Styria Verlag, 1966.

Harbison, E. Harris. *The Age of Reformation*. Ithica, NY: Cornell University Press, 1955.

Hardy, Thomas. *Jude the Obscure.* Edited by Patricia Ingham. New York: Oxford University Press, 1985.

Harper's Latin Dictionary: A New Latin Dictionary. Edited by E. A. Andrews. S.v. *"auctor,"* *"auctoritas,"* and *"augeo."*

Harvey, Barry A. "Insanity, Theocracy, and the Public Realm: Public Theology, the Church, and the Politics of Liberal Democracy," *Modern Theology* 10 (January 1994): 27–57.

Hauerwas, Stanley. *After Christendom?* Nashville, TN: Abingdon Press, 1991.

_____. *Christian Existence Today: Essays on Church, World, and Living in Between.* Durham, NC: The Labyrinth Press, 1988.

_____. *The Peaceable Kingdom: A Primer in Christian Ethics.* Notre Dame: University of Notre Dame Press, 1983.

_____, and Willimon, William H. *Resident Aliens: Life in the Christian Colony.* Nashville, TN: Abingdon Press, 1989.

Hays, Richard B. *Echos of Scripture in the Letters of Paul.* New Haven, CN: Yale University Press, 1989.

Healy, F. G., ed. *Prospect for Theology: Essays in Honor of H. H. Farmer.* Digswell Place: James Nisbet and Co., Ltd., 1966.

Hesse, Mary. *Revolutions and Reconstructions in the Philosophy of Science.* Bloomington: Indiana University Press, 1980.

Hill, Samuel S., ed. *Encyclopedia of Religion in the South.* Macon, GA: Mercer University Press, 1984.

Hinson, E. Glenn. *The Integrity of the Church.* Nashville: Broadman Press, 1978.

Holl, Karl. *Gesammelte Aufsätze zur Kirchengeschichte.* 3 vols. Tübingen: J. C. B. Mohr, 1923–1928.

Holmer, Paul L. *The Grammar of Faith.* San Francisco: Harper & Row, 1978.

Holmes, Arthur B. *"Nos Extra Nos:* Luther's Understanding of the Self as Conscience." *The Drew Gateway* 53 (Fall 1982): 18–30.

Horkheimer, Max, and Adorno, Theodor W. *Dialectic of Enlightenment.* Translated by John Cumming. New York: Herder and Herder, Inc., 1972.

Hudson, Winthrop. "Walter Rauschenbusch and the New Evangelism." *Religion in Life* 30 (Summer 1961): 412–430.

Hunsinger, George. *How to Read Karl Barth: The Shape of His Theology.* New York: Oxford University Press, 1991.

James, William . *The Meaning of Truth.* New York: Longmans, Green and Co., 1909.

_____. *Pragmatism.* New York: Longmans, Green and Co., 1908.

Jameson, Fredric. *The Political Unconscious: Narrative as a Socially Symbolic Act.* Ithica, NY: Cornell University Press, 1981.

Jennings, Theodore W. *Beyond Theism: A Grammar of God-Language.* New York: Oxford University Press, 1985.

Jeremias, Joachim. *New Testament Theology: The Proclamation of Jesus.* Translated by John Bowden. New York: Charles Scribner's Sons, 1971.

Jewett, Robert. *Paul's Anthropological Terms: A Study of Their Use in Conflict Settings.* Leiden: E. J. Brill, 1971.

Jones, L. Gregory. *Transformed Judgment: Toward a Trinitarian Account of the Moral Life.* Notre Dame, IN: University of Notre Dame Press, 1990.

Jordan, Clarence. *The Cotton Patch Version of Paul's Epistles.* Piscataway, NJ: Association Press, 1968.

Jüngel, Eberhard. *God as the Mystery of the World: On the Foundation of the Theology of the Crucified One in the Dispute Between Theism and Atheism.* Translated by Darrell L. Guder. Grand Rapids: William B. Eerdmans Publishing Company, 1983.

Kant, Immauel. *Kritik der reinen Vernuft.* Riga: Johann Friedrich Hartknoch, 1781.

Kaufmann, Walter, trans. and ed. *Basic Writings of Nietzsche.* New York: The Modern Library, 1968.

_____. *Nietzsche: Philosopher, Psychologist, Antichrist.* 4th edition. Princeton: Princeton University Press, 1974.

_____, trans. *The Portable Nietzsche.* New York: Penquin Books, 1954.

Ker, I. T. Introduction to *An Essay in Aid of a Grammar of Assent,* by John Henry Newman. Oxford: Claredon Press, 1985.

Kingdon, Robert M., ed. *Transition and Revolution.* Minneapolis: Burgess, 1974.

Lamb, Matthew. *Solidarity with Victims.* New York: Crossroads Publishing Company, 1982.

Laney, James T. "A Critique of Radical Contextualist Ethics." Ph.D. dissertation, Yale University, 1966.

Lapide, Pinchas, and Moltmann, Jürgen. *Jewish Monotheism and Christian Trinitarian Doctrine.* Translated by Leonard Swidler. Philadelphia: Fortress Press, 1981.

Lash, Nicholas. *Believing Three Ways in One God: A Reading of the Apostles' Creed.* Notre Dame, IN: University of Notre Dame Press, 1993.

_____. *Easter In Ordinary: Reflections on Human Experience and the Knowledge of God.* Charlottesville: University Press of Virginia, 1988.

_____. Introduction to *An Essay in Aid of a Grammar of Assent,* by John Henry Newman. Notre Dame: University of Notre Dame Press, 1979.

_____. *Theology on the Way to Emmaus.* London: SCM Press Ltd, 1986.

Lee, Dallas. *The Cotton Patch Evidence.* New York: Harper & Row, 1971.

Lee, Hillary Page. "A Study in the Methodology of Christian Ethics: The Ethics of Paul Lehmann." Ph.D. dissertation, The Southern Baptist Theological Seminary, 1968.

Lehmann, Paul L. "Betrayal of the Real Presence." *The Princeton Seminary Bulletin* 49 (January 1956): 20–25.

_____. *Christianity and Community.* Chapel Hill: The Committee on Convocations and Lectures of the University of North Carolina at Chapel Hill, 1947.

_____. "The Commandments and the Common Life." *Interpretation* 34 (October 1980): 341–355.

_____. "The Context of Theological Inquiry." *Harvard Divinity School Bulletin* (1956–57): 63–73.

_____. "A Critical Comparison of the Doctrine of Justification in the Theologies of Albrecht Ritschl and Karl Barth." Ph.D. dissertation, Union (NY) Theological Seminary, 1936.

_____. *Ethics in a Christian Context.* New York: Harper & Row, 1963.

_____. "Evanston: Problems and Prospects." *Theology Today* 11 (July 1954): 143–153.

_____. *Forgiveness: Decisive Issue in Protestant Thought.* New York: Harper & Brothers, 1940.

_____. "The Formative Power of Particularity." *Union Seminary Quarterly Review* 18 (March 1963): 306–319.

_____. "Harvey Cox, Martin Luther and a Macro-Sociological Appropriation of the Decalogue." *Sociological Analysis* 45 (Summer 1984): 85–90.

_____. *Ideology and Incarnation: A Contemporary Ecumenical Risk.* Geneva: The John Knox Association, 1962.

_____. "Karl Barth, Theologian of Permanent Revolution." *Union Seminary Quarterly Review* 28 (Fall 1972): 67–81.

_____. "Law as a Function of Forgiveness." *Oklahoma Law Review* 12 (February 1959): 102–112.

_____. "The Metaphorical Reciprocity Between Theology and Law." *The Journal of Law and Religion* 3 (1985): 179–191.

_____. "Piety, Power, and Politics: Church and Ministry Between Ratification and Resistance." *Journal of Theology for Southern Africa* 44 (September 1983): 58–72.

_____. "The Politics of Easter." *Dialog* 19 (Winter 1980): 37–43.

_____. "A Protestant Critique of Anglicanism." *Anglican Theological Review* 26 (July 1944): 151–159.

_____. *The Transfiguration of Politics.* New York: Harper & Row, 1975.

_____. "The Tri-unity of God." *Union Seminary Quarterly Review* 21 (November 1965): 35–49.

_____. "Truth is in Order to Goodness: Reflections on the Church and the University." *Theology Today* 6 (October 1949): 348–360.

_____. *Your Freedom is in Trouble.* New York: National Student Council of the YMCA and YWCA, 1954.

Lentricchia, Frank. *Ariel and the Police.* Madison: The University of Wisconsin Press, 1988.

_____. *Criticism and Social Change.* Chicago: The University of Chicago Press, 1983.

Leuba, Jean-Louis. *New Testament Pattern: An Exegetical Inquiry in the "Catholic" and "Protestant" Dualism.* Translated by Harold Knight. London: Lutterworth Press, 1953.

Lewis, David L. *King: A Critical Biography.* Baltimore: Penquin Press, 1970.

Lindbeck, George A. *The Nature of Doctrine: Religion and Theology in a Postliberal Age.* Philadelphia: The Westminster Press, 1984.

Lohse, Bernhard. *A Short History of Christian Doctrine.* Translated by F. Ernest Stoeffler. Philadelphia: Fortress Press, 1966.

Lortz, Joseph. *The Reformation in Germany.* Translated by Ronald Walls. 2 vols. London: Darton, Longman & Todd; New York: Herder and Herder, 1968.

Luther, Martin. *Luther's Works.* Edited by Jaroslav Pelikan and Helmut T. Lehmann. 55 vols. St. Louis: Concordia Publishing House; Philadelphia: Fortress Press, 1955–1986.

_____. *Three Treatises.* 2nd edition. Philadelphia: Fortress Press, 1970.

MacIntyre, Alasdair. *Three Rival Versions of Moral Enquiry.* Notre Dame, IN: University of Notre Dame Press, 1990.

_____. *Whose Justice? Which Rationality?* Notre Dame, IN: University of Notre Dame Press, 1988.

MacQuarrie, John, ed. *Realistic Reflections on Church Union.* Published privately for the Episcopal Church, 1967.

Marcuse, Herbert. *Negations: Essays in Critical Theory.* Boston: Beacon Press, 1968.

_____. *One-Dimensional Man.* Boston: Beacon Press, 1964.

_____. *Studies in Critical Philosophy.* Boston: Beacon Press, 1973.

Marion, Jean-Luc. *God Without Being: Hors-texte.* Translated by Thomas A. Carlson. Chicago: The University of Chicago Press, 1991.

Maurer, Wilhelm, and Bergstrasser, Elisabeth, eds. *Der Ausgang der altkirchelichen Christologie.* 1st edition. Berlin: Lutherisches Verlaghaus, 1957.

McCabe, Herbert, OP. *God Matters.* London: Geoffrey Chapman, 1987.

McClendon, James Wm., Jr. *Biography as Theology.* Nashville: Abingdon Press, 1974.

_____. *Ethics: Systematic Theology.* Nashville: Abingdon Press, 1986.

McConnell, Frank, ed. *The Bible and the Narrative Tradition.* New York: Oxford University Press, 1986.

McFague, Sallie. *Models of God: Theology for an Ecological, Nuclear Age.* Philadelphia: Fortress Press, 1987.

McGovern, Arthur F. *Marxism: An American Christian Perspective.* Maryknoll, NY: Orbis Books, 1980.

McKim, Donald K., ed. *A Guide to Contemporary Hermeneutics.* Grand Rapids, MI: William B. Eerdmans Publishing Company, 1986.

McNeill, John T. *Unitive Protestantism.* Richmond, VA: John Knox Press, 1964.

Metz, Johann Baptist. *Faith in History and Society: Toward a Practical Fundamental Theology.* Translated by David Smith. New York: The Seabury Press, 1980.

Meyendorff, John. *Christ in Eastern Christian Thought.* Crestwood, NY: St. Vladimir's Seminary Press, 1975.

Míguez Bonino, José. *Toward a Christian Political Ethics.* Philadelphia: Fortress Press, 1983.

Milbank, John. *Theology and Social Theory: Beyond Secular Reason.* Cambridge, MA: Basil Blackwell Inc., 1990.

Miller, Samuel H., and Wright, G. Ernest, eds. *Ecumencial Dialogue at Harvard: The Roman Catholic-Protestant Colloquium.* Cambridge: Belknap Press, Harvard University Press, 1964.

Minear, Paul S. *Images of the Church in the New Testament.* Philadelphia: The Westminster Press, 1960.

Moltmann, Jürgen. *The Trinity and the Kingdom.* Translated by Margaret Kohl. San Francisco: Harper & Row, 1981.

Moody, Dale. *The Word of Truth: A Summary of Christian Doctrine Based on Biblical Revelation.* Grand Rapids: William B. Eerdmans Publishing Company, 1981.

Morris, Charles. *The Pragmatic Movement in American Philosophy.* New York: George Braziller, 1970.

Morse, Christopher. *The Logic of Promise in Moltmann's Theology.* Philadelphia: Fortress Press, 1979.

Müller, Reinhart. *Walter Rauschenbusch: ein Betrag zur Begegnung des deutschen und des amerikanischen Protestantismus.* Leiden: E. J. Brill, 1957.

Mullins, Edgar Young. *The Axioms of Religion: A New Interpretation of the Baptist Faith.* Philadelphia: American Baptist Publication Society, 1908.

_____. *The Christian Religion in its Doctrinal Expression.* Philadelphia: The Judson Press, 1917.

Newman, John Henry. *Apologia Pro Vita Sua.* Edited by Charles Frederick Harrold. New York; Longmans, Green and Co., 1947.

_____. *An Essay in Aid of a Grammar of Assent.* Edited by Charles Frederick Harrold. New York: Longmans, Green and Co., 1947.

_____. *Fifteen Sermons Preached Before the University of Oxford.* London: Longmans, Green, and Co., 1900.

_____. *A Letter Addressed to His Grace the Duke of Norfolk.* London: B. M. Pickering, 1895.

Niebuhr, H. Richard. *The Kingdom of God in America.* New York: Harper and Brothers, 1935.

Niebuhr, Reinhold. *Faith and History.* New York: Charles Scribner's Sons, 1949.

Nietzsche, Friedrich. *The Will To Power.* Edited by Walter Kaufmann. New York: Vantage House, 1968.

Ogletree, Thomas W., ed. *Openings for Marxist-Christian Dialogue.* Nashville: Abingdon Press, 1968.

Ozment, Steven E. *Homo Spiritualis: A Comparative Study of the Anthropology of Johannes Tauler, Jean Gerson and Martin Luther (1509–1516) in the Context of their Theological Thought.* Studies in Medieval and Reformation Thought. Vol. 6. Leiden: E. J. Brill, 1969.

Pannenberg, Wolfhart. *Theology and the Philosophy of Science.* Translated by Francis McDonagh. Philadelphia: The Westminster Press, 1976.

Peacocke, A. R., ed. *The Sciences and Theology in the Twentieth Century.* Notre Dame: University of Notre Dame Press, 1981.

Percy, Walker. *Love in the Ruins.* New York: Farrar, Straus & Giroux, Inc., 1971; Avon Books, 1978.

_____. *The Message in the Bottle.* New York; Farrar, Straus & Giroux, 1954.

Perrin, Norman. *Jesus and the Language of the Kingdom.* Philadelphia: Fortress Press, 1976.

Pierce, Claude Anthony. *Conscience in the New Testament.* London: SCM Press, Ltd., 1955.

Pinnock, Clark H. *The Scripture Principle.* San Francisco: Harper & Row, 1984.

Placher, William. "Revisionist and Postliberal Theologies and the Public Character of Theology," *The Thomist* 49 (July 1985): 392–416.

Polanyi, Michael. *Personal Knowledge: Toward a Post-Critical Philosophy.* Corrected edition. Chicago: The University of Chicago Press, 1962.

_____, and Prosch, Harry. *Meaning.* Chicago: The University of Chicago Press, 1975.

Poteat, William H. *A Philosophical Daybook: Post-Critical Investigations.* Columbia: University of Missouri Press, 1990.

_____. *Polanyian Meditations: In Search of a Post-Critical Logic.* Durham, NC: Duke University Press, 1985.

Powell, Jouett L. "Cardinal Newman on Faith and Doubt: The Role of Conscience." *The Downside Review* 99 (April 1981): 137–148.

The Presbyterian Church (U.S.A.). *The Constitution of the Presbyterian Church (U.S.A.).* New York: The Office of the General Assembly of the Presbyterian Church (U.S.A.), 1981.

Rahner, Karl. *Theological Investigations.* Translated by Cornelius Ernst et al. 20 vol. to date. London: Darton, Longman & Todd; Baltimore: Helicon Press, 1961–.

Rajchman, John, and West, Cornel, eds. *Post-Analytic Philosophy.* New York: Columbia University Press, 1985.

Rauschenbusch, Walter. *A Theology for the Social Gospel.* New York: The Macmillan Co., 1917.

Rawls, John. *A Theory of Justice.* Cambridge: Harvard University Press, 1971.

Reagan, Charles E. and Stewart, David, ed. *The Philosophy of Paul Ricouer: An Anthology of his Work.* Boston: Beacon Hill Press, 1978.

Reardon, Bernard M. G. *From Coleridge to Gore: A Century of Religious Thought in Britain.* London: Longman, 1971.

Ricoeur, Paul. "The Critique of Religion." *Union Seminary Quarterly Review* 23 (Spring 1973): 203–224.

_____. *The Symbolism of Evil.* Translated by Emerson Buchanan. New York: Harper & Row, 1967.

Ritschl, Albrecht. *Justification and Reconciliation.* Translated by D. C. Macintosh. Vol. 3. Edinburgh: T. & T. Clark, 1902.

Robinson, J. "Newman's Use of Butler's Arguments." *The Downside Review* 76 (Spring 1958): 161–180.

Rorty, Richard. *Consequences of Pragmatism.* Minneapolis: University of Minnesota Press, 1982.

_____. *Philosophy and the Mirror of Nature.* Princeton: Princeton University Press, 1979.

Rosen, Stanley. *Hermeneutics as Politics.* New York: Oxford University Press, 1987.

Rouse, Joseph. *Knowledge and Power: Toward a Political Philosophy of Science.* Ithaca, NY: Cornell University Press, 1987.

Rumscheidt, Martin, ed. *Footnotes to a Theology: The Karl Barth Colloquium of 1972.* Waterloo, Ontario: The Corporation for the Publication of Academic Studies in Religion in Canada, 1974.

Rupp, E. Gordon. "Newman through Non-conformist Eyes." *Rediscovery of Newman: An Oxford Symposium.* Edited by Sidney John Coulson and Arthur MacDonald Allchin. London: Sheed & Ward, 1967.

Schipani, Daniel S. *Conscientization and Creativity: Paulo Freire and Christian Education.* Lanham, MD: University Press of America, 1984.

Schmemann, Alexander. *Church, World, Mission: Reflections on Orthodoxy in the West.* (Crestwood, NY: St. Vladimir's Seminary Press, 1979.

Sharpe, Dores Robinson. *Walter Rauschenbusch.* New York: The Macmillan Co., 1942.

Shestov, Lev. *Athens and Jerusalem.* Translated by Bernard Martin. Athens, OH: Ohio University Press, 1966.

Shinn, Roger L., ed. *Faith and Science in an Unjust World.* 2 vols. Philadelphia: Fortress Press, 1980.

Silver, James W. *Confederate Morale and Church Propoganda.* Tuscaloosa, AL: Confederate Publishing Co., 1957.

Smith, H. Shelton. *In His Image, But...: Racism in Southern Religion, 1780–1910.* Durham, NC: Duke University Press, 1972.

Snider, P. Joel. *The "Cotton Patch" Gospel: The Proclamation of Clarence Jordan.* Lanham, MD: University Press of America, 1985.

Soskice, Janet Martin. *Metaphor and Religious Language.* Oxford: Oxford University Press, 1985.

Stackhouse, Max L. Introduction to *The Righteousness of the Kingdom,* by Walter Rauschenbusch. Nashville: Abingdon Press, 1968.

Steinmetz, David C. "The Superiority of Pre-critical Exegesis." *Theology Today* 37 (April 1980): 27–38.

Stendahl, Krister. "The Apostle Paul and the Introspective Conscience of the West." *Harvard Theological Review* 56 (July 1963): 199–215.

Stoeffler, F. Ernest. *The Rise of Evangelical Pietism.* Leiden: E. J. Brill, 1965.

Stout, Jeffrey. *Ethics After Babel.* Boston: Beacon Press, 1988.

_____. *The Flight from Authority: Religion, Morality, and the Quest for Autonomy.* Notre Dame: University of Notre Dame Press, 1981.

Stringfellow, William. *An Ethic for Christians and Other Aliens in a Strange Land.* Waco, TX: Word Books, 1973.

_____. *The Politics of Spirituality.* Philadelphia: The Westminster Press, 1984.

Surin, Kenneth. *Theology and the Problem of Evil.* New York: Basil Blackwell Inc., 1986.

The "Summa Theologica" of St. Thomas Aquinas. Translated by Fathers of the English Dominican Province. London: Burns, Oates and Washbourne, Ltd., 1914–1942.

Talbert, Charles H. "The Church and Inclusive Language for God?" *Perspectives in Religious Studies* 19 (Winter 1992): 421–439.

Taylor, Charles. *Sources of the Self: The Making of the Modern Identity.* Cambridge, MA: Harvard University Press, 1989.

Theological Dictionary of the New Testament. Edited by Gerhard Kittel and Gerhard Friedrich. S.v. *"synoida, syneidesis,"* by Christian Maurer; and *"leitourgeo, leitourgia,"* by Hermann Strathmann and Rudolf Meyer.

Thistlethwaite, Susan Brooks. *Metaphors for the Contemporary Church.* New York: The Pilgrim Press, 1983.

Thompson, E. P. *The Making of the English Working Class.* New York: Random House, 1963.

_____. *The Poverty of Theory and Other Essays.* New York: Monthly Review Press, 1978.

Tilley, Terrence. "Why American Catholic Theologians Should Read 'baptist' Theology." *Horizons* 14 (1987): 129–137.

Tucker, Robert C., ed. *The Marx-Engel Reader.* 2nd edition. New York: W. W. Horton & Company, 1978.

Verhey, Allen Dale. "The Use of Scripture in Moral Discourse: A Case Study of Walter Rauschenbusch." Ph.D. dissertation, Yale University, 1975.

West, Cornel. *The American Evasion of Philosophy.* Madison: The University of Wisconsin Press, 1989.

_____. *Prophesy Deliverance!* Philadelphia: The Westminster Press, 1982.

_____. *Prophetic Fragments.* Grand Rapids, MI: William B. Eerdmans Publishing Co., 1988.

_____. Review of *In Memory of Her,* by Elisabeth Schüssler Fiorenza. *Religious Studies Review* 11 (January 1985): 1–4.

Wicker, Brian. *The Story-Shaped World: Fiction and Metaphysics: Some Variations on a Theme.* Notre Dame, IN: University of Notre Dame Press, 1975.

Wilkin, Robert L. *"Conscientia* in Ambrose's *de officiis* and in Stoic Ethics." Paper presented at Duke University, Durham, North Carolina, 27 September, 1985.

Williams, Raymond. *Marxism and Literature.* New York: Oxford University Press, 1977.

Williams, Rowan. *Resurrection: Interpreting the Easter Gospel.* New York: The Pilgrim Press, 1982.

_____. *The Wound of Knowledge.* 2nd edition. Boston: Cowley Publications, 1990.

Wilmore, Gayraud S. and Cone, James H., eds. *Black Theology: A Documentary History, 1966–1979.* Maryknoll, NY: Orbis Press, 1979.

Winter, Gibson. *Liberating Creation.* New York: Crossroads Publishing Company, 1981.

Wittgenstein, Ludwig. *Culture and Value.* Translated by Peter Winch. Chicago: The University of Chicago Press, 1980.

_____. *Philosophical Investigations.* Translated by G. E. M. Anscombe. 3rd edition. New York: Macmillan Publishing Co., 1958.

Wolff, Hans Walter. *Anthropology of the Old Testament.* Translated by Margaret Kohl. Philadelphia: Fortress Press, 1974.

Wolff, Robert Paul; Moore, Barrington, Jr.; and Marcuse, Herbert. *A Critique of Pure Tolerance.* Boston: Beacon Press, 1969.

Wolterstorff, Nicholas. *Until Justice and Peace Embrace.* Grand Rapids: William B. Eerdmans Publishing Company, 1983.

Wood, Charles M. *Vision and Discernment: An Orientation in Theological Study.* Atlanta: Scholars Press, 1985.

Wren, Brian *What Language Shall I Borrow?* London: SCM Press, Ltd., 1989.

Yoder, John Howard. *The Original Revolution: Essays on Christian Pacifism.* Scottdale, PA: Herald Press, 1970, 1977.

_____. *The Priestly Kingdom.* Notre Dame, IN: University of Notre Dame Press, 1984.

_____. "Sacrament as Social Process: Christ the Transformer of Culture." *Theology Today* 48 (April 1991): 31–44.

INDEX

Adorno, Theodor W., 52–53, 197
Advent, 130
aesthetics, art, 185–186, 191, 203
Alter, Robert, 212, 236
Althaus, Paul, 83–84, 166
Altizer, Thomas, 16
Alves, Rubem, 38, 54
Ansbro, John J., 55
Aquinas, Thomas, 26, 52, 69–70, 81, 93, 181
arbitration, 13–14
Arendt, Hannah, 144, 165
Aristotle, 11, 72, 75, 105, 124–126, 169, 181, 226–227, 238
asceticism, 24
assent, intellectual, 86–87, 89–90, 92, 94, 156
Auden, W. H., 142, 164, 210, 246–247
Augustine, 26, 121, 203
authority, 145–150, 153, 155, 161, 164, 182, 189, 196, 215–216, 241
autonomy, 68, 79, 83, 94, 120, 153
Ayer, Alfred Jules, 52

Bacon, Francis, 24–25, 34, 36, 54
Baconian science. See Francis Bacon
baptism, 11, 67
baptist, Baptist, 7–13, 17, 20–24, 39, 41, 43, 46–47, 51, 56, 240–242, 245
Barth, J. Robert, 106
Barth, Karl, 5, 27, 133, 139, 144, 150, 160, 164–165, 170, 196, 203, 218, 236
Baum, Gregory, 15
Baylor, Michael, 69, 76–77, 79, 81–84
being, 19, 29, 61, 64, 67, 91, 188, 205, 228, 233
Bellah, Robert, 232, 238
Berger, Peter, 103, 108
Bernstein, Richard J., 97, 107, 137, 144, 165, 181, 196–197
Biel, Gabriel, 69–70
Bieler, Andre, 55
Blau, Peter, 166

Bloesch, Donald, 233, 238
Bloom, Harold, 9, 17
Boesak, Allan, 55
Boff, Clodovis, ix, 15
Bonhoeffer, Dietrich, 12, 27, 37, 43, 52, 54, 56, 78, 83, 131, 138, 160, 162, 167, 190, 198
Bremond, Henri, 105–106
Brightman, Edgar S., 47
Brown, Robert McAfee, 107
Brueggemann, Walter, 236
Buber, Martin, 81, 98, 127, 137, 229–231, 238
Bultmann, Rudolf, 43, 56
Burke, Kenneth, 1
Burrell, David, 11, 173, 196, 203, 238
Butler, Joseph, 87

Calkins, Arthur Burton, 106
Calvin, John, 71, 80, 84, 172, 196, 198, 221
Campbell, Will D., 243, 247
canon (of Scripture), 67, 80, 136, 203, 215–217, 223, 245
Capra, Fritjof, 35, 54
Cartesianism. See René Descartes
Case, Shirley Jackson, 21
Cauthen, Kenneth, 9–10, 17, 51
Chalcedon, Chalcedonian christology, 11, 114, 122, 204
Childs, Brevard, 16, 138
Chomsky, Noam, 220
Christocentrism, 131–132
church, ix–x, 2–3, 7–9, 11–15, 38, 42, 45, 48, 51, 55, 63–65, 91–95, 98–99, 102–104, 106, 111–126, 128–129, 130–138, 141, 145–146, 148–149, 152, 156–159, 161–164, 166, 169, 171–181, 192–193, 194–195, 201–202–203, 207, 212, 214–218, 221–227, 230, 234, 239–246
Cicero, 166
Clarke, William Newton, 21–22, 51
Cobb, John, 15–16

Cochrane, Charles, 238
Coleridge, Samuel Taylor, 87, 104, 106, 108
Commager, Henry Steele, 23, 25, 52
Comte, Auguste, 27, 52
Cone, James H., 55, 144
Conner, Walter T., 21, 51
conscience, 12–13, 20–21, 39, 44–45, 49–51, 55, 59–83, 85–95, 99, 101, 104, 105–106, 108–112, 114–117, 120, 122–123, 129–130, 133–134, 141, 145, 148, 152–153, 159–161, 163–164, 166, 170, 172–175, 179–180, 185–187, 192–196, 201–202, 205, 210, 214, 219, 221, 229, 239–240, 242, 244, 246
conscientization, 95–103, 107
conscientia, 50, 69
Constantine, 121
Corleone, Vito, 14
Cormie, Lee, 167
Cox, Harvey, 7, 16, 51, 210
Cranfield, C. E. B., 81
creation, creature, ix–x, 12, 17, 21, 25, 45, 67, 110, 118, 138, 142, 153–154, 162, 171, 186, 191, 212, 222, 224, 226, 233–234, 238, 244, 246
Crites, Stephen, 236

D'Ailly, Pierre, 25
Darwin, Charles, 27
Darwinian biology. *See* Charles Darwin
Daube, David, 61, 80, 240, 246
Davies, W. D., 61, 80, 83
De Certeau, Michel, 18
deconstruction, 3–6
Derrida, Jacques, 16
Descartes, René, 11, 26, 29–31, 36; Cartesianism, 29–31, 36, 46–48, 50, 54, 86, 97, 103–104, 111, 115, 119, 124, 153–154, 163, 171, 182–184, 189–191, 194, 207–208, 215, 219–220, 229, 240
Dewey, John, 1, 98, 107, 181–182, 197
DeWolf, L. Harold, 47
différance, 5
doctrine, dogma, 6, 10–11, 22, 24, 26, 40, 42, 44, 46–47, 92, 112, 160, 173, 177–179, 191, 196, 201–202, 218–220, 222, 227–228, 241–243
dogmatic or systematic theology, 125, 177, 179–180, 203, 218–234, 244
Dreyfus, Hubert L., 56
Duff, Nancy J., 18
Dulles, Avery, 11
Durkheim, Emile, 27

Easter, 100, 102, 164
Ebeling, Gerhard, 83–84
ecclesiola in ecclesia, 117, 122, 136
Eckstein, Hans-Joachim, 80–81
ecumenism, 122–123, 137, 178
election, 115–116, 143–144, 162–163, 193, 243
Elert, Werner, 238
Emerson, Ralph Waldo, 11
Enlightenment, 4–5, 23, 26, 28–29, 48, 68, 154, 157, 178, 183, 215, 219, 232
epistemology, 5–6, 19–20, 25, 47–48, 50, 69, 96, 109, 164, 171–172, 180–181, 183, 185, 187, 190, 227, 242
Erikson, Erik, 68, 81
eschatology, 112, 115, 121, 124, 127–130, 132, 133, 142–143, 147, 149, 154, 161, 164, 194, 210–212, 217, 221, 225, 228, 230
ethics, 5, 110, 112, 125, 156, 159, 178–183, 185, 191, 220, 229–230, 244
Eucharist, 11–13, 116–117, 119–120, 124, 133–134, 143, 149, 158–159, 164, 174–175, 202, 217, 241, 239, 241–246
eucharistic community. *See* church
Exodus, 102, 127, 130

faith, ix, 125–126, 134, 186, 188, 192, 195, 204, 218
Farley, Edward, 15, 146, 165
Feuerbach, Ludwig, 172, 196, 244
filioque, 115, 227
Fiorenza, Elisabeth Schüssler, 158, 167
Fosdick, Harry Emerson, 21
Foster, George B., 21
Foucault, Michel, 1, 16, 32–33, 53–54, 110–111, 134
freedom, xi, 114, 120, 126, 129, 144–145, 147–150, 152–156, 159, 161–162, 166, 171, 173–174, 178, 186, 189, 194, 207, 210–213, 218, 220, 223, 232, 238, 243
Frei, Hans, 16, 219, 236–237
Freire, Paulo, 60, 95–103, 107–108
Freud, Sigmund, 60, 94, 110

Gadamer, Hans-Georg, 32
genealogy of rules, 220
Gilkey, Langdon, 15, 51
Gilson, Etienne, 26, 52
Giurlanda, Paul 16
Gnosticism, 9, 17, 182–183, 190
God, ix, 11–13, 15, 19–20, 22, 24–25, 29, 35, 38, 40, 42–43, 47–50, 61–68, 71–80, 86–93, 102–103, 105–106,

109–122, 124–137, 141–164, 166,
169–182, 185–190, 192–196, 202,
204–205, 207–214, 216–218, 220–
234, 238, 239–240, 242–246
Goldberg, Michael, 213–214, 236
Gottwald, Norman K., 137–138
Graham, W. Fred, 55
grammar, theology as, 173–174, 194–
195, 201, 203, 218–220, 222, 226–
227, 231–232, 235, 239, 244–245
Gramsci, Antonio, 39
Green, Garrett, 16
Griffin, David Ray, 15–16
Gutiérrez, Gustavo, 11

Habermas, Jürgen, 7, 23, 52, 116, 135
Hacker, Paul, 81
Harbison, E. Harris, 68, 81
Hardy, Thomas, 107
Harper, William Rainey, 21
Hauerwas, Stanley, 2, 3, 12, 15, 18,
112, 135, 138, 158–159, 166–167,
179, 183, 189, 197–198, 203, 236,
238
Hays, Richard, 66, 81
Hegel, G. W. F., 36, 172
Heidegger, Martin, 32
Henry, Carl F. H., 51
hermeneutics, 19, 31, 34, 45, 47, 56,
130, 141, 149, 152, 161, 164, 171–
172, 202–204, 215, 242
hermeneutics of suspicion, 22, 110
Herzog, Frederick, x, 16
Hesse, Mary, 33, 54
historicity, 32, 93, 96–97
history, 32, 93, 113, 116, 122–123,
174–175, 180, 186–187, 191, 194,
211, 226–227, 230, 233, 243
Hobbes, Thomas, 25
Holl, Karl, 68–69, 81, 85
Holmer, Paul, 16, 219, 237
Holmes, Arthur B., 82–84
Holy Spirit, 40, 42, 74, 78, 103, 112–
114, 117, 120, 123–124, 127–128,
132–133, 137–138, 170–172, 175–
176, 191, 202, 216–217, 223, 227,
229, 234, 242
Horkheimer, Max, 52–53
Hudson, Winthrop, 43, 55–56
Hume, David, 26
Hunsinger, George, 16, 165

ideology, 177–178, 193–194
idolatry, 12, 132, 231–232, 242
illative sense, 86, 91, 93, 105
integrity of the human person, 120, 153,
241

James, William, 11, 14, 181–182, 184,
190, 197–198
Jennings, Theodore, 219, 237
Jerome, 81
Jesus Christ, 15, 20, 38, 40, 47, 61, 63–
67, 71–72, 74–78, 94, 102, 104,
112–126, 128–133, 135–136, 148–
149, 151–152, 157–159, 161–164,
171–173, 175–178, 180, 186–187,
189–190, 192, 195, 204, 207, 212–
214, 222–225, 227, 229, 234, 239–
244
Jewett, Robert, 80
Jones, L. Gregory, 135, 211, 236
Jordan, Clarence, 39–40, 43–45, 47, 55–
56, 245
Jüngel, Eberhard, 53–54, 244, 247
justice, 12, 91, 114, 124, 129, 132, 149,
153–154, 156–157, 161–162, 212–
213, 222, 224, 243

Kant, Immanuel, 4–5, 26, 85, 93, 99,
166, 183; Kantianism, 138
Kaufman, Gordon, 15
Kelsey, David, 16
Ker, I. T., 105–106
Kierkegaard, Soren, 48
King, Martin Luther, Jr., 39–40, 43–45,
47, 55–56, 245
knowledge, 13, 19–20, 22–23, 26, 28–
35, 37–39, 45, 49–50, 61–63, 65,
69–70, 76, 95, 97–99, 104, 107, 119,
129, 134, 141, 145, 154, 158, 169,
173, 177–178, 180, 182–185, 190,
192, 203–204, 208–209, 219–220,
231, 238, 240, 242–243
koinonia, 11, 71, 113–126, 128–129,
131–135, 143, 147, 149, 152, 154–
155, 157–164, 169, 171, 175, 178,
180–181, 186, 192, 201–202, 204–
205, 207–208, 210–214, 216–218,
220, 222, 229, 240–242, 245–246
Kuhn, Thomas, 213
Küng, Hans, 15

La Mettrie, Julien de, 25
laboratory of maturity, 119, 133, 143,
154, 158, 164, 169, 184, 192
Lamb, Matthew, 28, 36, 48, 53–54, 56,
197, 228, 238
Langford, Thomas, 16
Lapide, Pinchas, 229, 238
Lash, Nicholas, 4, 7, 16, 20, 48, 50–51,
53, 56–57, 102, 108, 112, 115–116,
118, 126, 131, 135–138, 158, 164,
167, 170–171, 173, 180, 193, 196–

197, 199, 201, 208–209, 226, 230–
231, 233–236, 238, 244, 247
Lee, Dallas, 55
Lehmann, Paul, xi, 3, 11–13, 17–18,
48–50, 55–57, 59–60, 62, 65, 70–71,
80–82, 85, 94, 104–105, 107, 109–
139, 141–162, 164–167, 169–174,
176–180, 182–199, 201–205, 207–
229, 231–232, 235–238, 239–243,
245–247
Lentricchia, Frank, 1, 14–15, 18, 107
Lewis, David L., 56
lex orandi, lex credendi, 179
liberal theology, 3, 7, 10, 13, 21, 218,
220
liberalism, liberal capitalism, ix–x, 2, 47,
54, 98, 108, 153–155, 158, 164, 181,
233
Lindbeck, George, 5–7, 16, 219, 237
Locke, John, 25–26
Lohse, Bernhard, 238
Loomer, Bernard, 51
Lortz, Joseph, 81
Lueders, Edward, 235
Luther, Martin, 60, 68–69, 71–80, 81–
85, 94, 104, 153, 166, 221

Macintosh, Douglas Clyde, 21
MacIntyre, Alasdair, 2, 11, 15, 184–185,
191–193, 197–199, 220, 226, 237
Marcuse, Herbert, 29, 35, 37, 53–55,
83, 107
Marion, Jean-Luc, 19, 51
Marx, Karl, 5, 110, 134, 177; Marxism,
13, 97, 102–103, 138, 144–145, 150,
Mathews, Shailer, 21, 43, 56
maturity, 11, 48, 118–120, 124, 126,
129, 132, 134–135, 141, 143, 148–
149, 151, 153, 166, 178, 191, 194,
210–212, 217, 229, 240–241, 244
Mauer, Christian, 62–64, 66, 67, 80–81
McCabe, Herbert, 11, 15, 18, 20, 51,
176, 197, 226, 237
McClendon, James, 9–10, 12, 17–18,
44, 55–56, 135
McFague, Sallie, 15, 232, 238
McGovern, Arthur F., 54, 95, 107
McMullin, Ernan, 237
McNeill, John T., 119, 121, 136
Mead, George, 181
Meland, Bernard, 51
memory, 174–175
messiah, messianism, 12, 49, 113–114,
128–131, 133, 142–143, 145, 148,
151, 154, 157, 159, 172–173, 179,
189–190, 207, 210–212, 214, 217,

222, 224, 227–228, 230, 239, 242–
245
messianic community. *See* church
messianic politics. *See* politics
metaphor, 12, 126–128, 142, 170–171,
174, 179, 189–191, 195–196, 201–
210, 224, 226, 230–232, 235, 237,
244–245
metaphysics, 5, 20, 48, 50, 171–172,
183, 185, 187, 203, 219, 226–228
Metz, Johann Baptist, 174, 196
Meyendorff, John, 136
Meyer, Rudolf, 136
Milbank, John, 2, 11, 15, 25, 34, 52,
54, 57, 83, 108, 137–139, 158, 167,
186, 198, 234, 238, 246
modern thought, modernity, 19–20, 28–
29, 31, 47, 62, 79, 103, 110, 119,
129, 132, 146–147, 151, 155, 186,
209, 214–215, 220
Moltmann, Jürgen, 238
Moody, Dale, 21–22, 51
Morse, Christopher, 135
Müller, Reinhard, 55
Mullins, Edgar Young, 21–22, 47, 51,
56
mystery (of God), 13, 20–21, 50, 64,
111, 113, 116–117, 119, 142, 146,
157, 170–171, 176, 178, 181, 188,
193, 195, 205, 208–209, 217, 227–
230, 233, 245–246

narrative, ix, 7, 12, 45, 60, 101–103,
117, 120, 126–127, 136, 142–143,
147, 155, 164, 172–173, 196, 202,
208–217, 222, 224, 226–227, 230–
232, 243–245
Newman, John Henry, 60, 85–94, 105–
107, 134, 156
Newton, Isaac, 27, 29
Newtonian mechanics. *See* Isaac Newton
Nicaea, Nicene theology, 11, 226
Niebuhr, H. Richard, 12, 43, 56
Niebuhr, Reinhold, 12
Nietzsche, Friedrich, 110, 151, 165
normalization, 2, 4, 9, 15

Ockham, William of, 69–70
Ogden, Schubert, 15
ontology, 20, 50, 101, 103, 171–172,
180, 227, 233, 237, 242
organic intellectuals, 39, 54–55
Origen, 203

Pannenberg, Wolfhart, 15, 27, 52, 183,
197
parabolic image. *See* metaphor

Pascal, Blaise, 131
Paul, 49, 60–67, 69, 71–72, 78, 80–81, 94, 150, 185
Peirce, Charles, 181
Percesepe, Gary, 16
Percy, Walker, 28, 53
performance ix, 19, 49–50, 67, 86, 104, 110–112, 115, 126, 130, 141, 148, 173–174, 178–180, 184, 185, 191, 194–196, 202–203, 206, 214–217, 220–221, 224, 228–230, 239, 243
Perrin, Norman, 43, 56
Philo, 61
philosophical or fundamental theology, 178, 180, 244
philosophy, 23, 29, 32, 181, 182, 188–189, 228
phronesis, 105, 183
Pierce, Claude Anthony, 80–81
Pietism, 8–13, 17, 39–48, 55, 135, 240
piety, 3, 11–12, 40–48, 50, 132, 147–148, 157, 160, 162–163, 223, 240–242
Pinnock, Clark, 51, 146, 165
Placher, William, 15–16
Plato, 80, 226
poetic(s), 10, 197, 185, 187, 220, 226, 229, 243
Polanyi, Michael, 35, 54
political anatomy, 110–111, 159
political economy, 27, 45
politics, ix, 2–3, 11–12, 14, 17, 47, 50, 97–99, 116, 123–134, 141–142, 144, 146–147, 149, 151–158, 160–164, 171, 174–176, 179–181, 186–189, 191–192, 194, 202, 205, 208, 210–212, 214, 217–218, 224, 227–229, 231, 233, 235, 239–244, 246
positivism, 27–29, 38, 52, 103, 160
postliberal theology, 5–7, 170, 219–220
(post)modern thought, (post)modernity, 2–5, 7, 10–11, 13, 15, 19–20, 28–29, 31, 47, 51, 60, 103–104, 110–111, 134, 145, 151–152, 155, 159, 164, 174–175, 178, 219, 232, 239, 242
Poteat, William H., 5, 16, 30, 53, 80, 108, 220, 235–236
Powell, Jouett, 86
power, 13, 31–38, 59, 97, 101, 103, 114, 118–119, 129–130, 134, 141–160, 163–165, 177–179, 187, 189, 193–194, 202, 211–213, 218, 223, 227, 232, 241–243, 245
pragmatism and theological inquiry, 181–188, 192, 245
praxis, 95, 97–99, 102, 108, 125, 138, 169, 228, 232

praxis pietatis, 8, 11, 20, 40, 46–47, 132
priesthood of the believer, 47, 119, 241
Protestantism, 9, 21, 25, 40, 68
Puritanism, 20, 24–26, 39–41, 46, 55

Quine, W. V., 181

Rabinow, Paul, 56
Rahner, Karl, 231, 238
Ramm, Bertrand, 51
Raschke, Carl, 16
rationality, reason, 7, 14–15, 19, 48, 50, 59, 61, 69–70, 73, 79, 86–87, 89, 93–94, 105, 119, 156, 182–188, 190, 193–194, 219–221, 224, 232, 242
Rauschenbusch, Walter, 17, 39–40, 43–45, 47, 55–56, 245
Rawls, John, 166
realism, 187, 189
Realpolitik, 187–189
Reardon, Bernard, 85–87, 105–106
reconciliation, 75, 82, 117–118, 122, 142, 144, 149, 154, 156–157, 160–161, 166, 173, 212–213, 222
regula fidei, 222
religion, religious experience, ix, 6–7, 21–22, 46, 48, 66, 68, 86, 90, 93, 110, 119, 180, 182, 186, 218–219, 233, 243
revelation, 19, 26, 86, 92, 117, 128, 130, 180, 216, 225, 230, 233
revisionist theology, 3–4, 5, 7, 10, 15, 19, 170, 218, 233
revolution, 144–147, 149–150, 152, 156–157, 159–161, 165, 189, 213
Ricoeur, Paul, 44, 51, 56, 134, 215, 236
Ritschl, Albrecht, 47
Robertson, Pat, 2
Robinson, J., 87, 106
Rorty, Richard, 23, 51–52, 178, 181, 183–185, 187, 197–198
Rosen, Stanley, 4–5, 16, 45, 56
Rouse, Joseph, 18, 32, 34, 36–37, 53–54, 165, 177, 184, 197–198, 237
Ruether, Rosemary, 15
Rupp, E. Gordon, 105

sacrament, 41, 111, 113, 158, 161, 174–175, 209, 217, 242, 244
Sartre, Jean-Paul, 207
Scharlemann, Robert, 16
Schaull, Richard, 95, 107
Schipani, Daniel S., 107–108
Schleiermacher, Friedrich, 3, 47, 170, 203, 205
Schmemann, Alexander, 83

scholastic theology, scholasticism, 68–70, 72–75, 77, 79
science, scientific method, 19–30, 34–39, 44–45, 48, 50–52, 59, 86, 104, 183, 213, 232
scientia, 25, 50, 52
scientism, 25, 27, 37, 45, 52, 215
Sharpe, Dores Robinson, 17
Sheilaism, 232
Shestov, Lev, 26, 52
silence, 150–152, 213
Silver, James W., 247
Smith, H. Shelton, 247
Snider, P. Joel, 55
Spong, John, 2
social differentiation, 155, 158, 221–222, 241
Socrates, 62, 182
Soskice, Janet, 205–209, 235
soul competency, 46–47
Stackhouse, Max L., 56
Steinmetz, David C., 215, 236
Stendahl, Krister, 61, 66, 80, 83
Stoeffler, F. Ernest, 17, 39–44, 55–56
Stout, Jeffrey, 5, 16, 52, 146, 165
Strathmann, Hermann, 136
Stringfellow, William, 125, 137, 147, 165
Strong, Augustus Hopkins, 21–22, 51
subject, human being as, 4–7, 20, 23, 26, 29–32, 36, 45–48, 50, 78, 80, 86, 95, 97–98, 100–101, 103–104, 115, 124, 153–154, 182, 184, 205, 219–220, 232
submission, 150–152, 213
Surin, Kenneth, 52
syneidesis, 61–67, 81
synteresis, 69, 73, 81

Taylor, Charles, 17, 24–25, 39, 41, 52, 55
Taylor, Mark C., 16
the-anthropology, 170–171
theocracy, theopolitics, 66, 81, 127, 148
theoria, 97, 183, 227
Thiemann, Ronald, 16, 219, 237
Thistlethwaite, Susan, 15, 131, 138
Thompson, E. P., 107
Tilley, Terrence, 17
Tillich, Paul, 47
Torbet, Robert G., 56
Toy, Crawford H., 21
Tracy, David, 15, 19, 51
transfiguration, 3, 129–130, 132, 144–145, 147–154, 156–158, 161, 213, 235, 243–245
transubstantiation, 116, 241

Trinity, 112, 114–115, 130–132, 170, 176, 179, 181–182, 208, 217–218, 222–231, 233–234
truth, 5, 23, 28, 45, 86, 89, 91–92, 129, 144, 149–153, 164, 176, 178–179, 182, 185, 187–195, 204, 207, 210, 213–214, 221, 230, 243–244

Vatican II, 113
via negativa, 230–231, 233
violence, 147, 156–157, 159, 166
Voltaire, 25

Warford, Malcolm L., 107
Weber, Max, ix, 24
West, Cornel, 4–5, 7, 16, 29, 32, 34, 35, 53–56, 164, 167, 181, 197, 245, 247
Wicker, Brian, 174, 196
Wilkin, Robert L., 80
Wilkins, John, 25
Williams, Raymond, 53
Williams, Rowan, 11, 20, 51, 167, 174, 196, 221, 227, 233, 237–238
Willimon, William, 3, 15
Winquest, Charles, 16
Winter, Gibson, 37, 53–54
Wittgenstein, Ludwig, 199, 219, 237
Wolff, Hans Walter, 57, 80–81
Wolterstorff, Nicholas, 54–55
Wood, Charles, 16, 219, 237, 244, 247
Wren, Brian, 232, 238

Yoder, John Howard, 9, 12, 17, 56, 83, 112, 135–137, 158–159, 167, 246–247

DATE DUE